CONTEMPORARY COMPOSITION STUDIES

A Guide to Theorists and Terms

Edith Babin
and
Kimberly Harrison

Greenwood Press
Westport, Connecticut · London

Library of Congress Cataloging-in-Publication Data

Babin, Edith H.
    Contemporary composition studies : a guide to theorists and terms /
Edith Babin and Kimberly Harrison.
        p.   cm.
    Includes bibliographical references (p.   ) and index.
    ISBN 0–313–30087–9 (alk. paper)
    1. English language—Rhetoric—Study and teaching.   2. English
language—Rhetoric—Study and teaching—Terminology.   3. English
language—Composition and exercises.   I. Harrison, Kimberly.
II. Title.
PE1404.B23   1999
808'.042'07—dc21   99–27183

British Library Cataloguing in Publication Data is available.

Library of Congress Catalog Card Number: 99–27183
ISBN: 0–313–30087–9

First published in 1999

Greenwood Press, 88 Post Road West, Westport, CT 06881
An imprint of Greenwood Publishing Group, Inc.
www.greenwood.com

Printed in the United States of America

The paper used in this book complies with the
Permanent Paper Standard issued by the National
Information Standards Organization (Z39.48–1984).

10 9 8 7 6 5 4 3 2 1

Contents

Preface
vii

Acknowledgments
xi

Journal Abbreviations
xiii

Part I
Leading Scholars in Composition Studies
1

Part II
Important Terms in Composition Studies
113

*Appendix: Scholars Outside Composition Studies
Who Have Influenced the Field*
271

Works Cited
285

Name Index
315

Subject Index
325

Preface

This reference work is a result of our experiences as students in a graduate seminar on composition theory at Louisiana State University. At the time, one of us was a third-year graduate student in composition studies. The other, a writing teacher and administrator with twenty-five years' experience in the classroom, was trying to keep up with changes in the theoretical underpinnings of the discipline. Our experience in the class convinced us of the need for a reference work that would define key terms and concepts and provide information about scholars in the field. We intend this text as an invitation into composition studies for newcomers who wish to explore and perhaps contribute to the discipline, for those in other disciplines who wish to familiarize themselves with the field of composition studies, and for seasoned writing teachers who wish to review the field, possibly making new connections between theory and practice.

CONTENT

Taking the early 1960s as the beginning of composition studies, we introduce leading scholars and researchers, identify their areas of interest and expertise, and briefly review their major contributions. We also include brief entries for late nineteenth- and early twentieth-century scholars and teachers whose work has influenced our discipline. We define commonly used terms as they are understood by those in the field and, when appropriate, place them in the context of the field's development. In an appendix, we provide brief entries introducing scholars from other fields who have contributed significantly to composition studies. This information, we believe, should make it easier to converse, read, and write in composition studies.

SCHOLARS IN COMPOSITION STUDIES

Although composition studies is a relatively new field, many people have contributed to its development. To determine what figures among these to include in this work, we used a method of peer evaluation. Beginning by establishing minimal criteria, we listed the names of 200 women and men who have contributed to the field themselves or have influenced the work of those who have. On the list were scholars who have been most frequently published and most often cited in major professional journals, editors of major essay collections in the field and authors included therein, and leaders in professional organizations like CCCC. Also included were scholars from other disciplines who were often cited in the literature of our field. We first asked representatives of programs listed in the Consortium of Doctoral Programs in Rhetoric and Composition to identify which of these we should include in our project. Next, we consulted the fifty scholars they most often selected, asking them to choose other scholars on the list and to add names to the list. We mailed those they most frequently selected a shorter list of scholars who had often been mentioned and whom we were still considering. In each group we consulted, over 50 percent responded. Since publishers' restrictions limited us to approximately 500 manuscript pages, our final list could include only the 100 or so scholars who received the most "votes" from their colleagues. We recognize, of course, that many others besides these have contributed significantly to composition studies.

Once we determined the persons we would include, we asked them, whenever possible, to tell us the areas in which they have made their greatest impact and to name the works they consider their most influential. Sixty-six percent complied with our request.

Format for Scholar's Entries

Each entry for an individual is divided into three sections. Section (a) lists areas in which the scholar has made important contributions. Since a number of scholars have been leaders in composition studies since its beginnings, they have shaped many areas of the discipline. To make our categories useful, we included only the areas with which their names are usually associated. Section (b) briefly describes their contributions, focusing on books and articles most cited and, wherever possible, those the scholars themselves selected. The discussion of each scholar's work is arranged chronologically, as is the bibliography of representative works in section (c) so that readers can trace the progression of the scholar's thought and, sometimes, in the publications of those who have been in the profession the longest, the history of the developing discipline. Because textbooks influence our discipline by introducing theory to practice, we have frequently included textbooks by these scholars. To make the works in section (c) more accessible to our readers, we have included recent editions and reprints of our entries.

TERMS IN THE FIELD

In compiling the list of terms defined, we have included both terms problematic for those of us already reading and writing in the discipline and those likely to confuse persons new to composition studies. We began with a list of approximately 250 terms, selected from our major journals, conferences, and books. We consulted such journals as *College Composition and Communication, College English, Research in the Teaching of English, Journal of Advanced Composition, Rhetoric Review, Rhetoric Society Quarterly, PRE/TEXT, Journal of Basic Writing, Written Communication*, and *The Writing Instructor*. To narrow the list of entries, we also consulted the ERIC database to see how often these terms were mentioned, removing those seldom used. In a few cases, however, we retained a word either not cited in ERIC or with few citations (such as *god-term*) because experience indicated that the term is likely to confuse new readers in the field. We also retained an entry if the term has been frequently used in leading publications even though it is not catalogued in ERIC.

Format for Term Entries

Each definition is divided into four sections. Section (a) offers a working definition of the term. If it has a long history in composition conversations, this section also describes how the disciplinary context has shaped the way the term has been used and indicates connotations the term may carry. Section (b) gives variant definitions or explanations of the term offered by established compositionists, and section (c) provides examples of the term in context. The definitions and examples selected for (b) and (c) come from either our leading journals or other publications relevant to composition studies. When the term has been coined in another discipline, we often go outside the discipline in selecting examples. For instance, when discussing *thick description*, we quote Clifford Geertz, an anthropologist. Section (d) of each definition provides an alphabetical list of the scholars associated with the term, including those who originated the term and those who have redefined it. Neither the lists nor the definitions are exhaustive, but they provide a starting point for readers who wish to explore the concepts more fully.

In conducting a historical survey of the terms, we have relied heavily on the ERIC database, even while realizing its limitations. To supplement this source, we have also consulted the Longman/CCCC and Bedford bibliographies, as well as other bibliographic collections, such as Gary Tate's *Teaching Composition: 12 Bibliographical Essays*.

For ease of use, the two sections are alphabetical and cross-referenced. In the section on scholars, terms printed in **boldface** indicate that a fuller discussion appears in the section on terms. In the discussion of terms, the name of the scholar who coined it and the names of those most often associated with it are also printed in **boldface** if Part I includes entries on these figures. Asterisks (*) after scholars' names indicate that their names appear in the appendix. Terms defined elsewhere in the glossary are placed in bold print as well.

Acknowledgments

We would like to thank those who have helped us in this work: Lori Bianchini from NCTE for supplying the lists of awards given by NCTE and Barbara Lamar for giving us the list of past editors of NCTE journals; Frank Farmer, Eleanor Howes, and Jan Shoemaker for suggestions about entries in their areas of expertise; Bonnie Noonan and Helen Constantinides for reading and commenting on the usefulness of our definitions; Mary Sue Garay and Dennis Hall for using our manuscript in their graduate seminars; and George Butler and David Palmer at Greenwood Press for their encouragement and patience. Kimberly would like to thank members of the Mississippi College English Department for support and the library staff at Mississippi College for graciously answering many questions. Edith thanks Janine Conant for secretarial help, and Smitty Bolner, Bill Thompson, and other library staff at Louisiana State University for their expert assistance.

Our families have responded encouragingly every time we assured them that this project was nearing an end. Our husbands, Jim Babin and Jeremy Rowan, have provided support and excellent editing advice. They have uncomplainingly read and commented on draft after draft and have continued to believe in us and in the value of our undertaking. We would like to thank them. We also thank Sarah Liggett, Director of the First-Year Writing Program at Louisiana State University, and Carol Mattingly, in whose course this work was conceived. Both have read and commented on numerous drafts of our manuscript. Without their encouragement, inspiration, unfailing patience, and wise advice, we could not have completed this project. We know they are as grateful as we are that we have completed it.

We also thank the following members of the composition studies community for helping us select the scholars and/or providing us with information about their contributions to the discipline: Arthur Applebee, David Bartholomae, Lloyd Bitzer, Patricia Bizzell, Lynn Bloom, Wayne Booth, Lil Brannon, Linda Brodkey, Kenneth Bruffee, William Coles, Joseph Comprone, Charles Cooper, Edward P. J. Corbett, William Covino, Sharon Crowley, Frank D'Angelo, Ann Dobie, Lisa Ede, Bruce Edwards, Peter Elbow, Theresa Enos, Lester Faigley, Linda Ferreira-Buckley, Toby Fulwiler, Ann Ruggles Gere, Walker Gibson, Maxine Hairston, S. Michael Halloran, Gail Hawisher, John Hayes, Shirley Brice Heath, Bruce Herzberg, E. D. Hirsch, Jr., Catherine Hobbs, Winifred Bryan Horner, William Irmscher, Susan Jarratt, Stephen Tchudi, Albert Kitzhaber, C. H. Knoblauch, Richard Larson, Janice Lauer, Richard Lloyd-Jones, Andrea Lunsford, Elaine Maimon, Ruth Mirtz, James Moffett, Donald Murray, Jasper Neel, Lee Odell, Richard Ohmann, Walter Ong, Sondra Perl, Louise Weatherbee Phelps, Kenneth Pike, George Pullman, James Raymond, Paul Ranieri, Mike Rose, Louise Rosenblatt, Hephzibah Roskelly, Cynthia Selfe, Ira Shor, Joseph Williams, W. Ross Winterowd, Art Young, Richard Young, and two unidentified respondents.

Journal Abbreviations

ADE Bulletin	Association of Departments of English Bulletin
AJEd	American Journal of Education
Argumentation	Argumentation
C&C	Computers and Composition
CCC	College Composition and Communication
CCSJ	Central States Speech Journal
CE	College English
CL	College Literature
CritI	Critical Inquiry
EdRev	Education Review
EdT	Educational Theory
EEd	English Education
EJ	English Journal
FEN	Freshman English News
Focuses	Focuses
GR	Georgia Review
HER	Harvard Educational Review
JAC	Journal of Advanced Composition
JBW	Journal of Basic Writing
JEd	Journal of Education
JGenEd	Journal of General Education

JR	Journal of Reading
LangS	Language in Society
Leaflet	The Leaflet
NDCC	New Directions in Community Colleges
P&R	Philosophy and Rhetoric
PhSS	Philosophy of the Social Sciences
PMLA	Publications of the Modern Language Association of America
PRE/TEXT	PRE/TEXT: A Journal of Rhetorical Theory
QJS	Quarterly Journal of Speech Communication
RER	Review of Educational Research
RR	Rhetoric Review
RSQ	Rhetoric Society Quarterly
RTE	Research in the Teaching of English
SL&LB	Studies in Language and Language Behavior
SSJ	Southern Speech Communication Journal (Formerly SSB, Southern Speech Bulletin)
TETYC	Teaching English in the Two-Year College
WC	Written Communication
WE	Writing on the Edge
WI	Writing Instructor
WJSC	Western Journal of Speech Communication (formerly WSJ, Western Speech Journal)
Word	Word
WPA	Journal of the Council of Writing Program Administrators

Part I

Leading Scholars in Composition Studies

FORMAT

The name of the scholar

(a) The area(s) in which the scholar has made an impact on the field

(b) Significant contributions

(c) Representative works

APPLEBEE, ARTHUR N.

(a) Composing Processes, History of Rhetoric and/or Composition, Research Methodology

(b) In *Tradition and Reform in the Teaching of English* (1974), Applebee traces the history of American English instruction in elementary school, high school, and college, pointing out the constant tension between its two aims—to preserve a "high literary culture" and to develop a democratic society—and documenting the movement of English instruction to literary studies. In several studies, he describes the writing high school students do in major subject areas, noting that few teachers in any subject give writing assignments longer than a paragraph and that most teachers, even writing teachers, still focus on usage. In "Writing and Reasoning" (1984), Applebee reviews current research on the relationship between writing and reasoning, calling for continued investigation of how literacy affects culture, how specific writing experiences affect students' learning, and how writing in school affects students' cognitive development. In

How Writing Shapes Thinking: A Study of Teaching and Learning (1987), written with Judith Langer, Applebee suggests strategies teachers can use to incorporate **writing to learn** into content areas. Discussing **process** approaches to writing, he concludes that although process-oriented instruction is neither widely used nor, in general, effectively implemented, it does improve student writing. Applebee cites a need for reconceptualizing the nature of writing processes, of process instruction, and of writing itself that will make it easier to implement effective process approaches. In *Curriculum as Conversation: Transforming Traditions of Teaching and Learning* (1996), he argues for development of curricula that focus on knowledge in context. Such curricula, he says, would teach students about past traditions so that they can enter into conversations using the tools of the past to transform the future. *Curriculum as Conversation* won the **NCTE** David H. Russell Award for Distinguished Research in the Teaching of English for 1998. Applebee co-edited *Research in the Teaching of English* from 1984 to 1991.

(c) Applebee, Arthur N. *Tradition and Reform in the Teaching of English: A History.* Urbana: NCTE, 1974.

Applebee, Arthur N., Anne Auten, and Fran Lehr. *Writing in the Secondary School: English and the Content Areas.* NCTE Research Report No. 21. Urbana: NCTE, 1981.

Applebee, Arthur N. "Writing and Reasoning." *RER* 54 (1984): 577–96.

Applebee, Arthur N., and Judith A. Langer. *How Writing Shapes Thinking: A Study of Teaching and Learning.* Urbana: NCTE, 1987.

Applebee, Arthur. "Problems in Process Approaches: Toward a Reconceptualization of Process Instruction." *The Teaching of Writing: Eighty-fifth Yearbook of the National Society for the Study of Education.* Ed. Anthony Petrosky and David Bartholomae. 85, pt. 2. Chicago: NSSC, 1986. 95–113.

———. *Curriculum as Conversation: Transforming Traditions of Teaching and Learning.* Chicago: University of Chicago Press, 1996.

BAIN, ALEXANDER

(a) Arrangement, Pedagogy, Style

(b) Bain, who held the Chair of Logic (which included Rhetoric) at Aberdeen University from 1860 to 1880, influenced the teaching of writing by introducing or popularizing notions of the paragraph. In *English Composition and Rhetoric* (1886), Bain discusses six principles of paragraph construction: explicit reference, parallel construction, indication of the theme, unity, consecutive arrangement, and marking of subordination. These principles developed into **current-traditional rhetoric**'s dictates that all paragraphs, virtually without exception, must begin with topic sentences and follow principles of unity, coherence, and emphasis. Bain's division of prose writing into the **modes of discourse** (probably based on the work of George Campbell) also became part of the current-traditional **paradigm**.

(c) Bain, Alexander. "Rhetoric." *Information for the People*. Ed. W. and R. Chambers.
      Vol. 2. Edinburgh: W. and R. Chambers, 1849. 689–704.
———. *English Composition and Rhetoric: A Manual*. 1866. 2nd ed. London: Long-
      mans, Green and Co., 1888.
———. *Practical Essays*. London: Longmans, Green and Co., 1884.
———. *On Teaching English*. London: Longmans, Green and Co., 1887.

BARTHOLOMAE, DAVID

(a) Basic Writing, Literacy, Rhetoric and/or Composition Theory

(b) In his work on **basic writing**, Bartholomae emphasizes the need to reunite
the arts of speaking, writing, reading, and thinking. In his 1980 article "The
Study of Error" (which won the 1981 Braddock Award), he uses research on
error analysis and miscue analysis to compare student errors in writing and in
reading aloud and argues that having students read their work aloud is a valuable
diagnostic and instructional technique. In **"Inventing the University"** (1985),
he describes what he (like Bizzell) calls the **academic discourse community**
and says that the errors of basic writers result from their struggle to approximate
the discourse of that community. In that work and in *Facts, Artifacts and Counterfacts: Theory and Method for a Reading and Writing Course* (1986), he and
Anthony Petrosky argue that teachers should provide many opportunities for
basic writers to read and analyze **academic discourse** and should evaluate basic
writers on how well they succeed in approximating ("inventing") that discourse.
Bartholomae and Petrosky's 1987 textbook, *Ways of Reading*, applies recent
theories of reading and writing and asks first-year writers to make connections
between readings and their own experience, to learn to construct their own
readings of a text, and to develop their own voices. "Producing Adult Readers:
1930–50" (1990) provides a rationale for the difficult selections in the textbook
as it traces the history of the construction of the "adult reader" and argues against
giving these readers access only to those texts determined to be "right" for them.
"Writing with Teachers: A Conversation with Peter Elbow" (1995) and "Response" are the published texts of Bartholomae's half of a 1991 CCCC debate
with Elbow over whether academic writing or personal writing should be taught
in undergraduate writing courses. In arguing for academic writing, Bartholomae
says that he wants students to see how what they write has been **"socially
constructed"** by what they have read and heard and to learn to read critically
(skeptically) so that they can resist the voices that "write" them. Bartholomae
chaired the second MLA Literacy Conference in 1990 and **CCCC** in 1988. He
is one of the fifty most-cited authors in *CCC* articles from 1980–93.*

*This information and all future references to most frequently cited authors in *CCC* and to most
frequently published authors of major authors in *CCC* are from Donna Burns Phillips, Ruth Greenberg, and Sharon Gibson's 1993 article "College Composition and Communication: Chronicling a
Discipline's Genesis."

(c) Bartholomae, David. "The Study of Error." *CCC* 31 (1980): 253–69. Rpt. in *The Writing Teacher's Sourcebook*. Ed. Gary Tate and Edward P. J. Corbett. 2nd ed. New York: Oxford University Press, 1988. 303–17.

———. "Inventing the University." *When a Writer Can't Write: Studies in Writer's Block and Other Composing Process Problems*. Ed. Mike Rose. New York: Guilford Press, 1985. Rpt. in *Cross-Talk in Comp Theory: A Reader*. Ed. Victor Villanueva, Jr. Urbana: NCTE, 1997. 589–619.

Bartholomae, David, and Anthony R. Petrosky. *Facts, Artifacts and Counterfacts*. Upper Montclair, NJ: Boynton/Cook, 1986.

———. *Ways of Reading: An Anthology for Writers*. 1987. 4th ed. Boston: Bedford Books, 1996.

Bartholomae, David. "Producing Adult Readers, 1930–1950." *The Right to Literacy*. Ed. Andrea A. Lunsford, Helene Moglen, and James Slevin. New York: MLA, 1990. 13–28.

———. "Writing with Teachers: A Conversation with Peter Elbow." *CCC* 46 (1995): 62–71. "Response." *CCC* 46 (1995): 84–92. Rpt. in *Cross-Talk in Comp Theory: A Reader*. Ed. Victor Villanueva, Jr. Urbana: NCTE, 1997. 479–88 and 501–4.

BAZERMAN, CHARLES

(a) Rhetoric and/or Composition Theory, Writing Across the Curriculum, Writing in the Workplace

(b) Bazerman has reviewed the literature in the sociology of science, examining what it can teach about scientific and technical writing and what it suggests about new directions for research. He has analyzed both past and current texts from various disciplines, looking at the relationship of the language of texts to four contexts—reality (the object being studied), tradition (previous literature on the subject), society (**audience**), and the mind of the writer—and showing how strategies and conventions differ from one discipline to another and even within subcommunities of the same discipline. Bazerman suggests that new writing in a discipline enters into a **conversation** with all previous writing in the field. To take part in the conversation in the language community of a discipline, writers must learn the discipline's rhetorical strategies and discourse conventions. His textbook, written for courses in **writing across the curriculum**, emphasizes the connection between learning to read and to write in a discipline. In *Shaping Written Knowledge: The Genre and Activity of the Experimental Article in Science* (1988), Bazerman draws on a study of genre and of the persuasive strategies of scientists to argue that scientific writing is rhetorical. It won the American Medical Writers Association's McGovern Award and the 1989 NCTE Award for the Best Book in Technical Writing. *Textual Dynamics of the Professions* (1991), which he co-edited, makes the case that texts both constitute and are constituted by professions. In *Constructing Experience* (1994), a collection of his essays, Bazerman examines four perspectives—from that of the individual writer to that of the observer theorizing about literate practices—to see how each perspective contributes to an understanding of writing.

(c) Bazerman, Charles. "What Written Knowledge Does: Three Examples of Academic Discourse." *PhSS* 11 (1981): 361–81.

———. *The Informed Writer: Using Sources in the Disciplines.* 1981. 5th ed. Boston: Houghton Mifflin, 1995.

———. "Scientific Writing as a Social Act." *New Essays in Technical and Scientific Communication.* Ed. Paul V. Anderson, R. John Brockman, and Carolyn R. Miller. Farmingdale, NY: Baywood, 1983. 156–84.

———. *Shaping Written Knowledge: The Genre and Activity of the Experimental Article in Science.* Madison: University of Wisconsin Press, 1988.

Bazerman, Charles, and James Paradis, eds. *Textual Dynamics of the Professions: Historical and Contemporary Studies of Writing in Professional Communities.* Madison: University of Wisconsin Press, 1991.

———. *Constructing Experience.* Carbondale: Southern Illinois University Press, 1994.

BECKER, ALTON L.

(a) Invention, Rhetoric and/or Composition Theory

(b) With Richard Young and Kenneth Pike, Alton Becker is best known for the particle/wave/field **heuristic** in *Rhetoric: Discovery, and Change* (1970) and for that work's emphasis on **invention** and hence on the **process** of writing. This heuristic draws on **Rogerian rhetoric**'s emphasis on looking at more than one side of an issue. Becker is also influential for his work on the English paragraph. In "A **Tagmemic** Approach to Paragraph Analysis" (1965) and in "Toward a Modern Theory of Rhetoric" (1965) with Richard Young, Becker applies tagmemic theory (from linguistics) to paragraph analysis; he describes paragraphs as illustrating patterns such as topic-restriction-illustration (TRI) and problem-solution (PS). These patterns, Becker says, are not inflexible; students can be taught to recognize and manipulate them by deletion, reordering, addition, and combination. With Frank Koen and Richard Young, he has investigated the extent to which the paragraph forms a psychological unit that can be recognized even without paragraph markers, such as indentation, and the degree to which formal and semantic cues determine paragraph structure. He is one of the most frequently cited authors in *CCC* articles from 1965–79 and 1980–93.

(c) Becker, Alton. "A Tagmemic Approach to Paragraph Analysis." *CCC* 16 (1965): 237–42.

Becker, Alton, and Richard Young. "Toward a Modern Theory of Rhetoric: A Tagmemic Contribution." *HER* 35 (1965): 450–68. Rpt. in *The Writing Teacher's Sourcebook.* Ed. Gary Tate and Edward P. J. Corbett. New York: Oxford University Press, 1981. 129–48.

Becker, Alton, Frank Koen, and Richard Young. "The Psychological Reality of the Paragraph." *Stud Lang & Lang Behav* 3 (1967), Part I: 526–38.

———. "The Psychological Reality of the Paragraph." *Stud Lang & Lang Behav* 4 (1968), Part II: 482–98.

Becker, Alton, Richard Young, and Kenneth Pike. *Rhetoric: Discovery, and Change.* New York: Harcourt Brace, 1970.

BERKENKOTTER, CAROL

(a) Composing Processes, Research Methodology, Rhetoric and/or Composition Theory

(b) Berkenkotter has written on the relation between writer and **audience** in the **processes** of composing and revising and on how **discourse communities** affect the way their participants write and think. In "Decisions and Revisions: The Planning Strategies of a Publishing Writer" (1983), she reports on her study of Donald Murray's writing processes. In the study, she couples Linda Flower and John Hayes' think-aloud **protocols** with Murray's introspective accounts of his composing in natural settings over a two-month period and in a laboratory setting during a one-hour writing assignment. She emphasizes the conditions under which writing occurs, and, acknowledging that she cannot generalize from single-subject research, she calls for more qualitative studies of skilled and unskilled writers in natural settings. With Thomas N. Huckin and John M. Ackerman, in "Conventions, **Conversations**, and the Writer: Case Study of a Student in a Rhetoric PhD Program" (1988), Berkenkotter traces the process by which Nate, a new graduate student in a rhetoric program, changes his writing to reflect the conventions of his new discourse community. Her 1991 essay "Paradigm Debates, Turf Wars, and the Conduct of Sociocognitive Inquiry in Composition" examines the origins of disputes between cognitive and social perspectives on language learning and between the quantitative and qualitative methodologies with which they are identified. Alone and with Huckin, Berkenkotter has written several articles on genre theory. A number of these essays became chapters in her book with Huckin, *Genre Knowledge in Disciplinary Communication: Cognition/Culture/Power* (1995). In this work, they describe their approach to genre as sociocognitive; because they see genre as dynamic, both shaping and shaped by writers, readers, and disciplinary discourse communities, they study context as well as text. The authors identify five characteristics of genre and report on a number of case studies that investigate the way readers, writers, text, and discourse communities interact with genre. *Genre Knowledge in Disciplinary Communication* won the **NCTE** Award for the Best Book in Technical Writing for 1996. Berkenkotter is one of the most frequently published authors of major articles in *CCC* from 1980 to May 1993.

(c) Berkenkotter, Carol. "Understanding a Writer's Awareness of Audience." *CCC* 32 (1981): 388–99.

———. "Decisions and Revisions: The Planning Strategies of a Publishing Writer." *CCC* 34 (1983): 156–69. Rpt. in *The Writing Teacher's Sourcebook*. Ed. Gary Tate and Edward P. J. Corbett. 2nd ed. New York: Oxford University Press, 1988. 128–39.

Berkenkotter, Carol, Thomas N. Huckin, and John M. Ackerman. "Conventions, Conversations, and the Writer: Case Study of a Student in a Rhetoric PhD Program." *RTE* 22 (1988): 9–41.

Berkenkotter, Carol. "Paradigm Debates, Turf Wars, and the Conduct of Sociocognitive Inquiry in Composition." *CCC* 42 (1991): 151–69.

Berkenkotter, Carol, and Thomas Huckin. *Genre Knowledge in Disciplinary Communities: Cognition/Culture/Power.* Hillsdale, NJ: L. Erlbaum and Associates, 1995.

BERLIN, JAMES

(a) Bibliography, Cultural Studies, History of Rhetoric and/or Composition, Rhetoric and/or Composition Theory

(b) Berlin has done work in taxonomies, in the history of rhetorical theory, and in cultural studies. His 1981 bibliography of nineteenth-century rhetoric in England and America is a much-cited early bibliography of nineteenth-century forms of discourse. In *Writing Instruction in Nineteenth-Century American Colleges* (1984), he builds on Albert R. Kitzhaber's dissertation ("Rhetoric in American Colleges: 1850–1900") but amplifies Kitzhaber by arguing that every rhetoric assumes a closed "noetic field" specifying the character of language, what is knowable and who can know, and the relation between rhetor and audience. Based on which part of the noetic field a rhetoric emphasizes (its epistemological assumptions), Berlin classifies three rhetorics he says shaped nineteenth-century writing instruction: classical, psychological-epistemological, and romantic. He traces their influence on nineteenth-century thought and pedagogy, concluding with a discussion of contemporary writing pedagogies. In *Rhetoric and Reality: Writing Instruction in American Colleges, 1900–1985* (1987), he divides writing pedagogy of the twentieth century into objective theories, subjective theories, and **transactional** theories; and he further divides transactional theories into classical, **cognitive**, and **epistemic** (which he calls **new rhetoric**). In "Rhetoric and Ideology in the Writing Class" (1988), Berlin focuses on cognitive psychology, **expressionism**, and what he calls **social epistemic** rhetoric; Berlin's use of "epistemic" (a term coined by Robert L. Scott in 1967) for **social constructivist** theory has become part of the vocabulary of the discipline. In other work, Berlin draws on Raymond Williams, Gerald Graff, Pierre Bourdieu, and Robert Scholes to trace the split between **poetic** and rhetoric in English departments and the valorization of poetic over rhetoric. He says that the poetic-rhetoric division has caused English departments, consciously or not, to serve the interests of the managerial class by preserving its hegemony. Berlin argues that in reformulating the poetic-rhetoric relationship, social epistemic rhetoric demonstrates that all texts are about politics and power, that the poetic should not be privileged, and that the job of English studies should be to develop students' **critical literacy**—their ability to read and write critically about both the literary and the rhetorical. *Rhetorics, Poetics, and Cultures: Refiguring College English Studies* (1996) considers ways English studies could be "refigured" to give students the critical abilities to participate in and so to strengthen democracy. It won the **CCCC** Outstanding Book Award for 1998.

Berlin has written and edited a number of articles and anthologies on cultural studies and its applications for teaching English. He is one of the fifty authors most cited in *CCC* articles from 1980–93.

(c) Berlin, James. "A Bibliography of Rhetoric in England and America in the Nineteenth Century: The Primary Sources." *RSQ* 11 (summer 1981): 193–203.

———. "Contemporary Composition: The Major Pedagogical Theories." *CE* 44 (1982): 765–77. Rpt. in *Cross-Talk in Comp Theory: A Reader*. Ed. Victor Villanueva, Jr. Urbana: NCTE, 1997. 233–248.

———. *Writing Instruction in Nineteenth-Century American Colleges*. Carbondale: Southern Illinois University Press, 1984.

———. *Rhetoric and Reality: Writing Instruction in American Colleges, 1900–1985*. Carbondale: Southern Illinois University Press, 1987.

———. "Rhetoric and Ideology in the Writing Class." *CE* 50 (1988): 477–94. Rpt. in *Cross-Talk in Comp Theory: A Reader*. Ed. Victor Villanueva, Jr. Urbana: NCTE, 1997. 679–99.

Berlin, James, and Michael J. Vivion, eds. *Cultural Studies in the English Classroom*. Portsmouth, NH: Boynton/Cook Heinemann, 1992.

Berlin, James. *Rhetorics, Poetics, and Cultures: Refiguring College English Studies*. Urbana: NCTE, 1996.

BERTHOFF, ANN E.

(a) Invention, Pedagogy, Rhetoric and/or Composition Theory

(b) Ann Berthoff's main work has been the study of how meaning is made. She has written extensively on the work of I. A. Richards and Paulo Freire. In her textbook, *Forming, Thinking, Writing* (1978), she draws on I. A. Richards for her discussion of "the composing imagination," asserting that anyone who teaches writing teaches the making of meaning and that the process of composing is an act of knowing; it is the active mind, the imagination, that enables us to perceive and conceive. Berthoff wrote the essay on Richards for *Traditions of Inquiry* in 1985 and edited a collection of his essays in 1991. *Forming, Thinking, Writing* has been called one of the clearest expressions of "**epistemic** rhetoric." The first section of Berthoff's *The Making of Meaning* (1983) consists of a collection of metaphors, models, and maxims designed to help teachers translate theory into practice, the second section presents a number of her own talks and articles about teaching writing, and the final section includes a collection of essays and parts of essays from "great teachers." In several articles, including "The Problem of Problem Solving" (1971), Berthoff discusses the dangers of relying on models of cognitive development as a pedagogical concept. In "The Problem with Problem Solving," a response to Janice Lauer's "Heuristics and Composition" (1970), Berthoff argues that the invention techniques Lauer presents reduce creativity to problem solving. Berthoff's essay began a well-known debate between the two scholars. In *Reclaiming the Imagination* (1984), Berthoff aims to free the imagination from the captivity of the psychologists and return it to philosophy; she introduces essays and excerpts from philosophers, historians, scientists, artists, and others that provide philosophical perspectives from which writing teachers can consider the nature of the composing process and how to teach it. In her discussions of Paulo Freire's liberation pedagogy, she says that the only real learning is that which produces a **critical consciousness** that transforms both the individual and the world. *The Sense of Learning* (1990) is a collection of many of Berthoff's best-known essays, including "Is Teaching Still Possible?" "Abstraction as a Speculative Instrument," and " 'Reading the World . . . Reading the Word': Paulo Freire's Pedagogy of Knowing." Berthoff won the **CCCC** Exemplar Award in 1997. She is one of the fifty authors most cited in *CCC* articles from 1980–93.

(c) Berthoff, Ann E. "The Problem of Problem Solving." *CCC* 23 (1971): 237–42. Rpt. in *Contemporary Rhetoric: A Conceptual Background with Readings.* Ed. W. Ross Winterowd. New York: Harcourt Brace Jovanovich, 1975. 91–97.

———. *Forming/Thinking/Writing: The Composing Imagination.* 1978. 2nd ed. Rochelle Park, NJ: Hayden, 1988.

———. *The Making of Meaning: Metaphors, Models, and Maxims for Writing Teachers.* Upper Montclair, NJ: Boynton/Cook, 1981.

———. *Reclaiming the Imagination: Philosophical Perspectives for Writers and Teachers of Writers.* Upper Montclair, NJ: Boynton/Cook, 1984.

———. "I. A. Richards." *Traditions of Inquiry.* Ed. John Brereton. New York: Oxford University Press, 1985. 50–80.

———. *The Sense of Learning.* Portsmouth, NH: Boynton/Cook, 1990.

BITZER, LLOYD F.

(a) History of Rhetoric and/or Composition, Rhetoric and/or Composition Theory

(b) Bitzer, in the discipline of speech communication, has contributed to composition studies, particularly to the discussion of rhetorical context. His early work on Aristotle's enthymemes in "Aristotle's Enthymeme Revisited" (1959) emphasizes the role of the presuppositions of the **audience** in producing premises, and his critical introduction to *The Philosophy of Rhetoric of George Campbell* (1963) discusses the relationship of Campbell's theory of rhetoric to Campbell's views on the philosophies of his day, on human nature, and on religion. In "The Rhetorical Situation" (1968), Bitzer challenges the autonomy of the text. He describes what he considers the three critical components of any rhetorical situation: "exigence," or the circumstance that produces a need for the discourse; the audience to whom the discourse is addressed and who can respond to the circumstances if it is sufficiently moved by the discourse; and "constraints"—both the dominant assumptions, customs, and practices of the audience and the restrictions imposed on the rhetor by his own historical situation and the genre of his discourse. While Bitzer's discussion of this topic has been influential and mostly supported, it has been attacked as subordinating language to the politics and economics of a particular time and place or for giving independent, objective existence to the rhetorical situation. Bitzer's 1978 essay "Rhetoric and Public Knowledge" won the Speech Communication Association's Anniversary Essay Award for 1979. In this essay, Bitzer examines the notions of "a public" and "public knowledge" as he explores the relationship between rhetoric and public knowledge. The task of rhetoric, he suggests, is to rediscover and generate public truths and values and to make them available to the public; rhetoric should preserve and nurture wisdom in the public life. With Edwin Black, Bitzer edited *The Prospect of Rhetoric*, the proceedings of the 1970 "Wingspread Conference" and the 1970 National Conference on Rhetoric, which includes essays on the theory of rhetoric by key scholars in a variety of disciplines.

(c) Bitzer, Lloyd F. "Aristotle's Enthymeme Revisited." *QJS* 45 (1959): 399–408.

———, ed. *The Philosophy of Rhetoric of George Campbell*. 1963. Rev. ed. Carbondale: Southern Illinois University Press, 1988.

———. "The Rhetorical Situation." *P & R* 1 (1968): 1–14. Rpt. in *Contemporary Theories of Rhetoric*. Ed. Richard L. Johannesen. New York: Harper & Row, 1971. 381–93.

Bitzer, Lloyd R., and Edwin Black, eds. *The Prospect of Rhetoric: Report of the National Developmental Project*. Englewood Cliffs, NJ: Prentice-Hall, 1971.

———. "Rhetoric and Public Knowledge." *Rhetoric, Philosophy, and Literature*. Ed. Don M. Burks. West Lafayette: Purdue University Press, 1978. 67–93.

BIZZELL, PATRICIA

(a) Basic Writing, Bibliography, History of Rhetoric and/or Composition, Literacy, Rhetoric and/or Composition Theory

(b) A strong proponent of social theories of language, in "Cognition, Convention, and Certainty: What We Need to Know About Writing" (1982) Bizzell lays out the debate between **cognitive** and social theorists, using the terms **"inner-"** and **"outer-" directed** to characterize the two positions. Like David Bartholomae, she argues that **basic writers'** difficulties are not caused by problems of cognitive or linguistic development but by unfamiliarity with the conventions and practices of the **academic discourse community**. These writers need to gain an "academic worldview," to be introduced to the academic discourse community. Mastery of academic writing would lead to what Paulo Freire calls a **"critical consciousness"** or distance that would allow these writers to challenge and transform the world. This view supports one of the trends in basic writing—deemphasis on drills and workbooks and increased emphasis on **collaboration** and the integration of reading, writing, speaking, and thinking. When she discusses literacy, Bizzell distinguishes between those who argue rhetorically and those who argue **foundationally**. The former, she says, understand that their arguments are **socially constructed** and therefore always open to "dialectical revision." The latter, however, because they base their arguments on transcendent standards true for all times and places, believe that their arguments can prove an opponent wrong "absolutely." Bizzell advocates a rhetorical rather than a foundationalist point of view. By the time she writes "Beyond Anti-Foundationalism to Rhetorical **Authority**: Problems Defining 'Cultural Literacy' " in 1990, she argues that those who reject foundationalism must engage in a rhetorical process that produces trustworthy, but nonfoundational, knowledge. "Beyond Anti-Foundationalism" is the final essay in a collection, *Academic Discourse and Critical Consciousness* (1992), in which she traces the evolution of her thinking on the relationship between academic discourse and critical consciousness. In 1983, Bizzell began editing, with Bruce Herzberg, *The Bedford Bibliography for Teachers of Writing*. In 1990, Bizzell and Herzberg edited *The Rhetorical Tradition: Readings from Classical Times to the Present*. Intended for graduate courses in rhetoric in English departments, it is a chronologically presented interdisciplinary collection of primary readings from classical to twentieth-century rhetoric. It shared the **NCTE** Outstanding Book Award for 1992. Her 1996 collection of readings from periods of cultural conflict in America (also with Herzberg), teaches students to negotiate inherently unequal conflicts. Bizzell is one of the fifty authors most cited in *CCC* articles from 1980–93.

(c) Bizzell, Patricia. "Cognition, Convention, and Certainty: What We Need to Know About Writing." *PRE/TEXT* 3 (fall 1982): 213–43. Rpt. in *Cross-Talk in Comp Theory: A Reader*. Ed. Victor Villanueva, Jr. Urbana: NCTE, 1997. 365–89.

Bizzell, Patricia, and Bruce Herzberg. *The Bedford Bibliography for Teachers of Writing*. 1984. 4th ed. Bizzell, Patricia and Bruce Herzberg. Boston: Bedford Books, 1996. Online. WWW.BedfordBooks.Com/BB/online.HTML. 1997.

Bizzell, Patricia. "What Happens When Basic Writers Come to College?" *CCC* 37 (1986): 294–301.

Bizzell, Patricia, and Bruce Herzberg. *The Rhetorical Tradition: Readings from Classical Times to the Present*. Boston: Bedford Books, 1990.

Bizzell, Patricia. *Academic Discourse and Critical Consciousness*. Pittsburgh: University of Pittsburgh Press, 1992.

Bizzell, Patricia, and Bruce Herzberg. *Negotiating Difference: Cultural Case Studies for Composition*. Boston: Bedford Books, 1996.

BLAIR, HUGH

(a) Literature and Composition, Rhetoric and/or Composition Theory, Style

(b) Blair was a Scottish clergyman and teacher whose *Lectures on Rhetoric and Belle-Lettres* (1783) contains forty-seven classroom lectures presented over twenty years as Regius Professor of Rhetoric and Belle-Lettres at Edinburgh University. This comprehensive and practical work, which went through more than 130 editions and which was widely used as a textbook in England, Europe, and the United States, has been called one of the sources of **current-traditional rhetoric**. Blair was one of the first rhetoricians to join rhetoric and belle-lettres, and the *Lectures*, written for beginning writers, emphasizes the connection between reading and writing. Beginning writers should develop "taste," which they can do by practicing literary criticism—by using their reason to discover what, in a text, produces the sensory pleasure they feel when they read it. Through analysis and imitation of effective writing, they learn to write well themselves. Blair's influence has been felt mainly in his emphasis on style, but also in his slighting of rhetorical **invention** and in his focus on written discourse over oratory. He is one of three rhetoricians (see also George Campbell and Richard Whately) credited with beginning modern rhetoric.

(c) Blair, Hugh. *Lectures on Rhetoric and Belle-Lettres*. 2 vols. London and Edinburgh: Ridgeway, 1783. Rev. ed. Ed. Harold Harding. 2 vols. Carbondale: Southern Illinois University Press, 1965. Facsimile Reproduction. Introduction by Charlotte Downey. New York: Scholars' Facsimiles and Rpts., 1993.

BOOTH, WAYNE C.

(a) Literature and Composition, Rhetoric and/or Composition Theory

(b) Booth's work in the early 1960s did much to revive English departments' interest in rhetoric. By focusing on a close analysis of examples from many literary texts, his *Rhetoric of Fiction* (1961), which won both the Christian Gauss Award and **NCTE**'s David H. Russell Award for Distinguished Research in the Teaching of English, shows how authors of fiction use rhetorical techniques to create "voices" that in turn create "readers" by determining the way they respond to characters in the works. Booth's "The Rhetorical Stance" (1963) also contributed to the increased interest in rhetoric. This essay describes effective writing as that in which a writer achieves and maintains the "rhetorical stance"—a balance between the demands of the subject, the character of the **audience**, and the voice (the "implied character") of the speaker. Booth's *Moral Dogma and the Rhetoric of Assent* (1974) analyzes theories of rhetoric and epistemology of the late 1960s. In several works, Booth argues for the benefits of "critical pluralism" but also argues that writers, especially modern/postmodern writers, must be "morally responsible" and careful not to mislead or confuse their readers. In all his works, Booth reiterates the close connection between reading and writing and between literature/literary criticism and rhetoric/composition. He suggests the teaching of rhetoric as a way to unify the university curriculum. Booth's *The Craft of Research* (1995, with Joseph Williams and Gregory Colomb) describes the process of doing and reporting research. It won the National Critics Award.

(c) Booth, Wayne C. *The Rhetoric of Fiction*. 1961. 2nd ed. Chicago: University of Chicago Press, 1983. Rpt. London: Penguin, 1991.
———. "The Rhetorical Stance." *CCC* 14 (1963): 139–45. Rpt. in *The Writing Teacher's Sourcebook*. Ed. Gary Tate and Edward P. J. Corbett. New York: Oxford University Press, 1981. 108–16. 2nd ed. 1988. 151–57.

———. *Modern Dogma and the Rhetoric of Assent*. Notre Dame: University of Notre Dame Press, 1974.

Booth, Wayne C., and Marshall W. Gregory. *The Harper & Row Rhetoric*. 1987. 3rd ed. New York: HarperCollins, 1992.

———. "The Idea of a University as Seen by a Rhetorician." *The 1987 Ryerson Lecture*. Chicago: University of Chicago Press, 1987. Rpt. in *Professing the New Rhetorics: A Sourcebook*. Ed. Theresa Enos and Stuart Brown. Englewood Cliffs, NJ: Prentice Hall, 1994. 229–52.

Booth, Wayne C., Joseph Williams, and Gregory Colomb. *The Craft of Research*. Chicago: University of Chicago Press, 1995.

BRADDOCK, RICHARD

(a) Bibliography, Research Methodology

(b) Braddock was an early leader in composition studies whose contributions to the field have been discussed by Richard Lloyd-Jones in the 1985 *Traditions of Inquiry*. With Lloyd-Jones and Lowell Schoer, Braddock edited one of the earliest bibliographies of composition research, *Research in Written Composition* (1963), a work that oriented the discipline toward research and which many see as marking the beginning of composition studies. In this survey of 504 studies completed before 1963, Braddock shows most research to be concerned with presenting pedagogical techniques, not with demonstrating their effectiveness or with grounding them in theory. He asserts that the methodology of the sciences, with its insistence on "controlled experimentation," is the only valid research method; Braddock explains the methodology and warns of some of the problems of experimental research in composition. He recommends "frequency counts" of error types as an objective method for evaluating writing and thus reveals his roots in the empirical tradition. In the section evaluating school grammar instruction, however, he suggests that grammar is the least effective focus of instruction. Under the heading "Unexplored Territory," Braddock and his colleagues raise such issues as the relations of motivation and audience to writing. Braddock continued his leadership in the area of composition research by helping to establish and serving as the first editor for **NCTE**'s new journal, *Research in the Teaching of English*, from 1967 to 1972. The Braddock Award was established in his honor; he himself won the award in 1975 for "The Frequency and Placement of Topic Sentences in Expository Prose." In this article, Braddock analyzes the paragraphs of twenty-five professional essays written from 1964 to 1965, demonstrating that professional writers do not use topic sentences in many of their paragraphs. He warns writing teachers to "exercise caution" in making claims about the universality of topic sentences in professional writing. Braddock is one of the most frequently published authors of major articles in *CCC* from 1950–64. He chaired **CCCC** in 1967.

(c) Braddock, Richard, ed. *Introductory Readings on the English Language*. Englewood Cliffs, NJ: Prentice-Hall, 1962.

Braddock, Richard, Richard Lloyd-Jones, and Lowell Schoer, eds. *Research in Written Composition*. Urbana: NCTE, 1963.

Braddock, Richard. "The Frequency and Placement of Topic Sentences in Expository Prose." *RTE* 8 (1976): 287–304. Rpt. in *Cross-Talk in Comp Theory: A Reader*. Ed. Victor Villanueva, Jr. Urbana: NCTE, 1997. 167–81.

BRANNON, LIL

(**a**) History of Rhetoric and/or Composition, Literacy, Response and Evaluation, Rhetoric and/or Composition Theory

(**b**) *Rhetorical Traditions and the Teaching of Writing* (1984), written with C. H. Knoblauch, is Brannon's most influential work. In it, the authors argue that the epistemological revolution of René Descartes and John Locke reduced the relevance of classical rhetoric for teachers of composition. Adapting classical rhetoric to modern concerns, they say, might continue a "discredited distinction" between form and content and a mechanistic view of composing, so adhering to classical notions while drawing on later theory sends mixed and confusing messages. They conclude that the cognitive reorientation that took place in some late eighteenth- and early nineteenth-century rhetorics, like that of George Campbell, has led to methods more relevant for composition teaching, such as the writing **workshop**. Brannon and Knoblauch have also written on responding to student writing. Their 1982 essay "On Students' Rights to Their Own Texts" suggests that teachers give feedback during the writing **process** so that students can see how well their writing fulfills their intentions. In a 1983 essay, "Writing as Learning through the Curriculum," they argue that teachers in content areas should use writing as a way to help students make discoveries and to encourage further study. Brannon's essay in *Perspectives on Research and Scholarship in Composition* (1985) analyzes the way composition researchers from three philosophical perspectives—empirical-experimental, phenomenological-**ethnographic**, and philosophical-historical—have tried to answer questions about the composing process, the development of writers, and the best way to teach writing. In "Knowing Our Knowledge: A Phenomenological Basis for Teacher Research" (1988), Brannon and Knoblauch defend the legitimacy of **teacher research**. They argue that positivism's unfounded belief in empirical science's "objectivity" leads to criticisms of teacher inquiry, and they contend that storytelling is a valid way of "knowing." In their work on literacy and **critical pedagogy**, they argue for new "stories" that retheorize the practice and methods of testing and redefine the nature and importance of literacy. Brannon founded *The Writing Center Journal*, which she co-edited from 1980–85. She is one of the fifty authors most cited in *CCC* articles from 1980–93.

(**c**) Brannon, Lil, and C. H. Knoblauch. "On Students' Rights to Their Own Texts: A Model of Teacher Response." *CCC* 33 (1982): 157–66.

———. "Writing as Learning Through the Curriculum." *CE* 45 (1983): 465–74.

————. *Rhetorical Traditions and the Teaching of Writing*. Upper Montclair, NJ: Boynton/Cook, 1984.

Brannon, Lil. "Toward a Theory of Composition." *Perspectives on Research and Scholarship in Composition*. Eds. Ben McClelland and Timothy Donovan. New York: MLA, 1985. 6–25.

Brannon, Lil, and C. H. Knoblauch. "Knowing Our Knowledge: A Phenomenological Basis for Teacher Research." *Audits of Meaning*. Ed. Louise Z. Smith. Portsmouth, NH: Boynton/Cook, 1988. 17–28.

————. *Critical Teaching and the Idea of Literacy*. Portsmouth, NH: Boynton/Cook, 1993.

BRIDWELL-BOWLES (BRIDWELL), LILLIAN S.

(a) Bibliography, Technology and Composition, Research Methodology, Revision

(b) Bridwell-Bowles is noted for her work on computers and composition, especially for her bibliographies and her work with their use in composing and revising. In a 1980 essay, Bridwell-Bowles draws on and adds to Nancy Sommers' classification system for her own study of the revision strategies of twelfth-grade writers. In several later essays, she discusses the effects of writing with computers and word processors on students' composing and revising strategies and on research in revision. In essays with Paula Reed Nancarrow and Donald Ross, Bridwell-Bowles provides a comprehensive annotated bibliography of word processing and summarizes current research on using word processors to teach writing. With Helen Schwartz, she publishes and later updates "A Selected Bibliography on Computers in Composition" (1984 and 1987). Bridwell-Bowles also has edited, with Richard Beach, a collection of research studies, *New Directions in Composition Research* (1984). The studies in this collection reflect a broadening of the discipline's research models since *Research in Written Composition* (Braddock et al., 1963). Bridwell-Bowles wrote the chapter on issues and research methods in composition studies from the 1960s through the 1980s for *An Introduction to Composition Studies* (1991). In 1992 and 1995, she published two essays that have been reprinted in collections focusing on women as writers and teachers of writing. In the earlier essay, she describes why and how she encourages students in her classes to experiment with "diverse" ways of writing. Bridwell-Bowles chaired **CCCC** in 1994, and in the second essay, the text of her 1994 CCCC chair's address, she gives an autobiographical "literacy history" and discusses why she and others in composition studies must write in a wide variety of forms and from different perspectives. She is one of the most frequently published authors of major articles in *CCC* from 1980–93.

(c) Bridwell (Bowles), Lillian S. "Revising Strategies in Twelfth Grade Students' Transactional Writing." *RTE* 14 (1980): 197–222.

Bridwell (Bowles), Lillian S., and Helen Schwartz. "A Selected Bibliography on Computers in Composition." *CCC* 35 (1984): 71–77. "An Update." *CCC* 38 (1987): 453–57.

Bridwell (Bowles), Lillian S., and Richard Beach, eds. *New Directions in Composition Research*. New York: Guilford Press, 1984.

Bridwell (Bowles), Lillian S., Geoffrey Sirc, and Robert Brooke. "Revising and Computing: Case Studies of Student Writers." *The Acquisition of Written Language: Revision and Response*. Ed. Sarah Warshauer Freedman. Norwood, NJ: Ablex, 1985. 172–94.

Bridwell-Bowles, Lillian S. "Research in Composition: Issues and Methods." *An Introduction to Composition Studies*. Ed. Erika Lindemann and Gary Tate. New York: Oxford University Press, 1991. 94–117.

————. "Discourse and Diversity: Experimental Writing Within the Academy." *CCC* 43 (1992): 349–68. Rpt. in *Feminine Principles and Women's Experience in American Composition and Rhetoric*. Eds. Louise Weatherbee Phelps and Janet Emig. Pittsburgh: University of Pittsburgh Press, 1995. 43–66.

BRITTON, JAMES

(a) Composing Processes, Writing Across the Curriculum, Rhetoric and/or Composition Theory

(b) In *The Development of Writing Abilities (11–18)* (1975), Britton and a group of researchers at the University of London examine 2,100 papers written in eighty-five different classes by students between the ages of 11 and 18. Their work has resulted in an increased emphasis on **expressive writing**, particularly in elementary and secondary schools; on the composing **process**; and on **writing across the curriculum**, especially at the secondary level. One of the first groups to point out deficiencies in **current-traditional "modes of discourse"** and in **"T-units,"** Britton and these researchers develop a method of classifying texts according to function and **audience**. Their research also suggests an order of development in types of writing. Britton defines **"transactional"** language and argues that this kind of language (like **"poetic"** language) can come only as an outgrowth of "expressive" writing. These three function categories—transactional, expressive, and poetic—form a sliding scale: transactional<—expressive—>poetic. Although the expressive function is fundamental, Britton says students should practice writing of all sorts. In a 1980 essay, "Shaping at the Point of Utterance," he says that concern for multiple drafts and revision might lead theorists to discount the importance of "spontaneous inventiveness," the intuitive insights that allow writers to shape "at the point of utterance." He suggests that research into how writers develop their "inner voice" might lead to better understanding of invention. In "Spectator Role and the Beginnings of Language" (1982), Britton differentiates the role of spectator from that of participant, claiming that to play the role of spectator of events is to be in the realm of literature. He argues that when children tell stories in words and pictures, listen to stories, and later read and write stories, they are acting in the role of spectators. Britton contends that it is their activities as spectators that develop children's desire to master written language. Britton's work on the relationship of reading and writing argues that remembering what one has read, particularly aloud, carries over into the way one creates structure and meaning in one's own writing. *Prospect and Retrospect* (1982) collects twenty of Britton's essays on a variety of issues ranging from pedagogy to politics. Britton is one of the fifty authors most cited in *CCC* articles from 1980–93.

(c) Britton, James. *Language and Learning.* 1970. 2nd ed. Montclair, NJ: Boynton/Cook, 1993.

Britton, James, et al. *The Development of Writing Abilities (11–18).* London: Macmillan Education, 1975. Rpt. Urbana: NCTE, 1992.

Britton, James. "The Composing Process and the Functions of Writing." *Research on Composing: Points of Departure.* Ed. Charles Cooper and Lee Odell. Urbana: NCTE, 1978. 13–28.

———. "Shaping at the Point of Utterance." *Reinventing the Rhetorical Tradition.* Ed. Aviva Freedman and Ian Pringle. Ottawa: Canadian Council of Teachers of English, 1980. 61–65. Rpt. in *Composition in Four Keys: Inquiring into the Field.* Ed. Mark Wiley, Barbara Gleason, and Louise Weatherbee Phelps. Mountain View, CA: Mayfield, 1996. 29–33.

———. *Prospect and Retrospect: Selected Essays of James Britton.* Ed. Gordon Pradle. Montclair, NJ: Boynton/Cook, 1982.

———. "Spectator Role and the Beginnings of Writing." *What Writers Know: The Language, Process, and Structure of Written Discourse.* Ed. Martin Nystrand. New York: Academic, 1982. 149–69. Rpt. in *Cross-Talk in Comp Theory: A Reader.* Ed. Victor Villanueva, Jr. Urbana: NCTE, 1997. 129–51.

———. "Theories of the Disciplines and a Learning Theory." *Writing, Teaching, and Learning in the Disciplines.* Ed. Anne Herrington and Charles Moran. New York: MLA, 1992. 47–60.

BRODKEY, LINDA

(a) Gender and Composition, Literacy, Rhetoric and/or Composition Theory

(b) In all her work, Brodkey stresses writing as social practice. In "Modernism and the Scene(s) of Writing" (1987), she debunks the modernist metaphor of the **solitary author** alone in a garret, arguing that this picture ignores or denies that all writing takes place in the context of a **conversation** with other writers and readers. Brodkey's *Academic Writing as Social Practice* (1987) focuses on the scene of writing (and reading) in the academic community and on what forces govern who is allowed to participate in the largely written conversation of that community. Her work on **ethnography** points out the presence of narrative in all research traditions and argues that the centrality of narrative in ethnographic research does not make it inferior. In her work on literacy, she focuses on social and political concerns and on the need to recognize and explore differences. In "On the Subjects of Class and Gender in 'The Literacy Letters' " (1989), she reports on research informed by postmodern theories of subjectivity.

By examining a series of letters between white middle-class teachers and white
working-class women enrolled in an adult education class, she explores the
unconscious tactics the teachers use to preserve their privileged subject positions
and the ways the students **resist** how they are represented. Brodkey suggests
that by refusing to acknowledge differences in class, race, and gender, well-
meaning teachers actually "silence" students by not responding to their voices.
In the title article in *Writing Permitted in Designated Areas Only* (1996), a
collection of her work, she takes to task composition instruction that, she says,
too often teaches students to dislike writing by reducing it to a set of rules and
exercises.

(c) Brodkey, Linda. "Modernism and the Scene(s) of Writing." *CE* 49 (1987): 396–418.
———. *Academic Writing as Social Practice.* Philadelphia: Temple University Press,
     1987.
———. "Writing Ethnographic Narratives." *WC* 4 (1987): 25–50.
———. "On the Subjects of Class and Gender in 'The Literacy Letters.' " *CE* 51 (1989):
     125–41. Rpt. in *Cross-Talk in Comp Theory: A Reader.* Ed. Victor Villanueva,
     Jr. Urbana: NCTE, 1997. 639–58.
———. *Writing Permitted in Designated Areas Only.* Minneapolis: University of Min-
     nesota Press, 1996.

BRUFFEE, KENNETH A.

(a) Bibliography, Collaboration, Rhetoric and/or Composition Theory, Writing Program Administration

(b) Bruffee discusses both the history of **collaborative learning** and its conceptual framework and provides collaborative models for teachers. He agrees
with the philosophical movement that sees meaning as **socially constructed**.
Drawing on Lev Vygotsky, Thomas Kuhn, and, especially, Richard Rorty, he
argues that children develop the ability to think by conversing with others, that
they internalize these **conversations** to think reflexively, and that they exter-
nalize their thought again when they write. In "Collaborative Learning and the
'Conversation of Mankind' " (1984), he says that collaborative learning provides
the "conversations" that allow students to enter the **academic discourse community** and thus must form part of an effective pedagogy. In collaborative
learning, group members ideally arrive at collective decisions through negotiation, or **consensus**, a notion that draws criticism from those who argue that such
a process often silences minority voices. Bruffee advocates peer tutors as an
effective form of collaborative learning, since peers are united by social as well
as intellectual interests. His 1986 bibliographical essay "Social Construction,
Language, and the **Authority** of Knowledge" presents an overview of social
construction and its texts. In *Collaborative Learning: Higher Education, Interdependence, and the Authority of Knowledge* (1993), Bruffee discusses the implications of social construction and collaborative learning for college and
university education. He was the founder and editor of *Journal of the National*

Council of Writing Program Administrators (WPA) from 1978–83. Bruffee is one of the fifty authors most cited in *CCC* articles from 1980–93.

(c) Bruffee, Kenneth A. *A Short Course in Writing*. Cambridge, MA: Winthrop, 1972. 4th ed. *A Short Course in Writing: Composition, Collaborative Learning, and Constructive Reading*. New York: Reading, MA: Addison Wesley, 1993.

———. "Writing and Reading as Collaborative or Social Acts." *The Writer's Mind: Writing as a Mode of Thinking*. Ed. Janice N. Hays et al. Urbana: NCTE, 1983. 159–69.

———. "Collaborative Learning and the 'Conversation of Mankind.' " *CE* 46 (1984): 635–52. Rpt. in *Cross-Talk in Comp Theory: A Reader*. Ed. Victor Villanueva, Jr. Urbana: NCTE, 1997. 393–414.

———. "Social Construction, Language, and the Authority of Knowledge: A Bibliographical Essay." *CE* 48 (1986): 773–90.

———. *Collaborative Learning: Higher Education, Interdependence, and the Authority of Knowledge*. 1993. 2nd ed. Baltimore: Johns Hopkins University Press, 1998.

BURKE, KENNETH

(a) Argument, Invention, Rhetoric and/or Composition Theory

(b) Burke defines human beings as "symbol-using animals"; their "potential for speech and reason" sets them apart from other animals, and the symbolic action that language makes possible allows them to build their identities. Although designed to analyze texts rather than as an invention technique, Burke's accessible **heuristic**, the "**dramatistic pentad**"—act, scene, agent, agency, purpose—is the most widely known practical application of his theory. In *A Grammar of Motives* (1945), he discusses the permutations and implications of the pentad. This system for analyzing motives, whether an extension of Aristotelian rhetoric, as he has said, or of Nietzschean or Marxist philosophy, as has also been claimed, has influenced both theory and practice. In *A Rhetoric of Motives* (1950), Burke, one of the originators of the **new rhetoric**, replaces the "persuasion" of classical rhetoric with **"identification,"** a term that calls attention to the relation between rhetor and **audience**. A rhetor, he says, persuades an audience through structural and stylistic identifications designed to cause the audience to identify with the rhetor's interests. The rhetor then uses this identification of interests to establish rapport with her audience. In Burke's terms, rhetor and audience become "consubstantial," or "substantially one" while remaining uniquely themselves. Burke's discussion of "dialectics," which he sometimes describes as "abstract thinking," also has been influential. Through the symbolic action of language (abstract thinking), a person is able to reconcile what seem to be contradictions and to make the necessary, complex choices to grow morally. In his discussion of **"terministic screens,"** Burke points out that the terms we use to talk about an act will define (and limit) the way we perceive it. **"God-terms"** is his phrase for the ultimate rhetorical terms of a society that motivate its members and unite them. *Language as Symbolic Action* (1966) is a collection of Burke's articles. In 1968, he wrote the article on dramatism for the *International Encyclopedia of Social Sciences*, and in a 1978 essay he continues to answer questions about the pentad. He is one of the ten authors most often cited in *CCC* articles from 1965–79 and one of the fifty most cited from 1980–93.

(c) Burke, Kenneth. *A Grammar of Motives*. Englewood Cliffs, NJ: Prentice-Hall, 1945. Rpt. Berkeley: University of California Press, 1969.
———. *A Rhetoric of Motives*. Englewood Cliffs, NJ: Prentice-Hall, 1950. Rpt. Berkeley: University of California Press, 1969.
———. "Rhetoric—Old and New." *JGenEd* 5 (1951): 202–9.
———. *Language as Symbolic Action: Essays on Life, Literature, and Method*. 1966. Rpt. Berkeley: University of California Press, 1968.
———. *Dramatism and Development*. Barre, MA: Clark University Press, 1972.
———. "Questions and Answers about the Pentad." *CCC* 29 (1978): 330–35.

CAMPBELL, GEORGE

(a) Rhetoric and/or Composition Theory
(b) Campbell, a Scottish clergyman and preacher who was principal of Marischal College in Aberdeen from 1759 to 1795, is one of three rhetoricians (see **Hugh Blair** and **Richard Whately**) whose work marks a move to modern rhetoric. One of the first to classify discourse by its purpose or end, Campbell is also significant for his discussion of the way rhetors achieve the ends of discourse by understanding the psychology of their **audience**. He is best known for *The Philosophy of Rhetoric* (1776), a work anchored in both **Scottish common sense realism** and faculty psychology. In this work, Campbell maintains that the human mind comes to know reality through careful observation of sensory experience. Under such an epistemology, rhetorical **invention** ceases to be, in its original sense of topical invention, a part of rhetoric. The object of rhetoric is to recreate through language the vividness of the experience of the rhetor in the mind of his audience. Rhetoric achieves this end by appealing to the innate faculties shared by the rhetor and his audience—understanding, imagination, passion, and will. To persuade, discourse must move the will, which can be done only by appealing successfully, in turn, to each of the other three faculties. With its emphasis on the rhetorical strategy of establishing a bond of sympathy between rhetor and audience, Campbell's discussion of ethos seems to foreshadow Kenneth Burke's **identification**. His commentary on usage as social custom—what he calls reputable use, national use, and present use—has been important in American education. Robert Connors traces the roots of the **modes of discourse** to Campbell's rhetoric.

(c) Campbell, George. *The Philosophy of Rhetoric*, 2 vols. London: 1776. Landmark Ed. Ed. Lloyd Bitzer. Carbondale: Southern Illinois University Press, 1963.

CHRISTENSEN, FRANCIS

(a) Arrangement, Linguistics, Rhetoric and/or Composition Theory, Style

(b) Christensen is known for his generative grammar based on structural linguistics. In "A **Generative Rhetoric** of the Sentence" (1963), he describes what he says is the typical sentence of modern English, the "cumulative sentence," which has a sentence base or main clause that advances the discussion. This sentence pattern also includes "free modifiers," modifying words, phrases, or clauses that can occur at the beginning, within, or after the sentence base. Christensen argues that the form of this sentence alone is able to generate ideas. In "A Generative Rhetoric of the Paragraph" (1965), he argues that the paragraph has basically the same structure as the cumulative sentence, with supporting sentences structurally related to a topic sentence and to each other by either subordination or coordination. He identifies three kinds of paragraphs: those with coordinate, subordinate, and mixed sequences of sentences. By analyzing these sequences, he maintains, writers can learn where their paragraphs lack coherence and where they need additional development. Christensen has been among the first to argue that **T-units** are not accurate measures of syntactic maturity, since they ignore "free modifiers." He also warns that **sentence-combining** exercises might result in overwritten prose. *Notes Toward a New Rhetoric*: *Six Essays for Teachers* (1967) is a collection of his essays; the 1978 revised edition includes three additional essays. He is among the ten most cited authors in *CCC* from 1965–79 and is one of the fifty most cited authors in *CCC* from 1980–93. He is one of the most frequently published authors of major articles in *CCC* from 1980–93.

(c) Christensen, Francis. "A Generative Rhetoric of the Sentence." *CCC* 14 (1963): 155–61. Rpt. in *The Writing Teacher's Sourcebook*. Ed. Gary Tate and Edward P. J. Corbett. New York: Oxford University Press, 1981. 353–367.

———. "A Generative Rhetoric of the Paragraph." *CCC* 16 (1965): 144–56. Rpt. in *Teaching Freshman Composition*. Ed. Gary Tate and Edward P. J. Corbett. New York: Oxford University Press, 1967. 200–216.

———. *Notes Toward a New Rhetoric: Six Essays for Teachers*. 1967. Rev. ed. *Notes Toward a New Rhetoric: Nine Essays for Teachers*. Ed. Bonniejean Christensen. New York: Harper & Row, 1978.

COLES, WILLIAM E., JR.

(a) Composing Processes, Essay and Personal Writing, Pedagogy

(b) Coles is often associated with **expressivism**. Although his earlier work, including *Composing: A Guide to Teaching Writing as a Self-Creating Process* (1974), pioneered the expressivist approach, Coles is probably best known for *The Plural I* (1978), a set of thirty writing assignments on the same topic, sequenced to move toward greater complexity. Written for writing teachers, this work seems to have been a reaction to **current-traditional** theory, which, Coles says, often produces the empty, formulaic writing he calls "themewriting" (and Macrorie "Engfish") and which contradicts the teacher's own experience with writing. His work is based on the premise that though writing is an art that cannot be directly taught, it can be fostered by helping students become aware of how they use language to create themselves (their **authentic voices**) and their reality. In *The Plural I*, the students' own writing becomes the text over the course of a semester. The role of a writing teacher in such a course is to comment on the content of student writing, to encourage students to feel free to comment on one another's work, and to let students see how language has shaped the teacher's own life by letting them hear the teacher's "voice." Coles advocates that teachers be trained by taking the same sort of course they will teach their students. *The Plural I—and After* (1988) includes two additional essays, one about how the book originated and one discussing the nature of literacy. *What Makes Writing Good* (1985) is a collection of student essays chosen by writing teachers for their quality. After each essay, the teacher who chose it discusses why it is "good" writing. *Seeing Through Writing* (1988), like *The Plural I*, is designed primarily for teachers; its assignments ask students to look at their own writing from a variety of perspectives in order to gain power over and through their use of language.

(c) Coles, William E., Jr. *Composing: Writing as a Self-Creating Process.* Rochelle Park, NJ: Hayden, 1974. Upper Montclair, NJ: Boynton/Cook, 1983. Rpt. on demand by Boynton/Cook, 1996.

———. *The Plural I: The Teaching of Writing.* New York: Holt, Rinehart and Winston, 1978.

Coles, William E., and James Vopat, eds. *What Makes Writing Good.* Lexington, MA: D. C. Heath and Co., 1985.

———. *Seeing Through Writing.* New York: HarperCollins, 1988.

———. *The Plural I—and After.* Portsmouth, NH: Heinemann, Boynton/Cook, 1988.

COMPRONE, JOSEPH

(a) Bibliography, Composing Processes, Literature and Composition, Writing Across the Curriculum

(b) Comprone has written several articles on media and composition, and his textbook *From Experience to Expression* (1974) asks students to use in their own writing the forms they have found in different types of media. He wrote the bibliographical chapters "The Uses of Media in Teaching Composition" in *Teaching Composition: 10 Bibliographical Essays* (1976) and "Literary Theory and Composition" in *Teaching Composition: 12 Bibliographical Essays* (1987). "Literature and the Writing **Process**: A Pedagogical Reading of William Faulkner's 'Barn Burning' " (1982) suggests ways that writing can help readers move through what he describes as three stages in the process of constructing meaning from a work of literature. Comprone's work on composing includes several studies of Kenneth Burke's work, especially applications of his **dramatistic pentad**, discussion of **terministic screens**, and concept of **identification**. Comprone has also written on teacher training and **writing across the curriculum**. In a 1993 essay, "Where Do We Go Next in Writing Across the Curriculum?" (with Robert Jones), he warns that WAC programs must succeed in coordinating administration, teaching, and research. Comprone and Jones discuss goals for the next stage of development in writing across the curriculum, including integrating expressive **writing-to-learn** teaching aims and methods with rhetorical approaches that are the result of research into discipline-specific conventions.

(**c**) Comprone, Joseph. "Using Painting, Photography, and Film to Teach Writing." *CE* 35 (1973): 174–78.

————. *From Experience to Expression: A College Rhetoric*. Dubuque, IA: W. C. Brown, 1974. 2nd ed. Boston: Houghton Mifflin, 1981.

————. "The Uses of Media in Teaching Composition." *Teaching Composition: 10 Bibliographical Essays*. Fort Worth: Texas Christian University Press, 1976. 169–95. "Literary Theory and Composition." *Teaching Composition: 12 Bibliographical Essays*. Fort Worth: Texas Christian University Press, 1987. 291–330.

————. "Kenneth Burke and the Teaching of Writing." *CCC* 29 (1978): 336–40.

————. "Literature and the Writing Process: A Pedagogical Reading of William Faulkner's 'Barn Burning.' " *CL* 9 (1982): 2–21.

————, and Robert Jones. "Where Do We Go Next in Writing Across the Curriculum?" *CCC* 44 (1993): 59–68.

CONNORS, ROBERT J.

(**a**) Essay and Personal Writing, Gender and Composition, History of Rhetoric and/or Composition, Rhetoric and/or Composition Theory

(**b**) Connors' most influential work has been in the history of composition. In "The Rise and Fall of the **Modes of Discourse**," which won the Braddock Award in 1982, Connors surveys popular rhetoric textbooks to trace the history of writing instruction in American colleges and universities from the 1800s to the 1950s. Perhaps responding to criticism that he relied too heavily on textbooks to determine the nature of writing instruction in this period, Connors has written also on the way textbooks both reflect and recreate the interests of writing teachers. Among other historical studies, he has traced changes in the nature of writing assignments, the forces that produced the emphasis on mechanical correctness in writing courses, and the growth of a rhetoric of explanation (as opposed to a rhetoric of persuasion). Connors has also argued that the discipline of composition studies is not a science and has pointed out problems with the concept of **paradigm**. He won the Mina Shaughnessy Award in 1984 (with Lisa Ede and Andrea Lunsford) for *Essays on Classical Rhetoric and Modern Discourse*, which argues for the compatibility of classical and modern rhetoric. In 1989, he edited *The Selected Essays of Edward P. J. Corbett*. In 1989, he coauthored a handbook (with Andrea Lunsford) and a teaching guide to writing (with Cheryl Glenn), both for St. Martin's Press. Connors also wrote the chapter on the history of composition studies for Erika Lindemann and Gary Tate's *An Introduction to Composition Studies*. In "Teaching and Learning as a Man" (1996), he examines how a culture's definition of "manhood" affects the relationship of male teachers and their male students. *Composition-Rhetoric: Backgrounds, Theory, and Pedagogy* (1997) focuses on the rhetoric of written composition as it was taught in American colleges after 1780. One of Connors' purposes in this work is to reexamine and reevaluate nineteenth-century (**current-traditional**) rhetoric. He is one of the fifty authors most cited in *CCC* articles from 1980–93 and one of the most frequently published authors of major articles in *CCC* for the same period.

(c) Connors, Robert, J. "The Rise and Fall of the Modes of Discourse." *CCC* 32 (1981): 444–63. Rpt. in *The Writing Teacher's Sourcebook*. Ed. Gary Tate and Edward P. J. Corbett. 2nd ed. New York: Oxford University Press, 1988. 24–34.

Connors, Robert J., Lisa Ede, and Andrea Lunsford. *Essays on Classical Rhetoric and Modern Discourse*. Carbondale: Southern Illinois University Press: 1984.

Connors, Robert, J. "Textbooks and the Evolution of the Discipline." *CCC* 37 (1986): 178–94.

———, ed. *The Selected Essays of Edward P. J. Corbett*. Dallas: Southern Methodist University Press, 1989.

———. "Writing the History of Our Discipline." *An Introduction to Composition Studies*. Ed. Erika Lindemann and Gary Tate. New York: Oxford University Press, 1991. 49–71.

———. "Teaching and Learning as a Man." *CE* 58 (1996): 137–57.

———. *Composition-Rhetoric: Backgrounds, Theory, and Pedagogy*. Pittsburgh: University of Pittsburgh Press, 1997.

COOPER, CHARLES R.

(a) Composing Processes, Research Methodology, Response and Evaluation

(b) Charles Cooper, with Lee Odell, has edited two well-known collections of essays: *Evaluating Writing* (1977) and *Research on Composing: Points of Departure* (1978). In his essay in the first collection, Cooper argues for the use of student essays rather than multiple-choice instruments to evaluate writing competency. He explains **holistic** scoring and **analytic** scales, offers suggestions for improving their reliability, and suggests their advantages and disadvantages. The second collection reviews composition research from 1963, the publication date of *Research in Written Composition* (Braddock et al.), to 1978 and contains essays exhorting researchers to question the basic assumptions of the field and to devise more diverse research methodologies. Cooper's essay in this collection, written with Lee Odell and Cynthia Courts, proposes four focuses for research questions: the composing **process**, published writing, writing done at different age levels, and elicitation and assessment of writing. In other articles, often collaborations, Cooper examines various systems of evaluation, reviews linguistic approaches to text analysis, and describes the application of these approaches. In 1975 and 1985, Cooper co-authored two **NCTE** studies that describe instruments for research and evaluation in the language arts. These volumes, intended for researchers in English education, arrange instruments by category and age group; consider each instrument's validity, reliability, and normative data; and provide ordering information. *Researching Response to Literature and the Teaching of Literature* (1985) reviews response theories and discusses research methods for studying response and classroom instruction in literature. Cooper and Rise Axelrod's **process**-based textbook *The St. Martin's Guide to Writing* (1988), has been widely used. Cooper is one of the fifty authors most cited in *CCC* articles from 1980–93.

(c) Cooper, Charles R., and Lee Odell, eds. *Evaluating Writing: The Role of Teachers' Knowledge about Text, Learning, and Culture.* Urbana: NCTE, 1998. Rpt. of *Evaluating Writing: Describing, Measuring, Judging.* 1977.

———, eds. *Research on Composing: Points of Departure.* Urbana: NCTE, 1978.

Cooper, Charles R., William T. Fagan, and Julie M. Jensen. *Measures for Research and Evaluation in the English Language Arts.* 2 vols. Urbana: NCTE, 1975–85.

Cooper, Charles R., ed. *Researching Response to Literature and the Teaching of Literature: Points of Departure.* 1983. Norwood, NJ: Ablex, 1985.

Cooper, Charles R., and Rise B. Axelrod. *The St. Martin's Guide to Writing.* 1985. 5th ed. New York: St. Martin's Press, 1997.

CORBETT, EDWARD P. J.

(a) Bibliography, History of Rhetoric and/or Composition, Pedagogy, Rhetoric and/or Composition Theory, Style

(b) Edward P. J. Corbett's *Classical Rhetoric for the Modern Student* (1965) was instrumental in reawakening interest in classical rhetoric and its relevance for contemporary rhetoric and composition studies. In that work, Corbett gives a history of classical rhetoric, including sections on classical ideas of "form" and "topics," and provides an influential explanation of the classical division of figures of speech into schemes and tropes. In a 1971 essay, he traces the history of using prose models for imitation and suggests that activities such as **sentence-combining** are not new. His introduction (with James Golden) to *The Rhetoric of Blair, Campbell, and Whately* (1968) explores the contributions of these eighteenth- and nineteenth-century rhetoricians. Corbett wrote the bibliographical essay on style "Approaches to the Study of Style" in both the 1976 and 1987 editions of *Teaching Composition*, and his and Tate's *The Writing Teacher's Sourcebook* (1981) has often served as an introduction to the teaching of composition. Corbett's *The Little English Handbook* (first published in 1973) has undergone several editions. A number of Corbett's essays have been collected, with headnotes from his 1987 interview with Andrea Lunsford and Lisa Ede, in *The Selected Essays of Edward P. J. Corbett* (1989). Corbett chaired CCCC in 1971 and edited *CCC* from 1974–79. He won the **NCTE** Distinguished

Service Award in 1986 and the **CCCC** Exemplar Award in 1996. Corbett is one of the fifty authors most cited in *CCC* articles from 1980–93 and one of the most frequently published authors of major articles in *CCC* from 1965–79 and 1980–93.

(c) Corbett, Edward P. J. *Classical Rhetoric for the Modern Student.* 1965. Corbett, Edward P. J., and Robert Connors. 4th ed. New York: Oxford University Press, 1999.

Corbett, Edward P. J., and James Golden. *The Rhetoric of Blair, Campbell, and Whately.* 1968. Landmarks in Rhetoric and Public Address. Carbondale: Southern Illinois University Press, 1990.

————. *The Little English Handbook.* New York: Wiley, 1973. 8th ed., Ed. Edward P. J. Corbett and Sheryl L. Finkle. New York: Longman, 1998.

Corbett, Edward P. J. "Approaches to the Study of Style." *Teaching Composition: 10 Bibliographical Essays.* Ed. Gary Tate. Fort Worth: Texas Christian University Press, 1976. 73–109. Rev. ed. *Teaching Composition: 12 Bibliographical Essays,* 1987. 83–130.

Corbett, Edward P. J., and Gary Tate, eds. *The Writing Teacher's Sourcebook.* 1981. 4th ed. Ed. Corbett, Tate, and Nancy Myers. New York: Oxford University Press, 1999.

Corbett, Edward P. J. *Selected Essays of Edward P. J. Corbett.* Ed. Robert J. Connors. SMU Studies in Composition and Rhetoric. Dallas: Southern Methodist University Press, 1989.

CORDER, JAMES W.

(a) Argument, Bibliography, Rhetoric and/or Composition Theory

(b) The relationship of literary studies and rhetoric, the meaning of *ethos* in rhetoric, and the dangers of searching for **authority** in education have been recurring themes in Corder's work. Corder won the Braddock Award in 1976 for "What I Learned at School," an account of his experiences writing the same essays he assigned his students. His 1979 textbook, *Contemporary Writing: Process and Practice* was one of several published in the late 1970s and early 1980s that emphasize **invention** and mark a shift in the textbook market. In his bibliographical essays, "Rhetorical Analysis of Writing" (1976) and "Studying Rhetoric and Literature" (1987) in the first and second editions of *Teaching Composition,* Corder says that all writing is rhetorical and thus all analysis of writing is rhetorical analysis, a theme he also develops in later essays. In one of those essays, "On the Way, Perhaps, to a **New Rhetoric**, but Not There Yet, and If We Do Get There, There Won't Be There Anymore" (1985), he argues that although there are "modern" rhetorics, there is not yet a "new" rhetoric and there won't be one until rhetoricians meet certain conditions. Among them are seeing rhetoric as a door to other fields and understanding that the indeterminacy of knowledge makes all forms of study forms of rhetoric. In several works, Corder discusses the lack of community in English departments and suggests ways to increase communication between those in rhetoric and those in literary studies. He advocates a generative, open *ethos* that encourages rather than shuts down discussion, a view in keeping with his position in "Audience as Emergence, Rhetoric as Love" (1985). In this work, Corder discusses the difficulties of achieving the dispassion and objectivity called for in **Rogerian** argument. In such situations, Corder suggests, argument should become "emergence," an opening of ourselves to the other. He argues against attempts to find an authority that justifies, "fixes," and prescribes a certain type of writing or education. In several works, he "hunts" for *ethos*, asking whether it can ever be found in the "text" or whether all readers can know is what they themselves bring to the text.

(c) Corder, James W. "What I Learned at School." *CCC* 26 (1975): 330–34. Rpt. in *The Writing Teacher's Sourcebook*. Ed. Gary Tate and Edward P. J. Corbett. New York: Oxford University Press, 1981. 163–69.

———. "Rhetorical Analysis of Writing." *Teaching Composition: 10 Bibliographical Essays*. Ed. Gary Tate. Fort Worth: Texas Christian University Press, 1976. 223–40. "Studying Rhetoric and Literature." *Teaching Composition: 12 Bibliographical Essays*. Ed. Gary Tate. Fort Worth: Texas Christian University Press, 1987. 331–52.

———. *Contemporary Writing: Process and Practice*. 1979. Glenview, IL: Scott, Foresman, 1983.

———. "Audience as Emergence, Rhetoric as Love." *RR* 4 (1985): 16–32. Rpt. in *Professing the New Rhetorics*. Ed. Patricia Enos and Stuart C. Brown. Englewood Cliffs, NJ: Prentice Hall, 1994. 412–28.

———. "On the Way, Perhaps, to a New Rhetoric, but Not There Yet, and If We Do Get There, There Won't Be There Anymore." *CE* 47 (1985): 162–70.

COVINO, WILLIAM A.

(a) History of Rhetoric and/or Composition, Invention, Rhetoric and/or Composition Theory

(b) The major thrust of Covino's work has been to argue for a dialogic-dialectic rhetoric that tolerates ambiguity and encourages novelty and open, free discussion and critique. In his early articles such as "Making Differences in the Composition Class: A Philosophy of **Invention**" (1981), he views invention as "the unifying term for the whole **process** of composition," and in *The Art of Wondering: A Revisionist Return to the History of Rhetoric* (1988), he traces what he sees as an alternate course for the history of rhetoric—from Plato, Aristotle, and Cicero through Michel de Montaigne, Giambattista Vico, David Hume, Lord Byron, and Thomas De Quincey to Kenneth Burke, Jacques Derrida, Paul Feyerabend, and Clifford Geertz. The work of these figures, he suggests, does not force discussion to closure, but encourages exploration and continuing conversation. In "Magic, Literacy, and the National Enquirer" (1991) and *Magic, Rhetoric, and Literacy: An Eccentric History of the Composing Imagination* (1994), Covino identifies magic with rhetoric (and its incantatory language) and draws on Burke in his discussion of "true/correct" magic and "false/incorrect" magic. **Critical literacy** "invites" true/correct magic that leads to the kind of thought that expands the possibilities for action; false/incorrect magic (the kind Covino sees in media, governments, and teachers and scientists who allow only "authorized" knowledge) coerces into conformity those with least power to **resist** and reduces their possibilities for action. Covino's 1995 anthology with David A. Joliffe, *Rhetorical Concepts, Definitions, Boundaries*, provides a glossary of concepts, periods, and rhetors and includes essays by well-known scholars in rhetoric and related fields.

(c) Covino, William A. "Making a Difference in the Composition Class: A Philosophy of Invention." *FEN* 10.1 (spring 1981): 1–4, 13.

————. *The Art of Wondering: A Revisionist Return to the History of Rhetoric*. Portsmouth, NH: Heinemann, Boynton/Cook, 1988.

————. "Magic, Literacy, and the National Enquirer." *Contending with Words: Composition and Rhetoric in a Postmodern Age*. Ed. Patricia Harkin and John Schilb. New York: MLA, 1991. 23–37.

————. *Magic, Rhetoric, and Literacy: An Eccentric History of the Composing Imagination*. New York: SUNY Press, 1994.

————, and David A. Joliffe. *Rhetorical Concepts, Definitions, Boundaries*. Boston: Allyn and Bacon, 1995.

CROWLEY, SHARON

(a) History of Rhetoric and/or Composition, Invention, Rhetoric and/or Composition Theory

(b) Writing from a postmodern perspective, Crowley has done work on classical rhetoric and on modern rhetoric and composition. She has also written, with Linda Robertson and Frank Lentricchia, the 1987 **Wyoming Conference Resolution**, which calls for salary and working condition standards and grievance procedures for postsecondary writing teachers; she has chaired the **CCCC** Committee on Professional Standards. In "A Plea for the Revival of Sophistry" (1989), which suggests similarities between the older sophists and postmodern theorists such as Michel Foucault and Jacques Derrida, Crowley calls for reviving the sophistic awareness of the great role teachers' value judgments play in what they teach. In several works, including a book specifically written to introduce deconstruction, she attempts to make literary theory accessible and useful to teachers of composition and literature. In essays on nineteenth-century rhetoric, Crowley traces the evolution of **invention** that resulted in its diminished position in **current-traditional rhetoric**. *The Methodical Memory: Invention in Current-Traditional Rhetoric* is her deconstruction of current-traditional rhetoric. It was named "best book in the field" for 1990 by the *Journal of Advanced Composition*. In a 1996 essay in *Composition in the Twenty-First Century: Crisis and Change*, she argues that the introduction of **process**-oriented pedagogies has still not produced a **paradigm shift** in composition studies and that a focus on process has simply been incorporated into current-traditional epistemology. Crowley's composition textbook, *Ancient Rhetorics for Modern Students* (1994), introduces students to rhetorical categories from classical rhetoric.

(c) Crowley, Sharon, Frank Lentricchia, and Linda R. Robertson. "The Wyoming Conference Resolution Opposing Unfair Salaries and Working Conditions for Post-Secondary Teachers of Writing." *CE* 49 (1987): 274–80. Rpt. in *Composition in Four Keys: Inquiring into the Field.* Ed. Mark Wiley, Barbara Gleason, and Louise Weatherbee Phelps. Mountain View, CA: Mayfield, 1996. 486–91.

Crowley, Sharon. "A Plea for the Revival of Sophistry." *RR* 7 (1989): 318–34.

———. *The Methodical Memory: Invention in Current-Traditional Rhetoric.* Carbondale: Southern Illinois University Press, 1990.

———. *Ancient Rhetorics for Contemporary Students.* 1994. Sharon Crowley and Debra Hawhee. 2nd ed. Boston: Allyn and Bacon, 1999.

———. "Around 1971: Current-Traditional Rhetoric and Process Models of Composing." *Composition in the Twenty-First Century: Crisis and Change.* Ed. Lynn Z. Bloom, Donald A. Daiker, and Edward M. White. Carbondale: Southern Illinois University Press, 1996. 64–74.

D'ANGELO, FRANK

(a) Arrangement, History of Rhetoric and/or Composition, Rhetoric and/or Composition Theory

(b) Much of D'Angelo's work has concerned the relationship between thinking and writing and the structure of writing. In his work on discourse theory, D'Angelo sees the **modes of discourse** as patterns of thought that both give writing direction and help to order ideas. In *A Conceptual Theory of Rhetoric* (1975), he theorizes that the classical *topoi* (topics for **invention**) are also plans for thinking and that writing teachers must understand the close relation among the *topoi*, the modes, and the schemes. He argues that teachers should not separate arrangement from invention and style. D'Angelo wrote the bibliographic essays "Modes of Discourse" in the 1976 edition of *Teaching Composition* and "Aims, Modes, and Forms of Discourse" in the 1987 edition. In "The Search for Intelligible Structure in the Teaching of Composition" (1976), he argues that teachers and scholars in composition must identify the fundamental principles and concepts that inform the discipline; he diagrams a tentative "structure of composition" that includes principles and forms (or modes) of discourse. The essay shared the Braddock Award for 1977. In his work on modes and elsewhere, D'Angelo also comments on the history of the relationship between literature and the teaching of composition. In several essays, he argues for the value of the *progymnasmata* of classical education, which used forms such as the fable, tale, and proverb to teach writing. In other essays, he extends Francis Christensen's work on **generative rhetoric**, suggesting that just as Christensen sees the paragraph as a macrosentence, one can see the essay as a macroparagraph, a sequence of sentences bound to each other by subordination and co-

ordination. This view of the relationship of sentences may be one reason
D'Angelo, in "The Topic Sentence Revisited" (1986), defends the value of topic
sentences in some kinds of writing. In a 1982 essay on the relation of rhetoric
and cognition, D'Angelo outlines a theory of rhetorical competence based on
cognitive processes. In "The Four Master Tropes: Analogues of Development"
(1992), he proposes a theory of rhetorical competence based on metaphor, me-
tonymy, synecdoche, and irony. His 1993 essay "Organizing Texts: Some Classical and Modern Perspectives" traces classical and modern thought about form
and structure in nonfiction texts, including the development of his own thought
on the subject. It won the Edward P. J. Corbett Award for best article in *Focuses*
in 1993. D'Angelo chaired **CCCC** in 1980. He is one of the fifty authors most
cited in *CCC* articles from 1980–93 and is one of the most frequently published
authors of major articles in *CCC* from 1965–79 and again from 1980–93.

(c) D'Angelo, Frank. *A Conceptual Theory of Rhetoric*. Cambridge, MA: Winthrop,
    1975.
———. "Modes of Discourse." *Teaching Composition: 10 Bibliographical Essays*. Ed.
    Gary Tate. Fort Worth: Texas Christian University Press, 1976. 111–35. "Aims,
    Modes and Forms of Discourse." *Teaching Composition: 12 Bibliographical Es-
    says*. 2nd rev. ed. 1987. 131–54.
———. "The Search for Intelligible Structure in the Teaching of Composition." *CCC*
    27 (1976): 142–47. Rpt. in *The Writing Teacher's Sourcebook*. Ed. Gary Tate
    and Edward P. J. Corbett. New York: Oxford University Press, 1981. 80–88.
———. "The Topic Sentence Revisited." *CCC* (1986): 431–41.
———. "The Four Master Tropes: Analogues of Development." *RR* 11.1 (1992): 91–
    107.
———. "Organizing Texts: Some Classical and Modern Perspectives." *Focuses* 6.1
    (1993): 3–15.

EDE, LISA

(a) Collaboration, History of Rhetoric and/or Composition, Rhetoric and/or
Composition Theory

(b) Ede and her frequent co-author Andrea Lunsford have been influential for
their work encouraging a reexamination of classical rhetoric, for their work on
audience, and for their work on **collaborative writing**. In discussing classical
rhetoric and **new rhetoric**, they note both the similarities (both rhetorics are
cross-disciplinary) and the differences (unlike the new rhetoric, classical rhetoric
was concerned with oral language and the search for absolutes), and they argue
for their essential compatibility. *Essays on Classical Rhetoric and Modern Discourse*, co-edited with Andrea Lunsford and Robert Connors, won the Mina
Shaughnessy Award in 1984. In "Audience Addressed/Audience Invoked: The
Role of Audience in Composition Theory and Pedagogy" (which won the Braddock Award in 1985), Ede and Lunsford take a stance somewhere between two
current competing views of audience: views of audience as an entity the writer

discovers and addresses and audience as a fiction created by the writer. In a 1996 essay, "Representing Audience: 'Successful' Discourse and Disciplinary Critique," they reread "Audience Addressed / Audience Invoked," noting how their personal and professional commitments and identifications shaped the earlier essay and arguing for the value of such rereading as a way to reveal "exclusions and repressions." In work on collaborative writing, including *Singular Texts / Plural Authors* (1990), Ede and Lunsford contrast single-author writing, which they see as privileged by the patriarchal system, with collaborative writing, which they argue is more congenial to women. Within collaborative writing, they contrast hierarchical and **dialogic** collaboration, claiming that most women prefer the latter. Ede and Lunsford also have conducted research on writing in the workplace, arguing from this research that collaborative classroom models more closely approximate real-world writing and that writing teachers need to rethink their image of the writer working alone in the garret. Ede's chapter, "Teaching Writing," in *An Introduction to Composition Studies* (1991) discusses questions raised by competing theories and research about writing. Ede is one of the fifty authors most cited in *CCC* articles from 1980–93.

(c) Ede, Lisa, and Andrea Lunsford. "Audience Addressed / Audience Invoked: The Role of Audience in Composition Theory and Pedagogy." *CCC* 35 (1984): 155–71. Rpt. in *Cross-Talk in Comp Theory: A Reader*. Ed. Victor Villanueva, Jr. Urbana: NCTE, 1997. 77–95.

Ede, Lisa, Robert Connors, and Andrea Lunsford, eds. *Essays on Classical Rhetoric and Modern Discourse*. Carbondale: Southern Illinois University Press, 1984.

Ede, Lisa. *Work in Progress: A Guide to Writing and Revising*. 1989. 4th ed. New York: St. Martin's Press, 1998.

Ede, Lisa, and Andrea Lunsford. *Singular Texts / Plural Authors: Perspectives on Collaborative Writing*. Carbondale: Southern Illinois University Press, 1990.

Ede, Lisa. "Teaching Writing." *An Introduction to Composition Studies*. Ed. Erika Lindemann and Gary Tate. New York: Oxford University Press, 1991. 118–34.

Ede, Lisa, and Andrea Lunsford. "Representing Audience: 'Successful' Discourse and Disciplinary Critique." *CCC* 47 (1996): 167–79.

EHNINGER, DOUGLAS

(a) Argument, History of Rhetoric and/or Composition, Rhetoric and/or Composition Theory

(b) Writing in speech communications journals, Ehninger discusses the rhetorics of George Campbell, Hugh Blair, and Richard Whately. He provides the introduction for the Landmarks edition of Whately's *Elements of Rhetoric*. In several essays on these figures, Ehninger traces a shift in emphasis—from speaker to hearer—that, he says, took rhetoric in a new direction. He is one of the first to use the term "psychological-epistemological" to characterize these eighteenth-century rhetorics. With Wayne Brockriede, Ehninger was instrumental in introducing the **Toulmin model of argument**—from Stephen Toulmin's

The Uses of Argument (1958)—to speech departments and ultimately to composition programs. His essay "On Systems of Rhetoric" (1968), anthologized in *Professing the New Rhetorics* (1994), compares and contrasts classical rhetoric, the "new British rhetoric" of the later eighteenth century, and rhetoric(s) since the 1930s. Characterizing classical rhetoric as "grammatical," eighteenth-century rhetoric as "psychological," and rhetoric since the 1930s as "social" or "sociological," Ehninger argues that each rhetoric has been shaped by the place and time in which it developed, that each emphasizes one rhetorical element at the expense of others, and that each succeeding rhetoric attempts to right the imbalance produced by the focus of the previous rhetoric. The article has served as a call for more and better historical studies.

(c) Ehninger, Douglas. "Campbell, Blair, and Whately: Old Friends in a New Light." *WSJ* 19 (1955): 263–69.

Ehninger, Douglas, and Wayne Brockriede. "Toulmin on Argument: An Interpretation and Application." *QJS* 46 (1960): 44–53. Rpt. in *Contemporary Theories of Rhetoric*. Ed. Richard L. Johannesen. New York: Harper & Row, 1971. 241–55.

Ehninger, Douglas. "Campbell, Blair, and Whately Revisited." *SSJ* 28 (1963): 169–82.

———. Introduction. *Elements of Rhetoric*. By Richard Whately. *Landmarks in Rhetoric and Public Address*. Ed. David Potter. Carbondale: Southern Illinois University Press, 1963. ix–xxx.

———. "On Systems of Rhetoric." *P & R* 1 (1968): 131–44. Rpt. in *Professing the New Rhetorics: A Sourcebook*. Ed. Theresa Enos and Stuart Brown. Englewood Cliffs, NJ: Prentice Hall, 1994. 319–30.

ELBOW, PETER

(a) Composing Processes, Essay and Personal Writing, Response and Evaluation, Rhetoric and/or Composition Theory

(b) Elbow is associated with **"expressive"** theory. Both *Writing Without Teachers* (1973) and *Writing with Power* (1981) emphasize helping writers develop their own **real voices**. Both offer practical exercises and ways of responding to writing, encourage peer evaluation, and suggest changing roles for teachers. In *Writing Without Teachers*, Elbow popularizes Macrorie's **heuristic, freewriting**, and introduces new terms such as "cooking," the **"doubting game,"** and the **"believing game."** *Writing with Power* suggests additional ways that mastering their own voices can help writers move **audiences**, but in "Closing My Eyes as I Speak: An Argument for Ignoring Audience" (1987), Elbow cautions that focusing on audience too early in the writing **process** can sometimes be inhibiting, and he suggests that considering the audience may be more helpful during revision. In general, he advises writers to suspend their critical voices until they have finished composing. Elbow's 1985 essay "The Shifting Relationships Between Speech and Writing" argues paradoxical claims—that writing is unlike speech because it is more permanent, that it is unlike speech because it is more ephemeral, and that it is like speech in crucial ways. The mentalities represented in each of these claims, he says, are all valid, and it is the technology of writing that allows writers to move back and forth among these mentalities in ways that enhance writing. The essay won the Braddock Award in 1986. In a number of articles, several with Pat Belanoff, Elbow discusses and argues for **portfolio** grading, and in a textbook, also with Belanoff, he describes a **workshop** approach to teaching writing. Twelve of his early essays, nine of them previously published, have been collected in *Embracing Contraries: Explorations in Learning and Teaching* (1986). *What Is English* (1990) is his reflection on the 1987 **English Coalition Conference**. In "The War Between Reading and Writing—and How to End It" (1993), Elbow argues that reading is favored over writing in schools and colleges, not just because students spend more time reading than writing, but because of conflicts over who, readers or writers, get to say what texts "mean" and over whether students should be taught to trust—or distrust—language. Elbow says that correcting the imbalance between reading and writing will benefit both and suggests ways to end the "war" by changing curriculum and teaching practices. A section of this article formed part of a debate at the 1991 CCC Conference between Elbow and David Bartholomae over whether to teach academic discourse or expressive writing in first-year writing courses. "The War Between Reading and Writing" won the James A. Berlin Prize for best essay of the year in *Rhetoric Review*. Elbow is among the ten authors most cited in *CCC* articles from 1980–93.

(c) Elbow, Peter. *Writing Without Teachers*. New York: Oxford University Press, 1973. 2nd ed. New York: Oxford University Press, 1998.

———. *Writing with Power: Techniques for Mastering the Writing Process*. New York: Oxford University Press, 1981. 2nd ed. New York: Oxford University Press, 1998.

———. "The Shifting Relationships between Speech and Writing." *CCC* 36 (1985): 283–303. Rpt. in *Composition in Four Keys: Inquiring into the Field*. Ed. Mark Wiley, Barbara Gleason, and Louise Weatherbee Phelps. Mountain View, CA: Mayfield, 1996. 68–83.

———. *Embracing Contraries: Explorations in Learning and Teaching*. New York: Oxford University Press, 1986.

———. "Closing My Eyes as I Speak: An Argument for Ignoring Audience." *CE* 49 (1987): 50–69. Rpt. in *Teaching with the Bedford Guide for College Writers II: Background Readings*. Ed. Shirley Morahan. Boston: Bedford Books, 1996. 114–132.

———. *What Is English*? New York: MLA, 1990.

———. "The War Between Reading and Writing—And How to End It." *RR* 12 (1993): 5–24.

EMIG, JANET

(a) Composing Processes, Research Methodology, Rhetoric and/or Composition Theory

(b) Emig was one of the first to argue that composing is a **"recursive" cog-**

nitive process that should be studied and taught. Her most influential work, *The Composing Process of Twelfth Graders* (1971), draws upon the work of James Britton. In it, Emig presents a case study of the writing habits of eight high school seniors. Her "compose aloud" methodology (one of the first devised to look carefully at single episodes of composing) leads her to distinguish between writing that she calls "reflexive" (writers writing about their own feelings and experience) and "extensive" (writers writing to convey information to a reader). In "Writing as a Mode of Learning" (1977), Emig draws on the work of Lev Vygotsky, A. R. Luria, Jerome Bruner, and others to argue that unique correspondences between writing and successful learning strategies make writing a valuable way of learning. In "Hand, Eye, and Brain" (1978), she speculates about the part each plays in the writing process, and thus she calls attention to the importance of biology and physiology for those doing research on writing. In "The **Tacit** Tradition" (1980), she discusses the contributions of the modern thinkers who, she says, have provided the "tacit" tradition for composition research. These theorists have all been multidisciplinarians; it is inevitable, she maintains, that the discipline's approach to research should be multidisciplinary. In "Inquiry **Paradigms** and Writing" (1982), she argues that paradigms such as case study and **ethnography** are merely different from, and not inferior to, **positivistic inquiry**. Each of the eleven essays in the 1983 collection *The Web of Meaning: Essays on Writing, Teaching, Learning, and Thinking*, which traces her thought from 1963 to 1982, is introduced by a brief interview between Emig and one of the two editors. The collection won the Mina Shaughnessy Prize in 1983. Her textbook with Janice Lauer, Gene Montague, and Andrea Lunsford, *Four Worlds of Writing* (1981), which emphasizes process over product and the importance of the writer's purpose, has been widely used. In *Feminine Principles and Women's Experience in American Composition and Rhetoric* (1995), Emig and co-editor Louise Weatherbee Phelps introduce and write the concluding "reflections" to a collection of essays that explore women's contributions to composition studies. Emig won **CCCC**'s Exemplar Award for 1992. She is among the ten authors most cited in *CCC* articles from 1980–93.

(c) Emig, Janet. *The Composing Process of Twelfth Graders*. Urbana: NCTE, 1971.

———. "Writing as a Mode of Learning." *CCC* 28 (1977): 122–28. Rpt. in *Cross-Talk in Comp Theory: A Reader*. Ed. Victor Villanueva, Jr. Urbana: NCTE, 1997. 7–15.

———. "Hand, Eye, and Brain: Some Basics in the Writing Process." *Research on Composing: Points of Departure*. Urbana: NCTE, 1978. 59–71.

———. "The Tacit Tradition: The Inevitability of a Multi-Disciplinary Approach to Writing Research." *Reinventing the Rhetorical Tradition*. Ed. Aviva Freedman and Ian Pringle. Conway, AR: L & S Books 1980. 9–18.

Emig, Janet, Janice Lauer, Andrea Lunsford, and Gene Montague. *Four Worlds of Writing*. New York: Harper & Row, 1981. 3rd ed. Reading, MA: Addison-Wesley, 1991.

Emig, Janet. "Inquiry Paradigms and Writing." *CCC* (1982): 64–75.

———. *The Web of Meaning: Essays on Writing, Teaching, Learning, and Thinking*.

Ed. Dixie Goswami and Maureen Butler. Upper Montclair, NJ: Boynton/Cook, 1983.

Emig, Janet, and Louise Weatherbee Phelps. *Feminine Principles and Women's Experience in American Composition and Rhetoric*. Pittsburgh: University of Pittsburgh Press, 1995.

ENOS, RICHARD LEO

(a) Bibliography, History of Rhetoric and/or Composition

(b) Richard Leo Enos has done research in the history of rhetoric, especially classical rhetoric. Viewing all rhetoric as **epistemic**, he has argued that conventional methods of historical and philological research cannot answer all the questions in rhetoric's history, and he has urged historical researchers to look for new methodologies. He has written extensively on the sophists, studying them in their historical contexts, defending them against Plato's charges, and pointing out their contributions to rhetoric. In *The Literate Mode of Cicero's Legal Rhetoric* (1988), Enos provides the first detailed study of the relationship of a rhetor's theory to his practice. His other works on classical rhetoric include studies of Greek rhetoric before Aristotle, of Aristotelian rhetoric, and of the influence of Greek rhetoric on Roman rhetoric. Enos has also written bibliographies and bibliographical essays, among them "The Classical Period" (with Ann Blakeslee) for *The Present State of Scholarship in Historical and Contemporary Rhetoric* (1983; rev. ed., 1990) and "**Heuristic** Procedures and the Composing **Process**: A Selected Bibliography" (Enos et al., 1982), one of several special bibliographical issues published by *RSQ*. "Heuristic Procedures" is an extensive and useful bibliography of works on invention techniques from 1970–80. The essays in *Oral and Written Communication: Historical Approaches*, a collection Enos edited in 1990, begin with pre-history; the chapter by Enos discusses sophistic rhetoric's contributions to literacy.

(c) Enos, Richard Leo, et al. "Heuristic Procedures and the Composing Process: A Selected Bibliography." *RSQ* Special Issue No. 1 (1982).

Enos, Richard Leo, and Ann Blakeslee. "The Classical Period." *The Present State of Scholarship in Historical and Contemporary Rhetoric*. Ed. Winifred Bryan Horner. 1983. Rev. ed. Columbia: University of Missouri Press, 1990. 9–44.

Enos, Richard Leo. *The Literate Mode of Cicero's Legal Rhetoric*. Carbondale: Southern Illinois University Press, 1988.

———, ed. *Oral and Written Communication: Historical Approaches*. Newbury Park, CA: Sage Publications, 1990.

———. *Greek Rhetoric Before Aristotle*. Prospect Heights, IL: Waveland Press, 1993.

———. "Viewing the Dawns of Our Past Days Again: Classical Rhetoric as Reconstructive Literacy." *Defining the New Rhetorics*. Ed. Theresa Enos and Stuart C. Brown. Newbury Park, CA: Sage Publications, 1993. 8–21.

ENOS, THERESA

(a) Basic Writing, Gender and Composition, History of Rhetoric and/or Composition, Rhetoric and/or Composition Theory

(b) Enos is the founder and editor of *Rhetoric Review*. She is also the editor of a number of influential collections of essays, including *A Sourcebook for Basic Writing Teachers* (1987); essays and bibliographies on theory, research, and practice written for both teachers and researchers; and essays in honor of Winifred Bryan Horner. The essays in *Defining the New Rhetorics* (1993) emphasize the different definitions and uses of modern rhetoric. *Professing the New Rhetorics* (1994) again illustrates the diverse sources of twentieth-century rhetoric: It presents selections from figures who shaped the "new rhetorics" and essays by scholars in composition and speech communication who discuss and apply these rhetorics. Enos has also edited the *Encyclopedia of Rhetoric and Composition: Communication from Ancient Times to the Information Age* (1996). The *Encyclopedia*'s 467 alphabetical entries by scholars from rhetoric, composition, speech communication, and philosophy present the history, theory, major terms, and major figures in the field of rhetoric. The work includes a selected bibliography after each entry. Enos has also explored how the fact that most teachers of composition are women has influenced the way the discipline is perceived and the way its researchers, scholars, and, practitioners are treated and rewarded. In *Gender Roles and Faculty Lives in Rhetoric and Composition* (1996), she presents the results of a four-part national survey of writing teachers, telling their stories and providing the statistics that demonstrate the role their gender has played in their professional lives.

(c) Enos, Theresa, ed. *A Sourcebook for Basic Writing Teachers*. New York: Random House, 1987.

————, ed. *Learning from the Histories of Rhetoric: Essays in Honor of Winifred Bryan Horner*. Carbondale: Southern Illinois University Press, 1993.

————, and Stuart Brown, eds. *Defining the New Rhetorics*. Newbury Park, CA: Sage Publications, 1993.

————, eds. *Professing the New Rhetorics: A Sourcebook*. Englewood Cliffs, NJ: Prentice Hall, 1994.

Enos, Theresa, ed. *Encyclopedia of Rhetoric and Composition: Communication from Ancient Times to the Information Age*. New York: Garland, 1996.

————. *Gender Roles and Faculty Lives in Rhetoric and Composition*. Carbondale: Southern Illinois University Press, 1996.

FAIGLEY, LESTER

(a) Assessment, Cultural Studies, Response and Evaluation, Rhetoric and/or Composition Theory, Technology and Composition

(b) Faigley's early work includes research on coherence and cohesion, revision, writing apprehension, and assessment (of both writing programs and student writing). His study of coherence and cohesion (with Stephen Witte) emphasizes the importance of context and **audience** and argues that coherence and cohesion are necessary to good writing and thus a distinguishing feature of highly rated essays. One implication of the study is that problems with cohesion come from problems with thinking and that simply to teach students cohesive devices is insufficient. Faigley and Witte's work on revision synthesizes work in text analysis and in psycholinguistics. Their study makes it possible to interpret, not just to count, revisions. With John Daly, Faigley has researched how writing apprehension (fear of writing) affects writing performance, noting that personal narratives and descriptive essays, where a personal style is required, are most affected. In *Evaluating College Writing Programs* (1983), he and Witte point out the inadequacies of traditional methods of assessing programs and argue for methods of evaluation suggested by changes in research in writing and in the nature of writing courses. *Assessing Writers' Knowledge and Processes of Composing* (1985), with Roger Cherry, David Joliffe, and Anna Skinner, also warns against assessment that does not take into account current research. Beginning with an overview of research on writers' knowledge and processes of composing, the text presents, demonstrates, and critiques methods of assessing writing performance (such as **holistic, analytic**, and **primary-trait** scoring), describes approaches to assessing changes in composing processes, and calls for a new theory of writing assessment. In "Competing Theories of Process" (1986), Faigley voices reservations about the process approach and gives an overview of **expressive, cognitive**, and social theories of composing, focusing on theories and methods (poststructuralism, sociology of science, **ethnography**, and Marxism) that inform social theory. In *Fragments of Rationality: Postmodernity and the Subject of Composition* (1992), he discusses how changes in American culture, especially developments in electronic technology such as the networked classroom, have changed the way writing is taught. This work won the **CCCC** Outstanding Book Award (1994), the Mina Shaughnessy Prize (1992), and the ATAC W. Ross Winterowd Award (1992). Faigley served as CCCC chair in 1996. In his 1996 CCCC chair's address, published in 1997, he dealt again with the impact of the digital revolution and what he called the "revolution of the rich," urging members of the profession to use technology such as the internet to promote literacy and social equality. He is among the ten authors most cited in *CCC* articles from 1983–90 and one of the most frequently published authors of major articles in *CCC* for the same period.

(c) Faigley, Lester, and Stephen Witte. "Coherence, Cohesion, and Writing Quality." *CCC* 32 (1981): 189–204. Rpt. in *Cross-Talk in Comp Theory: A Reader*. Ed. Victor Villanueva, Jr. Urbana: NCTE, 1997.

———. *Evaluating College Writing Programs*. Carbondale: Southern Illinois University Press, 1983.

Faigley, Lester, Roger D. Cherry, David A. Joliffe, and Anna M. Skinner. *Assessing Writers' Knowledge and Processes of Composing*. Norwood, NJ: Ablex, 1985.

Faigley, Lester. "Competing Theories of Process: A Critique and a Proposal." *CE* 48

(1986): 527–42. Rpt. in *Rhetoric and Composition*. Ed. Richard L. Graves. 3rd ed. Portsmouth, NH: Boynton/Cook, 1990. 38–53.

———. *Fragments of Rationality: Post Modernity and the Subject of Composition*. Pittsburgh: University of Pittsburgh Press, 1992.

———. "Literacy After the Revolution." *CCC* 48 (1997): 30–43.

FLOWER, LINDA S.

(a) Composing Processes, Research Methodology, Revision, Rhetoric and/or Composition Theory, Service Learning

(b) Working with the psychologist John Hayes, Linda Flower was the first to relate modern cognitive psychology (and its research method) to composing. With Hayes, she adapted **"protocol analysis"** (a process by which researchers analyze tapes of writers describing their successive thoughts while writing) as a tool for investigating the composing process. Their work substantiates Janet Emig's claims that the writing process is hierarchical and provides one of the most extensive models of composing. Terms that Flower and her group of researchers have introduced into the field include **"writer-based** prose" (the writer writing for herself) and **"reader-based** prose" (the writer aware of and writing for an **audience**) and the writer's "monitor" (which regulates the whole composing process). (Terms like "monitor" and the use of a computer flowchart model to describe the composing process suggest roots in information theory.) Flowers views composing as problem solving and uses her analyses of professional writers to develop problem-solving strategies for student writers (her study includes both), arguing that if professional writers compose in certain ways, student writers can improve their writing by using the same composing strategies. Her textbook, *Problem Solving Strategies for Writing* (1981), attempts to make students more aware of their own intellectual processes and how those processes affect their writing. Perhaps in response to criticism by social theorists, Flower acknowledges that early **cognitive process** models did not sufficiently account for the influence of the writing situation on composing, and in several articles and books she reports research that uses talk-aloud protocols to examine the ways cognition and context interact to construct or "negotiate" meaning and the "strategic knowledge"—goals, strategies, and awareness—that students use to construct meaning. Based on this research, she argues for a "sociocognitive" theory of reading and writing. "Detection, Diagnosis, and the Strategies of Revision" discusses why beginning writers have difficulty identifying problems in their texts, understanding the nature of the problems, and forming strategies to solve them. It won the Braddock Award for 1987. In "Rhetorical Reading Strategies and the Construction of Meaning" (1988), Flower and Christina Haas report research on the way experienced college readers (graduate students) and student readers (first-year college students) "construct" the meaning of a text. Their results suggest that student readers read primarily for content and do not employ strategies of rhetorical reading, the strategies that lead to constructive reading. This essay won the Braddock Award for 1989. *The Construction of Negotiated Meaning* (1994), like "Rhetorical Reading Strategies and the Construction of Meaning," focuses on the interaction of the cognitive and the social, the voice of the individual and of the community, in what Flower calls the negotiation of meaning. In her work in intercultural **collaboration** and service learning, Flower adapts the writer's process of identifying a problem and solving it for use by communities. She is the author most cited in *CCC* articles from 1980–93 and one of the most frequently published authors of major articles in *CCC* for the same period.

(c) Flower, Linda, and John Hayes. "Writer-Based Prose: A Cognitive Basis for Problems in Writing." *CE* 41 (1979): 19–37. Rpt. in *The Writing Teacher's Sourcebook*. Ed. Gary Tate and Edward P. J. Corbett. New York: Oxford University Press, 1981. 268–92.

———. "Identifying the Organization of Writing Processes." *Cognitive Processes in Writing*. Ed. Lee W. Gregg and Erwin Steinberg. Hillsdale, NJ: Lawrence Erlbaum, 1980. 3–30.

———. "The Pregnant Pause—An Inquiry into the Nature of Planning. *RTE* 15 (1981): 229–43.

———. "A Cognitive Process Theory of Writing." *CCC* 32 (1981): 365–87. Rpt. in *Cross-Talk in Comp Theory: A Reader*. Ed. Victor Villanueva, Jr. Urbana: NCTE, 1997. 251–75.

Flower, Linda. *Problem Solving Strategies for Writing*. 1981. 4th ed. Fort Worth, TX: Harcourt Brace Jovanovich, 1993.

Flower, Linda, John Hayes, Linda Carey, Karen Schriver, and James Stratman. "Detection, Diagnosis, and the Strategies of Revision." *CCC* 37 (1986): 16–55.

Flower, Linda, and Christina Haas. "Rhetorical Reading Strategies and the Construction of Meaning." *CCC* 39 (1988): 167–83.

Flower, Linda. *The Construction of Negotiated Meaning: A Social Cognitive Theory of Meaning*. Carbondale: Southern Illinois University Press, 1994.

FLYNN, ELIZABETH A.

(a) Gender and Composition, Rhetoric and/or Composition Theory

(b) Flynn has been one of the first to argue for a feminist rhetoric. With Patrocinio Schweickart, she edited *Gender and Reading* (1986). In the title essay, she reports on research begun in 1980 that uses reader-response theory, feminist literary studies, and composition studies to examine gender-based responses to literary texts. In a 1994 essay, she rereads "Gender and Reading" in the light of postmodern thought. In "Composing as a Woman" (1988), Flynn draws on feminist work on social and psychological gender differences by Nancy Chodorow, Carol Gilligan, Mary Belenky, and others to argue that **collaboration** is a way of composing that is suited to women and to suggest areas for future feminist investigation of composition. In "Composition Studies from a Feminist Perspective" (1991), she describes and demonstrates two strategies necessary for a feminist critique of composition studies: identifying the different varieties of androcentrism in the field and recuperating feminist approaches in the field. In "Feminism and Scientism" (1995), she builds on recent feminist analyses of composition studies to examine the field's early reliance on empirical research, describing it as an attempt of a "feminine" (abused and undervalued) discipline to achieve legitimacy and power through "masculinization," identification with more powerful, male-dominated fields, such as the sciences. Flynn suggests that discourses of **resistance**, such as feminism, can prevent some of the most unfortunate consequences of such identifications if these discourses themselves are not allowed to become new forms of "debilitating" identifications. In "Rescuing Postmodernism" (1997), she distinguishes between modernism, antimodernism, and postmodernism, and she argues that antimodernism, not postmodernism, is the binary opposite of modernism. Illustrating her distinctions by analyzing three articles in technical communication, Flynn argues that postmodernism does not reject the goal of achieving objectivity in research. Flynn has also contributed to discussions of writing across the curriculum. She is the editor of the journal *Reader*.

(c) Flynn, Elizabeth A., and Patrocinio Schweickart, eds. *Gender and Reading: Essays on Readers, Texts and Contexts*. Baltimore: Johns Hopkins University Press, 1986.

Flynn, Elizabeth A. "Composing as a Woman." *CCC* 39 (1988): 423–35. Rpt. in *Cross-Talk in Comp Theory: A Reader*. Ed. Victor Villanueva, Jr. Urbana: NCTE, 1997. 549–63.

———. "Composition Studies from a Feminist Perspective." *The Politics of Writing Instruction: Postsecondary*. Ed. Richard Bullock and John Trimbur. Portsmouth, NH: Heinemann, Boynton/Cook, 1991.

———. "Feminism and Scientism." *CCC* 46 (1995): 353–68.

———. "Rescuing Postmodernism." *CCC* 48 (1997): 540–55.

FREEDMAN, SARAH WASHAUER

(a) Research Methodology, Response and Evaluation, Revision

(b) In several works, Freedman has studied what most determines readers' responses to and evaluations of writing. Her research (with Ellen Nold), reported in "An Analysis of Readers' Responses to Essays" (1977), corroborates earlier studies indicating that the two variables that best predict rated quality are essay length and percent of words in final free modifiers. In "**Holistic** Assessment of Writing: Experimental Design and **Cognitive Theory**" (1983), Freedman and Robert Calfee stress the importance of research design as they report research that indicates that development, organization, and mechanics—in that order—affect raters' holistic judgments. "The Registers of Student and Professional Expository Writing: Influences on Teachers' Responses" (1984), also with Calfee, suggests that teachers may be biased against student writing that seems to threaten their **authority** by its tone and its force. Studies in *The Acquisition of Written Language: Response and Revision* (1985), which Freedman edited, look at how teachers' responses to students' oral and written communication affect revision. In the essay she contributed, Freedman analyzes student-teacher writing conferences, suggesting reasons why she believes they are more like real conversations, and thus more effective in improving writing, than other classroom dialogue between student and teacher. In other research, (on writing conferences), she shows how ethnicity, race, and gender affect writing conferences. In *Response to Student Writing* (1987), she reports on what surveys and **ethnographic** research reveal about the response practices of successful elementary and secondary teachers. She has written also on the differences in language minority policy in the United States and Great Britain; in *Exchanging Writing, Exchanging Cultures* (1994), she describes a project that paired writing students in the United States and Great Britain to compare how students learn to write in these two cultures.

(c) Freedman, Sarah Washauer, and Ellen W. Nold. "An Analysis of Readers' Responses to Essays." *RTE* 11 (1977): 164–74.

Freedman, Sarah Washauer, and Robert C. Calfee. "Holistic Assessment of Writing: Experimental Design and Cognitive Theory." *Research in Writing: Principles and Methods.* Ed. Peter Mosenthal, Lynne Tamor, and Sean A. Walmsley. New York: Longman, 1983. 75–98.

Freedman, Sarah Washauer. "The Registers of Student and Professional Expository Writing: Influences on Teachers' Responses." *New Directions in Composition Research.* Ed. Richard Beach and Lillian Bridwell. New York: Guilford Press, 1984. 334–47. Rpt. in *Composition in Four Keys: Inquiring into the Field.* Ed. Mark Wiley, Barbara Gleason, and Louise Weatherbee Phelps. Mountain View, CA: Mayfield, 1996. 302–10.

———, ed. *The Acquisition of Written Language: Response and Revision.* Norwood, NJ: Ablex, 1985.

———. *Response to Student Writing.* Urbana: NCTE, 1987.

———. *Exchanging Writing, Exchanging Cultures: Lessons in School Reform from the United States and Great Britain.* Cambridge, MA: Harvard University Press, 1994.

FULWILER, TOBY

(a) Essay and Personal Writing, Literature and Composition, Writing Across the Curriculum

(b) Fulwiler has been a major figure in **writing across the curriculum**, and, conjoined with his work in this area, he has advocated **expressive** journal writing as a way of **writing to learn**. In numerous articles on journal writing and in *The Journal Book* (1987), he both traces the history of journal writing and argues that expressive journal writing can help to develop autonomous thinking as writers explore the content of academic courses and relate it to their own experiences. He discusses ways that teachers may respond to journal writing, pointing out language and document features they can expect and cognitive activities that indicate learning. Many of his articles and the collections he edited with Art Young describe the history, problems, and successes of the WAC program at Michigan Technological University. Also edited with Young, *Programs That Work: Models and Methods for Writing Across the Curriculum* (1990) describes successful WAC programs at fourteen U.S. colleges and universities. In a number of works, Fulwiler discusses the assumptions underlying writing across the curriculum. He asserts that writing across the curriculum requires professors to change their attitudes about the relations between language and learning, between students and teachers, and between themselves and their colleagues; it requires them to rethink even the nature of the university itself. With teachers in disciplines such as biology and history, Fulwiler has co-authored articles on incorporating writing into their courses. Applying ideas from writing across the curriculum to teaching literature, he discusses ways to incorporate writing into literature classes, including the use of different kinds of writing (journals, analytic writing, and creative writing) and different ways of writing (**freewriting**, literature discussion groups that double as writing **workshops**, and **collaborative** writing groups). The essays in *When Writing Teachers Teach Literature: Bringing Writing to Reading* (1995), which he co-edited with Art Young, describe how the authors' training and experience in teaching writing has transformed the way they teach literature.

(c) Fulwiler, Toby. "Showing, Not Telling, at a Writing Workshop." *CE* 43 (1981): 55–63.

———, ed. *The Journal Book*. Portsmouth, NH: Boynton/Cook, 1987.

———. "Looking and Listening for My Voice." *CCC* 41 (1990): 214–220. Fulwiler, Toby, and Art Young, eds. *Programs That Work: Models and Methods for Writing Across the Curriculum*. Portsmouth, NH: Boynton/Cook, Heinemann, 1990.

———, eds. *When Writing Teachers Teach Literature: Bringing Writing to Reading*. Portsmouth, NH: Boynton/Cook, Heinemann, 1995.

GENUNG, JOHN FRANKLIN

(a) Argument, Arrangement, Grammar and Usage, Invention, Style

(b) Genung, who took a position at Amherst in 1881 as a language instructor, is one of the **"big four"** late nineteenth-century rhetoricians who helped establish the direction of writing instruction in America. His influential textbooks *The Practical Elements of Rhetoric* (1885), *Outlines of Rhetoric* (1893), and *The Working Principles of Rhetoric* (1900) helped to establish what came to be called **current-traditional rhetoric**. *The Practical Elements of Rhetoric* is the only major textbook of the time to include sections on grammar and on **invention**. Like A. S. Hill at Harvard, however, Genung sees invention not as a way of generating material but as a means of arranging and shaping material found by thought and observation to suit a particular **audience**. With this view, Genung makes the paragraph, of which he distinguishes four types, a unit of invention. *Outlines of Rhetoric*, which includes some **sentence-combining**, emphasizes prescriptive grammar even more than his earlier text. Unlike Hill, Genung considers persuasion the essence of rhetoric, but because he sees it as tied inextricably to oratory, he relegates it to departments of speech.

(c) Genung, John Franklin. *The Practical Elements of Rhetoric*. Amherst, MA: J. E. Williams, 1885. Facsimile reproduction. Intro. Charlotte Downey. Delmar, NY: Scholars' Facsimiles and Reprints, 1995.

———. *The Study of Rhetoric in the College Course*. 1887. Rpt. Boston: D. C. Heath, 1892.

———. *Handbook of Rhetorical Analysis: Studies in Style and Invention*. 1888. Rpt. Boston: Ginn and Co., 1903.

———. *Outlines of Rhetoric*. Boston: Ginn and Co., 1893.

———. *The Working Principles of Rhetoric*. Boston: Ginn and Co., 1900.

GERE, ANNE RUGGLES

(a) Collaboration, Gender and Composition, Writing Across the Curriculum

(b) Gere has written and edited works on **writing across the curriculum** and writing outside the academy. In *Roots in the Sawdust: Writing to Learn Across the Disciplines* (1985), she describes how writing is used to promote learning in different disciplines. In *Writing Groups: History, Theory, and Implications* (1987), she demonstrates that interest in **collaborative** learning is not a recent phenomenon and shows its occurrence in writing groups inside and outside of academic institutions. She also supports, by theoretical arguments, the claim that group work makes students write better. Gere has done research on grading and evaluation and on how teachers' attitudes affect their choice of teaching methods, their evaluation of students' writing, and their students' achievements in writing. In her research she has noted that the basis of evaluation in a writing program is frequently not articulated. Gere argues for a definition of literacy that takes account of social and cognitive factors. She traces the way empirical research in composition has changed, and she says that these changes have led to a broader definition of acceptable scientific research. The essays in *Into the Field: Sites of Composition Studies* (1993) replace the bridge-building metaphor for the relationship between composition and other disciplines with Geoffrey Squires' "restructuring," which Gere says reconceptualizes the discipline by looking at it from multiple perspectives, deconstructing it by blurring the boundaries where composition interacts with other disciplines, and reconstructing it by reconceiving how theory and application relate to each other. Gere chaired **CCCC** in 1993. In "Kitchen Tables and Rented Rooms" (a revised version of her 1993 CCCC chair's address) and in *Intimate Practices: Literacy and Cultural Work in U.S. Women's Clubs, 1880–1920* (1997), she discusses the way nonacademic writing **workshops** and literary clubs have changed and continue to change members' lives and argues that those in composition studies can learn from studying the history and accomplishments of these "invisible" groups.

(c) Gere, Anne Ruggles, ed. *Roots in the Sawdust: Writing to Learn Across the Disciplines*. Urbana: NCTE, 1985.

———. *Writing Groups: History, Theory, and Implications*. Carbondale: Southern Illinois University Press, 1987.

———, ed. *Into the Field: Sites of Composition Studies*. New York: MLA, 1993.

———. "Kitchen Tables and Rented Rooms: The Extra Curriculum of Composition." *CCC* 45 (1994): 75–92.

———. *Intimate Practices: Literacy and Cultural Work in U.S. Women's Clubs, 1880–1920*. Urbana: University of Illinois Press, 1997.

GIBSON, WALKER

(a) Essay and Personal Writing, Rhetoric and/or Composition Theory, Style

(b) Gibson is often linked with **expressivists** Ken Macrorie, William Coles, Jr., Donald Murray, and Peter Elbow. Like these scholars, he suggests exercises such as **freewriting**, rewriting, journal writing, and group editing to encourage students to write about their personal experience in **authentic voices**. Gibson's *Seeing and Writing: Fifteen Exercises in Composing Experience* (1959) is a writing course whose assignments are designed to encourage students to recognize how language determines what they see. In *The Limits of Language* (1962), he presents selections in which scientists, artists, and writers testify to a "chaotic" world of experience and to the inability of language to describe that experience precisely and unambiguously. In his own final essay, he considers the style appropriate to a writer who is aware of the limits of language. Gibson's well-known work *Tough, Sweet, and Stuffy: An Essay on Modern American Prose Styles* (1966) introduces and demonstrates the use of The Style Machine, a method of identifying and classifying prose styles by sixteen grammatical-rhetorical qualities. In *Persona: A Style Study for Readers and Writers* (1969), Gibson argues that styles are determined by changing relations between speaker, subject, and **audience**, and he identifies styles that range from the most formal, "writer style," to the least formal, "speaker style," and from "honorific" to "pejorative." He wrote the essay on Theodore Baird for *Traditions of Inquiry* in 1985. Gibson was president of **NCTE** in 1972–73 and won the NCTE Distinguished Service Award in 1988.

(c) Gibson, Walker. *Seeing and Writing: Fifteen Exercises in Composing Experience*. 1959. 2nd ed. New York: David McKay, 1974.

———, ed. *The Limits of Language*. New York: Hill and Wang, 1962.

———. *Tough, Sweet, and Stuffy: An Essay on Modern American Prose Styles*. Bloomington: Indiana University Press, 1966.

———. *Persona: A Style Study for Readers and Writers*. New York: Random House, 1969.

———. "Theodore Baird of Amherst College." *Traditions of Inquiry.* Ed. John Brereton. New York: Oxford University Press, 1985. 136–152.

GOSWAMI, DIXIE

(a) Research Methodology, Writing in the Workplace

(b) With Lee Odell and others, Goswami has done research on writing in nonacademic settings. For their research, which describes the writing **process** in the workplaces where the writing is done, they developed the technique of discourse-based interviews. Their findings have implications for both teachers and theorists, especially those interested in **writing across the curriculum**. For these studies, Goswami and her colleagues collected and analyzed samples of on-the-job writing from employees of a social services agency, a state legislature, and a state department of labor. At intervals, they interviewed employees selected because of the writing their positions entail, and not for the quality of their writing. The discourse-based interviews reveal that the writers' stylistic choices are rhetorical and suggest that writing varies according to job description. "Studying Writing in Non-Academic Settings" (1983) describes their research, focusing on the complementary research strategies they designed to answer particular questions. It won the **NCTE** Award for Best Article on Research in Technical and Scientific Writing for 1984. One collection of essays Goswami and Odell edited, *Writing in Nonacademic Settings* (1985), describes research that uses **ethnographic**, quantitative, experimental, and other methodologies to investigate writing in the workplace. In another collection, *Reclaiming the Classroom: Teacher Research as an Agency for Change* (1987), Goswami presents samples of teacher research and encourages "teachers as researchers" to use the knowledge they have gained from classroom experience to do qualitative, descriptive research. In *Students Teaching, Teachers Learning* (1992), she co-edits stories of **collaborative** research between students and teachers from elementary through graduate school, followed by responses from teacher researchers. With Maureen Butler, Goswami edited a collection of Janet Emig's essays in 1983.

(c) Goswami, Dixie, and Lee Odell. "Writing in a Nonacademic Setting." *RTE* 16 (1982): 201–24. Rpt. in *New Directions in Composition Research.* Ed. Richard Beach and Lillian S. Bridwell. New York: Guilford Press, 1984. 233–58.

Goswami, Dixie, Lee Odell, Anne Herrington, and Doris Quick. "Studying Writing in Non-Academic Settings." *New Essays in Technological and Scientific Communication: Research, Theory, Practice.* Ed. P. V. Anderson, P. J. Brockman, and C. R. Miller. New York: Baywood Publishers, 1983. 17–40.

Goswami, Dixie, and Lee Odell, eds. *Writing in Nonacademic Settings.* New York: Guilford Press, 1985.

Goswami, Dixie, and Peter Stillman, eds. *Reclaiming the Classroom: Teacher Research as an Agency for Change.* Portsmouth, NH: Boynton/Cook, Heinemann, 1987.

Goswami, Dixie, N. Amanda Branscombe, and Jeffrey Schwartz, eds. *Students Teaching, Teachers Learning.* Portsmouth, NH: Boynton/Cook, Heinemann, 1992.

GRAVES, DONALD H.

(a) Composing Processes, Pedagogy, Research Methodology

(b) Like Janet Emig's descriptive study a few years earlier, Graves' 1972–73 case-study research on the writing **processes** of elementary school children has influenced the focus and methodology of later researchers and also the way writing is taught in elementary schools. Graves' research project focuses on process, and it has inspired a research method, sometimes called a "teaching case study" or "naturalistic" research, that has led to other **ethnographically** oriented studies. Before they wrote the final grant report to the National Institute of Education (NIE) (1982), Graves and his researchers reported their findings in articles and in a series of "Research Updates" in *Language Arts*. In their report to NIE, they emphasize the importance of generating ideas, which Graves calls "rehearsing," and of revision. The research suggests that developing writing skills is a natural process, and noting the variability of development in the subjects, Graves says that a teacher's best role is response. He argues for allowing students to choose their own topics and time for writing and advocates "process-conferences" as the best method for encouraging students to make meaning through writing. In *Writing: Teachers and Children at Work* (1982), he makes available to classroom teachers the implications of his NIE research and offers practical teaching advice based on the study. In *Balance the Basics: Let Them Write* (1978), he reports that most writing instruction includes little actual composing, and he urges a process-centered approach that has students writing from the first day of class. The book won the **NCTE** David H. Russell Award for Distinguished Research in the Teaching of English for 1982. In a 1980 essay, Graves advocates long-term observational studies like his own, arguing that the traditional scientific experimental research **paradigm** is often too decontextualized to be useful to teachers. Graves is the author of *The Reading/ Writing Teacher's Companion Series*, five books for teachers that explore the connection between reading and writing, and *A Fresh Look at Writing* (1994), which reevaluates and amplifies the advice he gave teachers in *Writing* in light of new research on children's writing processes. He won the first NCTE Award for Outstanding Educator in the Language Arts.

(c) Graves, Donald H. *Balance the Basics: Let Them Write*. New York: Ford Foundation, 1978.
———. *A Case Study Observing the Development of Primary Children's Composing, Spelling, and Motor Behaviors During the Writing Process*. Final Report for NIE Grant G–78–0174, Project 8–0343/9–0963, Feb. 1981. ED 1.310/2:218653. Durham, NH: University of New Hampshire Press, 1981.
———. *Writing: Teachers and Children at Work*. 1982. 2nd ed. Exeter, NH: Heinemann, 1993.
———. *The Reading/Writing Teacher's Companion Series*. 5 vols. Portsmouth, NH: Heinemann, 1989–92.
———. *A Fresh Look at Writing*. Portsmouth, NH: Heinemann, 1994.

HAIRSTON, MAXINE

(a) Argument, Composing Processes, Rhetoric and/or Composition Theory, Writing Program Administration

(b) In "The Winds of Change: Thomas Kuhn and the Revolution in the Teaching of Writing" (1982), Hairston was one of the first to talk about a **"paradigm shift"** (Thomas Kuhn's term for a revolution in scientific thinking) in the teaching of writing: in this case, a shift from emphasis on the product (the completed piece of writing) to the **process** of writing. She also considers why the methodology of the discipline has not kept pace with changes in the **paradigm**. Both Hairston's writing textbooks, *A Contemporary Rhetoric* (1974) and *Successful Writing* (1981), the latter a textbook designed for advanced writing students, present a process-centered approach. Her discussion of **Rogerian** argument, based on psychotherapist Carl Rogers' work, has helped to popularize nonthreatening argument in which the writer attempts to get the reader to understand the writer's point of view by demonstrating that the writer understands the reader's. In "Not All Errors Are Created Equal" (1981), Hairston reports that professional people responding to an informal questionnaire still have conservative views on mechanical correctness. Her 1986 essay "Different Products, Different Processes: A Theory about Writing" distinguishes different "classes" of writing and suggests that each requires a different writing process and a different pedagogy (a cognitive approach or an exploratory approach that "makes meaning"). Hairston chaired **CCCC** in 1985. In "Breaking Our Bonds and Reaffirming Our Connections," her chair's address to the 1985 CCCC Conference, she argues that the discipline should break its "emotional and intellectual" bonds to English studies, and perhaps its physical ties as well. "Diversity, Ideology, and Teaching Writing" (1992) argues against what Hairston sees as the dangers of using first-year writing classrooms as "vehicles for social reform" at the expense of the educational needs of students. She is one of the fifty authors most cited in *CCC* articles from 1980–93 and one of the most frequently published authors of major articles in *CCC* for the same period.

(c) Hairston, Maxine. *A Contemporary Rhetoric*. Boston: Houghton Mifflin, 1974. 4th ed. *Contemporary Composition*. Boston: Houghton Mifflin, 1986.

———. "Not All Errors Are Created Equal: Nonacademic Readers in the Professions Respond to Lapses in Usage." *CE* 41 (1981): 76–86.

———. *Successful Writing*. 1981. 4th ed. New York: W. W. Norton, 1998.

———. "The Winds of Change: Thomas Kuhn and the Revolution in the Teaching of Writing." *CCC* 33 (1982): 76–88. Rpt. in *Rhetoric and Composition*. Ed. Richard L. Graves. 3rd ed. Portsmouth, NH: Boynton/Cook, 1990. 3–15.

———. "Breaking Our Bonds and Reaffirming Our Connections." *CCC* 36 (1985): 272–82.

———. "Different Products, Different Processes: A Theory About Writing." *CCC* 37 (1986): 442–52.

———. "Diversity, Ideology, and Teaching Writing." *CCC* 43 (1992): 179–93. Rpt. in

Cross-Talk in Comp Theory: A Reader. Ed. Victor Villanueva, Jr. Urbana: NCTE, 1997. 659–75.

HALLORAN, S. MICHAEL

(a) History of Rhetoric and/or Composition, Rhetoric and/or Composition Theory

(b) Halloran has helped to restore rhetoric as the legitimate business of English departments and to revive interest in the classical rhetorical tradition. In "On the End of Rhetoric, Classical and Modern" (1975) and its 1976 companion piece, he says that classical rhetors and their **audiences** could rely on shared assumptions—that the world is "knowable," that values are stable and widely accepted by the community, and that one person is capable of knowing all that is worth knowing. In the second half of the twentieth century, neither rhetor nor audience can make those assumptions, he says, and therefore, through rhetorical choices, rhetors must shape their own world and their own selves and invite their audiences to share their worlds. In "Aristotle's Concept of *Ethos*, or If Not His Somebody Else's" (1982), he takes issue with several points in Louis Milic's argument that the tradition of classical rhetoric limits the teaching of composition to form, not content, and so only to matters of style. Halloran argues that *ethos* is the most important of Aristotle's three modes of appeal, and that, therefore, writing teachers must develop or assume a theory of *ethos*. Part of the work of modern writing teachers, he says, is to help students see how their rhetorical choices define their character and the world. In several essays, he analyses the rhetoric that defines the world of science, citing Cicero and current scientific writing to support claims that rhetorical tools such as figurative language are necessary to present scientific thought and to shape audience response. In "Rhetoric in the American College Curriculum: The Decline of Public Discourse" (1982), he describes the shift from classical rhetoric to **current-traditional rhetoric**, emphasizing the move from oral public discourse concerned with improving the life of the community to written private discourse concerned with improving the rhetor's own situation, and he argues for the return to a "rhetoric of citizenship." Halloran's contribution to *A Short History of Writing Instruction* (1990) again traces the movement from rhetoric to composition as it is reflected in the teaching of writing in America to 1900. In 1993, Halloran and Gregory Clark edited *Oratorical Culture in Nineteenth-Century America: Transformations in the Theory and Practice of Rhetoric*, a collection of essays that apply Kenneth Burke's concept of transformation to explain cultural change and explore the premise that the transformation of American culture (from an "oratorical culture" to a culture of individualism and later of professionalism) best explains changes in the theory and practice of rhetoric in America. Halloran served as president of the Rhetorical Society of America from 1992 to 1993.

(c) Halloran, S. Michael. "On the End of Rhetoric, Classical and Modern." *CE* 36 (1975): 621–31. Rpt. in *Professing the New Rhetorics: A Sourcebook*. Ed. Theresa Enos and Stuart C. Brown. Englewood Cliffs, NJ: Prentice Hall, 1994. 331–43.

———. "Aristotle's Concept of *Ethos*, or If Not His Somebody Else's." *RR* 1 (1982): 58–63.

———. "Rhetoric in the American College Curriculum: The Decline of Public Discourse." *PRE/TEXT* 3 (1982): 245–69. Rpt. in *PRE/TEXT: The First Decade*. Ed. Victor Vitanza. Pittsburgh: University of Pittsburgh/Press, 1993.

———. "From Rhetoric to Composition: The Teaching of Writing in America to 1900." *A Short History of Writing Instruction*. Ed. James Murphy. Davis, CA: Hermagoras Press, 1990. 151–82.

Halloran, S. Michael, and Gregory Clark, eds. *Oratorical Culture in 19th Century America: Transformation in the Theory and Practice of Rhetoric*. Carbondale: Southern Illinois University Press, 1993.

HARRIS, JOSEPH

(a) Basic Writing, History of Rhetoric and/or Composition, Pedagogy

(b) In his 1987 essay "The Plural Text, The Plural Self: Roland Barthes and William Coles," Harris develops one of several themes that run through much of his work. For both Barthes and Coles, Harris says, the self and the text are plural, defined but not wholly written by other texts and voices of their **discourse community**. "The Idea of Community in the Study of Writing" (1989) draws on the work of Raymond Williams and Stanley Fish to critique theories that depict an **"academic discourse community"** as a single, conflict-free unit with fixed boundaries. Harris suggests replacing the metaphor of "community" with that of "city"—a much more inclusive place of conflicting and competing beliefs and practices, where change and struggle are the norm. "The Idea of Community in the Study of Writing" won the Braddock Award in 1990. In "Negotiating the **Contact Zone**" (1995), Harris traces the way the metaphors of growth and initiation have been used in teaching **basic writing** and argues against a metaphor of initiation that suggests that students have to give up their old communities—their old "selves"—to become part of the new community. Using Mary Louise Pratt's description of classrooms as "contact zones," Harris argues for ways to enable students to see the value of reaching beyond their own communities to negotiate differences rather than only doing battle with the new. A second related theme in Harris's work examines the way Albert Kitzhaber's and James Britton's differing definitions of English at the 1966 **Dartmouth Seminar** illustrate conflicts in English studies that are still present today. Britton's definition, which Harris calls "performative," focuses on what teachers should be doing in the classroom, and while Harris favors this definition, he argues that it has sometimes led to an emphasis that ignores conflicting voices. In "The Theory of Rhetoric" (1994), Harris begins with the debate at the Dartmouth Seminar and argues for a performative theory, like Britton's, that comes out of practice and changes the way teachers teach. Harris's 1997 monograph, *A Teaching Subject, Composition Since 1966*, unites both the themes running through his work as he discusses how the terms "growth," "voice," "**process,**" "error," and "community" have been used in composition studies and how writing classrooms can become places where students learn to recognize and negotiate competing voices so that what goes on in the university has consequences beyond the classroom. Harris has edited *CCC* from 1994 to the present.

(c) Harris, Joseph. "The Plural Text/The Plural Self: Roland Barthes and William Coles." *CE* 49 (1987): 158–70.

———. "The Idea of Community in the Study of Writing." *CCC* 40 (1989): 11–22. Rpt. in *Rhetoric and Composition*. Ed. Richard L. Graves. 3rd ed. Portsmouth, NH: Boynton/Cook, 1990. 267–78.

———. "The Rhetoric of Theory." *Writing Theory and Critical Theory*. Ed. John Clifford and John Schilb. New York: MLA, 1994. 141–47.

———. "Negotiating the Contact Zone." *JBW* 14.1 (spring 1995): 27–42.

———. *A Teaching Subject: Composition Since 1966*. Upper Saddle River, NJ: Prentice-Hall, 1997.

HAYES, JOHN R.

(a) Composing Processes, Research Methodology, Rhetoric and/or Composition Theory

(b) Hayes, a psychologist, is best known in composition studies for his work with Linda Flower. The two researchers adapt the **protocol analysis** technique and the **cognitive process** model of cognitive psychology, typically used to study problem solving, to studying writing **processes**. In several essays, including "Identifying the Organization of Writing Processes" (1980), Hayes and Flower describe their process-tracing methodology and report on what it reveals about how writers compose. In other articles, they report what their think-aloud protocols show about the composing strategies of "good" and "poor" writers and suggest how writers can be taught to model the strategies of successful writers, especially their planning and revising strategies. In a 1986 essay, "Detection, Diagnosis, and the Strategies of Revision," Hayes, Flower, and other researchers analyze the reasons novice writers often fail to identify, understand, and form strategies to solve problems in their texts. It won the Braddock Award for 1987. In two essays that form the first two chapters of *The Science of Writing* (1996), Hayes presents revisions of the cognitive models he and Flower developed. "A New Framework for Understanding Cognition and Effect in Writing" describes a new framework for studying writing that, he believes, better describes the writing process. This new model gives more emphasis to the role of working memory and includes a place for visual-spatial representation and for motivation and affect. It also revises the cognitive-process section of Hayes' and Flower's 1980 model, replacing "revision" by "text interpretation" and subsuming "planning" under "reflection" and "translation" under "text production."

In "On the Nature of Planning in Writing," with Jane G. Nash, Hayes reviews and compares studies of planning in writing, proposes his own theoretical framework for understanding this part of the writing process, and suggests ways future researchers can improve the way they analyze data on planning in writing. Hayes has also researched how writers' personalities, as revealed by their texts, affect readers' acceptance of their message. He is one of the fifty most frequently published authors of major articles in *CCC* from 1980–93 and one of the most-cited authors in that journal for the same period.

(c) Hayes, John R., and Linda S. Flower. "Identifying the Organization of Writing Processes." *Cognitive Processes in Writing.* Ed. Lee W. Gregg and Erwin Steinberg. Hillsdale, NJ: Lawrence Erlbaum, 1980. 3–30.

Hayes, John R., and Linda Flower, Linda Carey, Karen Schriver, and James Stratman. "Detection, Diagnosis, and the Strategies of Revision." *CCC* 37 (1986): 16–55.

Hayes, John R., J. A. Hatch, and C. A. Hill. "When the Messenger Is the Message." *WC* 10 (1993): 569–98.

Hayes, John R. "A New Framework for Understanding Cognition and Affect in Writing." *The Science of Writing: Theories, Methods, Individual Differences, and Applications.* Ed. C. Michael Levy and Sarah Ransdell. Mahwah, NJ: Lawrence Erlbaum, 1996. 1–27.

Hayes, John R., and Jane G. Nash. "On the Nature of Planning in Writing." *The Science of Writing: Theories, Methods, Individual Differences, and Applications.* Ed. C. Michael Levy and Sarah Ransdell. Mahwah, NJ: Lawrence Erlbaum, 1996. 29–55.

HEATH, SHIRLEY BRICE

(a) Cultural Studies, Linguistics, Literacy, Research Methodology

(b) Shirley Brice Heath is best known for her work on literacy and for her use of **ethnography**. In ethnographic case studies, researchers immerse themselves in the culture they are studying, gathering data by a variety of methods. Often, the final report includes narrative. Heath's *Language in the USA* (1981) is an ethnographic investigation of language variation in American English. In *Ways with Words: Language, Life, and Work in Communities and Classrooms* (1983), Heath uses ethnography to investigate literacy in three working- and middle-class Piedmont communities in the Carolinas. Conducted over a ten-year period, her study demonstrates how children's literacy is shaped by home and community and how their literacy often differs from the literacy expected by schools. This study has become a model for ethnographic research in composition studies. It won the **NCTE** David H. Russell Award for Distinguished Research in the Teaching of English in 1985. In her concluding essay in *The Right to Literacy* (1990), she suggests that the workplace in the late 1980s was providing more opportunities to develop literacy than home, school, or community. In "What No Bedtime Story Means: Narrative Skills at Home and School" (1982) and in a 1982–91 case study reported in *The Braid of Literature:*

Children's World of Reading (1992), Heath investigates the ways that children interact with stories. *The Braid of Literature*, co-authored with Shelby Wolf, the mother of the two children in the case study, traces how the children respond in words and actions to the books their parents read to them each day. Heath's long-term **collaboration** with a classroom teacher, her investigation of literary societies formed by black women in the nineteenth and early twentieth centuries, and her study of theater groups that work with minority youth have results that are pertinent to English as a Second Language instruction and that clarify the relation between "extracurricular" lifelong learning and what goes on in composition classrooms. Heath is one of the fifty authors most cited in *CCC* articles from 1980–93.

(c) Heath, Shirley Brice, and Charles A. Ferguson, eds. *Language in the USA*. Cambridge: Cambridge University Press, 1981.

———. "What No Bedtime Story Means: Narrative Skills at Home and School." *LangS* 11 (1982): 49–76.

———. *Ways with Words: Language, Life, and Work in Communities and Classrooms*. New York: Cambridge University Press, 1983.

———. "The Fourth Vision: Literate Language at Work." *The Right to Literacy*. Ed. Andrea A. Lunsford, Helene Moglen, and James Slevin. New York: MLA, 1990. 288–306.

Heath, Shirley Brice, and Shelby Wolf. *The Braid of Literature*. Cambridge: Harvard University Press, 1992. Pbk., 1995.

HERRINGTON, ANNE J.

(a) Research Methodology, Writing Across the Curriculum, Writing in the Workplace

(b) In "Writing in Academic Settings" (1985) and elsewhere, Herrington draws on research on the writing done in two chemical engineering courses, one a lab and one a design course. The two courses, she suggests, represent different subcommunities, or "forums," of the discipline, and writers in these forums address different issues, use different lines of reasoning, assume different roles for themselves and their audiences, and try to achieve different social purposes. She studies how writing assignments in these courses help students to learn both the subject matter and the roles and purposes of the different forums. In other studies, she examines the way faculty in a variety of disciplines design courses, set course objectives, use peer review, and write and respond to assignments, and she attempts to determine how these factors affect the way students write and learn. With Lee Odell and others, Herrington has also researched writing in nonacademic settings; "Studying Writing in Non-Academic Settings" (1983) reports their findings and describes their research methodologies, including the discourse-based interview. It won the **NCTE** Award for Best Article on Research in Technical and Scientific Writing in 1984. In "The First Twenty Years of *Research in the Teaching of English* and the Growth of a Research Community in Composition Studies" (1989), she traces the way the research **paradigm** in composition studies has shifted from quantitative empirical research to the acceptance of qualitative research and how these primary methods may complement each other, as much of her own work illustrates. The essays in *Writing, Teaching, and Learning in the Disciplines* (1992), which Herrington edited with Charles Moran, provide an overview of **writing across the curriculum**, tracing its origins, examining its areas and methods of inquiry, and charting its boundaries. In the final essay, Moran and Herrington explain why they believe the field will continue to grow.

(c) Herrington, Anne J. "Writing to Learn: Writing Across the Disciplines." *CE* 43 (1981): 379–87.

Herrington, Anne J., Lee Odell, Dixie Goswami, and Doris Quick. "Studying Writing in Non-Academic Settings." *New Essays in Technical and Scientific Communication: Research, Theory, and Practice.* Ed. R. W. Bailey, P. J. Anderson, R. J. Brockman, and C. R. Miller. Farmingdale, NY: Baywood, 1983. 17–40.

Herrington, Anne J. "Writing in Academic Settings: A Study of the Contexts for Writing in Two College Engineering Courses." *RTE* 19 (1985): 331–61.

———. "The First Twenty Years of *Research in the Teaching of English* and the Growth of a Research Community in Composition Studies." *RTE* 23 (1989): 117–37.

Herrington, Anne J., and Charles Moran, eds. *Writing, Teaching, and Learning in the Disciplines.* New York: MLA, 1992.

HERZBERG, BRUCE

(a) Bibliography, History of Rhetoric and/or Composition, Rhetoric and/or Composition Theory, Service Learning

(b) With Patricia Bizzell, Herzberg has edited *The Bedford Bibliography for Teachers of Writing* (1984; 4th ed., 1996) and *The Rhetorical Tradition: Readings from Classical Time to the Present* (1990). *The Bedford Bibliography* provides writing teachers with an overview of the history, resources, and leading books and articles of the field. *The Rhetorical Tradition* includes works and parts of works from classical, medieval, Renaissance, Enlightenment, and twentieth-century rhetoric and provides introductions to the periods and the writers. One of the first texts to provide such an interdisciplinary collection of primary readings, it shared the **CCCC** Outstanding Book Award for 1992. Also with Bizzell, Herzberg has written two bibliographic essays on **writing across the curriculum**. Each includes a brief introduction to and history of writing across the curriculum, and one discusses the most popular textbooks in the field. In "Michel Foucault's Rhetorical Theory" (1990), Herzberg discusses Foucault's ideas about the relationship between discourse, knowledge, and power and suggests the implications of his ideas for modern rhetoric and composition theory and practice. In several essays, he considers how dominant social forces have influenced education in Europe and the United States. He argues that "socially-oriented" composition pedagogies, including service learning, should make students aware of systemic social problems and of the hidden agendas of the university curriculum and of the discipline(s) they are studying. By developing students' **critical consciousness**, he says, **critical pedagogies** should promote social change. In "Community Service and Critical Teaching" (1994), Herzberg describes one of those pedagogies, service learning, and its benefits for both students and the community organizations they serve. *Negotiating Difference: Cultural Case Studies for Composition*, with Pat Bizzell, presents readings selected to teach students to negotiate unequal conflicts.

(c) Herzberg, Bruce, and Patricia Bizzell. *The Bedford Bibliography for Teachers of Writing*. 1984. 4th ed. Boston: Bedford Books, 1996. Online. WWW. BedfordBooks.com/BB/online.HTML. 1997.

———, eds. *The Rhetorical Tradition: Readings from Classical Times to the Present*. New York: Bedford Books, 1990.

Herzberg, Bruce. "Composition and the Politics of the Curriculum." *The Politics of Writing Instruction*. Ed. Richard Bullock and John Trimbur. Portsmouth, NH: Boynton/Cook, 1991. 97–117.

———. "Michel Foucault's Theory of Rhetoric." *Contending with Words: Composition and Rhetoric in a Postmodern Era*. Ed. Patricia Harkin and John Schilb. New York: MLA, 1991. 69–81.

———. "Community Service and Critical Teaching." *CCC* 45 (1994): 307–19. Rpt. in *Service Learning in Composition*. Ed. Linda Adler-Kassner and Robert Crooks. Washington, DC: AAHE, 1996. 57–69.

———, Herzberg, Bruce, and Patricia Bizzell, eds. *Negotiating Difference: Cultural Case Studies for Composition*. Boston: Bedford Books, 1996.

HILL, ADAMS SHERMAN

(a) Arrangement, Grammar and Usage, Rhetoric and/or Composition Theory, Style

(b) Hill, who held the **Boylston professorship** at Harvard from 1876 to 1904, has been credited with being one of the **"big four"** rhetoricians (with John Genung, Fred Newton Scott, and Barrett Wendell) whose teaching and textbooks helped shape the direction of writing instruction in the late nineteenth century. In *The Principles of Rhetoric and Their Application* (1878), the first and most popular of his six textbooks, Hill emphasizes features that have come to be identified with **current-traditional rhetoric**: formal correctness, elegance of style, and the **modes of discourse**—description, narration, exposition, and argument. Persuasion, for Hill, becomes only a useful adjunct to argument, **invention** only a system of "management" in a rhetoric devoted to arrangement and style. In *The Foundations of Rhetoric* (1892), Hill joins Harvard colleague Barrett Wendell in focusing on words, sentences, and paragraphs rather than on the modes. In response to complaints about students' lack of preparation, Hill helped to institute a required freshman writing course at Harvard. This writing course led the way for mandatory freshman writing courses at other colleges.

(c) Hill, Adams Sherman. *The Principles of Rhetoric and Their Application.* New York: American Book Co., 1878.

———. *Our English.* New York: Harper and Brothers, 1888.

———. *The Foundations of Rhetoric.* New York: Harper and Brothers, 1892.

Hill, Adams Sherman, L. B. R. Briggs, and B. S. Hurlbut. *Twenty Years of School and College English.* Cambridge, MA: Harvard University Press, 1896.

———. *Beginnings of Rhetoric and Composition.* New York: American Book Co., 1902.

HILLOCKS, GEORGE, JR.

(a) Research Methodology, Rhetoric and/or Composition Theory

(b) Hillock's best-known work is *Research on Written Composition: New Directions for Teaching* (1986), which reviews research on composition teaching from 1963 to 1982 (1963 is the publication date of Braddock, Lloyd-Jones, and Schoer's *Research in Written Composition,* a work said to mark the beginning of composition studies). For the work, Hillocks screened 6,000 studies, classified and analyzed 2,000 of the 6,000, and performed meta-analyses for 60 of the 2000. Hillocks' most significant innovation is the application of meta-analysis to composition research. This methodology allows him to compare the results of studies in similar areas in order to discover and recommend the most effective methods of instruction. His meta-analysis indicates that of four modes of instruction—presentational, natural process, individualized, and **environmental**—the environmental mode is the most effective. Of six foci of instruction—grammar, models, **sentence-combining**, scales, inquiry, and **freewriting**—three, sentence-combining, scales, and inquiry, are significantly more effective than the others. His findings have been both controversial and influential. Although *Research on Written Composition* chronicles changes in research methodologies since 1963, the emphasis, like that of Braddock, Lloyd-Jones, and Schoer, is on empirical or experimental research. In several articles written between 1982 and 1984, Hillocks reviews experimental studies on teaching writing and identifies strategies that work, emphasizing especially the inquiry method. Among the strategies of inquiry, he identifies observing, describing, and comparing-contrasting, and he argues that these strategies work best when teachers design materials and initiate activities that actively engage students in their use. In "The Need for Interdisciplinary Studies of the Teaching of Writing" (1989), Hillocks broadens the research methodologies he recommends to include **ethnography**, which, he says, combines quantitative and qualitative research. Acknowledging that any such framework is provisional, in *Teaching Writing as **Reflective** Practice* (1995), he provides a "metatheory" that compares and combines current theories about writing. Hillocks won the 1997 **NCTE** David H. Russell Award for Distinguished Research in the Teaching of English for this work.

(c) Hillocks, George, Jr. "Inquiry and the Composing Process: Theory and Research." *CE* 44 (1982): 659–73.

———. "The Interaction of Instruction, Teacher Comment, and Revision in Teaching the Composing Process." *RTE* 16 (1982): 261–78.

———. "What Works in Teaching Composition: A Meta-Analysis of Experimental Treatment Studies." *AJEd* 93 (1984): 133–170.

———. *Research on Written Composition: New Directions for Teaching.* Urbana: NCTE, 1986.

———. "The Need for Interdisciplinary Studies of the Teaching of Writing." *RR* 7 (1989): 257–72. Rpt. in *Composition in Four Keys: Inquiring into the Field.* Ed. Mark Wiley, Barbara Gleason, and Louise Weatherbee Phelps. Mountain View, CA: Mayfield, 1996. 354–63.

———. *Teaching Writing as a Reflective Practice.* New York: Teachers College Press, 1995.

HIRSCH, E. D., JR.

(a) Cultural Studies, Literacy, Rhetoric and/or Composition Theory

(b) Hirsch has made significant contributions to discussions of **cultural literacy**. His early work was in literary theory, especially **hermeneutics**. In this work, he argues that the meaning of a text is determinate and can be ascertained; the work of the reader is to find the "semantic intention" of the writer by studying the text. In *The Philosophy of Composition* (1977), Hirsch draws on psycholinguistic research to formulate the notion of "relative readability," the ease with which sentences can be processed for meaning; if two sentences express the same meaning, the one whose meaning can be more easily understood is the better. Writers who understand the way readers read and adapt their language to their readers' processing needs are good writers. In the same work, he also argues that composition is a formalistic discipline, comprised of a set of skills that the writer must master. He attempts to reduce these to a few fundamental skills (found through empirical psycholinguistic research) that can be efficiently taught. By 1983, however, in "Reading, Writing, and Cultural Literacy," Hirsch urges the profession to end the division between teaching literature and teaching composition. He no longer believes in pedagogical formalism; he says that his research has shown that students with the same level of reading ability, reading books at the same level of difficulty, do not have similar responses to the texts. Hirsch argues that they do not understand the texts the same way because they do not share the same cultural background. In *Cultural Literacy: What Every American Needs to Know* (1987), Hirsch proposes a solution to the lack of cultural literacy: a teaching method in which form and content interact. The "content" would be a "canon" of works that would provide shared knowledge, a common background for all students. Such a canon would be arrived at through negotiation among national academies, MLA and **NCTE**, and state departments of education. *Cultural Literacy* has been a bestseller and much debated, as have his dictionaries of cultural literacy and his books in *The Core Knowledge Series* (1991–93). In *The Schools We Need and Why We Don't*

Have Them (1996), he proposes several reasons for the failure of U.S. public schools, including the idea that learning the tools of inquiry, "how to know," is sufficient. Hirsch suggests a program for renewing U.S. public schools that includes a national curriculum and a focus on core knowledge. He is one of the fifty most-cited authors in *CCC* articles from 1980–93.

(c) Hirsch, E. D., Jr. *The Philosophy of Composition.* Chicago: University of Chicago Press, 1977.

———. "Reading, Writing, and Cultural Literacy." *Composition and Literature: Bridging the Gap.* Ed. Winifred Bryan Horner. Chicago: University of Chicago Press, 1983. 141–47.

———. *Cultural Literacy: What Every American Needs to Know.* Boston: Houghton Mifflin, 1987. Pbk. New York: Vintage Books, 1988.

Hirsch, E. D., Jr., Joseph Kett, and James Trefil. *The Dictionary of Cultural Literacy.* 1989. 2nd rev. ed. Boston: Houghton Mifflin, 1993.

Hirsch, E. D. *The Core Knowledge Series.* New York: Doubleday, 1991–93.

———. *The Schools We Need and Why We Don't Have Them.* New York: Doubleday, 1996.

HORNER, WINIFRED BRYAN

(a) Bibliography, History of Rhetoric and/or Composition, Literature and Composition

(b) Horner has edited bibliographies of scholarship in historical and contemporary rhetoric and a collection of essays examining the theoretical and pedagogical connection between literature and composition. She has also written books and essays on the classical rhetorical tradition and on eighteenth-century and nineteenth-century rhetoric, especially Scottish rhetoric and its influence on twentieth-century composition and education. Horner's *Historical Rhetoric: An Annotated Bibliography of Selected Sources in English* (1980) provides annotated chronological entries for the primary works and annotated alphabetical entries of the secondary scholarship; *The Present State of Scholarship in Historical and Contemporary Rhetoric* (1983; 2nd ed., 1990) includes bibliographical essays by scholars in six historical periods. With Kerri Morris Barton, Horner wrote the essay on the eighteenth century for this volume. Horner's introduction to *Composition and Literature: Bridging the Gap*, which she edited in 1983, traces the historical reasons for the split between the teaching of reading and writing and the gradual widening of the "gap" between literature and composition in English departments; the collection consists of twelve essays by well-known scholars. Horner has written a number of essays on nineteenth-century Scottish rhetoric and rhetoricians, arguing that writing was taught in all subjects by instruction followed immediately by intensive writing practice. In *Nineteenth-Century Scottish Rhetoric: The American Connection* (1993), she considers why scholars know little about nineteenth-century Scottish rhetoric; she argues that it is the "missing link" between classical rhetoric and modern English language

studies and that the "roots" of modern English literature, criticism, and belletristic composition in America can be traced to the lecture notes of the
nineteenth-century professors she includes in this study.

(c) Horner, Winifred Bryan, ed. *Historical Rhetoric: An Annotated Bibliography of Selected Sources in English.* Boston: G. K. Hall, 1980.

————, ed. *Composition and Literature: Bridging the Gap.* Chicago: University of Chicago Press, 1983.

————. *Rhetoric in the Classical Tradition.* New York: St. Martin's Press, 1988.

————, ed. *The Present State of Scholarship in Historical and Contemporary Rhetoric.*
1983. Rev. ed. Columbia: University of Missouri Press, 1990.

————. "The Roots of Modern Writing Instruction: Eighteenth- and Nineteenth-Century
Britain." *RR* 8 (1990): 322–45.

————. *Nineteenth-Century Scottish Rhetoric: The American Connection.* Carbondale:
Southern Illinois University Press, 1993.

IRMSCHER, WILLIAM F.

(a) Invention, Pedagogy, Rhetoric and/or Composition Theory

(b) Irmscher was one of the first to introduce Kenneth Burke's theory of
rhetoric to writing teachers. *Ways of Writing*, his 1969 textbook, emphasizes
writing as self-discovery and suggests that the writing **process** will differ from
writer to writer. In *The Holt Guide to English: A Contemporary Handbook of
Rhetoric, Language, and Literature* (1972) and elsewhere, Irmscher adapts and
extends Kenneth Burke's **dramatistic pentad**; he also has written the essay on
Burke in *Traditions of Inquiry* (1985). In that essay, Irmscher presents Burke's
work and its consequences for rhetorical theory and for teaching writing, showing how key concepts from Burke have affected composition pedagogy and
distinguishing between Burke's use of the pentad as a way to analyze texts and
Irmscher's own use of it as an **invention** technique. In the first work written
for writing teachers, *Teaching Expository Writing* (1979), Irmscher offers beginning teachers advice on all areas of writing instruction. In "Finding a Comfortable Identity" (1987), he says that composition research in the preceding
twenty-five years failed to achieve academic "respectability" because it was
based on the wrong model, the experimental method of science. He sees promise
in new **ethnographic** approaches and offers a set of criteria and procedures for
future scholarly research. Irmscher was editor of *CCC* from 1965 to 1973. He
chaired **CCCC** in 1979 and was president of **NCTE** in 1982–83.

(c) Irmscher, William F. *Ways of Writing.* New York: McGraw, 1969.

————. *The Holt Guide to English: A Contemporary Handbook of Rhetoric, Language,
and Literature.* 1972. 3rd ed. New York: Holt, Rinehart, and Winston, 1981.
Alternate 3rd ed. Holt, Rinehart, and Winston, 1985.

————. *Teaching Expository Writing.* New York: Holt, Rinehart, and Winston, 1979.

————. "Kenneth Burke." *Traditions of Inquiry.* Ed. John Brereton. New York: Oxford
University Press, 1985. 105–35.

————. "Finding a Comfortable Identity." *CCC* 38 (1987): 81–87.

JARRATT, SUSAN

(a) Gender and Composition, History of Rhetoric and/or Composition

(b) Jarratt's work focuses on a recovery and reassessment of the sophists and on the argument that understanding their work will help scholars and writing teachers understand and use feminist discourse and pedagogy. In *Rereading the Sophists: Classical Rhetoric Refigured* (1991) and elsewhere, Jarratt points out parallels between sophist and feminist positions, maintaining that both use rhetorical argument to construct **knowledge** and to initiate change. In "Feminism and Composition: The Case for Conflict" (1991), Jarratt discusses the similarities between **expressivist** theory (for example, Peter Elbow's **"believing game"**) and feminist theories that reject confrontation, maintaining that either position may "silence" some voices in the writing classroom (including the voice of the teacher). Instead, Jarratt argues for an openly confrontational **critical pedagogy**, which she sees as a return to the informed debate central to sophistic rhetoric. She suggests ways to encourage dialogue in the political classroom in "Rhetorical Power: What Really Happens in Politicized Classrooms" (1992). In "Teaching Across and Within Differences," her contribution to "A Symposium on Feminist Experiences in the Composition Classroom" (1992), she describes her first "overtly" feminist writing class and examines the various factors that contributed to its success.

(c) Jarratt, Susan. *Rereading the Sophists: Classical Rhetoric Refigured.* Carbondale: Southern Illinois University Press, 1991.

————. "Feminism and Composition: The Case for Conflict." *Contending with Words: Composition and Rhetoric in a Postmodern Age.* Ed. Patricia Harkin and John Schilb. New York: MLA, 1991. 105–23.

————. "Rhetorical Power: What Really Happens in Politicized Classrooms." *ADE Bulletin* 102 (fall 1992): 34–39. Rpt. in *The Presence of Others.* Ed. Andrea Lunsford and John Ruskiewicz. New York: St. Martin's Press, 1994. 105–112.

Jarratt, Susan, Jill Eichhorn, Sara Farris, Karen Hayes, Adriana Hernandez, Karen Powers-Stubbs, and Marian Schiachitano. "A Symposium on Feminist Experiences in the Composition Classroom." *CCC* 43.3 (1992): 297–322.

————, and Lynn Worsham, eds. *Feminism and Composition Studies: In Other Words.* New York: MLA, 1998.

JUDY, STEPHEN (see TCHUDI, STEPHEN)

KINNEAVY, JAMES L.

(a) Bibliography, History of Rhetoric and/or Composition, Rhetoric and/or Composition Theory, Writing Across the Curriculum

(b) Kinneavy was one of the first to analyze and to trace the theory of discourse that began in classical rhetoric. In *A Theory of Discourse* (1971), he presents the communication triangle derived from Aristotle as fundamental to the use of language. Although often represented in a triangle, the structure consists of four elements: encoder (speaker), decoder (**audience**), and reality (thing spoken about)—which name the three points of the triangle—and signal (language), which interacts among the three. In chapter two, he calls the aims of discourse corresponding, respectively, to these elements "expressive," "persuasive," "referential," and "literary." He distinguishes these elements from the modes of discourse, which he renames "description," "narration," "classification," and "evaluation" and which he says are ways of thinking about reality. Each mode, he says, has its own pattern of organization, logic, and style. In several essays, including "*Kairos*: A Neglected Concept in Classical Rhetoric" (1986), Kinneavy traces *kairos*, situational context, from the Greeks to the present; and in "*Kairos* in Aristotle's '*Rhetoric*' " (1994) and elsewhere, he emphasizes the importance of this concept for contemporary rhetoric and for composition programs. In "Restoring the Humanities: The Return of Rhetoric from Exile" (1982), he describes the historical link between rhetoric and the humanities and argues that the "exile" of rhetoric has been one of the causes of the decline in the perceived relevance of the humanities. Kinneavy's work on **writing across the curriculum** includes a 1983 essay in which he discusses the character of writing across the curriculum and describes WAC programs at the University of Maryland and elsewhere, arguing that to write for a variety of **discourse communities**, students must learn both expository and persuasive writing. Kinneavy wrote "Writing Across the Curriculum" in *Teaching Composition: 12 Bibliographical Essays* (1987) and "Contemporary Rhetoric" for *The Present State of Scholarship in Historical and Contemporary Rhetoric* (1990). He is one of the fifty authors most cited in *CCC* articles from 1980–93 and won the **CCCC** Exemplar Award for 1995.

(c) Kinneavy, James. *A Theory of Discourse*. Englewood Cliffs, NJ: Prentice-Hall, 1971. New York: W. W. Norton, 1980.

———. "Restoring the Humanities: The Return of Rhetoric from Exile." *The Rhetorical Tradition and Modern Writing*. Ed. James J. Murphy. New York: MLA, 1982. 19–28.

———. "Contemporary Rhetoric." *The Present State of Scholarship in Historical and Contemporary Rhetoric*. Ed. Winifred Bryan Horner. 1983. Rev ed. Columbia: University of Missouri Press, 1990. 186–246.

———. "Translating Theory into Practice in Teaching Composition: A Historical View and a Contemporary View." *Essays on Classical Rhetoric and Modern Discourse*. Ed. Robert J. Connors, Lisa S. Ede, and Andrea A. Lunsford. Carbondale: Southern Illinois University Press, 1984. 69–81.

———. "*Kairos*: A Neglected Concept in Classical Rhetoric." *Rhetoric and Praxis: The Contribution of Classical Rhetoric to Practical Reasoning*. Ed. Jean Dietz Moss. Washington, DC: Catholic University of America Press, 1986. 79–105. Rpt. in *Composition in Four Keys: Inquiring into the Field*. Ed. Mark Wiley, Barbara

Gleason, and Louise Weatherbee Phelps. Mountain View, CA: Mayfield, 1996. 211–24.

———. "The Process of Writing: A Philosophical Base in Hermeneutics." *JAC* 7 (1987): 1–9.

———. "Writing Across the Curriculum." *Teaching Composition: 12 Bibliographical Essays*. Ed. Gary Tate. Fort Worth: Texas Christian University Press, 1987. 353–77.

Kinneavy, James, and Catherine R. Eskin. " '*Kairos*' in Aristotle's '*Rhetoric*' " *WC* 11 (1994): 131–42.

KITZHABER, ALBERT

(a) History of Rhetoric and/or Composition, Rhetoric and/or Composition Theory

(b) Kitzhaber's 1953 dissertation, *Rhetoric in American Colleges, 1850–1900*, is the earliest history of rhetoric and pedagogy in higher education in nineteenth-century America. Although not published until 1990, it has been a significant source for later historians such as James Berlin and Robert Connors. An early leader in the field, Kitzhaber served as **CCCC** chair in 1959 and **NCTE** president in 1964. He took a leading role in the 1966 **Dartmouth Seminar**, which he opened with an attempt to define English by bringing language, literature, and composition into a coherent, unified academic discipline. Kitzhaber sees writing courses as central to a university education but argues for a new rhetoric that would transform the **current-traditional** writing instruction of the 1960s. While maintaining that writing is an art, not a science, he also calls, in "4C, Freshman English, and the Future" (1963) and elsewhere, for more research on the writing **process**. In his 1959 debate with Warner G. Rice, recounted in "Death or Transfiguration" (1960), Kitzhaber responds to Rice's contention that first-year composition courses should be abolished. He agrees that most college writing instruction in the 1960s was ineffective, but, he argues, because writing is a way to discover and order knowledge, the answer is to improve, not eliminate, the instruction. In several articles and in *Themes, Theories, and Therapy: Teaching of Writing in College* (1963), based on a national survey of first-year composition programs, Kitzhaber describes the way writing was taught in the early 1960s and suggests changes that include more collaboration between high school and college writing teachers, more training in writing instruction for writing teachers, and more emphasis on making writing teachers writers themselves.

(c) Kitzhaber, Albert. *Rhetoric in American Colleges, 1850–1900*. Ph.D. diss, University of Washington, 1953. Dallas: Southern University Press, 1990.

———. "4C, Freshman English, and the Future." *CCC* 14 (1963): 129–38.

———. *Themes, Theories, and Therapy: Teaching of Writing in College*. New York: McGraw-Hill, 1963.

———. "The Government and English Teaching." *CCC* 18 (1967): 135–41.
———. "Teaching English Composition in College." *Teaching Freshman Composition.*
Ed. Gary Tate and Edward P. J. Corbett. New York: Oxford, 1967. 3–24.

KNOBLAUCH, C. H.

(a) Response and Evaluation, Rhetoric and/or Composition Theory

(b) Knoblauch's most influential work is *Rhetorical Traditions and the Teaching of Writing* (1984), written with Lil Brannon. In it, they argue that the classical rhetorical tradition, which they characterize as formalistic and prescriptive, is not compatible with or as useful for today's writing teachers as modern theory, which they describe as **epistemic** and nonprescriptive. Adhering to classical viewpoints and methods, often unconsciously, while also espousing modern rhetorical theory, they suggest, can lead only to inconsistency and confusion. In their work on responding to student writing, Knoblauch and Brannon argue that teachers should act as facilitators rather than as evaluators. As evaluators, they contend, teachers often compare student writing to an "ideal" text that students largely waste their time trying to approximate. Instead, Knoblauch and Brannon advocate responding to the work in progress at various points, giving "facilitative" feedback that allows a student to compare her intentions with her effect. By responding to specific writing problems in specific texts rather than by offering generalized advice about writing, teachers help students develop their capacity to think systematically. In another essay on the relation between writer and reader, "Intentionality in the Writing **Process**: A Case Study" (1980), Knoblauch considers ways to categorize discourse by analyzing proposals written by executives in a large consulting firm. In "Rhetorical Constructions: Dialogue and Commitment" (1988), he examines Paulo Freire's sense of **"praxis"** and the ways the ontological statements of Aristotle, the objectivist statements of René Descartes and John Locke, the expressionist statements of Immanuel Kant, and the sociological statements of Karl Marx can be applied to teaching rhetoric. Knoblauch and Brannon's "Knowing Our Knowledge: A Phenomenological Basis for **Teacher Research**" uses the phenomenological assumptions of quantum physics—that the object observed and the observer cannot be separated and thus that the terms "objective" and "subjective" become meaningless—to critique arguments against the legitimacy of teacher inquiry. Also with Brannon, Knoblauch's *Critical Teaching and the Idea of Literacy* (1993) reviews the debate concerning the meaning of "literacy," suggesting that different "stories" about the nature of literacy reveal the ideologies of those who tell them and that understanding the stories as rhetorical constructions makes it possible to "transform" pedagogy. Knoblauch is one of the fifty authors most cited in *CCC* articles from 1980–93.

(c) Knoblauch, C. H. "Intentionality in the Writing Process: A Case Study." *CCC* 31 (1980): 153–59.

Knoblauch, C. H., and Lil Brannon. "On Students' Rights to Their Own Texts: A Model of Teacher Response." *CCC* 33 (1982): 157–66.

———. *Rhetorical Traditions and the Teaching of Writing*. Upper Montclair, NJ: Boynton/Cook, 1984.

———. "Knowing Our Knowledge: A Phenomenological Basis for Teacher Research." *Audits of Meaning*. Ed. Louise Z. Smith. Portsmouth, NH: Boynton/Cook, 1988. 17–28.

Knoblauch, C. H., "Rhetorical Constructions: Dialogue and Commitment. *CE* 50 (1988): 125–40. Rpt. in *Composition in Four Keys: Inquiring into the Field*. Ed. Mark Wiley, Barbara Gleason, and Louise Weatherbee Phelps. Mountain View, CA: Mayfield, 1996. 582–93.

Knoblauch, C. H., and Lil Brannon. *Critical Teaching and the Idea of Literacy*. Portsmouth, NH: Boynton/Cook, 1993.

LARSON, RICHARD L.

(a) Arrangement, Bibliography, Rhetoric and/or Composition Theory, Pedagogy

(b) Larson wrote the first composition-specific bibliographies and an early (1971) MLA-sponsored study of the theory and procedures for evaluating the teaching of college composition. In five selected, annotated bibliographies published in the May issues of *CCC* (1975–79), Larson covers textbooks, reviews of books, and other material related to composition from 1973–78. He chaired the **NCTE** Committee on Teacher Preparation and Certification from 1966–70; and in a number of articles, he discusses training new teachers in writing comments on themes and in designing, sequencing, and presenting writing assignments. He advises new teachers to write themselves and to analyze their own writing **processes**. In 1967, Larson wrote the *Rhetorical Guide* to the first edition of *The Borzoi College Reader*, and the following year he edited a collection of essays from classical and contemporary theorists. In "Sentences in Action: A Technique for Analyzing Paragraphs" (1967), he expands Francis Christensen's discussion of the relationships among sentences in a paragraph. In his work on **invention**, "Discovery Through Questioning" (1968), Larson presents seven sets of questions designed to help students analyze their experiences and discover what is worth writing about and how to write about it effectively. In "The 'Research Paper' in the Writing Course: A Non-Form of Writing" (1982), he argues against the "generic" research paper. His "Structure and Form in Non-Fiction Prose" in *Teaching Composition* (1976, updated in 1987) is one of two major bibliographical essays of research on the paragraph. Larson chaired **CCCC** in 1974 and edited *CCC* from 1980–86. He won the NCTE Distinguished Service Award in 1994. Larson is one of the fifty most-cited authors in *CCC* articles from 1980–93; he is also one of the most frequently published authors of major articles in *CCC* from 1965–79.

(c) Larson, Richard L. "Sentences in Action: A Technique for Analyzing Paragraphs." *CCC* 18 (1967): 16–22.

————. *Rhetorical Guide to The Borzoi College Reader*. New York: Random House, 1967.

————. "Discovery Through Questioning: A Plan for Teaching Rhetorical Invention." *CE* 30 (1968): 126–34.

————. "Selected Bibliography of Research and Writing about the Teaching of Composition" (1973–78). *CCC* 26 (1975): 187–95. *CCC* 27 (1976): 171–80. *CCC* 28 (1977): 181–93. *CCC* 29 (1978): 181–94. *CCC* 30 (1979): 196–213.

————. "Structure and Form in Non-Fiction Prose." *Teaching Composition: 10 Bibliographical Essays*. Ed. Gary Tate. Fort Worth: Texas Christian University Press, 1976. 45–71. "Structure and Form in Non-Narrative Prose." *Teaching Composition: 12 Bibliographical Essays*. Rev. ed. Fort Worth: Texas Christian University Press, 1987. 39–82.

————. "The 'Research Paper' in the Writing Course: A Non-Form of Writing." *CE* 44 (1982): 811–16. Rpt. in *The Writing Teacher's Sourcebook*. Ed. Gary Tate and Edward P. J. Corbett. 2nd ed. New York: Oxford University Press, 1988. 361–66.

————. "Classifying Discourse: Limitations and Alternatives." *Essays on Classical Rhetoric and Modern Discourse*. Ed. Robert Connors, Lisa Ede, and Andrea Lunsford. Carbondale: Southern Illinois University Press, 1984. 203–14.

LAUER, JANICE

(a) History of Rhetoric and/or Composition, Invention, Research Methodology, Rhetoric and/or Composition Theory

(b) In "**Heuristics** and Composition"(1970), Lauer is one of the first to argue that writing teachers should draw from theoretical work in fields other than English and rhetoric as they attempt to reinstate rhetoric by resurrecting the art of **invention**. She proposes the term "heuristics," borrowed from the study of invention in other disciplines, and includes a bibliography of current work on heuristics in psychology. "Heuristics and Composition" provoked a well-known debate with Ann Berthoff, who characterizes Lauer's theory of knowledge as "problem-solving" and her understanding of heuristics as narrow and politically dangerous. In her response to Berthoff, Lauer suggests that Berthoff is reductionist both in her equating of Lauer's sense of heuristics to problem solving and in her depiction of problem solving. In a later article, in which she offers a metatheory of heuristic procedures, she proposes three criteria that would allow teachers, she says, to judge the adequacy of different heuristic models. Lauer wrote the chapter "Issues in Rhetorical Invention" in *Essays on Classical Rhetoric and Modern Discourse* (1984); in it she examines the differences in modern treatments of invention and traces the origins of those differences. In "Writing as Inquiry" (1982), she suggests that teachers of writing can use the questions raised by studies of the nature of the process of inquiry to design writing pedagogy. Lauer shows one way to do so in her chapter on "The Rhetorical Approach" in *Eight Approaches to Teaching Composition* (1980), in which she examines the implications of current rhetorical theory for methods of teaching.

Her textbook *Four Worlds of Writing* (1981), written with Gene Montague, Andrea Lunsford, and Janet Emig, presents a writing pedagogy based on premises from current theory. Lauer and J. William Asher wrote *Composition Research: Empirical Designs* (1988) for both novice and experienced researchers; it introduces eight empirical research designs in composition, illustrating each with current research studies and analyzing the strengths and weaknesses of each design in order to help researchers select appropriately. "Instructional Practices: Toward an Integration," also written in 1988, traces the history and current conceptions of four pedagogies—teaching writing as an art, helping students develop their natural processes, providing opportunities for practice, and using the imitation of prose models. Lauer argues for the value of integrating these four pedagogies rather than emphasizing one at the expense of the others. Lauer won the CCCC Exemplar Award in 1998. She is one of the most frequently published authors of major articles in *CCC* from 1980–93.

(c) Lauer, Janice. "Heuristics and Composition." *CCC* 21 (1970): 396–404.
———. "The Rhetorical Approach: Stages of Writing and Strategies for Writers." *Eight Approaches to Teaching Composition*. Ed. Timothy R. Donovan and Ben W. McClelland. Urbana: NCTE, 1980. 53–64.
Lauer, Janice, Janet Emig, Andrea Lunsford, and Gene Montague. *Four Worlds of Writing*. New York: Harper & Row, 1981. 3rd ed. Reading, MA: Addison-Wesley, 1991.
Lauer, Janice. "Writing as Inquiry: Some Questions for Teachers." *CCC* 33 (1982): 89–93.
———. "Composition Studies: Dappled Discipline." *RR* 3 (1984): 20–29.
———. "Issues in Rhetorical Invention." *Essays on Classical Rhetoric and Modern Discourse*. Ed. Robert Connors, Lisa Ede, and Andrea Lunsford. Carbondale: Southern Illinois University Press, 1984. 127–39.
Lauer, Janice, and J. William Asher. *Composition Research: Empirical Designs*. New York: Oxford University Press, 1988.
Lauer, Janice. "Instructional Practices: Toward an Integration." *Focuses* 1 (1988): 3–10.

LINDEMANN, ERIKA

(a) Bibliography, Rhetoric and/or Composition Theory, Pedagogy

(b) Erika Lindemann's *Longman Bibliography of Composition and Rhetoric* (1984–85, 1986), which became the *CCCC Bibliography of Composition and Rhetoric* in 1987 and continues under that title, was the first comprehensive bibliography of the field. The first volume, which covers 1984–85, contains 3,853 annotated entries by over 150 bibliographers. Later volumes cover works published, for the most part, in a single calendar year. The works provide descriptive annotations of each citation, cross-references when necessary, and indexes of subjects and authors and editors. In *A Rhetoric for Writing Teachers* (1982), she addresses questions that beginning writing teachers (and experienced teachers who have not been trained as writing teachers) often ask, she summarizes important research on composition theory and practice, and she suggests practical ways teachers can apply theory in their writing classes. As she does elsewhere, Lindemann asserts that teaching is itself a rhetorical act, and she reminds teachers that their writing assignments, evaluations of and responses to student writing, course designs, and classroom management all reflect their rhetorical stance. In this work and in later essays, Lindemann discusses different models for teaching composition, emphasizing not only how these approaches differ, but also what they have in common; she continues to insist on the primacy of writing (not talk about literature or talk about writing) in whatever approach teachers choose. Essays in *An Introduction to Composition Studies*, which Lindemann co-edited with Gary Tate in 1991, give an overview of the new discipline of composition studies, focusing on what distinguishes it from other fields, its history, theories, practice, research methods, and resources.

(c) Lindemann, Erika. *A Rhetoric for Writing Teachers*. 1982. 3rd ed. New York: Oxford University Press, 1995.
———. *Longman Bibliography of Composition and Rhetoric*. 1984–85, 1986. 2 vols. New York: Longman, 1987–88.
———, ed. *CCCC Bibliography of Composition and Rhetoric*. 1987, 1988, 1989, 1990. 4 vols. Carbondale: Southern Illinois University Press, 1990–92.
Lindemann, Erika, and Gary Tate, eds. *An Introduction to Composition Studies*. New York: Oxford University Press, 1991.

LLOYD-JONES, RICHARD

(a) Research Methodology, Response and Evaluation

(b) With Richard Braddock and Lowell Schoer, Lloyd-Jones edited *Research in Written Composition* (1963), which surveys research in composition before 1963, emphasizing the experimental methodology of the sciences. Many see this work as marking the emergence of composition and rhetoric as a research discipline. With Carl H. Klaus, Lloyd-Jones developed the design (and the scoring guides) for "**Primary Trait** Scoring." In *The Students' Right to Write* (1976), he discusses situations in which this form of **holistic** scoring can be particularly useful. He also wrote the essay on primary trait scoring for *Evaluating Writing: Describing, Measuring, Judging* (1977). In the essay, he describes the three-part model of discourse he and Klaus chose for the Primary Trait Scoring System, their considerations when developing writing prompts, and the scoring guides they produced. Lloyd-Jones wrote the bibliographical essay on writing tests in the revised edition of *Teaching Composition* (1987) and the essay on his colleague, Richard Braddock, in *Traditions of Inquiry* (1985), a collection of essays on major figures in rhetoric and composition. In "The Politics of Research into the Teaching of Composition" (1977), he reviews reasons why the educational establishment, including English departments, will have to begin supporting composition research. In 1989, he and Andrea Lunsford edited the report on the

1987 **English Coalition Conference** that examined English instruction at all levels and stressed the importance of English studies in a multicultural society. In several essays and conference presentations, he discusses the future of composition studies and chronicles important events in its past, including the meetings that produced the Students' Right to Write Resolution and the English Coalition Conference, noting the relevance of these deliberations to current issues. Lloyd-Jones was chair of **CCCC** in 1977 and president of **NCTE** in 1986; he won CCCC's first Exemplar Award in 1991. He is one of the most frequently published authors of major articles in *CCC* from 1965–79 and one of the fifty most-cited authors in *CCC* articles from 1980–93.

(c) Lloyd-Jones, Richard, Richard Braddock, and Lowell Schoer, eds. *Research in Written Composition*. Urbana: NCTE, 1963.

Lloyd-Jones, Richard. "Primary Trait Scoring." *Evaluating Writing: Describing, Measuring, Judging*. Ed. Charles Cooper and Lee Odell. Buffalo: State University of New York, 1977. 33–66.

———. "The Politics of Research into the Teaching of Composition." *CCC* 28 (1977): 218–22.

———. "Richard Braddock." *Traditions of Inquiry*. Ed. John Brereton. New York: Oxford University Press, 1985. 153–70.

———. "Tests of Writing Ability." *Teaching Composition: 12 Bibliographical Essays*. Ed. Gary Tate. Fort Worth: Texas Christian University Press, 1987. 155–76.

Lloyd-Jones, Richard, and Andrea Lunsford, eds. *The English Coalition Conference: Democracy Through Language*. New York: MLA, 1987.

LUNSFORD, ANDREA

(a) Basic Writing, Collaboration, Gender and Composition, History of Rhetoric and/or Composition, Rhetoric and/or Composition Theory

(b) Lunsford has contributed to many areas of composition studies, from her early work in **basic writing** to her 1996 discussion of intellectual property. In several essays, she has examined issues in basic writing, including the implications of theories of cognitive development for teaching and research. She updated Mina Shaughnessy's 1976 article on basic writing in *Teaching Composition* (1987). Lunsford has done work on both nineteenth century and classical rhetoric. With Lisa Ede, she argues that classical rhetoric and the **"new rhetoric"** are more similar than dissimilar and that the features they share mark any viable theory of rhetoric. *Essays on Classical Rhetoric and Modern Discourse* (edited with Robert Connors and Lisa Ede) won the MLA Mina Shaughnessy Award in 1985. Lunsford and Ede's essay on **audience**, "Audience Addressed / Audience Invoked," won the Braddock Award for 1984. In this essay, they argue that both those who emphasize audience (audience addressed) and those who do not (audience invoked) oversimplify the role of audience; instead, Lunsford and Ede present a model that, they argue, illustrates the shifting, interrelated role of audience in the composing **process**. In a 1996 essay, they critique their earlier essay on audience, examining how personal and professional allegiances influenced their work and suggesting the value of such revealing rereadings. In other studies, Lunsford and Ede conclude that **collaborative** writing in the classroom best prepares writers for the workplace. In "Singular Texts / Plural Authors" (1990), they argue against privileging single-author writing and for the acceptance of collaborative writing, especially **dialogic** collaboration, which they see as particularly suited to women. The essays in *Reclaiming Rhetorica: Women in the Rhetorical Tradition*, which Lunsford edited in 1995, discuss the work of women who, she suggests, have been excluded from the rhetorical tradition because their ways of and purposes for communicating have not fit the traditional "masculinist" definition of "rhetoric." With Richard Lloyd-Jones, Lunsford edited the report of the 1987 **English Coalition Conference**; with Helene Moglen and James Slevin, Lunsford edited a collection of essays from the 1988 Right to Literacy Conference. Her 1981 textbook, *Four Worlds of Writing*, with Janice Lauer, Gene Montague, and Janet Emig, and *The St. Martin's Handbook* (1989), with Robert Connors, have been widely used. In her discussion of intellectual property (with Susan West), Lunsford traces the history of rights of ownership and examines how poststructuralist theory, debate over patent law in the scientific community, and changes in technology are challenging those notions. She calls on teachers of composition to join in the public debate about intellectual property law. Lunsford was **CCCC** chair in 1989 and won the CCCC Exemplar Award in 1994. She served on the Executive Council of MLA from 1994–97. She is among the ten authors most cited in *CCC* articles from 1980–93 and is one of the most frequently published authors of major articles in *CCC* for the same period.

(c) Lunsford, Andrea. "Cognitive Development and the Basic Writer." *CE* 41 (1979): 38–46. Rpt. in *Cross-Talk in Comp Theory: A Reader*. Ed. Victor Villanueva, Jr. Urbana: NCTE, 1997. 277–88.

Lunsford, Andrea, Janet Emig, Janet Lauer, and Gene Montague. *Four Worlds of Writing*. New York: Harper & Row, 1981. 3rd ed. Reading, MA: Addison-Wesley, 1991.

Lunsford, Andrea, and Lisa Ede. "Audience Addressed / Audience Invoked: The Role of Audience in Composition Theory and Pedagogy." *CCC* 35 (1984): 155–71. Rpt. in *Cross-Talk in Comp Theory: A Reader*. Ed. Victor Villanueva, Jr. Urbana: NCTE, 1997. 77–95.

Lunsford, Andrea, Robert J. Connors, and Lisa Ede, eds. *Essays on Classical Rhetoric and Modern Discourse*. Carbondale: Southern Illinois University Press, 1984.

Lunsford, Andrea. "Basic Writing Update." *Teaching Composition: Twelve Bibliographical Essays*. Fort Worth: Texas Christian University Press, 1987. 207–26.

Lunsford, Andrea, and Robert Connors. *The St. Martin's Handbook*. 1989. 3rd ed. New York: St. Martin's Press, 1996.

Lunsford, Andrea, and Lisa Ede. *Singular Texts / Plural Authors: Perspectives on Collaborative Writing*. Carbondale: Southern Illinois University Press, 1990.

Lunsford, Andrea, ed. *Reclaiming Rhetorica: Women in the History of Rhetoric*. Pittsburgh: University of Pittsburgh Press, 1995.

Lunsford, Andrea, and Susan West. "Intellectual Property and Composition Studies." *CCC* 47 (1996): 383–411.

MACRORIE, KEN

(a) Essay and Personal Writing, Invention, Pedagogy

(b) As an early editor of *CCC* (1962–64), Macrorie helped to make the journal a leader in the field of writing instruction. One of the earliest to talk of writing as **process**, in all his work he emphasizes teaching students to write by encouraging them to make connections between their subject and their own experience. In early articles and his first book, he argues for delaying correction of spelling, grammar, and mechanics so that students will feel free to write more naturally. His **expressivist** emphasis on letting students discover who they are and what they want to say through writing freely has influenced all levels of writing instruction. *Writing to Be Read* (1968), written for high school students, and *Telling Writing* (1970), written for college students, reflect Macrorie's experience that most classroom writing assignments do not produce **real voices** or real communication, but encourage students to use **"Engfish,"** his term for pretentious language that says nothing. Instead, he advocates the **heuristic "freewriting,"** which he says provides students with freedom and discipline; he makes it part of his student-centered **Third Way** of teaching writing. In *Uptaught* (1970), Macrorie chronicles his experience as a writing teacher, showing how it led him to challenge traditional ways of teaching and, almost by accident, to develop freewriting. In *A Vulnerable Teacher*, (1974) he discusses his failures as well as his successes and what he has learned from each. In both *Searching Writing* (1980) and *Twenty Teachers* (1984), based on case studies of the practice of students and teachers, he continues to connect theory and practice as he has in his earlier work. In *Searching Writing*, Macrorie argues against the traditional research paper and for what he calls the "I-Search" paper, beginning with what the student needs to know at the moment and leading to a variety of resources, including, but not limited to, the library. In *Twenty Teachers*, he reports what writing teachers whose students do good work have told him about their approaches to teaching and, largely in their own words, describes what goes on in their classrooms.

(c) Macrorie, Ken. *Writing to Be Read.* 1968. 3rd ed. Upper Montclair, NJ: Boynton/ Cook, 1984.

———. *Telling Writing.* 1970. 4th ed. Upper Montclair, NJ: Boynton/Cook, 1985.

———. *Uptaught.* 1970. New ed. Portsmouth, NH: Boynton/Cook, 1996.

———. *A Vulnerable Teacher.* Rochelle Park, NJ: Hayden, 1974.

———. *Searching Writing: A Contextbook.* Rochelle Park, NJ: Hayden, 1980. Rpt., 1986.

———. *Twenty Teachers.* Oxford: Oxford University Press, 1984.

MAIMON, ELAINE

(a) Collaboration, Writing Across the Curriculum

(b) Maimon is best known for her work in **writing across the curriculum** and in **collaborative learning**, which she sees as central to successful WAC programs. In "Maps and Genres: Exploring Connections in the Arts and Sciences" (1983), she argues that writing in various disciplines can profitably be studied as literary genres whose knowledge, conventions, and assumptions have been collaboratively constructed by the members of the discipline. Students are often as unfamiliar with these genres as they are with literary genres because they have not yet "heard" the voices of their communities and cannot "speak" their languages and so cannot enter their **conversations**. The teacher's role becomes, first, to make clear the concept of genre, and, second, to introduce students to the various **discourse communities** and to give them practice in the new languages. In this process, students' peers can function as an intermediate community, and collaborative learning can help students enter discussions within the disciplines. Written with colleagues from various disciplines, each of Maimon's textbooks, *Writing in the Arts and Sciences* (1981) and *Readings in the Arts and Sciences* (1984), asks students to investigate writing in the humanities, the social sciences, and the natural sciences in order to learn and then to practice their discourse conventions. With Finnbar O'Connor and Barbara Nodine, Maimon has edited *Thinking, Reasoning, and Writing* (1989), essays on the teaching of thinking by authors in cognitive psychology, composition, and logic. Maimon's autobiographical essay for *Women / Writing / Teaching* (1998), written with her daughter, herself a teacher, examines the way mothers and daughters, like teachers and students, create fictions for and about each other. Persons must learn, she says, to appreciate and to **resist** those fictions as, together, they author their lives. Maimon has written extensively about beginning and maintaining successful WAC programs and has served as consultant to colleges and universities interested in implementing such programs.

(c) Maimon, Elaine, Gerald L. Belcher, Gail W. Hearn, Barbara F. Nodine, and Finbarr
    W. O'Connor. *Writing in the Arts and Sciences*. Boston: Little, Brown, 1981.
Maimon, Elaine. "Maps and Genres: Exploring Connections in the Arts and Sciences."
    Composition and Literature: Bridging the Gap. Ed. Winifred Bryan Horner. Chicago: University of Chicago Press, 1983. 110–25.
Maimon, Elaine, Gerald L. Belcher, Gail W. Hearn, Barbara F. Nodine, and Finbarr W.
    O'Connor. *Readings in the Arts and Sciences*. Boston: Little, Brown, 1984.
Maimon, Elaine, Barbara Nodine, and Finbarr W. O'Connor. *Thinking, Reasoning, and
    Writing*. New York: Longman, 1989.
Maimon, Elaine. "Mothers, Daughters, Writing, Teaching." *Women / Writing / Teaching*.
    Ed. Jan Z. Schmidt. Albany: SUNY Press, 1998. 149–64.

McQUADE, DONALD

(a) Linguistics, Pedagogy, Research Methodology, Style

(b) McQuade edited an early collection of essays, *Linguistics, Stylistics, and the Teaching of Composition* (1979), that helped to make available to nonspecialist readers some of the leading composition-related research of the 1970s. Designed to introduce writing teachers to "assumptions, methods, and results" of research in linguistics and stylistics that might have classroom applications, the essays are by leading composition theorists, including David Bartholomae, Frank D'Angelo, James Kinneavy, Richard Larson, W. Ross Winterowd, and Richard Young. They encourage the development of new research methodologies to test the theories the authors present and discuss. In 1986, this original collection was issued in a new, enlarged edition as *The Territory of Language: Linguistics, Stylistics, and the Teaching of Composition*. With classroom composition teachers still its intended audience, the text contains new essays dealing with recent work in linguistics and stylistics. With Robert Atwan, McQuade edited *Popular Writing in America: The Interaction of Style and Audience* (1974), a collection of essays and articles from advertising, newspapers, and magazines, as well as excerpts from bestsellers, classics, and radio, television, and movie scripts presented as subjects for discussion and analysis and models for writing. With Nancy Sommers, he edited *Student Writers at Work: The Bedford Prizes* (1984; 3rd ed., 1989), and with Marie Ponsot, he reported on the Queen's English Project to train secondary teachers to teach **basic writing**. In "Composition and Literary Studies" (1992), McQuade traces academic boundary disputes between literary studies and rhetoric—often, he says, over the territory of composition—in order to provide the context for composition scholarship and research. In the second half of the article, he discusses the scholarship and research that has shaped and professionalized composition studies. McQuade served as chair of **CCCC** in 1991.

(c) McQuade, Donald, and Robert Atwan. *Popular Writing in America: The Interaction of Style and Audience.* 1974. 5th ed. New York: Oxford University Press, 1993.

McQuade, Donald, ed. *Linguistics, Stylistics, and the Teaching of Composition.* Akron, OH: L & S Books and the Department of English, University of Akron, 1979. Rev. ed. *The Territory of Language: Linguistics, Stylistics, and the Teaching of Composition.* Carbondale: Southern Illinois University Press, 1986.

McQuade, Donald, and Marie Ponsot. "Creating Communities of Writers: The Experiment of the Queen's English Project." *JBW* 3.2 (spring/summer 1981): 79–89.

McQuade, Donald, and Nancy Sommers, eds. *Student Writers at Work: The Bedford Prizes.* 1984. 3rd ed. With Michael Tratner. New York: Bedford Books, 1989.

McQuade, Donald. "Composition and Literary Studies." *Redrawing the Boundaries: The Transformation of English and American Literary Studies.* Ed. Stephen Greenblatt and Giles Gunn. New York: MLA, 1992. 482–519.

MILLER, SUSAN

(a) Cultural Studies, Gender and Composition, History of Rhetoric and/or Composition, Rhetoric and/or Composition Theory

(b) In her early essays (1980–82), Miller discusses and suggests uses of Lawrence Kohlberg's extension of Jean Piaget's stages of moral development; she proposes a unified model of product and **process** that writing and literature teachers can use to evaluate student writing in reference to context and desired outcome and to explain features of texts. She also calls for a history of composition studies focusing on classroom practices, on how textbooks were actually used in a class rather than on more studies of textbooks themselves. In *Rescuing the Subject: A Critical Introduction to Rhetoric and the Writer* (1989), she proposes rereading the history of rhetoric to examine the differences between oral rhetoric and written composition. Rhetoric, she says, accounts for the relations any piece of writing has to texts that have gone before it. She intends to "rescue" both rhetoric, as "subject" from an oral tradition that no longer "fits," and the writing "subject," who is neither as autonomous as the orator of classical rhetoric was thought to be nor as "written" as postmodern theory suggests. Miller's "The Feminization of Composition" (1990) and *Textual* **Carnivals:** *The Politics of Composition* (1991), which shared the **CCCC** Outstanding Book Award for 1992, both treat the "history, populations, and theories" of composition studies as a text that reveals the hegemonic agenda present from its beginnings and the attitudes that have kept it subordinate to literature. Recent attempts to improve the status of composition and composition teachers by establishing composition as the intellectual equal of other studies have failed. Instead, they have only sustained and reproduced the original hegemonic agenda. To change the "text" of composition studies, those in the discipline must uncover its beginnings and **resist** its traditional function of marginalizing nontraditional students who enter the academy. In *Assuming the Positions: Cultural Pedagogy and the Politics of Commonplace Writing* (1998), Miller provides an example of the kind of textual rhetoric she advocates: She examines a wide variety of writings from ordinary life to explore what they reveal about how earlier texts, cultural codes, and different genres of writing help to determine what a writer can and cannot say. Miller's anthology, *The Written World: Reading and Writing in Social Contexts*, offers students a similar variety of genres.

(c) Miller, Susan. *Rescuing the Subject: A Critical Introduction to Rhetoric and the Writer*. Carbondale: Southern Illinois University Press, 1989.

———. *The Written World: Reading and Writing in Social Contexts*. New York: Harper & Row, 1989. 2nd ed. *Written Worlds: Reading and Writing Culture*. New York: HarperCollins, 1993.

———. "The Feminization of Composition." In *The Politics of Writing Instruction: Postsecondary*. Ed. Richard Bullock and John Trimbur. Portsmouth, NH: Boynton/Cook, 1990. 39–53. Rpt. in *Composition in Four Keys: Inquiring into the*

Field. Ed. Mark Wiley, Barbara Gleason, and Louise Weatherbee Phelps. Mountain View, CA: Mayfield, 1996. 492–502.

———. *Textual Carnivals: The Politics of Composition*. Carbondale: Southern Illinois University Press, 1991.

———. *Assuming the Positions: Cultural Pedagogy and the Politics of Commonplace Writing*. Pittsburgh: University of Pittsburgh Press, 1998.

MOFFETT, JAMES

(a) Essay and Personal Writing, Literacy, Pedagogy, Rhetoric and/or Composition Theory

(b) Based on the principles that came out of the **Dartmouth Seminar** (a 1966 conference of writing teachers from the United States and Great Britain), Moffett's **process**-oriented *Teaching the Universe of Discourse* (1968) has influenced all levels of writing instruction. It provides the theoretical grounding for his work as well as for the work of other **expressivists** such as Peter Elbow and Donald Murray. In "I, You, and It" (1965) and elsewhere, Moffett suggests that stages of language development correspond to stages of discourse—from internal "reflection" to "conversation" to "correspondence" and finally to "publication"—each stage marking a greater distance between speaker and audience and a move to a higher level of abstraction. Reflecting Jean Piaget's work on cognitive development and his own experience as writer and teacher, Moffett sees the beginning of writing in speech and storytelling, saying that a child's first move toward writing occurs when she takes over a conversation and tells a story without the help of her **audience**. Moffett's 1968 textbook, *A Student-Centered Language Arts Curriculum* with its handbooks for teachers at various grade levels, puts his whole-language theory into practice, suggesting that children should begin by writing narratives about personal experiences and proceed through a sequence of writing tasks designed to help them move through the stages of language development. He warns of the dangers when teachers evaluate student writing and advocates peer feedback as well as teacher response, arguing that the teacher's role as **authority** figure and grade-giver sometimes makes her responses to student writing destructive to the student's development. His definitions of discourse as "any piece of verbalization complete for its original purpose" and of rhetoric as "acting on another through words" have often been quoted. Several of Moffett's textbooks outline curricula that combine teaching writing and literature, and in other works, Moffett has explored relationships between inner speech, reading, writing, and meditation. In *Storm in the Mountains* (1988), a case study of a 1974 controversy over textbooks in Kanawha County, West Virginia, that condemned some of his own work, he has analyzed the roots of censorship and suggested what he calls "spiritual" education as a corrective. *Storm in the Mountains* won the NCTE David H. Russell Award for Distinguished Research in the Teaching of English for 1992. In *The Universal Schoolhouse: Spiritual Awakening Through Education* (1994), Moffett describes the holistic education that he believes would help students to develop spiritually. *Coming on Center: English Education in Evolution* (1981) is a collection of Moffett's essays and talks on language arts education in the 1970s. Moffett is one of the fifty authors most cited in *CCC* articles from 1980–93.

(c) Moffett, James. "I, You, It." *CCC* 16 (1965): 243–48. Rpt. in *Composition in Four Keys: Inquiring into the Field.* Ed. Mark Wiley, Barbara Gleason, and Louise Weatherbee Phelps. Mountain View, CA: Mayfield, 1996. 24–28.

———. *A Student-Centered Language Arts Curriculum.* New York: Oxford University Press, 1968.

———. *Teaching the Universe of Discourse.* Boston: Houghton Mifflin, 1968. Rpt. Portsmouth, NH: Boynton/Cook, 1987.

———. *Coming on Center: English Education in Evolution.* Montclair, NJ: Boynton/ Cook, 1981. Rev. ed. *Coming on Center: Essays in English Education*, Montclair, NJ: Boynton/Cook, 1988.

———. *Storm in the Mountains: A Case Study of Censorship, Conflict, and Consciousness.* Portsmouth, NH: Boynton/Cook, 1988.

———. *The Universal Schoolhouse: Spiritual Awakening Through Education.* San Francisco: Jossey Bass, 1994. Rpt. Portland, ME: Calendar Islands, 1998.

MURPHY, JAMES J.

(a) Bibliography, History of Rhetoric and/or Composition

(b) Murphy's *Medieval Rhetoric: A Select Bibliography* (1971) and *Rhetoric in the Middle Ages* (1974) are standard works on the medieval period. He has also done work on Renaissance and classical rhetoric and on the theory and practice of eloquence in those periods. In his comprehensive works on rhetoric in the Middle Ages, Murphy describes how St. Augustine subsumed the rhetorics of Aristotle and Cicero to the Christian *ethos*, leading to medieval rhetoric's elevation of the art of preaching to equal status with the arts of letter-writing and prescriptive grammar. With Martin Camargo, he wrote the bibliographical essay on the Middle Ages for *The Present State of Scholarship in Historical and Contemporary Rhetoric* (1983). Murphy edited collections of essays in 1972, 1982, and 1990. Three essays in *A Synoptic History of Classical Rhetoric* are by Murphy; together the essays in the work review the field, summarizing major Greek and Roman works. The essays in *The Rhetorical Tradition and Modern Writing* discuss the relation between classical, eighteenth-century, and nineteenth-century rhetorics and modern writing pedagogy, identifying rhetoric's legacies to composition and indicating ways modern writers in America can learn from the rhetorical tradition. Murphy wrote the chapter giving Quintilian's description of Roman writing instruction for *A Short History of Writing Instruction from Ancient Greece to Twentieth Century America*, which he edited in 1990. The work ends with a survey of the teaching of writing in American schools and colleges from 1890 to 1985.

(c) Murphy, James J. *Medieval Rhetoric: A Select Bibliography.* 1971. 2nd ed. Toronto Medieval Bibliographies, 3. Toronto: University of Toronto Press, 1989.

————, ed. *A Synoptic History of Classical Rhetoric*. New York: Random House, 1972. Rpt. Davis, CA: Hermagoras Press, 1983. 2nd ed. With Richard A. Katula, Forbes I. Hill, Donovan J. Ochs, and Prentice Mendor. Mahwah, NJ: Lawrence Erlbaum, 1995.

————. *Rhetoric in the Middle Ages: A History of Rhetorical Theory from Saint Augustine to the Renaissance*. 1974. 2nd ed. Berkeley: University of California Press, 1981.

————, ed. *The Rhetorical Tradition and Modern Writing*. New York: MLA, 1982.

Murphy, James J., and Martin Camargo. "The Middle Ages." *The Present State of Scholarship in Historical and Contemporary Rhetoric*. Ed. Winifred Bryan Horner. Columbia: University of Missouri Press, 1983. Rev. ed., 1990. 45–83.

Murphy, James J., ed. *A Short History of Writing Instruction from Ancient Greece to Twentieth Century America*. Davis, CA: Hermagoras Press, 1990.

MURRAY, DONALD M.

(a) Composing Processes, Essay and Personal Writing, Pedagogy, Revision

(b) A Pulitzer Prize–winning journalist, a novelist, and a poet, Murray has emphasized the **processes** of composing and revision in his work on composition. In his early articles on revision, he claims that revision for the professional writer is most frequently "internal," discovering what he wants to say and how to say it, not "external," preparing the paper for the reader, a process that often becomes editing for surface errors. He wrote *The Craft of Revision* in 1991. Like the **expressivist** group that includes Peter Elbow, Ken Macrorie, and James Moffett, Murray believes that writing is an art and that the teacher's job is to provide the environment in which the writer can develop an **"authentic voice."** He too draws from his development as a writer and believes that students should be encouraged to write about their own interests. He encourages decentering the writing class by using techniques of **collaboration** and writing **workshops**. Like James Britton, he believes that writing cannot be programmed or controlled; he uses the term "surprise" to refer to the moments of insight that Britton calls "spontaneous inventiveness." He does, however, believe that writers can be taught strategies that encourage "surprises" as well as how to recognize and attend to such moments. *A Writer Teaches Writing* (1968, revised 1985), in which he explains his theory and offers practical teaching advice, has been a standard text for writing teachers. *Learning by Teaching* (1982) collects twenty-nine of his articles written over a period of fourteen years. A second collection of his essays, *Expecting the Unexpected* (1989), focuses, he says, on ways to teach writing students to expect and accept the unexpected and to be challenged and stimulated by it. In *Shoptalk, Learning to Write with Writers* (1990), Murray introduces thematically arranged collections of quotations on writing by authors from different times and places. He is among the ten authors most cited in *CCC* articles from 1980–93 and one of the most frequently published authors of major articles in *CCC* for the same period.

(c) Murray, Donald. *A Writer Teaches Writing*. 1968. 2nd ed. Boston: Houghton Mifflin, 1985.

———. *Learning by Teaching: Selected Articles on Writing and Teaching*. 1982. 2nd ed. Montclair, NJ: Heinemann, Boynton/Cook, 1989.

———. *Write to Learn*. 1984. 5th ed. Fort Worth, TX: Harcourt Brace, 1996.

———. *Expecting the Unexpected*. Montclair, NJ: Heinemann, Boynton/Cook, 1989.

———. *Shoptalk, Learning to Write with Writers*. Montclair, NJ: Heinemann, Boynton/Cook, 1990.

———. *The Craft of Revision*. 1991. 3rd ed. Fort Worth, TX: Harcourt Brace, 1998.

NEEL, JASPER

(a) History of Rhetoric and/or Composition, Rhetoric and/or Composition Theory

(b) In 1978, Neel edited *Options for the Teaching of English: Freshman Composition*, a collection of essays that reviews model writing programs of the 1970s. He has also done significant work on the connections between classical rhetoric, current literary theory, and composition studies. In *Plato, Derrida, and Writing* (1988), Neel discusses similarities and differences in Plato's and Derrida's views of writing, arguing that although both reject the possibility that one can discover transcendent truth through writing, only Derrida claims that such truth either does not exist or cannot be known. Although he agrees with Derrida's view of transcendent truth, Neel argues that "usable" truth can be arrived at through the sophistic method of testing claims through competing discourse. *Plato, Derrida, and Writing* won the Mina Shaughnessy Prize for 1989. Neel's other essays and books also introduce composition teachers to new critical and reading theories. His 1992 essay, "Dichotomy, Consubstantiality, Technical Writing, Literary Theory: The Double Orthodox Curse," which won the James Kinneavy Prize, compares pedagogies as different as those of technical writing and literary criticism to encourage dialogue about those differences. In 1995 he won the W. Ross Winterowd Prize for *Aristotle's Voice: Rhetoric, Theory, and Writing in America*. In this work, Neel takes Aristotle's theory as the starting point of his pedagogy and examines its social and political implications in order to allow it, he says, to reveal its inconsistencies; he concludes by arguing for the composition of the sophists as a response to the rhetoric of Aristotle. In "The Degradation of Rhetoric, or Dressing like a Gentleman, Speaking like a Scholar" (1995), he traces the prejudice against rhetoric and composition in modern-day English departments to the influence of Aristotelian rhetoric, which, he argues, is based on a social structure that elevates the philosopher (today's professor of literature) and degrades the rhetorician (today's teacher of rhetoric and composition).

(c) Neel, Jasper, ed. *Options for the Teaching of English: Freshman Composition*. New York: MLA, 1978.

―――. *Plato, Derrida, and Writing*. Carbondale: Southern Illinois University Press, 1988.

―――. "Dichotomy, Consubstantiality, Technical Writing, Literary Theory: The Double Orthodox Curse." *JAC* 12 (1992): 305–21.

―――. *Aristotle's Voice: Rhetoric, Theory, and Writing in America*. Carbondale: Southern Illinois University Press, 1994.

―――. "The Degradation of Rhetoric, or Dressing like a Gentleman, Speaking like a Scholar." *Rhetoric, Sophistry, Neopragmatism*. Ed. Steven Mailloux. Cambridge: Cambridge University Press, 1995. 61–81.

NORTH, STEPHEN M.

(a) History of Rhetoric and/or Composition, Pedagogy, Research Methodology, Rhetoric and/or Composition Theory, Writing Centers

(b) North has written on tutor training and writing centers and reported on and examined the use of case studies for composition research; he has also written an overview of composition studies and its methodological communities. In articles on tutor training, North describes how to teach tutors to talk about writing, including role playing, videotaping, and watching live tutorial sessions. In "The Idea of a Writing Center" (1984), he argues that the main purpose of writing centers is not to "fix" **basic writing** problems but to develop better writers by discussing the writing **process** with students who voluntarily come to the centers because they are ready to talk about writing. In a 1986 essay, he describes his study of writing done by three students in a philosophy class. Using the methods of literary criticism to interpret the texts students produce for a course, he says, reveals much about the way writers shape and are shaped by their writing; he also notes that reviewer response to this study suggests a bias against regarding such studies as "real" research. In *The Making of Knowledge in Composition: Portrait of an Emerging Field* (1987), his best-known work, North dates the beginning of modern composition to 1963, the year *Research in Written Composition* was published. He calls composition a "field" rather than a "discipline" because he says that the term "discipline" conveys the idea of preparation to *do* something, and in an attempt to legitimize composition as a discipline, researchers have turned away from its practical tradition of teaching. North identifies the accumulated knowledge of that practical tradition as **"lore"** and writing teachers as **"practitioners."** He argues that writing teachers' practice is a mode of inquiry that has been devalued, and he identifies two other methodological communities that have each privileged its own epistemology over that of practitioners: scholars (historians, philosophers, and critics); and researchers (experimentalists, clinicians, formalists, and ethnographers). Hailed by some as a way to look at teaching practices in a new and fruitful way, his defense of practice as a mode of inquiry has also been criticized both by those who question its legitimacy and by those who argue that he misrepresents what teachers know and how they know it.

(c) North, Stephen M. "Training Tutors to Talk About Writing." *CCC* 33 (1982): 434–41.

———. "Writing Center Diagnosis: The Composing Profile." *Tutoring Writing: A Sourcebook for Writing Labs*. Ed. Muriel Harris. Glenview, IL: Scott, Foresman, 1982. 42–52.

———. "The Idea of a Writing Center." *CE* 46 (1984): 433–46. Rpt. in *Rhetoric and Composition*. Ed. Richard L. Graves. 3rd ed. Portsmouth, NH: Boynton/Cook, 1990. 232–46.

———. "Designing a Case Study Method for Tutorials: A Prelude to Research." *RR* 4 (1985): 88–89.

———. "Writing in a Philosophy Class: Three Case Studies." *RTE* 20 (1986): 225–62.

———. *The Making of Knowledge in Composition: Portrait of an Emerging Field*. Upper Montclair, NJ: Boynton/Cook, 1987.

ODELL, LEE

(a) Composing Processes, Research Methodology, Response and Evaluation, Writing in the Workplace

(b) Lee Odell is the co-editor of three influential collections of essays. *Evaluating Writing: Describing, Measuring, Judging* (1977), with Charles Cooper, contains essays describing, among other assessment instruments, **holistic** scoring, **primary trait** scoring, and peer evaluation and asserting that the purpose of the evaluation should determine the method of assessment. *Research on Composing: Points of Departure* (1978), also with Cooper, is the sequel to the Richard Braddock, Richard Lloyd-Jones, and Lowell Schoer study of composition research. Besides providing a summary of empirical research completed between 1963 and 1978, essays in this work reject the **current-traditional** paradigm, argue that the experimental method should not be enshrined as the only viable methodology, and suggest possible areas of new research in composing and alternative research models. *Writing in Nonacademic Settings* (edited with Dixie Goswami in 1985) provides information on how to use a variety of research methodologies—**ethnographic**, qualitative, and experimental—to conduct research on writing in the workplace. The editors' own naturalistic research on writing in the workplace introduces the discourse-based interview as a research method and suggests that persons undertaking different writing tasks use different kinds of reasoning. Odell's 1983 essay, "Studying Writing in Non-Academic Settings" (with Goswami, Anne Herrington, and Doris Quick), won the **NCTE** Award for Best Article on Research in Technical and Scientific Writing for 1984. Many of Odell's early articles show the relevance to composition teaching of Jean Piaget's cognitive psychology. In "Teachers of Composition and Needed Research in Discourse Theory," which won the Braddock Award in 1980, Odell urges researchers to study the composing **process** rather than to analyze finished pieces of writing. In *Theory and Practice in the Teaching of Writing: Rethinking the Discipline* (1993), he discusses ways to teach strategy while encouraging surprise (moments of insight) and ways to make the process of assessment a learning experience. Odell is one of the fifty authors most cited in *CCC* articles from 1980–93 and one of the most frequently published authors of major articles in *CCC* for the same period. He chaired **CCCC** in 1986.

(c) Odell, Lee, and Charles Cooper, eds. *Evaluating Writing: Describing, Measuring, Judging.* Urbana: NCTE, 1977.

————, eds. *Research on Composing: Points of Departure.* Urbana: NCTE, 1978.

Odell, Lee. "Teachers of Composition and Needed Research in Discourse Theory." *CCC* (1979): 39–45. Rpt. in *The Writing Teacher's Sourcebook.* Ed. Gary Tate and Edward P. J. Corbett. New York: Oxford University Press, 1981. 53–61.

Odell, Lee, Dixie Goswami, Anne Herrington, and Doris Quick. "Studying Writing in Non-Academic Settings." *New Essays in Technical and Scientific Communication: Research, Theory, and Practice.* Ed. R. W. Bailey, P. J. Anderson, R. J. Brockman, and C. R. Miller. Farmingdale, NY: Baywood, 1983. 17–40.

Odell, Lee, and Dixie Goswami, eds. *Writing in Nonacademic Settings.* New York: Guilford Press, 1985.

Odell, Lee, ed. *Theory and Practice in the Teaching of Writing: Rethinking the Discipline.* Carbondale: Southern Illinois University Press, 1993.

O'HARE, FRANK

(a) Research Methodology, Style, Pedagogy

(b) O'Hare has done research and authored textbooks on **sentence-combining**. Triggered in part by Noam Chomsky's work in **transformational-generative grammar** and Kellogg Hunt's work with **T-units**, O'Hare's work replicates John C. Mellon's research, which tests the hypothesis that exercises in sentence-combining will improve writers' syntactic maturity. O'Hare's study differs from Mellon's in several important respects. Unlike Mellon, who uses grammatical terms from students' previous study as prompts, O'Hare uses no grammatical terms, relying instead on connecting words and other cues to prompt students. Using an analytic scale, O'Hare also had eight experienced readers read paired pre- and post-treatment essays; the results allow him to claim that sentence-combining produces not only an increase in syntactic maturity but gains in writing quality as well. O'Hare's study led to widespread experiments with and classroom use of this practice. Besides describing his own study and its results, *Sentence-Combining: Improving Student Writing Without Formal Grammar Instruction* (1973) reviews other research in this area and gives a rationale for using the technique. O'Hare's *Sentencecraft* (1975) and his textbook with Dean Memering, *The Writer's Work: Guide to Effective Composition* (1980), include methods for directing sentence-combining as well as sentence-combining exercises. O'Hare's 1979 television series on writing and sentence-combining for elementary students has won media awards. *How to Cut Hours off the Time You Spend Marking Papers* (1981) offers secondary writing teachers advice on correcting student essays.

(c) O'Hare, Frank. *Sentence-Combining: Improving Student Writing Without Formal Grammar Instruction*. Urbana: NCTE, 1973.

———. *Sentencecraft*. 1975. 2nd ed. Lexington, MA: Ginn and Co., 1985.

O'Hare, Frank, and Dean Memering. *The Writer's Work: Guide to Effective Composition*. 1980. 3rd ed. Englewood Cliffs, NJ: Prentice Hall, 1990.

———. *How to Cut Hours off the Time You Spend Marking Papers*. Englewood Cliffs, NJ: Scholastic, 1981.

———. *The Modern Writer's Handbook*. New York: Macmillan, 1986. 4th ed. Upper Saddle River, NJ: Simon & Schuster, 1995.

OHMANN, RICHARD

(a) Cultural Studies, History of Rhetoric and/or Composition, Literacy, Style

(b) Ohmann has done work on style, on the politics of writing instruction, and in cultural studies, where Marxist ideas have shaped his concerns. His early work in stylistics shows the relevance of linguistics, especially **transformational grammar**, to studies of style. Ohmann views style as **epistemic** choice, and he claims that the critic, by a close examination of a writer's stylistic choices, can understand his epistemology; he demonstrates his point in several studies, including an analysis of the style of George Bernard Shaw. In the 1970s, he suggests that **speech act theory** is also useful for stylistic analysis. His "In Lieu of a **New Rhetoric**" (1964), which he writes just as rhetoric is beginning to be viewed as a research discipline, examines how new ideas about rhetoric are similar to and different from those of the past. He then suggests a framework for a first-year writing course that reflects modern theory and that includes a consideration of what he calls "world views." In this course, students learn that people see the world differently, and they become aware of how they themselves see the world. By the time he writes *English in America: A Radical View of the Profession* (1976), Ohmann sees English departments in trouble—declining enrollments, shrinking budgets, jobless Ph.D.s. He argues for a rethinking of the kind of "acculturation" he sees being enforced by writing teachers with red pencils and handbooks and urges writing teachers to acknowledge the implications of their control of knowledge. He indicts the rhetorics of the period for discouraging vigorous expressions of opinion and "sociopolitical" agendas and the profession for adopting a problem-solution format for dealing with social issues that makes them seem less complex than they are. Ohmann suggests that, with the largely unconscious complicity of writing teachers, composition classes prepare students to fill the social slots assigned to them by the military-industrial governing classes. In *Politics of Letters* (1987), a collection of his essays, Ohmann argues that control is exercised through "habitual meanings" that by their very familiarity disguise domination. The essays in this collection examine the ways institutions and professions create class position, including "case studies" of how, in forming the canon, literary critics perpetuate the power structure; the essays also provide examples of the way Ohmann teaches his own American literature classes. Ohmann won the **CCCC** Exemplar Award in 1993. He was editor of *CE* from 1966–78; with his associate editor, W. B. Coley, he edited *Ideas for English 101: Teaching Writing in College*, a collection of articles that appeared in *CE* from 1963 to 1975. Ohmann is among the ten most-cited *CCC* authors from 1965–79 and one of the fifty most-cited *CCC* authors from 1980–93.

(c) Ohmann, Richard, Harold C. Martin, and James H. Wheatley. *The Logic and Rhetoric of Exposition*. 1957. 3rd ed. New York: Holt, Rinehart, and Winston, 1969.

Ohmann, Richard. "In Lieu of a New Rhetoric." *CE* 26 (1964): 17–22. Rpt. in *Contemporary Theories of Rhetoric: Selected Readings*. Ed. Richard L. Johannesen. New York: Harper & Row, 1971. 63–71.

Ohmann, Richard, and W. B. Coley, eds. *Ideas for English 101: Teaching Writing in College*. Urbana: NCTE, 1975.

Ohmann, Richard. *English in America: A Radical View of the Profession*. New York: Oxford University Press, 1976. 2nd ed. New introduction. Hanover, NH: Wesleyan University Press, 1995.

———. "Reflections on Class and Language." *CE* 44.1 (1982): 1–17.

———. *Politics of Letters*. Middletown, CT: Wesleyan University Press, 1987.

ONG, WALTER J., S.J.

(a) History of Rhetoric and/or Composition, Literacy, Rhetoric and/or Composition Theory, Technology and Composition

(b) Ong's work in Renaissance studies, especially his work on the French rhetorician Ramus and his followers, led him to rhetoric. In addition to his study of Ramus, Ong has influenced composition studies through his books and articles on orality, secondary orality, literacy and technology, and **audience**. Ong says that Ramus and Ramists were among the first to go from an oral to a visual medium, a transition that he says led to abstract logical thinking, to the empirical scientific method, and, by the middle of the twentieth century, to the exclusion of **invention** from composition classes. In *The Presence of the Word: Some Prolegomena for Cultural and Religious History* (1967), *Rhetoric, Romance, and Technology: Studies in the Interaction of Expression and Culture* (1971), and *Interfaces of the Word: Studies in the Interaction of Consciousness and Culture* (1977), Ong examines the effect the technologizing of the word through writing, print, and electronics has had on the consciousness of human beings, on oral tradition and literary forms, and on cultures. In *Fighting for Life: Contest, Sexuality, and Consciousness* (1981), Ong's discussion of the relation of what he calls "contest" in human life to sexuality and consciousness, especially as it is revealed in classroom teaching and political rhetoric, has been of particular interest to feminist scholars in composition studies. Drawing on Eric Havelock's speculations about the cognitive differences between oral and literate societies, Ong's *Orality and Literacy: The Technologizing of the Word* (1982), traces those differences from ancient to modern cultures and discusses their implications for literary and rhetorical theory. Two often reprinted articles, "The Writer's Audience Is Always a Fiction" and "Literacy and Orality in Our Times" have popularized Ong's ideas. In "The Writer's Audience Is Always a Fiction" (1975), Ong argues that writers always imaginatively create their audiences and the role they wish their audiences to play. He says that one proof of writers' success is an ability to persuade their audiences to play the roles they have created for them. In "Literacy and Orality in Our Time" (1978), Ong distinguishes between "primary orality" (orality untouched by writing or print); "literacy" (writing, print, electronics), which he says makes analytic, sequential thought possible; and what he calls "secondary orality" (sounded words reproduced by media such as radio, television, and computers), and he suggests ways that composition teachers can use these distinctions to help beginning students who may come from cultures of secondary orality.

(c) Ong, Walter J., S.J. *The Presence of the Word: Some Prolegomena for Cultural and Religious History*. New Haven, CT: Yale University Press, 1967. Pbk. Minneapolis: University of Minnesota Press, 1991.

————. *Rhetoric, Romance, and Technology: Studies in the Interaction of Expression and Culture*. 1971. 2nd ed. Ithaca, NY: Cornell University Press, 1990.

————. "The Writer's Audience Is Always a Fiction." *PMLA* 90 (1975): 9–21. Rpt. in *Cross-Talk in Comp Theory: A Reader*. Ed. Victor Villanueva, Jr. Urbana: NCTE, 1997. 55–76.

————. *Interfaces of the Word: Studies in the Evolution of Consciousness and Culture*. Ithaca, NY: Cornell University Press, 1977. Pbk. Ithaca, NY: Cornell University Press, 1982.

————. "Literacy and Orality in Our Times." *ADE Bulletin* 58 (Sept. 1978): 1–7. Rpt. in *The Writing Teacher's Sourcebook*. Ed. Gary Tate and Edward P. J. Corbett. 2nd ed. New York: Oxford University Press, 1988. 37–46.

————. *Fighting for Life: Contest, Sexuality, and Consciousness*. Ithaca, NY: Cornell University Press, 1981. Pbk. Amherst: University of Massachusetts Press, 1989.

————. *Orality and Literacy: The Technologizing of the Word*. New York: Methuen, 1982. Rpt. New York: Routledge, 1995.

PERELMAN, CHAIM

(a) Argument, Arrangement, History of Rhetoric and/or Composition, Rhetoric and/or Composition Theory

(b) Perelman, for the most part in collaboration with Lucie Olbrechts-Tyteca, has been credited with helping to revive the art of rhetoric through his work on argumentation, which he and Olbrechts-Tyteca call the "**new rhetoric**." Beginning with a search for a nonformal logic that would serve philosophy and the social sciences as formal logic serves the exact sciences, Perelman says that he and Olbrechts-Tyteca ended up rediscovering Aristotle's discussion of dialectical proofs or *topoi*. They argue that "truth" in human affairs is always contingent, never absolute. What is regarded as truth in human affairs is really accepted opinion that has been "tested" over time but that is always open to the possibility of modification or rejection. To change accepted opinion requires skill in argumentation, or rhetoric, for if truth is not absolute, neither is it completely arbitrary. Whether or not an opinion becomes accepted as truth depends on a rhetor's ability to convince a "universal **audience**." Perelman and Olbrechts-Tyteca in *The New Rhetoric: A Treatise on Argumentation* (1958), and later Perelman in *The Realm of Rhetoric* (1977), define this audience as composed of all reasonable human beings. Effective arguments, therefore, begin with rhetors' imagining, identifying with, and achieving "communion" with their audiences and with the "unquestioned beliefs" and "dominant opinions" of their **discourse communities**. Perelman and Olbrechts-Tyteca discuss ways the arrangement of arguments influences audiences and argue against general patterns of development that do not carefully consider particular audiences and purposes. They also consider the importance of stylistic choices, particularly the use of rhetorical figures, in securing "presence," the attention of their audiences, for what rhetors consider is central to their argument.

(c) Perelman, Chaim, and Lucie Olbrechts-Tyteca. *The New Rhetoric: A Treatise on Argumentation*. Trans. John Wilkinson and Purcell Weaver, 1958. Notre Dame, IN: University of Notre Dame Press, 1969. Excerpted in *Contemporary Theories of Rhetoric: Selected Readings*. Ed. Richard L. Johannesen. New York: Harper & Row, 1971. 119–221. Excerpted in *The Rhetorical Tradition: Readings from Classical Times to the Present*. Ed. Patricia Bizzell and Bruce Herzberg. Boston: Bedford Books, 1990.

Perelman, Chaim. "The New Rhetoric: A Theory of Practical Reasoning." *Professing the New Rhetorics: A Sourcebook*. Ed. Theresa Enos and Stuart Brown. Englewood Cliffs, NJ: Prentice Hall, 1994. 145–77. Excerpted from *Great Ideas Today*. Encyclopaedia Britannica. 1970 ed.

———. *The Realm of Rhetoric*. Trans. William Kluback. 1977. Notre Dame, IN: University of Notre Dame Press, 1982.

———. *The New Rhetoric and the Humanities*. Trans. William Kluback. Boston: D. Reidel, 1979.

———. "The New Rhetoric and the Rhetoricians: Remembrances and Comments." *QJS* 70 (1984): 188–96.

PERL, SONDRA

(a) Basic Writing, Composing Processes, Research Methodology, Rhetoric and/or Composition Theory

(b) Perl has done her most significant work on **cognitive processes** in composing. Her 1979 descriptive case study of "unskilled college writers" has been influential both for its methodology (tape-recorded talk-aloud **protocols** analyzed by her own coding system) and for its insights into composing **processes**. Perl's studies indicate that although unskilled writers do not spend much time on prewriting or revising, they do have consistent composing strategies. These writers' premature concern for mechanical correctness, however, frequently interferes with their attempts to "discover and construct" what they mean. This study and Perl's later work demonstrate the **recursiveness** of the composing process as the writers she studies move between structuring their thoughts as they write (projective structuring) and rereading and rewriting what they have written to make it say what they intend (retrospective structuring). Perl uses Eugene Gendlin's term **"felt sense"** to describe what writers attend to when they reread their writing and what they "write out of" when they rewrite. This "felt sense" seems to correspond to the inner voice of writers and describes their feeling that what they have written does or does not capture what they intended to say. Experienced writers, Perl says, rely on this "felt sense" during the revision process. *Through Teachers' Eyes: Portraits of Writing Teachers at Work* (with Nancy Wilson) is an **ethnographic** study of six writing teachers at work; the text examines the way these teachers move from theory to practice. In "Composing Texts, Composing Lives" (1994), Perl takes readers into her own university classroom as she "composes" the text of her own pedagogy, "reading" what she and her students say and write as the course unfolds. As they reflect on and write about what they read in the light of their own experience, Perl argues, they compose not just texts but themselves. *Landmark Essays on Writing Process*, which Perl edited in 1994, contains eighteen chronologically presented essays on the composing process. Perl is one of the fifty most-cited CCC authors from 1980–93. She is co-founder and co-director of the New York City Writing Project.

(c) Perl, Sondra. "The Composing Processes of Unskilled College Writers." *RTE* 13 (1979): 317–36. Rpt. in *Cross-Talk in Comp Theory: A Reader*. Ed. Victor Villanueva, Jr. Urbana: NCTE, 1997. 17–42.

———. "Understanding Composing." *CCC* 31 (1980): 363–69. Rpt. in *The Writing Teacher's Sourcebook*. Ed. Gary Tate and Edward P. J. Corbett. 2nd ed. New York: Oxford University Press, 1988. 113–18.

Perl, Sondra, and Nancy Wilson. *Through Teachers' Eyes: Portraits of Writing Teachers at Work*. Portsmouth, NH: Heinemann, 1986. Reissued with a new preface and corrections. Portland, ME: Calendar Island, 1998.

Perl, Sondra. "Composing Texts, Composing Lives." *HER* 64 (1994): 427–49.

———, ed. *Landmark Essays on Writing Process*. Davis, CA: Hermagoras Press, 1994.

PHELPS, LOUISE WEATHERBEE

(a) Gender and Composition, Rhetoric and/or Composition Theory

(b) Phelps has explored the psychological and philosophical underpinnings of composition theory in her attempt to delineate composition as a discipline, to map its contours, and to explore the geography of its knowledge. In early essays, she compares composition to the new physics to suggest a "dynamic, relativistic view of discourse" for composition; she provides an overview of the field of psychology to suggest what a psychology of composition might look like; she criticizes **process** theory for not being able to account for texts and textual studies and proposes a "dialectics of coherence" to develop a unified theory of composition; and she analyzes the situation of rhetoric in a postmodern world. *Composition as a Human Science* (1988) incorporates these essays in a still broader attempt to provide a theoretical frame for composition. Situating composition within postmodern contextualism, Phelps examines a role for and the importance of the discipline in this scene. She presents the dialectical "Third Way" of Paul Ricoeur as a "metamethod" that would adjudicate debates over methods of research and analysis in the discipline. In her final chapters, Phelps draws on the work of Hans-Georg Gadamer, John Dewey, and Paulo Freire to discuss the relationship between theory and practice in the discipline; she suggests that by reflecting on their own experience, teachers can establish a dialogue between inquiry into practice and practice itself. In a 1989 essay, "Images of Student Writing: The Deep Structure of Teacher Response," she illustrates what she calls the "arc," from practice to theory and back to practice (the "PTP arc") by considering the topic of responding to writing. In "Practical Wisdom and the Geography of Knowledge in Composition" (1991), she starts with North's study of knowledge-making in composition to present a phenomenology of knowledge that moves from teacher **lore** through the **reflective practice** she described in *Composition as a Human Science* to a "local knowledge" that differs from theoretical knowledge in its method of inquiry and context-bound product as well as in the breadth of the community that produces it and to which it is disseminated. Through her discussion, Phelps clarifies the mutual dependence of theory and practice. With Janet Emig, Phelps has edited *Feminine Principles and Women's Experience in American Composition and Rhetoric* (1995), a collection of essays based upon the premise that feminine principles are native to American composition and rhetoric. An exploration of those principles and of the experience of women in the profession, Phelps argues, will allow those in composition and rhetoric to connect with and to contribute to feminist scholarship. In *Composition in Four Keys: Inquiring into the Field* (1996), Phelps and her coeditors "map" the discipline for newcomers by grouping influential essays into four "keys": art, science, nature, and politics.

(c) Phelps, Louise Weatherbee. *Composition as a Human Science: Contributions to the Self-Understanding of a Discipline.* 1988. Rpt. New York: Oxford University Press, 1991.

———. "Images of Student Writing: The Deep Structure of Teacher Response." *Writing and Response: Theory, Practice, and Research.* Ed. Chris Anson. Urbana: NCTE, 1989. 37–67.

———. "Practical Wisdom and the Geography of Knowledge in Composition." *CE* 53 (1991): 863–85.

Phelps, Louise Weatherbee, and Janet Emig, eds. *Feminine Principles and Women's Experience in American Composition and Rhetoric.* Pittsburgh: University of Pittsburgh Press, 1995.

Phelps, Louise Weatherbee, Mark Wiley, and Barbara Gleason, eds. *Composition in Four Keys: Inquiring into the Field*. Mountain View, CA: Mayfield, 1996.

PIKE, KENNETH L.

(a) Invention, Linguistics, Rhetoric and/or Composition Theory

(b) Pike, a linguist, has written several books explaining **tagmemics** and tagmemic analytic methods. In two early (1964) articles, "A Linguistic Contribution to Composition" and "Beyond the Sentence," he applies tagmemic grammar to composition, suggesting ways this theory could be used to produce exercises to develop writing competence and to analyze language structures beyond the sentence. In *Rhetoric: Discovery and Change*, Richard Young, Alton Becker, and Pike use Pike's tagmemic theory to develop their particle/wave/field **heuristic**. In this textbook, they argue that by viewing the world from different perspectives, the writer comes to understand it differently; James Berlin sees this work as an expression of **epistemic** rhetoric. Pike is among the ten authors most cited in *CCC* articles from 1950–79; he is one of the fifty most-cited authors in *CCC* from 1980–93.

(c) Pike, Kenneth. "A Linguistic Contribution to Composition." *CCC* 15 (1964): 81–89.
———. "Beyond the Sentence." *CCC* 15 (1964): 129–35.
Pike, Kenneth, Richard Young, and Alton Becker. *Rhetoric: Discovery and Change*. New York: Harcourt Brace, 1970.
Pike, Kenneth, and Evelyn G. Pike. *Grammatical Analysis*. 1977. Rev. ed. Dallas: Summer Institute of Linguistics and University of Texas, Arlington, 1982.
Pike, Kenneth. *Linguistic Concepts: An Introduction to Tagmemics*. Lincoln: University of Nebraska Press, 1982. Ann Arbor, MI: UMI Books on Demand, 1997.
Pike, Kenneth, and Evelyn G. Pike. *Text and Tagmeme*. Norwood, NJ: Ablex, 1983.

RICHARDS, IVOR A.

(a) Literature and Composition, Rhetoric and/or Composition Theory

(b) Writing in the first half of the twentieth century, Richards was one of several early voices calling for a **new rhetoric**. His first book, *The Meaning of Meaning* (1923), was written with psychologist C. K. Ogden and focuses on Richards' lifelong concern—how words come to *mean*. In the work, they argue against what they call the "proper meaning superstition," the belief that each word has its own meaning about which everyone agrees. Instead, they suggest that meaning begins with sense impressions that leave a psychological trace on the mind. When a similar sense impression occurs, the mind recalls the context of the earlier event. Thus the meaning of a new experience is dependent on past experience; "thinking," which cannot be separated from language, becomes the process of "sorting" our new perceptions by comparing and contrasting them with our past experiences. This comparing and contrasting in order to discover analogies leads to more and more abstractness, and metaphor becomes the heart of language. Since no one's experiences are precisely like those of another, no two people assign exactly the same meaning to a word; the possibility of understanding depends on the number of shared experiences. Richards introduces the "semantic triangle" to show that there is no necessary connection between a symbol or word and the "thing" to which it refers (the "referent"). In *The Philosophy of Rhetoric* (1936), he argues that rhetoric must be broadened to include more than persuasion and that in the province of rhetoric should be also the study of misunderstanding and ways to alleviate it. In *Speculative Instruments* (1955), he maintains that "all studies are language studies" (pp. 115–16). Richards' *Practical Criticism* (1929) reports on an experiment in which he gave students unidentified poems and asked them to respond to the texts. His careful analysis of their responses (he called them **"protocols"**) reveal much misreading and indicates, he says, the need for teaching techniques of reading. He points out how context (the surrounding text) of a passage limits the possible meanings of the passage and urges readers to pay attention to context and to slow down enough to reflect on what is said. Richards suggests various techniques, such as paraphrase, designed to help readers see how changes in what is said affect meaning. Such thinking about thinking, he says, will lead to greater control of language as readers and writers see how their choices of words affect and generate meaning. This emphasis on the **heuristic** power of language is probably what has led historians of rhetoric to call his view of language **epistemic**. Richards' work with Basic English, a vocabulary of 850 words that can be used to define over 20,000 words, was an attempt to reduce the misunderstanding that is inevitable when speakers of different backgrounds and languages attempt to exchange ideas. His later work in education, which includes a series of elementary reading textbooks, illustrates his interest in making theory and practice dialectical.

(c) Richards, I. A., and C. K. Ogden. *The Meaning of Meaning.* London: Kegan Paul; New York: Harcourt Brace, 1923. Rpt. in *C. K. Ogden and Linguistics.* Ed. W. Terrence Gordon. Vol. 3 of 5 volumes. London: Routledge/Theimmes Press, 1994.

Richards, I. A. *Practical Criticism.* 1929. Rpt. London: Routledge and Kegan Paul, 1973.

———. *The Philosophy of Rhetoric.* 1936. New York: Oxford University Press, 1971.

———. *Interpretation in Teaching.* 1938. 2nd ed. London: Routledge and Kegan Paul; New York: Humanities Press, 1973.

———. *Speculative Instruments.* Chicago: University of Chicago Press, 1955.

———. *Richards on Rhetoric: Selected Essays, 1929–1974.* Ed. Ann E. Berthoff. New York: Oxford University Press, 1990.

ROSE, MIKE

(a) Basic Writing, Literacy, Pedagogy, Research Methodology

(b) Throughout his work on **basic writing**, Rose argues that basic writers should not be loosely labeled "remedial" or "illiterate." Because of social and cultural factors, he maintains, they are often simply unfamiliar with and so unprepared to enter the **academic discourse community**. Rose maintains that university courses for basic writers should make them familiar with **academic discourse** by including academic reading and writing (and speaking and thinking) and that course assignments should have "academic substance" and not be limited to **expressive** writing. The emphasis should be on meaning rather than on "inflexible rules and rigid plans" that may actually block students' writing. In his work on writer's block, Rose identifies causes of and cognitive behaviors or attitudes associated with blocking; however, he cautions that trying to find one cognitive explanation for writers' problems is always reductionist and often causes researchers to ignore social and cultural issues. He suggests a number of ways teachers can help students avoid or overcome writer's block. In 1985 he edited *When a Writer Can't Write: Studies in Writer's Block and Other Composing Process Problems*. In *Lives on the Boundary: The Struggles and Achievements of America's Underprepared*, Rose uses stories from his own life and from the lives of the "underprepared" students he has taught to make his case for the intellectual capacity of those in the educational underclass. *Lives on the Boundary* won the Mina Shaughnessy Award and the **NCTE** David H. Russell Award for Distinguished Research in the Teaching of English in 1989 and the first **CCCC** Outstanding Book Award in 1991. "This Wooden Shack Place," written with Glynda Hull, illustrates some of the ways the social and cultural backgrounds of basic writers cause them to misread academic discourse; the essay won the Braddock Award for 1991. "Remediation as Social Context," with Hull, Marisa Castellano, and Kay Losey Fraser, discusses ways that teachers' assumptions about literacy and students' abilities structure their pedagogies and limit students' learning. It won the Braddock Award for 1992. *Possible Lives: The Promise of Public Education in America* (1995) describes Rose's journey across the country, visiting schools at all levels. Through descriptions of the work being done in these public schools, Rose hopes to develop a new critical language that focuses on possibility rather than on failure in discussions about public education. Rose is among the ten authors most cited in *CCC* articles from 1980–93 and is one of the most frequently published authors of major articles in *CCC* for the same period.

(c) Rose, Mike, ed. *When a Writer Can't Write: Studies in Writer's Block and Other Composing Process Problems*. New York: Guilford Press, 1985.

Rose, Mike, Eugene Kintgen, and Barry Kroll, eds. *Perspectives on Literacy*. Carbondale: Southern Illinois University Press, 1988. Pbk. New York: Viking Penguin, 1990.

Rose, Mike. *Lives on the Boundary: The Struggles and Achievements of America's Underprepared*. New York: Free Press, 1989.

Rose, Mike, and Glynda Hull. " 'This Wooden Shack Place': The Logic of an Unconventional Reading." *CCC* 44 (1990): 287–98.

Rose, Mike, and M. Kiniry. *Critical Strategies for Academic Thinking and Writing:*

Cases, Assignments, and Readings. Boston: Bedford Books, 1990. 3rd ed. *Critical Strategies for Academic Thinking and Writing: A Sourcebook of Cross-Disciplinary Writing Materials*. Boston: Bedford Books, 1997.

Rose, Mike, Marisa Castellano, Glynda Hull, and Kay Losey Fraser. "Remediation as Social Construct: Perspectives from an Analysis of Classroom Discourse." *CCC* 42 (1991): 299–329.

Rose, Mike. *Possible Lives: The Promise of Public Education in America*. New York: Houghton Mifflin, 1995. Pbk. New York: Viking Penguin, 1996.

ROYSTER, JACQUELINE JONES

(a) Gender and Composition, Literacy

(b) Royster identifies the locus of her interest and work in composition studies as the intersection of literacy studies, women's studies, and the African diaspora. In "Perspectives on the Intellectual Tradition of Black Women Writers" (1990), she traces a history of black women whose writing, fiction and nonfiction, demonstrates a tradition of literacy and intellectualism. This tradition provides, she says, the "gardens" for the current flowering of black women writers and an intellectual legacy that can help society reenvision other marginalized groups now seen as illiterate. Royster co-edited *Double-Stitch: Black Women Write about Mothers and Daughters* in 1991 and in other essays has described how she draws her own inspiration from her parents and from the legacies of African-American women. In "To Call a Thing by Its True Name: The Rhetoric of Ida B. Wells" (1995), she aims to recover the eloquence and rhetorical strategies of the nineteenth-century anti-lynching campaign of Ida B. Wells and to suggest how Wells' rhetoric embodies the strategies of other black women speakers and writers fighting to change the societies of their day. In 1997 Royster edited and wrote the introduction for *Southern Horrors and Other Writings: The Anti-Lynching Campaign of Ida B. Wells, 1892–1900*. The published version of her chair's address to the **CCCC**, "When the First Voice You Hear Is Not Your Own" (1996), argues for transforming personal and professional cross-boundary discourse by giving others "subjectivity," the power and **authority** to speak; by treating them with respect, by accepting their right to know, and by listening to what they say. Royster chaired CCCC in 1995.

(c) Royster, Jacqueline Jones. "Perspectives on the Intellectual Tradition of Black Women Writers." *The Right to Literacy*. Ed. Andrea Lunsford, Helene Moglen, and James Slevin. New York: MLA, 1990. 103–12.

Royster, Jacqueline Jones, Patricia Bell-Scott, Beverly Guy-Sheftall, Janet Sims-Wood, Mirian DeCosta-Willis, and Lucille P. Fultz, eds. *Double-Stitch: Black Women Write about Mothers and Daughters*. Boston: Beacon Press, 1991.

Royster, Jacqueline Jones. "To Call a Thing By Its True Name: The Rhetoric of Ida B. Wells." *Reclaiming Rhetorica: Women in the Rhetorical Tradition*. Ed. Andrea A. Lunsford. Pittsburgh: University of Pittsburgh Press, 1995. 167–84.

———. "When the First Voice You Hear Is Not Your Own." *CCC* 44 (1996): 29–40.

——, ed. *Southern Horrors and Other Writings: The Anti-Lynching Campaign of Ida B. Wells, 1892–1900*. By Ida B. Wells. Boston: Bedford Books, 1997.

SCOTT, FRED NEWTON

(a) Pedagogy, Rhetoric and/or Composition Theory

(b) One of the **"big four"** nineteenth-century rhetoricians whose textbooks shaped composition studies, Scott, who headed the Department of Rhetoric at the University of Michigan from 1903–26, has been credited with developing a rhetoric that differed from both belles lettres and **current-traditional rhetoric**. This rhetoric, which James Berlin calls a forerunner of **epistemic** rhetoric because it sees reality as **socially constructed**, has its roots in Plato and in John Dewey's idea of **progressive education**. For Scott, to teach writing is to train students not simply to appreciate literature or to win arguments but to be good citizens committed to furthering the welfare of the community. In "Rhetoric Rediviva," a paper he gave at a 1909 MLA meeting, he traces to Plato the origin of rhetoric's concern with the public good, in contrast to Aristotle, whose focus on persuasion ignores, Scott believes, issues of morality. In this paper, Scott also discusses Plato's idea of organic form, agreeing that the content and form of a piece of writing are inseparable and arguing against teaching formulas such as the five-paragraph essay associated with current-traditional rhetoric. Although the fifteen textbooks on which Scott collaborated do not always reflect the advanced ideas of his rhetorical theory, Donald Stewart, who is largely responsible for reviving interest in Scott's work, says that even these textbooks contain much that has become a part of modern rhetoric. For instance, they emphasize rhetorical context and **audience**, spoken language as the basis of written language, and **process** rather than product; and like his well-known *Paragraph Writing* (1891), written with Joseph Denney, they incorporate ideas from other disciplines such as psychology and linguistics. Articles such as "The Standard of American Speech" and "English Composition as a Mode of Behavior" argue for such modern notions as students' right to their own language and for a multiplicity of dialects. They are included in *The Standard of American Speech and Other Papers* (1926), a collection of previously published essays. Scott was one of the leaders in the attempt to reform the secondary school curriculum by eliminating the teaching of the "Universal List of Works" required for entrance exams to eastern universities; his and others' successful efforts led to the founding of **NCTE** in 1911. Scott served as president of MLA in 1907 and from 1911 to 1913 as both the first and second president of NCTE.

(c) Scott, Fred Newton, and Joseph Villiers Denney. *Paragraph Writing*. Ann Arbor, MI: Register Publishing, 1891. 2nd ed. Boston: Allyn and Bacon, 1894.

——. *Composition-Rhetoric, Designed for Use in Secondary Schools*. 1897. Boston: Allyn and Bacon, 1898.

——. *Elementary English Composition*. 1900. New rev. ed. Boston: Allyn and Bacon, 1908.

————. *Composition-Literature*. Boston: Allyn and Bacon, 1902.

Scott, Fred Newton. *The Standard of American Speech and Other Papers*. Boston: Allyn and Bacon, 1926.

————. "Rhetoric Rediviva." Ed. Donald Stewart. *CCC* 31 (1980): 413–19.

SELFE, CYNTHIA L.

(a) Bibliography, Technology and Composition

(b) Selfe has been in the forefront of work with computers and composition teaching. Early in her career, she did research on writing apprehension and on reading as a writing strategy. She has also published on technical communication and **writing across the curriculum**. In her work on writing apprehension, Selfe suggests a connection between poor composing skills or strategies and high apprehension about writing. In 1986, she reexamines two case studies and determines that a student more afraid of writing also uses fewer and less effective strategies to write and revise than does a student with lower writing apprehension. Alone and with others, Selfe has authored and edited books and articles that discuss ways students adapt to composing on computers, that call for new software reflecting composition theory, and that report on the ways computers have changed and are changing composition studies—including the cultural and political implications of electronic environments and the effects of technology on literacy. In 1995 Selfe and Richard J. Selfe won the Ellen Nold Award for "The Politics of the Interface: Power and Its Exercise in Electronic Contact Zones." In this article, they argue that computer interfaces "map" the world in ways that privilege the dominant forces in American culture and suggest ways that those who use computers to teach composition can help to redraw those maps. With Gail Hawisher, Selfe has served as editor of *Computers and Composition: An International Journal for Teachers of English* from 1982 to the present. She is the editor and co-founder of Computers and Composition Press. With Hawisher, she has edited the *CCCC Bibliography of Composition and Rhetoric* from 1991–94. Selfe chaired CCCC in 1997.

(c) Selfe, Cynthia L. *Creating a Computer-Supported Writing Facility: A Blueprint for Action*. Houghton, MI: Computers and Composition Press, 1989.

Selfe, Cynthia L., and S. Hilligloss, eds. *Literacy and Computers: The Complications of Teaching and Learning with Technology*. New York: MLA, 1994.

Selfe, Cynthia L., and R. Selfe. "The Politics of the Interface: Power and Its Exercise in Electronic Contact Zones." *CCC* 45 (1994): 480–504.

Selfe, Cynthia L., and Gail E. Hawisher, ed. *CCCC Bibliography of Composition and Rhetoric*. 1991, 1992, 1993, 1994. 4 vols. Carbondale: Southern Illinois University Press, 1993–96.

Selfe, Cynthia L. "Theorizing E-Mail for the Practice, Instruction, and Study of Literacy." *Electronic Literacies in the Workplace*. Ed. P. Sullivan and J. Dautermann. Urbana: NCTE and Computers and Composition Press, 1996. 255–93.

Selfe, Cynthia L., and R. Selfe. "Writing as Democratic Social Action in a Technological

World: Politicizing and Inhabiting Virtual Landscapes." *Multidisciplinary Research in Nonacademic Writing*. Ed. A. Duin and C. Hansen. Mahwah, NJ: Lawrence Erlbaum, 1996. 325–58.

SHAUGHNESSY, MINA

(a) Basic Writing, Bibliography, Research Methodology

(b) "Diving In: An Introduction to Basic Writing," Shaughnessy's 1976 essay, proposes a "developmental scale" for college teachers faced with a class of nontraditional students, "basic writers" entering the university for the first time. She calls the stages of her scale "guarding the tower," "converting the natives," "sounding the depth," and "diving in" and shows how writing teachers, if they are to be successful, must themselves become students both of new disciplines and of their students. Published the following year, *Errors and Expectations: A Guide for Teachers of Basic Writing* (1977) is the most important early work on basic writing. Based on Shaughnessy's analysis of 4,000 essays written by first-year writing students in the open-admissions City University of New York system of 1970, this work changed the way people in the discipline look at basic writers. *Errors and Expectations* is also important because of Shaughnessy's research methodology. In her study, Shaughnessy identifies, classifies, and investigates the sources of the errors basic writers make, demonstrating that many of the errors are the result of students' experiments with reasonable, if incorrect, hypotheses about how language functions; these errors represent students' attempts to understand the patterns of English. She suggests that writing teachers focus on understanding why their students make errors, rather than assigning them grammatical exercises in workbooks. *Errors and Expectations* won the **NCTE** David H. Russell Award for Distinguished Research in the Teaching of English. Other researchers in basic writing, such as Patricia Bizzell, Mike Rose, Sondra Perl, and David Bartholomae, build on Shaughnessy's work, especially on her argument that these writers are not unintelligent, but simply unfamiliar with both forms and concepts of academic writing. Shaughnessy's bibliographic essay on basic writing in the first edition of *Teaching Composition* (1976) was one of the first bibliographies of postsecondary basic writing. The *Journal of Basic Writing* has published a collection of her speeches and writing about teaching, research, writing evaluation, and basic writing. MLA posthumously established the Mina Shaughnessy Award in her honor. She is among the ten authors most cited in *CCC* articles from 1980–93.

(c) Shaughnessy, Mina. "Diving In: An Introduction to Basic Writing." *CCC* 27 (1976): 234–39. Rpt. in *Cross-Talk in Comp Theory: A Reader*. Ed. Victor Villanueva, Jr. Urbana: NCTE, 1997. 289–95.

———. "Basic Writing." *Teaching Composition: Ten Bibliographic Essays*. Ed. Gary Tate. Fort Worth: Texas Christian University Press, 1976. 137–67. (This essay was updated by Andrea Lunsford in the 1987 revised edition of *Teaching Composition*.)

———. "Some Needed Research on Writing." *CCC* 28 (1977): 317–20.

———. *Errors and Expectations: A Guide for Teachers of Basic Writing.* New York: Oxford University Press, 1977.

———. "Selected Speeches and Essays of Mina Pendo Shaughnessy." *JBW* 3.1 (fall-winter 1980): 91–119.

SHOR, IRA

(a) Cultural Studies, Literacy, Pedagogy

(b) Shor was one of the first to translate Paulo Freire's education theory into a **critical pedagogy** for American education. James Berlin has called *Critical Teaching and Everyday Life* (1980), which grew out of Shor's experience teaching English to working-class students at the City University of New York, the best example of **epistemic** rhetoric in practice. Citing John Dewey's concern that education be more than a "pouring in" of knowledge to be "passively" absorbed by students (**"banking"**), Shor describes a **dialogic** pedagogy that reduces the teacher's **authority** and, in Paulo Freire's term, leads teachers and students to "problematize" all areas of study, to come to see everything they "know," including the way they define themselves, as **socially constructed** by the dominant ideology of the culture in which they live. Shor argues that traditional pedagogies serve the dominant ideology by teaching students to accept the way that it has constructed their economic, social, and political position. Critical pedagogy, in contrast, works to develop a **critical consciousness** that liberates students and empowers them to **resist** the dominant ideology and so to control their own lives and to create a more democratic culture. *Culture Wars: School and Society in the Conservative Restoration, 1969–84* (1986) chronicles what Shor argues were the damaging effects on education (reforms such as career education, illiteracy testing, and the back-to-basics movement) of the conservative response to the protest movement of the 1960s. Shor has edited or authored a number of works on Paulo Freire's pedagogy. *A Pedagogy for Liberation: Dialogues on Transforming Education* (1987) is a collection of taped and edited conversations between Shor and Freire on the most frequently asked questions about liberating education. The essays in *Freire for the Classroom: A Sourcebook for Liberatory Teaching* (1987) and Shor's *Empowering Education: Critical Teaching for Social Change* (1992) attempt to adapt Freire's pedagogy to composition classrooms in the United States. In *When Students Have Power: Negotiating Authority in a Critical Pedagogy* (1996), Shor tells the story of his problems and successes as he has attempted to transform the traditional "teacher-down" class into one in which teacher and students fully share authority and power.

(c) Shor, Ira. *Critical Teaching and Everyday Life.* 1980. Rpt. Chicago: University of Chicago Press, 1987.

———. *Culture Wars: School and Society in the Conservative Restoration, 1969–84.* 1986. Rpt. Chicago: University of Chicago Press, 1992.

Shor, Ira, and Paulo Freire. *A Pedagogy for Liberation: Dialogues on Transforming Education*. Westport, CT: Greenwood Press, 1987.

Shor, Ira, ed. *Freire for the Classroom: A Sourcebook for Liberatory Teaching*. Portsmouth, NH: Heinemann, Boynton/Cook, 1987.

———. *Empowering Education: Critical Teaching for Social Change*. Chicago: University of Illinois Press, 1992.

———. *When Students Have Power: Negotiating Authority in a Critical Pedagogy*. Chicago: University of Chicago Press, 1996.

SLEVIN, JAMES F.

(a) Cultural Studies, Literacy, Pedagogy, Rhetoric and/or Composition Theory

(b) Slevin has written on the political, social, and economic forces that shape graduate education in English studies; on literacy and approaches to literacy education; and on the realities of professional careers in composition studies. In *The Future of Doctoral Studies in English*, which he co-edited in 1989, his "Conceptual Frameworks and Curricular Arrangements" responds to the first five essays in the collection and argues for involving graduate students in an examination of their own curriculum, thus allowing them to see the relationships (or their lack) between the courses they are required to take and the theories they are learning. Such an examination would, he suggests, prepare students to transform the profession. Slevin has also co-edited *The Right to Literacy* (1990), a collection whose essays raise issues about how literacy is understood and how and why it is denied to some citizens. In essays including "Depoliticizing and Politicizing Composition Studies" (1991) and "The Politics of the Profession" (1991), Slevin says that inequality between reading and writing and between those who teach literature and those who teach writing is a central feature of the profession today. Arguing that there are neither economic nor ideological justifications for this inequality, Slevin urges professors in composition studies to restructure their institutions by making changes in pedagogy, curriculum, and graduate programs and to enlist the help of professional organizations such as MLA, **CCCC**, and **NCTE** to do so. In "Reading and Writing in the Classroom and the Profession" (1994), he analyzes a piece from a 1943 issue of the *New Yorker* to illustrate the difference between formalist reading and writing and critical literacy, a contextualized reading and writing that considers the social, political, and cultural circumstances of a work's production. With Art Young, he co-edited *Critical Theory and the Teaching of Literature: Politics, Curriculum, and Pedagogy* (1996), essays that discuss the ways pedagogy, politics, and culture interact in contemporary classrooms to generate theory.

(c) Slevin, James F., Andrea Lunsford, and Helene Moglen. *The Future of Doctoral Studies in English*. New York: MLA, 1989.

———. *The Right to Literacy*. New York: MLA and NCTE, 1990.

Slevin, James F. "Depoliticizing and Politicizing Composition Studies." *The Politics of*

Writing Instruction: Postsecondary. Ed. Richard Bullock and John Trimbur. General ed. Charles Schuster. Portsmouth, NH: Boynton/Cook, 1991. 1–21.

———. "The Politics of the Profession." *An Introduction to Composition Studies*. Ed. Erika Lindemann and Gary Tate. New York: Oxford University Press, 1991. 135–59.

———. "Reading and Writing in the Classroom and the Profession." *Writing Theory and Critical Theory*. Ed. John Clifford and John Schilb. New York: MLA, 1994. 53–72.

Slevin, James, and Art Young, eds. *Critical Theory and the Teaching of Literature: Politics, Curriculum, and Pedagogy*. Urbana: NCTE, 1995. Pbk., 1996.

SOMMERS, NANCY

(a) Composing Processes, Revision, Research Methodology, Response and Evaluation

(b) In her early research, Sommers notes the disparity between how writing textbooks teach composing and how experienced writers really compose, and she calls for careful research into **cognitive processes** in writing. From her research on revision strategies, she was one of the first to conclude that revision is **recursive**. She argues that student writers revise at the word or sentence level, while adult writers revise at the global level (reformulating their argument to present it most effectively for a particular **audience**). When student writers do focus on the form of the whole piece, she says, it is often not to consider how the essay serves their purpose in addressing a specific audience, but instead to make certain that their essays follow the prescribed textbook form: a thesis with examples developing it, for example. To encourage meaningful revision, teachers should emphasize audience and purpose and comment on global concerns before dealing with sentence-level problems; they should respond to student writing during the writing **process** rather than after the work is completed, letting concerns with the audience and purpose of a piece of writing rather than generalized rules and models shape the work. Sommers won the Braddock Award in 1983 for "Responding to Student Writing" and again in 1992 for "Between the Drafts," a personal essay in which she argues that students should be encouraged to use the **authority** of their own voices to "revise" their academic sources. In "I Stand Here Writing" (1993), Sommers again emphasizes that students should bring judgments based on their own experience to their writing of academic essays. With Donald McQuade, she has edited *Student Writers at Work: The Bedford Prizes* (1984; 3rd ed., 1989). With Linda Simon, she has written *The HarperCollins Guide to Writing* (1993). She is among the ten authors most cited in *CCC* articles from 1980–93 and is one of the most frequently published authors of major articles in *CCC* for the same period.

(c) Sommers, Nancy. *Revision in the Composing Process: A Case Study of College Freshmen and Experienced Adult Writers*. Ph.D. diss. Boston University, 1978. Ann Arbor: UMI, 1979. 7905022.

———. "Revision Strategies of Student Writers and Experienced Adult Writers." *CCC* 31 (1980): 378–88. Rpt. in *Cross-Talk in Comp Theory: A Reader*. Ed. Victor Villanueva, Jr. Urbana: NCTE, 1997. 43–54.

———. "Responding to Student Writing." *CCC* 32 (1982): 148–56.

Sommers, Nancy, and Donald McQuade, eds. *Student Writers at Work: The Bedford Prizes*. 1984. 3rd ed. With Michael Tratner. New York: Bedford Books, 1989.

Sommers, Nancy. "Between the Drafts." *CCC* 43 (1992); 23–31. Rpt. in *Feminine Principles and Women's Experience in American Composition and Rhetoric*. Ed. Louise Weatherbee Phelps and Janet Emig. Pittsburgh: University of Pittsburgh Press, 1995. 341–50.

———. "I Stand Here Writing." *CE* 55 (1993): 420–28.

Sommers, Nancy, and Linda Simon. *The HarperCollins Guide to Writing*. New York: HarperCollins, 1993.

STEWART, DONALD C.

(a) Bibliography, Essay and Personal Writing, History of Rhetoric and/or Composition

(b) Donald Stewart's *The Authentic Voice: A Pre-Writing Approach to Student Writing* (1972) is one of the best-known textbooks based on the **expressivist** and **process** theories of D. Gordon Rohman and Albert O. Wlecke. In "Composition Textbooks and the Assault on Tradition" (1978), written partly at least to provide composition teachers an overview of texts, Stewart maintains that writing textbooks have changed little since the nineteenth century; he says that contemporary textbooks do not, for the most part, reflect coherent rhetorical theory or current research. In a 1994 essay "revisiting" composition textbooks, he suggests that textbooks are becoming more innovative, but very slowly. Stewart has also contributed to scholarship in nineteenth-century rhetoric, particularly by his work on Fred Newton Scott (a leading educator in the early 1900s). His work on Scott includes an essay in *Traditions of Inquiry* (1985) and a co-edited book on Scott's life and legacy. Stewart has also written bibliographies of nineteenth-century rhetoric; the best known is probably "The Nineteenth Century" in *The Present State of Scholarship in Historical and Contemporary Rhetoric* (1983). Stewart's work on classical rhetoric includes "The Continuing Relevance of Plato's *Phaedrus*" (1984), in which he reviews the scholarship on this dialogue and argues for the relevance to teachers of writing of Plato's insistence on organic rather than mechanical unity in discourse and on truth arrived at by dialectic. His 1986 rhetoric, *The Versatile Writer*, includes sections on **tagmemics**, Burke's **dramatistic pentad**, and **heuristics** from classical rhetoric. In **"Collaborative Learning** and Composition: Boon or Bane" (1988), Stewart offers his assessment of the strengths and weaknesses of **social constructionism** and collaborative learning. He criticizes the movement's version of the history of authoritarianism in the classroom, definition of the term "collaboration," pedagogical limitations, moral relativism, political implications, and unsound psychology. Stewart is one of the fifty authors most cited in *CCC* articles from 1980–93; he is one of the most frequently published authors of major articles for the same period. He was chair of **CCCC** in 1983.

(c) Stewart, Donald C. *The Authentic Voice: A Pre-writing Approach to Student Writing.* Dubuque, IA: W. C. Brown Co., 1972.

———. "Composition Textbooks and the Assault on Tradition." *CCC* 29 (1978): 171–76. Rpt. in *The Writing Teacher's Sourcebook.* Ed. Gary Tate and Edward P. J. Corbett. New York: Oxford University Press, 1981.

———. "The Nineteenth Century." *The Present State of Scholarship in Historical and Contemporary Rhetoric.* Ed. Winifred Bryan Horner. 1983. Rev ed. Columbia: University of Missouri Press, 1990. 151–85.

———. "The Continuing Relevance of Plato's *Phaedrus.*" *Essays on Classical Rhetoric and Modern Discourse.* Ed. Robert J. Connors, Lisa S. Ede, and Andrea A. Lunsford. Carbondale: Southern Illinois University Press, 1984. 115–26.

———. "Fred Newton Scott." *Traditions of Inquiry.* Ed. John Brereton. New York: Oxford University Press, 1985. 26–49.

———. *The Versatile Writer.* Lexington, MA: D. C. Heath, 1986.

———. "Collaborative Learning and Composition: Boon or Bane?" *RR* 7 (1988): 58–85. Rpt. in *Composition in Four Keys: Inquiring into the Field.* Ed. Mark Wiley, Barbara Gleason, and Louise Weatherbee Phelps. Mountain View, CA: Mayfield, 1996. 98–113.

TATE, GARY

(a) Bibliography, Pedagogy, Rhetoric and/or Composition Theory

(b) Tate is the editor or co-editor of several essay collections. In 1967 and 1970, he and Edward P. J. Corbett edited two of the earliest collections of essays focusing on the theoretical and practical approaches to teaching high school and college composition. *Teaching Composition: 10 Bibliographical Essays*, which Tate edited in 1976, also breaks new ground. Focusing primarily on work done before 1973, the year that Richard Larson takes as a starting point for his bibliographical essays in 1975–79 issues of *CCC*, the essays in this volume demonstrate that much respectable scholarship in teaching composition had been done in the ten or twelve years before the book's publication. Written by leading scholars in the field, the essays critically examine the scholarship of the emerging discipline and indicate areas for future research. Some of the essays in the second edition of *Teaching Composition* (1987) start where those in the earlier volume ended; two of them, Mina Shaughnessy's review of the literature on basic writing (updated by Andrea Lunsford) and Corbett's essay on style, are reprinted and updated. Changes in the discipline are indicated by new material: two of the original authors write on new topics, the relationship between literary theory and composition and **writing across the curriculum**; and two bibliographical essays, one on evaluation and one on computers and composition studies, are added. In 1981, Tate and Corbett edited *The Writing Teacher's*

Sourcebook, another collection of essays on theory and pedagogy written since their earlier anthology. *An Introduction to Composition Studies*, which Tate edited with Erika Lindemann in 1991, contains essays that introduce newcomers to the distinguishing features, history, theories, practitioners, research methods, and resources of composition studies. In 1993 and 1995 essays, Tate examines the reasons for the elimination of literature from composition classes and argues for its reintroduction. In his 1997 essay, "Thinking About Our Class," he argues that composition teachers must come to understand their own class histories, the stories they tell themselves about their pasts, to introduce necessary discussions of social class into their classrooms.

(c) Tate, Gary, and Edward P. J. Corbett, eds. *Teaching Freshman Composition*. New York: Oxford University Press, 1967.
———. eds. *Teaching High School Composition*. New York: Oxford University Press, 1970.
Tate, Gary, ed. *Teaching Composition: 10 Bibliographical Essays*. Fort Worth: Texas Christian University Press, 1976. Rev. ed. *Teaching Composition: 12 Bibliographical Essays*, Fort Worth: Texas Christian University Press, 1987.
Tate, Gary, and Edward P. J. Corbett, eds. *The Writing Teacher's Sourcebook*. New York: Oxford University Press, 1981. 3rd ed. Ed. Tate, Corbett, and Nancy Myers. New York: Oxford University Press, 1994.
Tate, Gary, and Erika Lindemann, eds. *An Introduction to Composition Studies*. New York: Oxford University Press, 1991.
Tate, Gary. "Thinking About Our Class." *JBW* 16 (spring 1997): 13–17.
———, Alan Shepherd, and John McMillan, eds. *Coming to Class: Pedagogy and the Social Class of Teachers*. Portsmouth, NH: Boynton/Cook Heinemann, 1998.

TCHUDI (JUDY), STEPHEN

(a) History of Rhetoric and/or Composition, Pedagogy, Writing Across the Curriculum

(b) Tchudi has done work on nineteenth-century rhetoric in American secondary schools and, drawing on the work of psychologists and linguists, has argued for an experience-based writing program at all academic levels. His own writing instruction begins with the premise that good student writing comes from students' own feelings and experiences; teaching students to write, therefore, requires helping them to synthesize their own experiences, to communicate in different modes (including expository and academic as well as **expressive** modes), and to structure, shape, and edit each piece of writing with due regard for its content and **audience**. Tchudi's articles and textbooks demonstrate practical ways to incorporate these premises into course design, writing assignments, and writing assessment, and they have influenced, particularly, writing instruction in secondary schools. In *Planning and Assessing the Curriculum in the English Language Arts* (1989), Tchudi argues that English language arts curricula should vary in different schools according to the students they serve. As he examines the history of various curricula, describes successful programs, and reviews reports by curriculum leaders, he suggests ways to design, implement, and assess curricula. Tchudi has argued for an interdisciplinary approach to education, maintaining that English, with its focus on whole-language instruction and **writing across the curriculum**, is well-suited to take the lead in a revolutionary reformulation of curricula. In *The Interdisciplinary Teacher's Handbook* (1996), he offers advice on using language to foster interdisciplinary learning and to integrate curricula. In *The New Literacy: Moving Beyond the 3Rs* (1996), Tchudi and Paul Morris define literacy as how people communicate with words in real-life situations and suggest that most people do not develop this literacy through formal education as it is presently structured. Tchudi was president of **NCTE** in 1983 and editor of *English Journal* from 1973–80.

(c) Tchudi (Judy), Stephen. *Explorations in the Teaching of English.* 1975. 3rd rev. ed. With Diana Mitchell. New York: Harper & Row, 1989.

———. "The Experiential Approach: Inner Worlds to Outer Worlds." *Eight Approaches to Teaching Composition.* Ed. Timothy R. Donovan and Ben W. McClelland. Urbana: NCTE, 1980. 37–51.

———. *Planning and Assessing the English Language Arts Curriculum.* 1989. Pbk. Alexandria, VA: ASCD, 1991.

Tchudi (Judy), Stephen, and Stephen Lafor. *The Interdisciplinary Teacher's Handbook.* Portsmouth, NH: Heinemann, 1996.

Tchudi (Judy), Stephen, and Paul Morris. *The New Literacy: Moving Beyond the 3Rs.* San Francisco: Jossey Bass, 1996. Rpt. Portland, ME: Calendar Islands, 1998.

TOULMIN, STEPHEN

(a) Argument, Arrangement, Rhetoric and/or Composition Theory

(b) Toulmin, an English logician, believes that formal syllogistic logic is inadequate to assess rational arguments in the practical world. Instead, he proposes an "informal logic" that he says describes the "rational process" human beings employ when they make decisions. The success of Toulmin's *Uses of Argument* (1958) has largely been driven by its reception by rhetoricians, who have called his view of rationality **epistemic**. Originally drawing on law and jurisprudence to develop his model of argument, Toulmin analyzes arguments from many disciplines to distinguish those parts of an argument that are invariant and those that are field specific. The first three parts of the **Toulmin model** are essential, he argues, to any rhetorical argument. They are the *claim*, the point at issue in an argument; the *data*, the evidence used to support the claim; and the *warrant*, the authorization, sometimes simply assumed, for the movement from data to claim. The second three parts support or qualify the claim or the warrant. They are the *qualifier*, which acknowledges that the claim is probably, not certainly, true; the *reservation*, which indicates conditions under which the warrant may not apply; and the *backing*, which supports the warrant. Since Toulmin's six-part model of argument was introduced in the United States by

Wayne Brockriede and Douglas Ehninger in 1960, many argumentation text-books have used it to analyze and criticize rhetorical arguments. It was not until *An Introduction to Reasoning* (1979), however, that Toulmin himself considered the implications to rhetoric of his model of argument. In *Human Understanding, Volume I: The Collective Use and Evolution of Concepts* (1972), Toulmin takes issue with Thomas Kuhn's idea that concepts change by revolution, arguing instead for an evolutionary model of concept change. As in his evaluation of argument, Toulmin rejects the absolutism that results from the use of formal logic to evaluate concepts. Attempting to avoid a relativist approach as well, Toulmin suggests that a new concept be evaluated by comparing it with others to determine which concept has more explanatory power. People show their rationality, he says, by their willingness to modify or revise their concepts in the light of this rhetorical process of criticism and evaluation.

(c) Toulmin, Stephen. *The Uses of Argument*. 1958. Rpt. Cambridge, England: Cambridge University Press, 1974.

————. *Human Understanding, Volume I: The Collective Use and Evolution of Concepts*. 1972. 2nd ed. Princeton, NJ: Princeton University Press, 1977.

Toulmin, Stephen, Richard Rieke, and Allan Janik. *An Introduction to Reasoning*. 1979. New York: Macmillan, 1984.

Toulmin, Stephen. "The Layout of Arguments." *Professing the New Rhetorics: A Sourcebook*. Ed. Theresa Enos and Stuart C. Brown. Englewood Cliffs, NJ: Prentice Hall, 1994. 105–25.

TRIMBUR, JOHN

(a) Collaboration, Cultural Studies, Rhetoric and/or Composition Theory

(b) Much of Trimbur's work has been on the social relations of writing and writing instruction. In "**Collaborative Learning** and Teaching Writing" (1985), he traces the origins of collaborative learning to the distrust of power and **authority** of the 1960s. Because he sees tutoring in centers as further removed from institutional authority than peer tutoring in classrooms, Trimbur favors peer tutoring in learning centers. He says locating peer tutoring in centers allows more voices to speak and even, perhaps, to challenge institutional authority. In "**Consensus** and Difference in Collaborative Learning" (1989), he responds to criticisms of collaborative learning, especially the charge that attempts to reach consensus sometimes silence individual voices and can even reproduce patterns of oppression. Suggesting that genuine consensus is not achievable, Trimbur argues that "dissensus" is the normal state of affairs, both in collaborative classrooms and in society. Working toward consensus, however, can produce what Trimbur calls a "rhetoric of dissensus" that allows students in collaborative classrooms to hear and understand the differences between individuals and that fosters the commitment to give all voices an opportunity to be heard. *The Politics of Writing Instruction: Postsecondary*, which he co-edited in 1990, contains essays that examine the social relations of writing as a microcosm of social relations in general. It won the 1993 CCCC Outstanding Book Award. Trimbur was one of the first to point out similarities between cultural and composition studies; in "Composition Studies: Postmodern or Popular" (1993), he argues that though the view of composition studies as a postmodern discipline is appealing, the postmodern death of the subject does not allow for "agency" and "utopian aspirations." Trimbur suggests that cultural studies, with its conception of the "popular," the everyday ways people **resist** "hegemony" and so fashion "selves," provides a possible counter to this reduction of the self. In "Writing Instruction and the Politics of Professionalism" (1996), Trimbur cautions that the professionalization of composition studies, if embraced uncritically, can lead to specialization, monopolies of expertise, and stratification that exclude rather than include. Trimbur's work in **writing across the curriculum** has led to several essays and to a 1996 book on writing about chemistry in collaboration with chemistry professor Herbert Beall.

(c) Trimbur, John. "Collaborative Learning and Teaching Writing." *Perspectives on Research and Scholarship in Composition.* Ed. Ben W. McClelland and Timothy R. Donovan. New York: MLA, 1985. 87–109.

———. "Consensus and Difference in Collaborative Learning." *CE* 51 (1989): 602–16. Rpt. in *Cross-Talk in Comp Theory: A Reader.* Ed. Victor Villanueva, Jr. Urbana: NCTE, 1997. 439–56.

Trimbur, John, and John Bullock, eds. *The Politics of Writing Instruction: Postsecondary.* Portsmouth, NH: Heinemann, Boynton/Cook, 1990.

Trimbur, John. "Composition Studies: Postmodern or Popular." *Into the Field: Sites of Composition Studies.* Ed. Anne Ruggles Gere. New York: MLA, 1993. 117–32.

Trimbur, John, and Herbert Beall. *A Short Guide to Writing About Chemistry.* New York: HarperCollins, 1996.

Trimbur, John. "Writing Instruction and the Politics of Professionalization." *Composition in the Twenty-First Century: Crisis and Change.* Ed. Lynn Z. Bloom, Donald A. Daiker, and Edward M. White. Carbondale: Southern Illinois University Press, 1996. 133–45.

VITANZA, VICTOR J.

(a) History of Rhetoric and/or Composition, Rhetoric and/or Composition Theory

(b) Vitanza writes, as he says, not history but *about* history—his area is historiography of rhetoric. Writing from a postmodern perspective, Vitanza draws on Kenneth Burke, Helene Cixous, Gilles Deleuze, Felix Guatari, Jean-François Lyotard, and Friedrich Nietzsche, among others, to critique **foundational** and antifoundational rhetorics and the historians of rhetoric who write from these theoretical positions. In the former he includes **current-traditional, expressionist**, and **cognitive**; and in the latter **social epistemic** and Marxist. Although he is more in sympathy with the social epistemic and Marxist historians of rhetoric, even this group, Vitanza says, is finally foundational and "deterritorializes" only to "reterritorialize." All historians from these groups write "grand narratives" that aim to be *the* history of rhetoric, and the very structure necessary to create such narratives, he says, is made possible only by excluding, saying "no," to some "voices." As he attempts in his own writing about the history of rhetoric and as he advocates for all those writing histories of rhetoric, Vitanza wants to "denegate" (say "yes" to) all these voices—to be all-inclusive. This desire is manifest in a style that has been called "performative." Drawing on Jean-Francois Lyotard's discussion of **paralogy**, Vitanza aims to write like a stranger to his own language; he resists hypotactic organizational structures (subordination) and opts instead for parataxis (coordination). Calling himself a "nomad" who wanders and drifts in his writing, he experiments with orthography and capitalization; his writing is full of parenthetical comments and parentheses. Vitanza's two 1987 articles, "Critical Sub / Versions of the History of Philosophical Rhetoric" and " 'Notes' Towards Historiographies of Rhetorics; or, Rhetorics of the Histories of Rhetorics: Traditional, Revisionary, and Sub / Versive" have been called groundbreaking. In the first essay, Vitanza calls for a postmodern paralogic rhetoric, an "Antibody Rhetoric," a therapy, but not a cure, for the infection of philosophical rhetoric with its "logophilia"; he suggests that the roots of this therapeutic rhetoric can be found in sophistic rhetorics. In the second essay, Vitanza says that all historians of rhetoric write, consciously or unconsciously, from ideological positions. By examining the rhetorics of their histories of rhetorics, he places representative historians of rhetoric in (sometimes overlapping) categories of historiography, traditional, revisionary, and sub/versive, which he favors. In "Three Counter-Theses: or, A Critical In(ter)vention into Composition and Pedagogies" (1991) and elsewhere, Vitanza questions the relationship of theory to practice in composition teaching and calls for a subversive questioning of the notion of disciplinarity and of the way writing and reading are taught. *Writing Histories of Rhetoric*, which he edited in 1994, contains twelve essays on the historiography of rhetoric, including two by Vitanza. He is the founding editor of *PRE/TEXT: A Journal of Rhetorical Theory*; in *PRE/TEXT: The First Decade* (1993), he edits a collection of ten key articles from the journal's first ten years of publication. *Negation, Subjectivity, and the History of Rhetoric* (1997) presents his current thought about historiography and discourse; it reprints several of his previously published essays, including "Feminist Sophistic?" (1995).

(c) Vitanza, Victor J. "Critical Sub / Versions of the History of Philosophical Rhetoric." *RR* 6 (1987): 41–66.

———. " 'Notes' Towards Historiographies of Rhetorics; or, the Rhetorics of the Histories of Rhetorics: Traditional, Revisionary, and Sub / Versive." *PRE/TEXT* 8.1–2 (spring/summer 1987): 63–125.

———. "Three Countertheses: Or, a Critical In(ter)vention into Composition Theories and Pedagogies." *Contending with Words*. Ed. Patricia Harkin and John Schilb. New York: MLA, 1991. 139–72.

————, ed. *PRE/TEXT: The First Decade*. Pittsburgh: University of Pittsburgh Press, 1993.

————, ed. *Writing Histories of Rhetoric*. Carbondale: Southern Illinois University Press, 1994.

————. *Negation, Subjectivity, and the History of Rhetoric*. Albany: SUNY Press, 1997.

WEAVER, RICHARD

(a) Argument, Rhetoric and/or Composition Theory

(b) Weaver's political conservatism and his belief in Platonic idealism have shaped his rhetorical theory. His work, which also shows the influence of Kenneth Burke, has become increasingly cited for its insistence on the ethical dimensions of rhetoric. Weaver consistently argues that the persuasive speech of rhetors should lead their **audiences** to truth and justice and should create in their audiences a reasoned passion for the good. Believing in a world of transcendental reality, Weaver measures the truth of a thing or an action by how closely it conforms to "a conceptual ideal." By reference to a hierarchical order of "goods" topped by an "ultimate good," rhetors, he says, have a responsibility to determine the ethical course of action or position in a particular situation and to advise their audience in language that moves them toward the ultimate good. Thus, in Weaver's words, "language becomes sermonic." Weaver takes modern society to task for—among other things—scientism, semantic **positivism**, and cultural relativism. In particular, he indicts most social scientists for making value judgments while pretending to avoid them. Weaver's view of a hierarchical order of increasing abstraction topped by a **god-term** and his discussion of rhetoric as the process of making **identifications** are two of many echoes of Kenneth Burke's rhetorical theory. His work on rhetoric—which, like Burke's, has dialectic as its base—focuses mainly on **invention** and argumentation. He ranks *topoi* according to their ethical worth, from the best, genus or definition (which argues from the nature of a thing) to circumstances (which argues from the level of perception of fact), and he maintains that the ethical value of a rhetor can be determined by the method of argumentation he habitually chooses. In *The Ethics of Rhetoric* (1953), a collection of eight of his essays, he illustrates these argumentative forms by examining two speeches. Weaver's best-known work is probably his 1963 essay, "Language Is Sermonic." His last book, *Visions of Order: The Cultural Crisis of Our Time* (1964), is an indictment of the scientism, relativism, and other "isms" he sees as diseases of his society and a discussion of the rhetor's role in restoring society's health.

(c) Weaver, Richard. *Ideas Have Consequences*. 1948. Pbk. Chicago: University of Chicago Press, 1984.

————. "To Write the Truth." *CE* 10 (1948): 25–30.

————. *The Ethics of Rhetoric*. Chicago: Henry Regnery, 1953.

————. *Composition*. New York: Holt, Rinehart, and Winston, 1957.

————. "Language Is Sermonic." *Dimensions of Rhetorical Scholarship*. Ed. Robert E.

Nebergall. Norman: University of Oklahoma Department of Speech, 1963. 49–63. Rpt. in *Language Is Sermonic: Richard M. Weaver on the Nature of Rhetoric.* Ed. Richard L. Johannesen, Rennard Strickland, and Ralph Eubanks. Baton Rouge: Louisiana State University Press, 1970. 201–25.

———. *Visions of Order: The Cultural Crisis of Our Time.* Baton Rouge: Louisiana State University Press, 1964. Rpt. Bryn Mawr, PA: Intercollegiate Studies Institute, 1995.

WENDELL, BARRETT

(a) Arrangement, Grammar and Usage, Rhetoric and/or Composition Theory, Style

(b) Wendell, who was an instructor of composition and literature at Harvard from 1880 to 1917, has been cited as one of the "**big four**" influential teachers who shaped rhetoric and composition in the late nineteenth century. Based on his textbooks, he has been charged with helping to establish the **current-traditional** paradigm for writing instruction in America by emphasizing mechanical correctness and other formal features of the finished product. In his influential textbook *English Composition: Eight Lectures Given at the Lowell Institute* (1891), he stressed unity, mass (emphasis), and coherence (his term) in the expository and argumentative essay, as well as correct usage, clearness, force, and elegance of style. This popular text encouraged writing instruction that began with the word, moved to the sentence, to the paragraph, and finally to the essay. In recent years, David Joliffe and Thomas Newkirk's study of Harvard archives has led to a reevaluation of Wendell's teaching. Their research indicates that Wendell allowed students to choose their own topics, used a **workshop** format in his writing classes, and held individual conferences with students. They suggest that Wendell's teaching was much more **process**-oriented than had been thought.

(c) Wendell, Barrett. *English Composition: Eight Lectures Given at the Lowell Institute.* New York: Scribner's, 1891. New York: Ungar, 1983.

WHATELY, RICHARD

(a) Argument, Rhetoric and/or Composition Theory

(b) Although Whately wrote *Elements of Rhetoric* while he was principal of St. Alban's Hall, Oxford, in 1828, his name is often linked with those of two late eighteenth-century rhetoricians, Hugh Blair (1718–1800) and George Campbell (1719–1796), as the founders of modern rhetoric. In *Elements of Logic* (1826), Whately defends deductive logic (the syllogism), which Campbell had followed Bacon in rejecting in favor of induction. Following Aristotle, Whately says that rhetoric springs from logic, and in *Elements of Rhetoric* (1828), he focuses on ways of creating effective arguments. Like Campbell, Whately sees the discovery of reality (truth) as based on experience, and persuasion as requiring not only an appeal to reason but also to emotion. Also like Campbell, he sees topical **invention**—used to discover truth—as no longer a part of rhetoric. Rhetorical invention then becomes psychological, the investigation of the best means of appealing to the faculties of the **audience**, including both the understanding and the passions. *Elements of Rhetoric* becomes a practical textbook, discussing first the form and use of logical arguments to produce conviction, then the nature and use of emotional appeals to persuade, and finally style and correctness. This text's presentation of composing, with its emphasis on the correctness of the product, influenced **current-traditional rhetoric**.

(c) Whately, Richard. *Elements of Logic*. London: 1826. Facsimile Reproduction. Intro. by Ray E. McKerrow. Delmar, NY: Scholars' Facsimiles and Reprints, 1975.
———. *Elements of Rhetoric*. London: 1828. Rpt. in *Landmarks in Rhetoric and Public Address*. Ed. Douglas Ehninger. Carbondale: Southern Illinois University Press, 1963. Facsimile Reproduction. Intro. by Charlotte Downey and Howard Coughlin. Delmar, NY: Scholars' Facsimiles and Reprints, 1991.

WHITE, EDWARD M.

(a) Assessment, Response and Evaluation, Writing Program Administration

(b) White's work has focused on assessment: methods teachers can use to evaluate student writing, the connection between evaluating and teaching writing, and methods administrators can use to evaluate writing programs. In *Teaching and Assessing Writing* (1985), White reviews research in writing assessment and discusses the history of indirect (multiple-choice) and direct (writing sample) forms of writing assessment. He traces the development of **holistic** scoring, examining its similarities to **primary trait** scoring and its differences from **analytic** scoring, and gives advice on all aspects of evaluation and assessment. As he did in "Post-Structural Literary Criticism and the Response to Student Writing" (1984), he also discusses the ways that teaching writing and writing assessment can contribute to the other's effectiveness. Theories that emphasize the role of readers in producing meaning from texts, he suggests, complement composition teachers' growing awareness that no reading of a text—including their own—is "objective" and that students must, throughout the composing **process**, consider the ways that different groups of readers may respond to their drafts. In *Developing Successful College Writing Programs* (1989) and *Assigning, Responding, Evaluating: A Writing Teacher's Guide* (1992), White draws on his experience as a writing program administrator to discuss setting up writing programs, including program evaluation. The 1994 edition of *Teaching and Assessing Writing* continues to argue for holistic assessment of writing, but it also includes a chapter on **portfolio** assessment; it offers faculty in other disciplines advice on teaching writing. In "An Apologia for the Timed Impromptu Essay

Test" (1995), White, while agreeing that portfolio assessment is most appropriate at the college graduation level, argues for the value of holistic evaluation of impromptu essays over multiple-choice assessment for placement in freshman writing courses. In "Writing Assessment Beyond the Classroom"—from *Composition in the Twenty-First Century: Crisis and Change*, which White co-edited—he again argues for matching the assessment device to the context in which it will be used. Here and elsewhere, he urges writing faculty to unite to influence writing assessment beyond the classroom; if they fail to do so, he warns that this assessment will be done for them by those who know little about what writing faculty understand and value.

(c) White, Edward M. "Post-Structural Literary Criticism and the Response to Student Writing." *CCC* 35 (1984): 186–95. Rpt. in *The Writing Teacher's Sourcebook*. Ed. Gary Tate and Edward P. J. Corbett. 2nd ed. New York: Oxford University Press, 1988. 285–93.

———. *Teaching and Assessing Writing*. 1985. 2nd ed. *Teaching and Assessing Writing: Recent Advances in Understanding, Evaluating, and Improving Student Performance*. San Francisco: Jossey-Bass, 1994. 2nd rev. and expanded ed. Portland, ME: Calendar Islands, 1998.

———. *Developing Successful College Writing Programs*. San Francisco: Jossey-Bass, 1989. Rpt. New Intro. Portland, ME: Calendar Islands, 1998.

———. *Assigning, Responding, Evaluating: A Writing Teacher's Guide*. 1992. 3rd ed. New York: St. Martin's Press, 1995.

———. "An Apologia for the Timed Impromptu Essay Test." *CCC* 46 (1995): 30–45.

White, Edward M., Lynn Z. Bloom, and Donald Daiker, eds. *Composition in the Twenty-First Century: Crisis and Change*. Carbondale: Southern Illinois University Press, 1996.

WILLIAMS, JOSEPH M.

(a) Grammar and Usage, Linguistics, Style

(b) Williams has written extensively on grammar and style. From his early *The New English: Structure / Form / Style* (1970), which drew on the work of structuralists like Noam Chomsky, Williams has emphasized the social dimension of writing, arguing that grammar and usage, like etiquette, depend on social context. He was among the first to question the use of the **T-unit** to determine syntactic maturity, demonstrating in a number of articles that complex sentences do not necessarily mean better writing. In "The Phenomenology of Error" (1981), perhaps his best-known essay, Williams suggests that writing instructors should rethink their definition of error in students' papers. Without warning his readers to expect them, he includes 100 grammar errors in this essay, challenging readers to list the errors they noticed on first reading it. Williams argues that because he is a professional writer whose relationship to his readers is quite different from the teacher-student relationship, many of the errors in his article have gone undetected. Writing teachers, he maintains, should emphasize that grammar, like other aspects of writing, depends on the social relationship between writer and reader, and they should emphasize those grammar rules whose violation distracts most readers. In his popular textbook, *Style: Ten Lessons in Clarity and Grace* (1981), Williams focuses on helping writers avoid nominalization, wordiness, confusion, and complexity in sentence structure. In "Style and Its Consequences: Do as I Do, Not as I Say" (1981), Williams and Rosemary Hake report on research indicating that though writing teachers at all levels tell students to write in a direct style, they often reward a nominalized style. Williams' *The Craft of Research* (1995), written with Wayne C. Booth and Gregory Colomb, addresses the concerns of beginning and experienced researchers, focusing on the recursive nature of research and its reporting, on understanding and meeting the expectations of readers, and on the way attention to the formal elements of a report can direct writers through the process of writing it and lead to greater creativity. *The Craft of Research* won the National Critics Award.

(c) Williams, Joseph M. *The New English: Structure, Form, Style.* New York: Free Press, 1970.

Williams, Joseph M., and Rosemary Hake. "Style and Its Consequences: Do as I Do, Not as I Say." *CE* 43 (1981): 433–51.

Williams, Joseph M. *Style: Ten Lessons in Clarity and Grace.* Glenview, IL: Scott, Foresman, 1981. 5th ed. *Style: Toward Clarity and Grace.* New York: Longman, 1995.

———. "The Phenomenology of Error." *CCC* 32 (1981): 152–68. Rpt. in *Composition in Four Keys: Inquiring into the Field.* Ed. Mark Wiley, Barbara Gleason, and Louise Weatherbee Phelps. Mountain View, CA: Mayfield, 1996. 163–75.

———. "Non-linguistics and the Teaching of Style." *The Territory of Language: Linguistics, Stylistics, and the Teaching of Composition.* Ed. Donald A. McQuade. Carbondale: Southern Illinois University Press, 1986. 174–91.

Williams, Joseph M., Wayne C. Booth, and Gregory Colomb. *The Craft of Research.* Chicago: University of Chicago Press, 1995.

WINTEROWD, W. ROSS

(a) Bibliography, History of Rhetoric and/or Composition, Linguistics, Literacy, Pedagogy, Rhetoric and/or Composition Theory

(b) W. Ross Winterowd's *Rhetoric: A Synthesis* (1968) was one of the first texts to bring together all that was happening in rhetoric in the 1960s and to suggest its classroom applications. Also of early influence were his definition of form as the "set of consistent relationships" within any piece of writing or oratory and his argument that seven transitional relationships are responsible for coherence. In *Contemporary Rhetoric: A Conceptual Background with Readings* (1975) and elsewhere, Winterowd maintains that writing, especially composing, is **epistemic**, a way of discovering meaning. *Contemporary Rhetoric* includes essays by researchers in composition, yet does not espouse any one research methodology. Here and elsewhere, as Winterowd looks for a "unifying theoretical base" for composition teaching, he introduces theories and theoreticians such as Kenneth Burke, whose discussion of "form" (from *Counter-Statement*) he includes in *Contemporary Rhetoric*. Winterowd's 1975 textbook, *The Contemporary Writer*, applies composition research and theory—from **sentence-combining** to **invention** techniques such as Burke's **dramatistic pentad** and Richard Young, Alton Becker, and Kenneth Pike's **tagmemic** matrix. His bibliographical essays in *Teaching Composition* (1976 and 1987) survey research on linguistics and composition. A 1979 essay offers practical applications for research in neurophysiology, suggesting that study of left brain–right brain functions is useful to composition teachers as metaphors for two equally valuable ways of perceiving the world. In four 1983 essays, he explores Burke's dramatism, examines Paulo Freire's pedagogical method, discusses possible consequences for composition teaching of Jacques Derrida's "radical indeterminacy," and explores the ways sentence-combining and "accessibility" (readability) can be used to improve writing and reading ability. His Huntington Beach Project develops a writing **workshop**-lab model for teaching writing that relies on Stephen Krashen's distinction between language acquisition and language learning. In *Composition/Rhetoric: A Synthesis* (1986), in which Winterowd collects and reworks his previous essays, the evolution of his own thought provides a synthesis of issues in the field as he argues for the importance of theory in teaching literacy. His "The Purification of Literature and Rhetoric" (1987) traces the process he sees culminating in literary studies that are all theory and a rhetoric devoid of theory and reduced to stylistics. In *The Culture and Politics of Literacy* (1989), he argues that literacy can be defined only in the context of a social group; whether one reads and writes well, he suggests, depends to a large extent on whether one's culture has taught one to value those activities. Winterowd is among the ten authors most cited in *CCC* articles from 1965–79 and one of the fifty authors most cited from 1980–93; he is also one of the most frequently published authors of major articles in *CCC* from 1965–79.

(c) Winterowd, W. Ross. *Rhetoric: A Synthesis*. New York: Holt, Rinehart, and Winston, 1968.

———. "The Grammar of Coherence." *CE* 31 (1970): 328–35. Rpt. in *The Writing Teacher's Sourcebook*. Ed. Gary Tate and Edward P. J. Corbett. New York: Oxford University Press, 1981. 301–09.

———, ed. *Contemporary Rhetoric: A Conceptual Background with Readings*. New York: Harcourt, 1975.

———. *The Contemporary Writer*. 1975. 3rd ed. With John S. Nixon. San Diego: Harcourt, Brace, Jovanovich, 1989.

———. "Linguistics and Composition." *Teaching Composition: 10 Bibliographic Essays*. Ed. Gary Tate. 1976. 197–221. "Literacy, Linguistics, and Rhetoric." Rev. ed. *Teaching Composition: 12 Bibliographic Essays*. Fort Worth: Texas Christian University Press, 1987. 265–90.

———. "The Purification of Literature and Rhetoric." *CE* 49 (1987): 257–73.

————. *Composition/Rhetoric: A Synthesis*. Carbondale: Southern Illinois University Press, 1989.

————. *The Culture and Politics of Literacy*. New York: Oxford University Press, 1989.

YOUNG, ART

(a) Literature and Composition, Writing Across the Curriculum

(b) With his colleague Toby Fulwiler, Young has edited several essay collections on **writing across the curriculum**. In particular, he has focused on the **poetic** use of language in WAC courses. Drawn from their work in the WAC program at Michigan Technological University (MTU), essays in *Language Connections: Writing and Reading Across the Curriculum* (1982) present both theoretical and practical issues. Young's own contribution to the collection, "Considering Values: The Poetic Function of Language," argues for including creative as well as **expressive** and **transactional writing** in writing-intensive courses in different disciplines. The essays in *Writing Across the Disciplines: Research into Practice* (1986) describe the way the WAC program at MTU affected the humanities department and other participating departments. Young has two essays in that collection. In the first essay, "Building Community in the English Department," he suggests that English departments can build an internal and a universitywide community by studying and teaching writing, reading, and literature as one subject. In the second, "Writing Across the Disciplines," Young supports his earlier argument for poetic writing by describing an introductory psychology class that incorporates such assignments. Other collections of essays Young has co-edited, such as *Programs That Work: Models and Methods for Writing Across the Curriculum* (1990), describe successful WAC programs and continue to stress the connection between reading, writing, and literature. The essays in *When Writing Teachers Teach Literature: Bringing Writing to Reading* (1995), also co-edited with Fulwiler, suggest ways for writing teachers to apply to literature classes what they have learned from WAC programs. Young has also edited, with James Slevin, a 1996 collection of essays that investigate the connection between critical theory and teaching literature.

(c) Young, Art, and Toby Fulwiler, eds. *Language Connections: Writing and Reading Across the Curriculum*. Urbana: NCTE, 1982.

————. *Writing Across the Disciplines: Research into Practice*. Upper Montclair, NJ: Boynton/Cook, 1986.

————. *Programs That Work: Models and Methods for Writing Across the Curriculum*. Portsmouth, NH: Boynton/Cook, Heinemann, 1990.

Young, Art. *Writing Across the Curriculum*. 1994. 2nd ed. Englewood Cliffs, NJ: Blair Resources for Teaching Writing, A Blair Free Press Book, Prentice Hall, 1997.

Young, Art, and Toby Fulwiler, eds. *When Writing Teachers Teach Literature: Bringing Writing to Reading*. Portsmouth, NH: Boynton/Cook, Heinemann, 1995.

Young, Art, and James F. Slevin. *Critical Theory and the Teaching of Literature: Politics, Curriculum, and Pedagogy*. Urbana: NCTE, 1996.

YOUNG, RICHARD E.

(a) Bibliography, Composing Processes, Invention, Linguistics, Rhetoric and/ or Composition Theory

(b) With Alton Becker and Kenneth Pike, Richard Young is best known for the particle/wave/field **heuristic**, which comes from the application of Pike's **tagmemic** linguistic theory to rhetoric. This heuristic comes from the principle that the observer discovers pattern in the world, and thus meaning, and that to understand the world, she must view it from three perspectives: as "discrete contrastive bits" (particles); as "unsegmentable physical continua" (waves); and as "orderly systems of relationships" (fields). In *Rhetoric, Discovery, and Change* (1970), these three provide the writer with a "tagmemic grid," which she can use to see the topic and the reader from different perspectives. Young, Becker, and Pike have been seen as allied with **cognitive theorists** in their use of the tagmemic grid and the implication that writing becomes a matter of problem solving through use of the grid. Young's bibliographical essay on **invention** in *Teaching Composition: 10 Bibliographical Essays* (1976) examines ways theorists have differed in their understanding of classical "topics," some seeing them as cognitive and others as socially conditioned. His bibliographical essay in the 1987 edition of *Teaching Composition: 12 Bibliographical Essays* surveys new research on invention. In **"Paradigms** and Problems: Needed Research in Rhetorical Invention" (1978), Young is the first to herald a **paradigm shift** in the discipline; he criticizes the **current-traditional** paradigm for focusing on product and thus ignoring invention, and he suggests areas for further research on invention. In several essays, he traces the move from the current-traditional paradigm to the **"new rhetoric,"** identifying two contrasting positions in the new paradigm. One group sees the art of writing as mysterious and unteachable, the other as comprehensible and teachable. In "Why Write? A Reconciliation" (1984), with Patricia Sullivan, Young argues that writing is a way of learning, an idea that seems implicit in his earlier tagmemic grid, since the grid helps the writer to understand the world in different ways through different perspectives. In several essays, Young argues that the analysis of a writer's plan in a piece of writing can reveal his thought processes while writing and that problem solving is a procedure that organizes and structures much professional writing. In "Writing in the Content Areas: Some Theoretical Complexities" (1993), he and David Kaufer propose an "interactionist" model that relies on both general writing strategies and rhetorical situations specific to a discipline. Young is among the ten authors most cited in *CCC* articles from 1965–79 and one of the fifty most-cited authors in *CCC* articles from 1980–93.

(c) Young, Richard, Alton Becker, and Kenneth Pike. *Rhetoric: Discovery and Change.* New York: Harcourt, Brace, & World, 1970.

Young, Richard. "Invention: A Topographical Survey." *Teaching Composition: 10 Bibliographical Essays.* Ed. Gary Tate, 1976. 1–43. "Recent Developments in Rhetorical Invention." Rev. ed. *Teaching Composition: 12 Bibliographical Essays.* Fort Worth: Texas Christian University Press, 1987. 1–38.

———. "Paradigms and Problems: Needed Research in Rhetorical Invention." *Research on Composing: Points of Departure.* Ed. Charles R. Cooper and Lee Odell. Urbana: NCTE, 1978. 29–47.

———. "Concepts of Art and the Teaching of Writing." *The Rhetorical Tradition and Modern Writing.* Ed. James J. Murphy. New York: MLA, 1982. 130–41. Rpt. in *Composition in Four Keys: Inquiring into the Field.* Ed. Mark Wiley, Barbara Gleason, and Louise Weatherbee Phelps. Mountain View, CA: Mayfield, 1996. 176–83.

Young, Richard, and Patricia Sullivan. "Why Write? A Reconciliation." *Essays on Classical Rhetoric and Modern Discourse.* Ed. Robert J. Connors, Lisa S. Ede, and Andrea Lunsford. Carbondale: Southern Illinois University Press, 1984. 215–25.

Young, Richard, and David Kaufer. "Writing in the Content Areas: Some Theoretical Complexities." *Theory and Practice in the Teaching of Writing.* Ed. Lee Odell. Carbondale: Southern Illinois University Press, 1993.

Part II

Important Terms in Composition Studies

FORMAT

(a) working definition

(b) term as defined by speakers in the field

(c) term used in context by speakers in the field

(d) person(s) usually associated with term

ABNORMAL DISCOURSE (see NORMAL DISCOURSE)

ACADEMIC DISCOURSE

(a) Language spoken and written by members of an academic community that indicates their familiarity with particular academic conventions and validates their place among scholars. This discourse consists of discipline-specific jargon, knowledge of and reference to names of persons important in the field, and particular ways of communicating. The term "academic discourse" is widely used in composition studies. In her 1978 article "The Ethos of Academic Discourse," **Patricia Bizzell** was one of the first to use the term in composition studies, although **Mina Shaughnessy**, in 1977, had discussed the problems non-traditional students have adapting to "academic writing." In 1982, Bizzell argued in "College Composition: An Initiation into the **Academic Discourse Community**" that first-year composition should be an introduction to academic discourse. **Mike Rose** has argued that the difficulties of some student writers, especially **basic writers**, should be linked not to intellectual deficiency but to their unfamiliarity with academic discourse; (see especially "Remedial Writing Courses: A Critique and a Proposal" [1983] and *Lives on the Boundary* [1989]). Also, **David Bartholomae**'s 1985 article "Inventing the University," was seminal in composition's discussion of academic discourse (as well as **discourse communities**). According to Bartholomae, mastering conventions of academic writing often leads to academic success; therefore, he recommends that students "mimic" the language of the university, imitating it before they fully understand it (see **inventing the university**).

Other scholars argue that students should resist the urge to conform and should speak instead in their own voice and in their own language. In a later article, "Marxist Ideas in Composition Studies" (1991), Bizzell problematizes her earlier argument, suggesting that when confronted with requirements of academic discourse, some students are in danger of either completely sacrificing their own language or of giving up on the academy altogether. Also in 1991, **Peter Elbow** contends that while academic discourse has its place in first-year composition, it should not be the only kind of discourse taught ("Reflections on Academic Discourse"). Some feminists, including Gesa Kirsch (1993) and Patricia Sullivan (1992), have argued that academic discourse represents "masculine" language and that when speaking and writing in such language, women must take on a persona with which they are not completely comfortable. **Joseph Harris** (1997), however, questions the assumption of a wholly "academic" discourse (or a wholly nonacademic one), arguing that teachers' discourses are certainly influenced by factors other than the academy—such as home, media, and personal interests (105). Similarly, Harris points out that a student's discourse is not wholly outside the academy, but is influenced by former educational experience. Though the term "academic discourse" was used in the early and mid-1980s, it was most prevalent in the late 1980s through the mid 1990s, as scholars argued for and against a first-year composition curriculum centered around academic discourse.

(b) "Academic discourse seems to be characterized by a large, diverse, and highly literate vocabulary and by a richness of cohesive ties established through its vocabulary" (Stotsky, "Types" 440).

"ideas and information of authorities on a given subject" (Ritchie, "Beginning" 160).

(c) "I don't think that we risk creating bullshit artists by making the ethos of academic discourse available to beginning adult writers" (Bizzell, "Ethos" 354).

"It may very well be that some students will need to learn to crudely mimic the 'distinctive register' of academic discourse before they are prepared to actually and legitimately do the work of the discourse, and before they are sophisticated enough with the refinements of tone and gesture to do it with grace or elegance" (Bartholomae, "Inventing" 162).

"The academic discourses that men and women students must 'master' in order to succeed in the academy are largely inscriptions of male subjectivities; women have inherited modes of discourse that they have had little voice in shaping" (P. Sullivan, "Feminism" 40).

"There has been much debate in recent years over whether we need, above all, to respect our students' 'right to their own language,' or to teach them the ways and forms of 'academic discourse.' Both sides of this argument, in the end, rest their cases on the same suspect generalization: That we and our students belong to different and fairly distinct communities of discourse, that we have 'our' 'academic' discourse and they have 'their own' 'common' (?!) ones" (J. Harris, *Teaching* 105).

(**d**) David Bartholomae, Patricia Bizzell.

ACADEMIC DISCOURSE COMMUNITY

(**a**) A group within the university that speaks a common language, has common interests, and shares common beliefs. Some scholars propose that there is one academic discourse community within the university, whereas others see many such communities there. For example, colleagues in the English department who use common terms, read the same journals, go to the same conferences, and hold similar beliefs are considered fellow members of a particular academic discourse community. Mathematics faculty can be considered members of the university discourse community or members of the mathematics community. Often a goal of a **writing across the curriculum** program is to initiate students into their specific academic discourse community.

Unfortunately, communities are not always as warm and welcoming as the term implies, for, as **Patricia Bizzell** notes in 1991, "the academic neighborhood does not welcome everyone equally" ("Marxist" 59). Some critics, such as Geoffrey Chase (1988), also dispute the idealistic connotations of "community" and argue that the classroom is often a place of struggle and alienation. **Joseph Harris** (1989) questions the connotations implicit with the term "community," arguing that the term is both "warm and fuzzy" and loaded with rhetorical power. The term "academic discourse community" appears most frequently in composition conversations beginning in the late 1980s and extending to the mid-1990s.

(**b**) "a group of people who accept, and whose work is guided by, the same paradigms and the same code of values and assumptions" (Bruffee, "Collaborative" 642).

"are organized around the production and legitimization of particular forms of knowledge and social practices at the expense of others, and they are not ideologically innocent" (Chase, "Accommodation" 13).

(**c**) "The writings of [Kenneth] Bruffee, [Thomas] Farrell, and [Lionel] Trilling concur that the goal of education is to acculturate students to the kind of academic 'community' they posit. [Mina] Shaughnessy, on the other hand, attempts to eliminate students' conflicting feelings towards academic discourse by reassuring them that her teaching will only 'accommodate' but not weaken their existing relationships with their home cultures" (Lu, "Conflict" 299).

"Similarly, most of the 'communities' to which other current theorists refer exist at a vague remove from actual experience: The University, The Profession, The Discipline, The <u>Academic Discourse Community</u>. They are all quite literally utopias—nowheres, meta-communities—tied to no particular time or place, and thus oddly free of many of the tensions, discontinuities, and conflicts in the sorts of talk and writing that go on everyday in the classrooms and departments of an actual university" (J. Harris, "Idea" 14).

(d) David Bartholomae, Patricia Bizzell, **Kenneth Bruffee**, Geoffrey Chase, Joseph Harris.

ANALYTIC SCORING

(a) A method of writing assessment based on the assumption that the quality of an essay can be determined by examining individual features or writing sub-skills such as organization, voice, focus, and mechanics. According to Richard Lloyd-Jones, the formalization of analytic scoring methods can be traced to E. F. Lindquist's doctoral work after World War I; yet the concept behind the analytic method had been in practice prior to this date, as teachers gave separate grades for ideas and for mechanics ("Tests" 164). Lester Faigley and his colleagues designate as the most-known analytic scale that of Diederich, French, and Carlton (1961). This scale establishes five factors important for college-level essays—ideas, form, flavor, mechanics, and wording (*Assessing* 104). An initial step in analytic scoring is to establish criteria for specific essay genres or modes of writing. For example, to establish an analytic scale for persuasive essays, developers must decide what traits are commonly found in effective persuasive writing. Once consensus has been reached about desired features, developers must decide how to rate each feature and must test the scale and rating guidelines for reliability.

Establishing and agreeing upon an analytic scale, however, can be difficult, and questions remain regarding the transferability of established scales to different contexts. Critics question the usefulness of some essay traits to be analyzed; for example, Diederich and his colleagues' category of "flavor" has raised questions of validity and reliability. Additionally, developing analytic scales and applying analytic scoring are time-consuming activities and thus costly for large-scale testing. Some critics, including **Edward White** (1985), find fault with the concept inherent in analytic scoring that writing can be seen as a sum of its parts. Analytic scoring also has been criticized for failing to account for writer's content and thus ignoring the fact that essays, though the same genre, may be written to different audiences and with different purposes.

Benefits of analytic scoring include its specificity, which some see as leading to greater reliability, and its versatility, as it can be used for large-scale testing as well as in the individual classroom. Also, the method provides specific feedback for the writer, in contrast to **holistic grading**.

Scholars disagree on whether analytic scoring is a version of holistic scoring. Edward White (1985) concludes that as the method is "based on analytic premises," it should not be called holistic (120). Similarly, Richard Lloyd-Jones (1977) divides evaluation methods into "holistic" and "atomistic," with atomistic tests characterized as assessing particular features of the text. Charles Cooper (1997), in contrast, attempting to "broaden" the view of the term "holistic," classifies analytic scoring as a variation of holistic evaluation (4). Others follow Cooper's lead in such a classification. Though analytic scoring, at least in practice, has long been a part of writing instruction, the term has been most discussed in composition studies from the 1970s to the 1990s.

(b) "an attempt to gain a series of separate scores for separate subskills from each student writing sample" (White, *Teaching* 29).

"aims to provide more information about papers by having them scaled on numerous dimensions, usually including organization, spelling, ideas, mechanics, and wording" (Brown 126).

(c) "While we must acknowledge, then, that analytic scales lack certain kinds of precision, we can still demonstrate their usefulness as general or global guides for responding to a piece of writing" (Cooper, "Holistic" 14).

"in ways parallel to multiple-choice testing, analytic scoring imagines a model of writing that is neatly sequential and comfortably segmented" (White, *Teaching* 30).

"A second method of direct assessment—analytic scoring—attempts to overcome the descriptive limitations of holistic scoring by isolating and assessing particular qualities of written texts" (Faigley et al. 104).

(d) Charles Cooper, E. F. Lindquist, **Edward White**.

ANTI-ESSENTIALISM (see ESSENTIALISM)

ANTI-FOUNDATIONAL (see FOUNDATIONAL)

AUDIENCE

(a) A term that can refer to a group of real readers to which the successful writer must adapt. It can also refer to readers who are "fictional" or invented, as well as to a spectrum of meanings between the "real" and "invented." In **current-traditional** instruction, the concept of audience was not overtly emphasized as students wrote formal compositions with the teacher as the only audience for their work. However, with the growth of **process**, student-centered approaches to composition, audience became a key term in composition theory and practice. In the 1960s, with the interest in classical and **"new" rhetoric** came an emphasis on "the rhetorical situation," which includes audience. The "new rhetorics" cast audience in a slightly different and more amicable role than did classical rhetoric since, as explained by **Kenneth Burke, identification**, not persuasion, was the key to the new rhetoric.

Many composition scholars in the 1960s and early 1970s argued that students should not write in a void but should have a specific audience for their work. In such discussions, the term represents those "real" readers or listeners already assembled to respond to the text. For example, **Wayne Booth** (1963) criticizes the teaching of first-year English through essays that are directed to no one and finds a solution in having students read one another's work. Similarly, **Donald Stewart** (1965) emphasizes the need for composition students to write to a "real" audience, suggesting that students be required to submit an essay for publication. Contrary to **James Berlin**'s well-known explanations of **expressionist** thought and practice (see, for example, "Rhetoric and Ideology in the Writing Class" [1988]), leading expressionists also called for audience in the classroom to combat lifeless student prose. In "To Be Read" (1968), **Ken Macrorie** discusses the advantages of writing for a "real" audience, encouraging students to publish their work for the school "community." Lou Kelly (1973) writes about expanding the relevance and enjoyment of the first-year writing class by incorporating audiences other than the teacher. In such approaches, students work to recognize their audience's characteristics through the use of prewriting **heuristics**.

Attention to audience increased in the 1970s, mostly in the late 1970s, as cognitive development psychology gained influence in composition studies. For the cognitivists, audience was a real entity to which the writer must respond, but also important was the writer's mental representation of the audience. The influence of cognitive psychology led to changes in the conception of audience, as scholars no longer looked only to actual readers, but examined the writer's ability to mentally analyze and respond to these readers. For the cognitivists, the writer must be "mature" and not **"egocentric"** in order to have a full understanding of the audience's needs. For instance, in **Carol Berkenkotter**'s (1983) influential protocol research with **Donald Murray** as the subject, Berkenkotter stresses the importance of audience awareness in revision but concludes that for Murray, after years of writing experience, adapting writing to the audience was so basic as to seem almost effortless; whereas for an inexperienced writer, such a task was not so simple. Accordingly, scholars proposed adapting assignments to writers' cognitive maturity and helping them move from "egocentric," or **"writer-based prose"** to **"reader-based prose."** (**Peter Elbow** [1987] argues, however, that at times, a focus on reader-based prose may inhibit a writer and that the writer may be better served by "ignoring" the audience.)

By the late 1970s, most composition scholars writing about audience at least mention **Walter Ong**'s 1975 article "The Writer's Audience Is Always a Fiction," an article that has influenced discussion of audience since its publication.

Ong proposes that writers do not analyze and respond to an already existing audience but create a role for the reader to fill if the reader chooses. Ong's concept of audience as "invented" is most forcefully argued in composition studies by Russell Long in his 1980 article "Writer-Audience Relationships: Analysis or Invention." According to Long, the view of audience as "invented" gives the writer a larger and more creative role than does the classical definition in which the writer must conform to the audience's characteristics. In response to views of Long and Ong, many compositions scholars called for a middle ground. For example, Walter Minot, in his response to Long, claims effective writing involves both analysis and invention. In their 1980 article, Fred R. Pfister and Joanne F. Petrick (1980) make a similar point, arguing that the writer cannot ignore actual readers.

Through the influence of social theories of language, the concept of audience has further expanded. According to **social constructionists**, writers anticipate and respond to the **discourse community** to which they belong or wish to belong, writing in ways and about topics that this community sanctions. For social theorists, audience is a key factor because all language use is **collaborative** and social in nature, with the writer always writing in response to what has been said and in anticipation of what will be said. In his 1984 article "Collaborative Learning and the 'Conversation of Mankind,' " **Kenneth Bruffee** applies this view of writing as a collaborative act to pedagogy, advising techniques such as writing **workshops** and peer tutoring, techniques that were not new, although the theory behind them had changed.

In the late 1970s and especially by the mid-1980s, discussion of audience in composition studies greatly increased. With the increased interest came taxonomies of audience as scholars attempted to reconcile the real/invented contradiction. Douglas Park (1982), one of the first to propose a taxonomy of the term, offers two views of audience—as either external or internal to the text. He lays out these differing views—audience as real people whose characteristics shape the text and audience as defined by the text itself, or more simply as internal or external to the text. He offers four meanings of the term, moving from literal to more abstract, but he does not advocate a preferred view of the term. Barry Kroll (1984) offers another taxonomy, proposing three views of the concept: rhetorical, informational, and social. Perhaps the most well known taxonomy of audience is **Lisa Ede** and **Andrea Lunsford**'s (1984) audience addressed / audience invoked that was set forth in their article "Audience Addressed / Audience Invoked: The Role of Audience in Composition Theory and Practice." (Both Kroll's and Ede and Lunsford's articles appear in the May 1984 issue of *CCC* that also contains Ede's "Audience: An Introduction to Research.") Ede and Lunsford look at the two dominant methods of viewing audience, the traditional or rhetorical view, which they call "audience addressed," and the view that audience is the creation of the writer, naming this second view "audience invoked." They advocate a synthesis of these two positions.

By the late 1980s and 1990s, many compositionists recognized the various meanings of audience and saw the need to specify how they were using the term, recognizing that it was no longer (or maybe never was) self-explanatory. For example, in "The Evolving Audience: Alternatives to Audience Accommodation" (1987), Robert Roth argues against prewriting **heuristics** intended to analyze audience, claiming that they may limit the writer's **invention** and proposes that a view of audience as changeable, not static, may be helpful for the writer. He recommends that instructors clarify what they mean by the term "audience." In a 1996 *CCC* article, Lunsford and Ede also further explore the concept of audience as explained in their well-known 1984 article "Audience Addressed / Audience Invoked." Influenced by poststructuralism, they "revisit" their earlier work, examining the "cultural, disciplinary, and institutional forces at play in it" (169). They do not contradict their prior views but conclude that the article and the views of audience presented in it ignore possibilities for tension and conflict as writers negotiate their rhetorical situation.

While new theories such as deconstruction, social construction, and poststructuralism now color the meanings of audience, the term still possesses, as well, its traditional meaning of a real and waiting group of readers, sometimes adversarial and sometimes not. The additional meanings audience has taken on in the last thirty-five years reflect the field's pedagogical and theoretical developments and the need that these changing perspectives have created for new answers, even, as some seem to imply, if the answers are found in abstractions. While audience has been a staple in composition conversations since the beginnings of the **process** movement, it was most widely discussed during the 1980s.

(b) Whether we mean by 'audience' primarily something in the text or something outside it, 'audience' essentially refers not to people as such but to those apparent aspects of knowledge and motivation in readers and listeners that form the contexts for discourse and the ends of discourse (Park, "Meanings" 249).

"The term audience refers not just to the intended, actual, or eventual readers of a discourse, but to all those whose images, ideas, or actions influence a writer during the process of composition. One way to conceive of 'audience,' then, is an overdetermined or unusually rich concept, one which may perhaps be best specified through the analysis of precise, concrete situations" (Ede & Lunsford, "Audience" 111).

(c) "We want to suggest that one important dimension of development in writing ability is the growth of a sense of audience, the growth of the ability to make adjustments and choices in writing which take account of the audience for whom the writing is intended" (Britton et al., *Development* 58).

"*Every writer and every speaker needs an audience beyond the teacher, needs many responses to whatever they have to say on paper and in class*" (Kelly 53).

"This cognitive development orientation calls attention to the dependency of audience awareness on specific cognitive functions in a speaker or writer. . . . Hence, the crucial factors in an investigation of *audience* awareness are not salient characteristics of audiences, but the constructive processes operative in the mind of the writer" (Kroll, "Cognitive" 280).

"Long is right in suggesting that the writer needs to be aware of the possibilities of creating <u>audiences</u>, but he ignores the relationship between created <u>audiences</u> and actual readers" (Minot 337).

"By insisting that the concept of <u>audience</u> involves textual and material constraints as well as opportunities, and that it must always be considered in the context of the larger rhetorical situation, AA/AI [the article "Audience Addressed / Audience Invoked"] sets the scene—but then fails to explore—the ways in which <u>audiences</u> can not only enable but also silence writers and readers" (Lunsford & Ede, "Representing" 170).

(d) Carol Berkenkotter, **Lloyd Bitzer**, Wayne Booth, Kenneth Burke, Lisa Ede, **George Campbell**, Peter Elbow, **Linda Flower**, Barry Kroll, Russell Long, Andrea Lunsford, Walter Ong, Douglas Park, **Chaim Perelman** and Lucie Olbrechts-Tyteca.

AUTHENTIC VOICE (REAL VOICE)

(a) A term used by **expressivists** and popularized by **Ken Macrorie**, especially in *Uptaught* (1970) and *Telling Writing* (1970), by **Donald Stewart** in *The Authentic Voice: A Pre-Writing Approach to Student Writing* (1972), by **Peter Elbow** in *Writing Without Teachers* (1973) and *Writing with Power* (1981), and by **William Coles, Jr.**, in *The Plural I: Teaching Writing* (1978). The term is used to describe the "personal" and "true" voice of a writer or speaker. An underlying assumption of this idea is that the writer can express, in all honesty and through written discourse, her or his one true self. According to many expressivists, students gain access to their inner feelings and thoughts and learn to express them confidently through expressive writing such as **freewriting**. Elbow also uses the term "real voice" to express this idea.

Advocates of social theories of writing often disagree with the emphasis that the concept places on the individual and argue that it overlooks social influences on writing. For example, in his 1989 article "Judging Writing, Judging Selves," **Lester Faigley** argues, based on Marxist theory, against the focus on personal essays, claiming instead that students should learn how the "self" is created in discourse, historically, culturally, and in relation to power structures. Also, Don Bialostosky adapts Elbow's use of the term "authentic voice" from the personal, expressive realm to that of **social construction** (see especially his discussion in the 1991 article "Liberal Education, Writing, and the Dialogic Self"). In Bialostosky's view, the authentic voice is one that is actively and productively engaged in the ongoing conversation of a **discourse community**. As Bialostosky mentions, "authentic voice" had been popular enough to warrant a special CCCC session in 1984 but was "clearly marginalized" by the time of the 1987 national conference as the field's attention focused heavily on political, social theories (13). The term, however, while marginalized, has not disappeared. In the 1990s, as expressionist rhetoric undergoes a reevaluation, the term "authentic voice" remains in debate, as seen by Donald Stewart's 1992 article "Cognitive Psychologists, Social Constructionists, and Three Nineteenth-Century Advocates of Authentic Voice," in which Stewart maintains that writers need to find their own unique voice. In a 1994 article, Randall R. Freisinger argues that poststructural theory and expressive pedagogical techniques, such as those fostered by "authentic voice," need not be mutually exclusive. The term is most often used in major conference presentations and publications from the late 1980s to the mid 1990s.

(b) [For Elbow authentic voice] "is describable but not definable . . . possesses the drama and presence of speech in intimate contact with one's experience of the world" (Wiley 58).

"resonant and effortless expression in an utterance of the person uttering it" (Bialostosky, "Liberal" 13, describing Elbow's "self"-centered view).

"Both [Kenneth] Bruffee and Karen Burke LeFevre give clear indications of their attitudes toward what I would call an <u>authentic voice</u>, the expression of the essential individuality of a particular writer. They associate it with the concept of the writer as atomistic, pursuing truth in lonely isolation" (Stewart, "Cognitive" 283).

(c) "Those who encourage 'authentic voices' in student writing often speak of giving students 'ownership' of a text or 'empowering' students" (Faigley, "Judging" 410).

"It is obvious that we cannot simply cling to Romantic notions of self and Arnoldian concepts of culture and circle the wagons against Theorists, Philistines and Barbarians. Nor should we, as it seems to me both Berlin and Faigley are inclined to do, sever our connections with teachers of the <u>Authentic Voice</u> school—teachers like Macrorie and Elbow and Coles—and the pedagogical practices they advocate and which have served us well" (Freisinger 271).

(d) Don Bialostosky, William Coles, Jr., Peter Elbow, **Walker Gibson**, Ken Macrorie, **Donald Murray**, Donald C. Stewart.

AUTHORITATIVE WORD (DISCOURSE)

(a) A term used by Mikhail Bakhtin* in *The Dialogic Imagination* (translated in 1981) to describe discourse that does not invite dialogue but confines the listener to merely listening, accepting, and then repeating the information back to authorities. Bakhtin abhors such discourse because hearers are intimidated by its seemingly unquestionable authority and, therefore, never personalize or interact with it. The authoritative word, according to Bakhtin, is located in the "distance zone" where hearers can passively see and hear the information but not touch, mold, or shape it. Religion and education are arenas where discourse has potential to become authoritative. Contrary to this term, Bakhtin describes the "**internally persuasive word**," which can be touched and used productively.

In composition classrooms, many teachers encourage students to question and analyze authoritative discourses. Under contemporary **process** and post-process pedagogy, most teachers want students to think about the rhetorical situation and to adapt their writing accordingly, not to accept authoritative educational discourse that directs them to produce five-paragraph themes and to avoid first-person pronouns. In the politicized pedagogies that have characterized composition in the 1990s, instructors encourage students to question the authoritative discourses of dominant culture, with the goal of social change. The term appears most frequently in composition discussions during the early to mid-1990s in discussions of language and writing as social and postmodern activities.

(b) "It is, so to speak, the word of the fathers. Its authority was already acknowledged in the past. It is a prior discourse. . . . It is given (it sounds) in lofty spheres, not those of familiar contact" (Bakhtin, *Dialogic* 342).

"It is the voice of the textbook or the lecturer that students learn to parrot back on tests, the voice of the instructor's summary judgment, the voice of given rules and conventions that must be observed but that do not have to account for themselves" (Bialostosky, "Liberal" 15).

"By authoritative, Bakhtin means a discourse so powerful, so commanding, that it inspires only adoration and respect and thereby maintains the status quo" (Halasek 68).

(c) "If dialogue and unconscious stylistic imitation represent a human tendency toward interaction and intervention, 'authoritative discourse,' according to Bakhtin, limits the proclivity toward dialogue and appropriation. In other words, one shies away from answering, repeating, or even uttering the words of a 'sacred' text" (Minock 495).

"Though the teacher's discourse is inevitably authoritative, it is not always authoritative in all its aspects" (Edlund 62).

(d) Mikhail Bakhtin.

AUTHORITY

(a) A term in composition studies often used in discussions of classroom relationships and the field's disciplinary status. In the context of classroom relationships, authority is often used synonymously with power, and scholars have long debated ways to conceive authority and to use it productively in the writing classroom. The **current-traditional** classroom locates authority firmly in the hands of the instructor. In contrast, early **process** theorists, writing in the 1960s and early 1970s, emphasized student authority. Beginning in the 1970s, many scholars argued that traditional writing instruction negatively minimized student authority. For example, many **expressivist** scholars emphasized a break from traditional authority figures and proposed images of the instructor as partner, as fellow writer, and/or as coach. Expressivist texts placed emphasis on cultivating student power, helping student writers see themselves as authorities and as authors. Also, scholars emphasized the knowledge and authority students brought to the classroom, encouraging students to explore topics about which they were experts, such as popular culture. Many scholars of the 1960s and 1970s recognized that teachers could and should learn from their students. (See, for example, **Donald Murray** [1972] and **Peter Elbow** [1973].

Similarly, scholars argued that traditional forms and formats of composition instruction stripped authority from students. Keith Fort, in "Form, Authority, and the Critical Essay" (1971), argues that by teaching traditional forms of writing, instructors may be guilty of fostering students' competitive and hierarchical attitudes as well as a respect for authority that supports the existing power structure. John Rouse (1979) proposes that traditional "analytic" composition instruction oppresses students, leaving them with no authority. Rouse's argument drew attention, partly because he implicated **Mina Shaughnessy**'s popular and well-respected work *Errors and Expectations* as an example of a pedagogy that could "help produce a personality type acceptable to those who would maintain things as they are, who already have power" (11).

Beginning in the late 1970s and early 1980s, scholars also noted problems related to nontraditional teaching methods, seeming to propose a balance of authority between student and teacher. Both Gerald Graff* (1980) and Michael Allen (1980), in reply to Rouse, suggest that the teacher who refuses authority may only frustrate beginning writers. According to Allen, **basic writers** need the respect and support of "someone clearly in authority who helps the writer learn the structures and rules of authorship" (864). Looking at students' responses to peer reviews, **Carol Berkenkotter** in "Student Writers and Their Sense of Authority over Texts" (1984) acknowledges problems when student writers assume too much authority over their texts. She argues that students who maintain excessive authority over their writing often refuse to accommodate their audience's needs.

In contrast to expressivist theories that locate authority in the individual and encourage students to cultivate their sense of original authorship, **social constructionism** and discourse community theories locate authority in the concept of community. **David Bartholomae**, in his influential article "Inventing the University" (1985), asserts that students gain authority when they learn the conventions of the discourse community to which they seek to belong. Based on discourse community theory, the composition instructor's authority is a result of his or her role as representative of the **academic discourse community**. In the **collaborative** classroom, authority is seen as constructed through group consensus. Advocates of collaborative learning often emphasize that classroom authority is shared and negotiated. (See, for example, Harvey Wiener [1986] and Carol Stanger [1987].)

With the influence of feminist theory in the late 1980s, however, authority became a more common topic in composition conversations. Some feminists advocate a classroom in which authority is shared and minimized while others see conflict as a necessary ingredient in the feminist classroom. Those who promote a nonhierarchical environment often embrace expressivist theories, appreciating their emphasis on personal experience and on a nonhierarchical, non-confrontational classroom. Important feminist scholarship, including Carol Gilligan's *In a Different Voice* and Mary Belenky and her colleagues' *Women's Ways of Knowing*, support the idea that female students learn better in a non-confrontational, nurturing environment where traditional hierarchies of authority are minimized. (See especially Cynthia Caywood and Gillian Overing's 1987 collected edition *Teaching Writing, Pedagogy, Gender, and Equity*.)

Drawing from scholars such as bell hooks and influences such as the political turn in composition studies during the early 1990s, some scholars propose that a feminist agenda is sometimes better served through confrontation, pointing out that emphasis on **consensus**, community, and nurture can ignore voices of minority students and even of the teacher. Also, some compositionists have expressed anger at students for taking advantage of the teacher, often female, who attempts to share or give up her authority. In response to such concerns, scholars have looked to the concept of authority, attempting to see it based on the realization that power relations in the classroom are complex and multiple. **Susan Jarratt** [1991], for example, criticizes expressivism for failing to recognize differences of race, gender, and class and suggests that compositionists need a pedagogy better equipped to deal with difference and conflict. Dale Bauer (1990) and **Patricia Bizzell** ("Power" 1991) argue that to challenge the dominant patriarchal culture, feminist and **radical** instructors are justified in using their authority to promote their political and classroom goals. Similarly, many scholars advocate a pedagogy based on theories of **contact zones** in which conflict and difference are not ignored but become a productive part of the classroom.

Yet, in the 1990s some composition scholars have seen the need to define authority in a manner that recognizes classroom responsibility, multiple power relations, and political goals. For example, Peter Mortensen and Gesa E. Kirsch in their article "On Authority in the Study of Writing" (1993) argue for a "**dialogic**" model of authority based on an **ethic of care**. Peter Sotirou ("The Question" 1993) draws on the philosophy of Hans-Georg Gadamer to propose a view of authority that is based on knowledge and not obedience (7). Urging instructors to move beyond reliance on institutional authority, Dennis Lynch and Stephen Jukuri (1997) propose a concept of power based on the theories of Michel Foucault.*

As a discipline, composition studies has been criticized for claiming institutional authority by association with stronger disciplines. For example, Patricia Bizzell ("Cognition" 1982) criticizes cognitive scholars for placing too much faith in science, assuming that a scientific method will yield "authoritative" results. Similarly, Elizabeth Flynn (1995) claims that composition's "identifications with the sciences and social sciences were clear attempts to gain authority" (360). Until recently, the term "authority" largely has been left undefined. It has long been a topic of conversation, but until the 1980s it was not a focus of conversation.

(b) "authority itself is a social artifact" (Bruffee, "Collaborative" 649).

"a form of argumentation in which the teacher demonstrates links between his or her own historical circumstances and those of the students, to suggest that their joining together in a liberatory educational project will serve all of their best interests" (Bizzell, "Power" 58).

(c) "[to] speak with <u>authority</u> they [composition students] have to speak not only in another's voice but through another's code; and they not only have to do this, they have to speak in the voice and through the codes of those of us with power and wisdom" (Bartholomae, "Inventing" 156).

"We derive our <u>authority</u> as teachers from being certified representatives of the communities of knowledgeable peers that students aspire to join" (Bruffee, "Collaborative" 649–50).

"An ethic of care, we argue, presents one possibility for rethinking notions of objectified, stable, autonomous <u>authority</u>. And while imbuing <u>authority</u> with care is hardly unproblematic . . . we believe that doing so yields a plan for subverting authority conceived as singular and monologic" (Mortensen and Kirsch, "On Authority" 557).

(d) Patricia Bizzell, **Sara Washauer Freedman**, Susan Jarratt, Gesa Kirsch, Peter Mortensen, **Ira Shor, James Slevin, John Trimbur**.

BACK TO BASICS MOVEMENT

(a) A movement whose origin can be traced to the early to mid-1970s as popular magazines including *Newsweek* and *U.S. News and World Report* published articles asserting a literacy crisis resulting from lax standards in American education. Although supported by conservative educators and administrators including William Bennett, Allan Bloom, and **E. D. Hirsch**, this movement is highly criticized in the field of composition studies. Many compositionists see the "literacy" about which the popular media reminisced as based on memorization and grammar drills, not on critical reasoning and logic. The movement resulted in implementation of entrance and exit exams and publication of test scores, which often forced teachers to "teach to the test," preparing students for multiple choice tests on "skill" rather than for writing extended discourse. Such a skills-oriented approach is at odds with the goals of **process** and social-oriented writing instruction, and composition scholars have maintained opposition to the popular press's reductive approach to writing.

The term "back to basics" appears frequently in major journals and presentations between 1976 and 1979. In the 1980s and 1990s it often refers to this call for more grammar instruction but also redefines the literacy crisis as one lacking emphasis on critical pedagogy.

(b) "A countermovement to educational pluralism . . . [which] began in the popular media following the publication of 'Why Johnny Can't Write' in *Newsweek* in 1975, an article which sounded the alarm of a 'literacy crisis' " (Faigley, *Fragments* 61–62).

"A good part of the demand for a 'return to the basics' ... is a relatively harmless form of nostalgia. .... Another part of the demand for a 'return to the basics' is simple foolishness, another instance of the human predilection for measuring everything by ourselves" (Corder, "Outhouses" 476).

(c) "Many of the adherents of 'back to the basics' determine their philosophical direction on little more than a 'good old days' mindset and a personal, unexamined opinion that rigor and sternness as teaching techniques and 'the basics' as subject matter will solve the problem of teaching students to write" (Cowan 461).

"For something like six weeks early in 1976, a comic strip called 'The Jackson Twins' (McNaught Syndicate, Inc.) urged readers to get schools back on the right path and back to the basics, all the time attacking the National Council of Teachers of English and CCCC's pamphlet *The Students' Right to Their Own Language*" (Donelson 170).

"For twenty years at least we have been told to get back to the basics, but the great gains in our field have probably come from defining 'basics' in ways different from what is meant by most of the people telling us to go back to them" (Lloyd-Jones, "Who" 494).

(d) William Bennett, Allan Bloom, E. D. Hirsch.

BANKING CONCEPT OF EDUCATION

(a) A term coined by Paulo Freire* in his popular *Pedagogy of the Oppressed* (1968) to describe an approach to education in which students' ability to think critically is not developed and is even discouraged. To Freire, this approach to education, while appearing helpful and humane, is actually a tool used by the oppressors to enforce their own social, political, and economic authority. In this approach to education, both students and teachers assume that teachers hold the power, wisdom, and truth, whereas students are weak and ignorant. A classroom based on the banking method would be silent except for the voice of the teacher as students are encouraged to remain passive receptacles of the information dispensed by the teacher. In Freire's view, the goal of this type of education is to mold students into unquestioning, unthinking citizens of the dominant society. The opposite educational approach of the banking concept, in Freire's philosophy, is **problem-posing education**.

In composition studies, the term is often used to criticize the "teacher-centered" pedagogy often associated with **current traditionalism**, as opposed to the "student-centered" pedagogies encouraged in **process** teaching. The term also stands in opposition to a political pedagogy that cultivates **critical consciousness**, with the goal that students will participate in social reform. (See, for example, **James Berlin**'s work on cultural studies and **social epistemic** rhetoric.)

(b) "Education [as] an act of depositing, in which the students are the depositories and the teacher is the depositor. Instead of communicating, the teacher issues communiqués and makes deposits which the students patiently receive, memorize, and repeat" (Freire, *Pedagogy* 58).

"The teacher deposits valuable information" (Berthoff, "Is Teaching" 754).

(c) "Years of enduring the banking model of education have taken their toll so that, like the unschooled peasants that Freire tells us about, our students often refuse to speak" (Berlin, "Freirean Pedagogy" 172).

"The capability of banking education to minimize or annul the students' creative power and to stimulate their credulity serves the interests of the oppressors, who care neither to have the world revealed nor to see it transformed" (Freire, *Pedagogy* 60).

"Some pedagogical theories maintain that literacy is irrevocably bound up with culture. Paulo Freire, for example, eschews the 'banking' system of education where the teacher fills the student's head with the 'right' ideas for the 'dialogical' teacher-student relationship" (Nardini 45).

(d) Paulo Freire.

BASIC WRITERS (BASIC WRITING)

(a) Basic writers are those students who lack experience in communicating effectively in writing, both in academic and in everyday settings. Often those who occupy basic writing classrooms are nontraditional students. As an academic course, basic writing emerged in the early 1970s, largely as a result of the open admissions policies, especially at the City University of New York (CUNY). *The Journal of Basic Writing* began in 1975 under the leadership of **Mina Shaughnessy**, who in 1977 published the seminal research book on basic writing *Errors and Expectations: A Guide for the Teacher of Basic Writing*. In her book, Shaughnessy classifies the linguistic "errors" of basic writers, showing how their writing is actually rule-governed. Their errors, she explains, often result from a misunderstanding of the complexities of the assignment and context and/or apprehension about the writing situation. **Mike Rose** has also been influential in exposing the damaging assumptions about and stereotyping of basic or "remedial" writing and in calling for an understanding of the basic writer's situation. (See, for example, *Lives on the Boundary: The Struggles and Achievements of America's Underprepared* [1989].)

Recently, some composition scholars have proposed that "basic writing" began earlier than the 1970s, when the adjectives describing this writing and writer were "remedial" or "developmental," instead of "basic." The term "remedial" was used even in the late 1970s, as, for example, in **Andrea Lunsford**'s "What We Know—and Don't Know—About Remedial Writing" (1978).

In the late 1970s and early 1980s, scholars located the problems of basic writers in their cognitive development, focusing, for example, on their **egocentricity** and instructing them to develop **reader-based prose** (see, particularly,

Linda Flower and **John Hayes** [1977], Flower [1979], and Lunsford ["Cognitive" 1979, 1980]). Also in the early, but mostly in the mid-1980s, scholars, including **Patricia Bizzell** and **David Bartholomae**, encouraged instructors to introduce basic writers into the **academic discourse community(ies)**. In the late 1980s and 1990s, this method has been criticized for ignoring the culture of basic writers. Responding to this problem, Min-Zhan Lu (1987, 1992) has argued for a basic writing classroom that acknowledges students' marginalized cultures and accepts more than one form of discourse. David Bartholomae (1993) criticizes the "skills" approach to many basic writing courses, arguing instead that basic writers contend with the **contact zone**, acknowledging historical, political, and social factors that have created and maintained the classification "basic writer." Similarly, Bruce Horner (1996) cautions against overlooking the political implications of the field and the marginalized status of basic writing students and teachers. **Peter Elbow** (1996) envisions composition programs with no placement testing and in which all students participate in the regular first-year writing course; students who need extra help would receive extra attention without being segregated into a basic writing class. In composition studies, the term appears frequently, beginning in 1979.

(b) "I use the term 'basic writers' to refer to university students traditionally placed in remedial composition courses" (Bartholomae, "Inventing" 136).

"For the time being, let me suggest that 'basic writers' are those who are least well prepared for college . . . their salient characteristic is their 'outlandishness'—their appearance to many teachers and to themselves as the students who are most alien in the college community" (Bizzell, "What Happens" 294).

(c) "Not only do medical metaphors dominate the pedagogy (*remedial, clinic, lab, diagnosis,* and so on), but teachers and administrators tend to discuss basic-writing students much as doctors tend to discuss their patients, without being tinged by mortality themselves and with certainly no expectations that questions will be raised about the state of *their* health" (Shaughnessy, "Diving" 297).

"The words *basic writing* helped usher in a national enthusiasm for meeting the needs of underprepared students. The new term inspired research as well as renewed interest in teaching young men and women with adult interests but weak writing skills" (Troyka 3).

"The teaching of basic writing occupies a peculiar position in composition studies. It is the specialty of some of the leading figures in composition studies and, simultaneously, the province of teachers and students placed at the bottom of the academic institutional hierarchy" (B. Horner, "Discoursing" 199).

(d) David Bartholomae, Patricia Bizzell, **Theresa Enos, Joseph Harris**, Andrea Lunsford, **Sondra Perl**, Mike Rose, Mina Shaughnessy, Lynn Quitman Troyka.

BAY AREA WRITING PROJECT (see NATIONAL WRITING PROJECT)

BELIEVING GAME

(a) **Peter Elbow**'s term that describes the acceptance of an idea without argument and skepticism and that was coined in 1973 in his text *Writing Without Teachers*. The purpose of this stance is to evaluate fairly another's perspective instead of making hasty and ill-founded judgments. The successful player attempts to "get inside the head" of those with different opinions in order to understand their point of view. Elbow associates the term with femininity because the qualities needed to play the believing game—patience, commitment, nonaggression—are traits traditionally assumed to be feminine. Along the same line of thought, this game is often associated with **collaborative learning**, which is often considered a feminine way of learning. The believing game is the opposite of the **"doubting game,"** but Elbow explains that both games are necessary and important to the search for truth.

Whereas Elbow sees the term as positive, **Susan Jarratt**, in her 1991 article "Feminism and Composition: The Case for Conflict," criticizes the concept for its potential to silence women and other minorities. A feminist critique of the term suggests that by encouraging women and other minorities to play the believing game in the classroom, the teacher unfairly asks them to accept sometimes derogatory and even violent ideas and responses. Another view, however, is voiced by Thomas O'Donnell (1996) as he reevaluates the "believing game" in light of composition's more social perspective, claiming that it can be seen as a call to respect the multicultural voices of the classroom.

(b) "It is a way of coming up with right answers" (Elbow, *Writing Without* 76).

"a full acknowledgment of, a full response to, the authority of individual speakers and writers to produce meaningful samples of what native speakers— and the *community* of native speakers—do with their words" (O'Donnell 433).

(c) "It is this sort of generous and deliberate misreading—readings in which we go beyond the words' literal meanings to try to draw out possibilities in a text, to imagine what the text might be trying to become—that is the basis of . . . Elbow's 'believing game' " (Tobin, *Writing* 26, discussing reading student essays).

"Working against the standard teaching and writing practices of the literary criticism he inherited, Elbow encourages participants in the 'believing game' to give up the aggressive, combative, argumentative rigidity required for the 'doubting game.' . . . In doing so, they leave themselves open" (Jarratt, "Feminism" 110).

"Peter Elbow has argued that we neutralize potential hostility by emphasizing the believing game over the doubting game. While this position encourages students to listen to each other and to think about alternatives, [Susan] Jarratt points out that it also leaves unexamined the social origins of difference and untouched the existing structures of privilege and authority" (Lynch, George and Cooper 254).

(d) Peter Elbow, Mary Field Belenky, Blythe McVicker Clinchy, Nancy Rule Goldberger, Jill Mattuck Tarule, Susan Jarratt.

BIG FOUR

(a) **Albert Kitzhaber**'s title for **Adams Sherman Hill, Fred Newton Scott, Barrett Wendell**, and **John Franklin Genung**, who were writers of the most influential **current-traditional** textbooks in the composition field from the late 1800s to the early 1900s. Many of their ideas still influence classrooms today. The "big four" have been criticized for emphasizing rules, grammar, and "the right way to write." They are also criticized for assuming a rational and knowable reality that the writer attempts to mirror in words.

Recently, though, composition scholars are challenging this harsh criticism by arguing that, in some cases, the "big four's" textbooks do not represent their classroom practices and that they came to reject the rule-based practices they once advocated. For example, **Donald Stewart** (1979, 1985) and **James Berlin** (1984) urge a reevaluation of Fred Newton Scott, arguing that his views of composing differed from the **current-traditional** views of his time. Kitzhaber himself argues that of the four, Scott was the most "original" thinker, seeing writing instruction as more than simply a focus on grammatical correctness. In "Barrett Wendell's Theory of Discourse," Thomas Newkirk (1991) proposes that Wendell also tackled rhetorical issues more complex than stylistics. Kitzhaber uses the term "big four" in his influential 1953 dissertation, *Rhetoric in American Colleges, 1850–1900*, first published in 1990.

(b) "[Albert] Kitzhaber identifies four rhetoricians—Adams Sherman Hill, Barrett Wendell, John Franklin Genung, and Fred Newton Scott, whom he subsequently refers to as the 'big four'—who through the textbooks they published did the most to shape the theory and practice of composition teaching in the last third of the century" (Varnum 43).

(c) "Of the textbook authors that Kitzhaber calls 'The Big Four' of the late nineteenth century—Barrett Wendell, John Genung, Adams Sherman Hill, and Fred Newton Scott (who wrote his texts in collaboration with Joseph V. Denney)—all had implicitly accepted the modes [of discourse] by 1894, and by 1895 all except Wendell were using them as important parts of their texts" (Connors, "Rise and Fall" 447).

"The most influential current-traditional textbooks ever written are among the most pedantic and intellectually poverty-stricken examples of the tradition. I refer specifically to some of the textbooks composed by the 'big four' " (Crowley, *Methodological* 140).

"Genung may have been the only rhetorician of the '<u>Big Four</u>' to include grammatical elements in his rhetoric, but beginning in the late eighties other text authors made the jump from 'rhetoric' to 'composition' " (Connors, "Grammar" 11).

(**d**) John Genung, Adams Sherman Hill, Albert Kitzhaber, Fred Newton Scott, Barrett Wendell.

BOYLSTON PROFESSORSHIP

(**a**) A Harvard professorship of rhetoric and oratory established in 1804 through money left to Harvard by Nicholas Boylston, a Boston merchant. Though Boylston left the money to Harvard in 1771, the professorship was not established, partly because of the Revolutionary War, until the early 1800s. John Quincy Adams served as the first Boylston professor beginning in 1806, during the time that he was U.S. senator for Massachusetts. Reverend Joseph McKean was appointed as the second in 1809, followed by William Ellery Channing (1819–1851), Francis James Child (1851–1876), and **Adams Sherman Hill** (1876–1904).

Initially, the duties of the Boylston professor included instruction of undergraduates in speechmaking and of upper-level students, graduates, and the general public in classical rhetoric and oratory. During Channing's professorship, composition was included in the position, with a shift from emphasis on oratory; but Child, with his interest in literature, switched emphasis again. In the late nineteenth and early twentieth century, beginning with Hill's professorship, classical training in oratory became less popular, and the Boylston chair became part of the English department. By the 1890s, professors who held the professorship were relieved of instruction in written composition after a recommendation by a Harvard committee (J. Murphy, "Rhetorical" 5).

Eventually then, the emphasis on rhetoric and composition was lost, leaving basically a professorship of literature and poetry (see **Edward Corbett**, "What Is Being Revived?"; Ronald Reid, "The Boylston Professorship of Rhetoric and Oratory"; and Paul Ried, "The Boylston Professor in the Twentieth Century"). It is in Harvard's change of focus from rhetoric to literature that some compositionists locate current problems with the status of composition studies in university English departments. Also, many see Harvard's influence during the late nineteenth century as contributing to the trivialization of writing instruction in English departments, including the focus on superficial correctness and grammar and the separation of writing from social context. For example, in his article "Two Model Teachers and the Harvardization of English Departments," **Donald Stewart** (1982) argues that Boylston Professor Francis James Child greatly contributed to the decline of rhetoric studies by urging a literary focus in the English department. Stewart contends that English departments across America became "Harvardized," resulting in writing instruction that largely focused on superficial correctness. In his 1992 article "Harvard's Influence on English Studies: Perceptions from Three Universities in the Early Twentieth Century," Stewart strengthens his earlier argument and takes issue with S. Michael Halloran's claim developed in "From Rhetoric to Composition: The Teaching of Writing in America to 1900" (1990) that Harvard's influence has been exaggerated. The Boylston professorship is a key concept in discussions of the history of composition studies as well as the history of English studies as a whole.

(b) "This, the most famous chair of rhetoric in America, was made possible by a grant from Nicholas Boylston, a wealthy Boston merchant, in 1771 and was formally activated in 1806" (Corbett, "What" 169).

(c) "The history of the Boylston Professorship at Harvard University is virtually a paradigm of the history of English departments themselves" (J. Murphy 4).

"In my discussion I shall treat the Statute of the Boylston Professorship as marking the initial assimilation into the academic tradition of certain ideas in eighteenth-century rhetoric that seem to me to be essential, constitutive elements in the idea of composition" (Ohmann, *English* 99).

"We can see the change that has obtained between 1840 and 1890: From an honored professoriate, the Boylston Chair has descended—even in the mind of the Harvard president—to the status of an academic sweatshop, which wears out its people like ball bearings, which then have to be replaced" (Connors, "Overwork" 111).

(d) Boylston Professors; see above for first five.

CCCC (FOUR C'S OR 4 C'S) / *CCC*

(a) CCCC, also written as Four C's and 4 C's, stands for Conference on College Composition and Communication, an organization and an annual conference for those whose interests are in the field of composition studies. The origins of CCCC can be traced to the 1948 **NCTE** conference where the discussion about the growing student population in American universities and thus in first-year English classes refused to end. In "Who We Were, Who We Should Become," **Richard Lloyd-Jones** (1992) explains that those attending were "desperate" because of the increase in enrollment and had little idea of how to deal practically with the large number of students, many underprepared, in the required composition course. This conversation began in a session entitled "Three Views of Required English," which was chaired by John Gerber, soon to become the first chair of CCCC. Session participants encouraged Gerber to call another meeting, and in the spring of 1949 the conversation continued at an NCTE-sponsored conference specifically on first-year English. As **David Bartholomae** (1989) explains, this is considered the first meeting of CCCC even though the organization was not yet official. In November 1949, NCTE approved, although initially on a trial basis, Gerber's request that those interested in first-year English have their own organization. This signaled, not a break with NCTE, but an extension of the parent group's focus and signified the growing strength of composition studies as a field. George Wykoff, also a contributing participant in the 1948 discussion, was the second chair of the new organization. CCCC publishes a quarterly journal entitled *College Composition and Communication* (*CCC*), which, like the organization itself, focuses mostly on issues relating to composition instruction on the college level.

Recently the organization and the annual conference have been criticized for perpetrating a hierarchical relationship within composition studies. For example, some have criticized the organization for becoming too similar to MLA and for fostering a "star system" in which a few prominent voices are heard often while others are kept silent (see especially "CCCC: Voices in the Parlor, and Responses" and "The Conversation Continues: Voices in the Parlor" in 1988 and 1989 issues of *Rhetoric Review*). CCCC has also been faulted for neglecting needs of nontenured writing instructors in its dealing with the **Wyoming Resolution**.

(b) "an organization whose original concern, as [Jane] Peterson notes, was the pedagogical issue of what to do with first year English" (Ray, *Practice* 3).

"our forty-year-old professional organization and home" (Lunsford, "Composing" 76).

(c) "CCCC was born out of the need to have a certain kind of discussion that existing venues were not making possible (not NCTE, not MLA). In fact, 4 C's could be said literally to begin in conversation that would not fit into the 1948 annual meeting of NCTE" (Bartholomae, "Freshman" 39).

"CCCC is an appropriate forum. We have been in the forefront of academic challenge for almost half a century, and we have adapted well—often like canaries in a mine providing early warning of trouble to our more esteemed colleagues" (Lloyd-Jones, "Who" 496).

"Changes within the discipline will succeed, finally, only to the extent that the actions (curricular, pedagogical, and institutional) initiated by individual members of the profession are supported by professional associations like CCCC, MLA, and NCTE" (Slevin, "Depoliticizing" 15).

(d) The past chairs of CCCC include John Gerber (1949 & 1950), George S. Wykoff (1951), Harold B. Allen (1952), Karl W. Dykema (1953), T. A. Barnhart (1954), Jerome W. Archer (1955), Irwin Griggs (1956), Francis Shoemaker (1957), Robert E. Tuttle (1958), **Albert R. Kitzhaber** (1959), Glen Leggett (1960), Erwin R. Steinberg (1961), Frances E. Bowman (1962), Priscilla Tyler (1963), Robert M. Gorrell (1964), Richard S. Beal (1965), Gordon Wilson (1966), **Richard Braddock** (1967), Dudley Bailey (1968), Wallace W. Douglas (1969), Ronald E. Freeman (1970), **Edward P. J. Corbett** (1971), Elisabeth McPherson (1972), James D. Barry (1973), **Richard Larson** (1974), Lionel Sharp (1975), Marianna W. Davis (1976), Richard Lloyd-Jones (1977), Vivian I. Davis (1978), **William Irmscher** (1979), **Frank D'Angelo** (1980), Lynn Quitman Troyka (1981), James Lee Hill (1982), **Donald Stewart** (1983), Rosentene

Purnell (1984), **Maxine Hairston** (1985), **Lee Odell** (1986), Miriam T. Chaplin (1987), David Bartholomae (1988), **Andrea Lunsford** (1989), Jane E. Peterson (1990), **Donald McQuade** (1991), William W. Cook (1992), **Anne Ruggles Gere** (1993), **Lillian Bridwell-Bowles** (1994), **Jacqueline Jones Royster** (1995), **Lester Faigley** (1996), Nell Ann Pickett (1997), **Cynthia Selfe** (1998).

CARNIVAL

(a) Mikhail Bakhtin* uses the term in reference to the carnivals of the Middle Ages and Renaissance. Though he mentions carnival in several essays, his most sustained, developed treatment of the concept is found in *Rabelais and His World* (translated in 1968). For Bakhtin, these carnivals allowed the people, mostly from the underclass, to rebel momentarily against social conventions and the class and financial hierarchies that structured society. As Bakhtin explains, in medieval times, carnival offered a "second world and a second life" for the people in which to participate during certain times of the year. Play, mockery, inversion, laughter, and profanity are all elements in Bakhtin's carnival. In composition studies, the concept of carnival can be used to describe a resistance to dominant discourses, or a playful, even subversive, use of language. The term is useful in feminist and Marxist works because it implies inversion of hierarchies and ridicule of traditional icons of respect. For example, in *Textual Carnivals: The Politics of Composition*, **Susan Miller** (1991) uses the concept of carnival to reread the history of composition studies and to reveal and urge resistance to the hegemonic agenda that has subordinated composition to literature. However, Frank Farmer (1998) reiterates the familiar charge that carnival overlooks complexities of power structures and that it actually reinforces and legitimizes the dominant power, since with the end of carnival, traditional order is reinstated (194). In composition studies, the term most frequently appears in the late 1980s and early 1990s with the field's emphasis on social theories and **critical pedagogy**.

(b) "Carnival, which for Bakhtin is the purest expression of popular culture, features the inversion of normal hierarchies and the exchange of established social roles" (Ewald, "Writing" 333).

"the place where hierarchy is suspended and with it the distance between people" (Lamb 15).

(c) "Carnival is not a spectacle seen by the people; they live in it, and everyone participates because its very idea embraces all the people. . . . It has a universal spirit; it is a special condition of the entire world, of the world's revival and renewal, in which all take part" (Bakhtin, *Rabelais* 7).

"Similarly, the concept of 'carnival'—necessary rebellion and subversion—corroborates a feminist agenda of social, linguistic, and political rebellion" (Halasek 67).

"The carnival features of active participation, free and familiar contact among people, and a playful, familiar relation to the world are also prominent and positive features of writing workshops. Profanation, however, is not a prominent characteristic of workshops" (Lensmire 375–76).

"Subversive laughter . . . may not be all that subversive when at <u>carnival</u>'s end, the temporarily-suspended hierarchies of a dominant order return with a ferocity that is happily assented to by all" (Farmer, "Dialogue" 194).

(d) Mikhail Bakhtin.

COGNITIVE PROCESS THEORY (COGNITIVE THEORY)

(a) A theory of the writing process with roots in cognitive psychology, especially in the theories of Jean Piaget* and Jerome Bruner.* Cognitive process theorists study the mental steps individual writers go through to write texts and often present writing as a problem-solving, goal-directed activity. Most assume that once these processes that successful writers go through to produce texts are discovered, they can be taught. Cognitive process theory research, based on social science and psychological models, is often conducted by the **protocol method** and focuses on discovering the mind's activities during the writing process. In composition, this theory emerged in the early 1970s, due largely to **Janet Emig**'s study, *The Composing Process of Twelfth Graders* (1971). Other early cognitive research includes **Sondra Perl**'s "The Composing Process of Unskilled College Writers" (1979), Emig's "Writing as a Mode of Learning" (1977), and **Nancy Sommers**' "Revision Strategies of Student Writers and Experienced Adult Writers" (1980).

In 1981, **Linda Flower** and **John R. Hayes** published their influential article "A Cognitive Process Theory of Writing" in which, based upon protocols of writers' mental activities during writing, they devised a cognitive process model that stressed that the composing process was hierarchical, goal-directed, and **recursive.** Flower and Hayes' model raised hopes among composition scholars and teachers that the writing process could be defined and that a proven method for effectively teaching writing could be developed.

In the early 1980s, when cognitive process theory was at its height of popularity, reservations about the method began to surface. **Patricia Bizzell** objected to the method's lack of social emphasis as early as 1982 ("Cognition, Convention, and Certainty: What We Need to Know about Writing"). Bizzell faults Flower and Hayes (and other "**inner-directed**" theorists) for separating the thinking process from writing and for seeing students' problems with writing as cognitive deficiency. Bizzell argues instead that such problems result from social differences and are the result of **discourse community** membership, or lack thereof. In general, critics of the cognitive approach, including many **social constructionists**, argue that cognitive theory ignores the influence of the social environment on writing and assumes that writing is solely an individual act. Some also point out that Flower and Hayes' model assumes unchanging cognitive activities even when the writing assignment changes, and others question the validity of the protocol methodology.

While scholarship on the cognitive process continued in the 1980s, the focus began to shift to social contexts by the mid-1980s. In response, Linda Flower, in "Cognition, Context, and Theory Building" (1989), defends her work in cognitive process, disagreeing with those who call for an abandonment of cognitive theory and arguing instead for a theory of the writing process that combines a cognitive and contextual perspective. Drawing on the work of Lev Vygotsky,* Flower continues this call for a "social cognitive" perspective in later work, as do other scholars including Judith Langer, Karen Schriver, **Carol Berkenkotter**, and Deborah Brandt. Such a view attempts to combine the benefits of both the social and cognitive approaches, arguing that one perspective by itself is incomplete. In her 1991 article "Paradigm Debates, Turf Wars, and the Conduct of Sociocognitive Inquiry in Composition," Carol Berkenkotter proposes that the tendency of compositionists to dichotomize social and cognitive perspectives may result from a "deeper epistemological schism" as scholars debate the benefits and dangers of quantitative versus qualitative research (152). As do the scholars listed above, Berkenkotter questions the need to choose one side or the other in the social-versus-cognitive debate.

(b) "Our cognitive process theory rests on four key points. . . . 1. The process of writing is best understood as a set of distinctive thinking processes. . . . 2. These processes have a hierarchical, highly embedded organization. . . . 3. The act of composing itself is a goal-directed thinking process. . . . 4. Writers create their own goals in two key ways: by generating both high-level goals and supporting sub-goals which embody the writer's developing sense of purpose, and then, at times by changing major goals" (Flower & Hayes, "Cognitive" 366).

"[Cognitive process theory] regards writing as the activation of innate, universal psychological processes and leads to the view, expressed by Andrea Lunsford, that basic writers are egocentered and deficient in reasoning skills" (Harned 14).

(c) "The difference between saying that language has a social context and that language is a social construct defines a key difference between cognitive and social constructionist work in composition" (Bruffee, "Social Construction" 784).

"Using results from think-aloud protocols, the cognitive process model attempts to show how writers bring complex and recursive mental activities to bear on composing" (Brand 439).

"Currently, our competing images of the composing process reflect a cognitive/contextual polarization that seems to shrink understanding and threatens to break up our vision of writing into floating islands of theory" (Flower, "Cognition" 282).

(d) Carol Berkenkotter, Janet Emig, Linda Flower, John Hayes, Sondra Perl, Nancy Sommers.

COLLABORATION (COLLABORATIVE WRITING / COLLABORATIVE LEARNING)

(a) Collaboration in the classroom can mean many things, from peer review to multiple-authored essays. Some argue that all writing is collaborative in that writers are always responding to and are influenced by what has been said and anticipating future discussion of their topic. According to **Kenneth Bruffee**, the term "collaborative learning" and the "basic idea" of how it should work was developed in Britain during the 1950s and 1960s. The motivation for the method of teaching in Britain, Bruffee explains, was political—a democratic move ("Collaborative" 636). **Anne Ruggles Gere**, however, in her 1987 book *Writing Groups: History, Theory, and Implications*, traces the roots of collaborative writing to the eighteenth and nineteenth centuries. Where one traces the origin of collaborative writing, however, often depends on how one defines it. Yet, regardless of the origin, collaboration did not largely influence American higher education pedagogy until the 1980s.

Kenneth Bruffee has led the call for a collaborative approach to composition since the 1970s. In his influential articles "Writing and Reading as Collaborative or Social Acts" (1983), "Collaborative Learning and the 'Conversation of Mankind'" (1984), and "Social Construction, Language, and the Authority of Knowledge: A Bibliographical Essay" (1986), Bruffee uses Thomas Kuhn's* and Richard Rorty's* theories of the social nature of knowledge as a basis for his idea of the social nature of writing. Bruffee argues that collaborative learning is the "natural" extension of this philosophy in the classroom.

As with all pedagogical practices and theories once seen as a panacea, collaboration has undergone some critique. For example, initially, collaboration in composition included the idea of **consensus** or agreement among group members, but critics, including Greg Myers (1986) and **John Trimbur** (1989), argue that the requirement of consensus necessarily silences difference. Insistence on consensus can be seen as perpetuating the power structures existing outside the supposedly egalitarian collaborative classroom. In a 1989 article, David W. Smit questions Bruffee's and other political-minded scholars' claims that collaboration in the classroom can lead to a more egalitarian, critically aware society. Scholars also point out that when collaboration "works," it works well, but that it must be carefully planned for progress to result. For example, Sue Hum Yin, in her 1992 article "Collaboration: Proceed with Caution," reminds instructors that traditional education has not prepared students to accept and succeed in collaborative classrooms. (See also Harvey Wiener [1986] and Irene Clark [1993].)

Collaborative learning is frequently discussed in contexts of feminism. Some feminists argue that women, in general, learn and work better in a collaborative situation. Carol Gilligan's *In a Different Voice* (1982) and Mary Field Belenky, Blythe McVicker Clinchy, Nancy Rule Goldberger, and Jill Mattuck Tarule's

Women's Ways of Knowing: The Development of Self, Voice, and Mind (1986) are popular studies often cited as supporting this view. In her study, Gilligan concludes that women often make decisions based on relationships, and Belenky and her colleagues find that women learn better in a collaborative, cooperative setting, as opposed to a competitive one. Some scholars propose as well that small-group collaboration frees students from the teacher's final **authority**, and that collaboratively, they feel free to challenge teacher authority.

Although the practice and theory of collaboration in composition studies is quite widespread, not all in the academy value co-authored texts. As **Lisa Ede** and **Andrea Lunsford** recognize in their preface to *Singular Texts / Plural Authors* (1990), collaboration in publishing can be a problem in larger academic circles because collaborative authorship is not highly regarded by all tenure and promotion committees. In composition studies, the term appears frequently, often in titles of special collections, as the focus of special journal issues, and in calls for conference papers. Though used in composition conversations beginning in the early 1970s, "collaboration" did not become a key term until the 1980s.

(b) "a generic term, covering a range of techniques that have become increasingly visible in the past ten years, practices such as reader response, peer critiques, small writing groups, joint writing projects, and peer tutoring in writing centers and classrooms. . . . By shifting initiative and responsibility from the group leader to the members of the group, collaborative learning offers a style of leadership that actively involves the participants in their own learning" (Trimbur, "Collaborative" 87).

"the institutionalized counterpart of the social or collaborative nature of knowledge and thought, [which] is not merely a helpful pedagogical technique incidental to writing. It is essential to writing" (Bruffee, "Writing" 165).

(c) "Collaborative learning is messier in practice than in theory; no one can 'live' the theory as clearly as the model suggests" (Wiener, "Collaborative" 246).

"Even if we grant the tenets of social construction, however, it is not at all clear that collaborative methods best implement that philosophy. . . . By the definitions of social construction, all pedagogies use language socially, and the collaborative theorist must demonstrate how collaborative methods more closely model the 'real world' than other pedagogies" (Smit, "Some Difficulties" 49–50).

"In terms of composition pedagogy, as John Schilb points out, we usually associate the term 'collaboration' with something that is *good* for students—people who espouse collaboration in our profession are the 'good guys' " (I. Clark 519).

(d) Pat Belanoff, Kenneth Bruffee, Lisa Ede, **Peter Elbow**, Anne Ruggles Gere, Andrea Lunsford, **Elaine Maimon**, Harvey Wiener; for critiques, see, for example, David Smit, Greg Myers, John Trimbur.

CONSENSUS

(a) A term with disciplinary origins in philosophy and history of science, but adopted into composition vocabulary in the early- to mid-1980s for discussion of **social construction** and **collaboration**. The term refers to a community's agreement about accepted commonplaces such as rules, beliefs, and discourse. According to philosopher of science Thomas Kuhn,* through consensus, the scientific community determines scientific "truths," and according to philosopher Richard Rorty,* consensus is the way that all discourse communities regulate their conventions. In association with collaborative learning, the term refers to negotiation among group members that results in a collective decision. Such negotiation is said to occur through **conversation**.

Ideally, the decision reached by consensus fairly represents all members' ideas and judgments, but as critics, especially Marxists and feminists, point out, this is not always the case. For example, Greg Myers argues in his 1986 article "Reality, Consensus, and Reform in the Rhetoric of Composition Teaching" that consensus, as defined above, restricts individualism and silences minority voices. Similarly, in "Consensus and Difference in Collaborative Learning" (1989), **John Trimbur** proposes a "revised" notion of consensus that facilitates recognition of and conversation about difference. These critics redefine the term to include conflict, differences, and disagreements, and by the late 1980s and into the 1990s, "consensus" is most often used with a recognition that "dissensus" should be valued and even encouraged in the composition classroom.

(b) "We need to see consensus, I think, not as an agreement that reconciles differences through an ideal conversation but rather as the desire of humans to live and work together with differences" (Trimbur, "Consensus" 615).

"Consensus, within the system as it is, must mean that some interests have been suppressed or excluded" (Myers, "Reality" 156).

(c) "[The community's interpretive conventions] are not arbitrary because they are always conditioned by the on-going work in the community and sanctioned by consensus" (Bizzell "Cognition" 226).

"Of course, science does not operate as neatly as the scientific method suggests. Scientific knowledge results from a consensus-building enterprise that often consists of resistance and an ongoing process of negotiation" (Greene 157).

"When difference is stressed over consensus, however, what emerges, often with difficulty, and not always without anguish, is a profusion of voices, none of which claims authority over the others, but all of which claim a subjective space within the vacant statement of the classroom" (Walters 833).

(d) Stanley Fish, Thomas Kuhn, Richard Rorty, and social constructionists such as **Charles Bazerman, Kenneth Bruffee**, Harvey Wiener; for critiques, see, for example, Greg Myers, Carol Stanger, John Trimbur.

CONSUBSTANTIAL (see IDENTIFICATION)

CONTACT ZONES

(a) A term that stems from the sociolinguistic concept of contact language and that was popularized by literary theorist and linguist Mary Louise Pratt in her 1991 article "Arts of the Contact Zone." She uses the term to describe the meeting, negotiation, and sometimes "clash" of different cultures in a social space (Pratt 34). The term implies a valuing of difference as well as a recognition that the cultures that come together are often unequal in power. However, in this meeting, it is not only the representative of the powerful culture that is changed or influenced; both cultural representatives are potentially impacted by this contact.

Composition studies adopted the term in the early- to mid-1990s to refer to this meeting and clash of cultures within the composition classroom, within discourse, and within **discourse communities**. In this context, the concept of the contact zone implies a confrontation of difference (race, class, and gender) in the classroom, leading to a new understanding and social change. This concept also challenges the idea of a unified discourse community. **Patricia Bizzell**, in her 1994 article " 'Contact Zones' and English Studies" argues for a restructuring of English departments based on the concept of contact zones, in which students would study literary texts in relation to the historical contact zone from which they emerge. Bizzell's suggested approach to literature would be a rhetorical one—a studying of literature as "efforts of rhetoric." In composition studies, the term was most used as the topic of articles and presentations at significant conferences in the mid-1990s, although the concept is still widely discussed in the late 1990s. Most of these discussions focus on the benefits of structuring the composition course around the concept of contact zones, although in the late 1990s, some scholars have critiqued contact zone pedagogies for essentializing and failing to contextualize cultural differences (see, for example, **Joseph Harris** [1995, 1997] and Bruce Horner [1997]).

(b) "social spaces where cultures meet, clash, and grapple with each other, often in contexts of highly asymmetrical relations of power, such as colonialism, slavery, or their aftermaths" (Pratt 34).

"those borderlands on the margins of communities in which it is conflict and difference that bind, but do not unite, participants" (F. Sullivan 427).

(c) "In fact, life in the <u>contact zone</u> is by definition dynamic, heterogeneous, and volatile. Bewilderment and suffering as well as revelation and exhilaration are experienced by everyone, teacher and students, at different moments" (Lu, "Professing" 456).

"If we understand that we are teaching in, and about, <u>contact zones</u>, Pratt suggests that we must stop imagining our job to be transmitting a unitary literature and literacy" (Bizzell, "Contact" 166).

"[The] first intellectual move for those interested in composition studies is to explore collaboration/cooperation as principles, to construct a writing scene that is not a Hirschean shrine, an Elbowian soul search, or a Flower and Hayes storehouse, but a conversational grouping, a Burkean parlor or even a 'contact zone' " (Lunsford, "Intellectual" 72).

"And while expressivist pedagogies, for example, claim to remove the class-room from the operation of social pressures, contact zone pedagogies aim explicitly to identify those pressures within the classroom, re-imagined as a contact zone. Where these latter pedagogies can run into trouble, however, is in failing to recognize the operation of such pressures within individual student consciousness as well as within the classrooms, and in failing to recognize the contact zone itself . . . as an historically specific strategic response" (B. Horner, "Students" 516–17).

(d) Mary Louise Pratt, social theorists including Patricia Bizzell, Joseph Harris, Min-Zhan Lu, and Richard Miller.

CONTEXT STRIPPING

(a) A term used by Elliot G. Mishler in his 1979 article "Meaning in Context: Is There Any Other Kind?" to describe and to criticize the tendency of experimental research in the social and behavioral sciences to disregard the subject's natural environment both in the experiment itself and in analyzing the results. The term often refers to experiments that apparently assume that the phenomenon is best tested in isolation and that general laws can be found and applied without regard to individual contexts. An assumption of context-stripping experiments is that isolating the subject allows for purer results and, therefore, more true and useful information. The issue of context stripping questions the presumptions that general laws can be found that are applicable from context to context. In his article, Mishler discusses alternative research methods, such as ethnomethodology and a phenomenological approach, that attempt to take context into consideration.

Mishler's critique of context stripping influenced and signaled the increased use of descriptive studies, such as **ethnography**, in composition and the emphasis on providing "**thick description**" of the research site. In her 1982 article "Inquiry Paradigms and Writing," **Janet Emig**, citing Mishler, also cautions against ignoring the effect of context on research.

(b) "When researchers remove writers from their natural settings (the study, the classroom, the office, the dormitory room, the library) to examine their thinking processes in the laboratory" (Berkenkotter, "Decisions" 156).

"Context stripping is a key feature of our standard methods of experimental design, measurement, and statistical analysis. To test the generality of our hypotheses, we remove the subjects of our studies from their natural social settings; their normal roles and social networks are left behind as they enter our experimental laboratories, much as we leave our shoes outside on entering a shrine" (Mishler 2, with a tone of irony).

(c) "A major reason for its [case study] lack of status was the domination in the post–World War II period by behaviorist psychology with its tenet that only large-scale experimental studies conducted under ostensibly controlled and context-stripped conditions provided validity and generalizability of findings" (Birnbaum & Emig 195).

"Mischler criticized the positivistic assumptions upon which experimentation is based; meaning is contextual, and to 'strip' the context, as experimental designs do, is to distort the phenomenon the researcher sets out to explain" (Newkirk, "Politics" 124).

"Theorists . . . have argued that experimental inquiry emphasizes hypothesis testing, control of variables, 'stripping' of contexts, educational outcomes, generalizability, reductionism, and researcher detachment from objects of study; while naturalistic inquiry is concerned with hypothesis generating, grounded theory, educational processes, unique and multidimensional features of contexts, and the involvement of researcher with subject required by participant-observation" (Kantor, Kirby & Goetz 294)

(d) Elliot G. Mishler, **Janet Emig**.

CONVERSATION

(a) Richard Rorty's* term adopted from Thomas Kuhn* and used by **social constructionists** to describe the way **knowledge** is made, or the way **consensus** is reached, in a community. This conversation can take place both internally in our thoughts or externally in speech and writing. According to Rorty, conversation is always ongoing within a community. In Rorty's view, conversation continues smoothly without the need for corrective intervention. In **discourse community** theories of communication, scholars view teaching as inviting students to join the academic conversation (or the conversation of the students' prospective disciplines). Such an invitation is issued through teaching students academic (or professional) discourse conventions. Left-wing critics disagree with Rorty's assumption that conversation flows smoothly; they argue that it includes social conflicts, struggle, and differences that are "normalized" or silenced in the process of conversation and consensus.

(b) "a social constructionist code word to talk about knowledge and teaching and learning as social—not cognitive—acts. Knowledge is not the result of the confrontation of the individual mind with reality but of the conversation that organizes the available means we have at any given time to talk about reality" (Trimbur, "Consensus" 605).

(c) "To see keeping a conversation going as a sufficient aim of philosophy, to see wisdom as consisting in the ability to sustain a conversation, is to see human beings as generators of new descriptions rather than beings one hopes to be able to describe accurately" (Rorty 379).

"In short, reading books with comprehension, making arguments, writing papers, and making comments in a class discussion are *social* activities. They involve entering into a cultural or disciplinary <u>conversation</u>, a process not unlike an initiation into a social club" (Graff, *Beyond* 77).

"When we ask students to engage in inquiry, to locate issues and conflict, or to enter the <u>conversations</u> of a discipline, we expect that they will be able to recognize and understand others' points of view and to adapt what they know, even transform their knowledge for knowledgeable readers. But our expectations may not be realistic" (Greene 162).

(d) Charles Bazerman, Linda Brodkey, Kenneth Bruffee, Richard Rorty, **John Trimbur**.

CRITICAL CONSCIOUSNESS

(a) A term developed by Paulo Freire* to describe a goal of his **problem-posing**, liberatory pedagogy. The term is developed in several of his publications, including *Pedagogy of the Oppressed* (1968) and *Education for Critical Consciousness* (1973). Critical consciousness refers to an awareness of how meaning is made through language as well as to an awareness of how meaning is made and maintained in a society for the benefit of the elite. Through such a realization, one can make changes; with a critical consciousness, one does not see the world or a certain situation as given and unchangeable but questions the dominant order and perceives how and why the majority accepts it. With critical consciousness, the oppressed can take action to correct injustices; without it, any action would be futile or would never even take place. According to Freire, other Marxist educators, and social theorists, the purpose of education is to create within students a questioning nature and critical consciousness so that they will not adhere passively to an inequitable social order. In composition studies, the term appears most frequently in the late 1980s and early 1990s. Scholars including Henry Giroux,* Stanley Aronowitz, and **Ira Shor** have furthered the use and development of this concept in education theory; composition scholars who have developed the term for the writing classroom include **Ann E. Berthoff, Patricia Bizzell**, and **William Covino**.

(b) "Paulo Freire's term for the process of becoming aware of a culture's structure of domination and oppression" (Leverenz 298).

"comes from understanding language as symbolic action, as having the power to revise the self and the world" (Warnock & Warnock 18).

(c) "It [the literature classroom] aims at creating a <u>critical consciousness</u> of the institution of literature, including its political manifestations in schools, literary establishments, and the 'industry' of literature production and reception" (Knoblauch, "Rhetorical" 135–36).

"Aronowitz and Giroux, while acknowledging the importance of <u>critical consciousness</u>, argue that false consciousness is not the best way to describe students' apparent unreflectiveness about large social and political forces controlling their lives" (Jarratt, *Rereading* 108).

"Hence, in writing courses, teaching our students to value convention alone may not lead to the kind of writing or learning that we want them to exhibit. ... Rather, we may need to provide students the opportunity to develop a 'critical consciousness' (Freire) about discourse and its societal functions" (Cooper & Selfe 850).

(d) Stanley Aronowitz, Ann E. Berthoff, Patricia Bizzell, William Covino, Paulo Freire, Henry Giroux, **Bruce Herzberg**, Ira Shor.

CRITICAL LITERACY

(a) A term often used to describe the literacy program of Paulo Freire.* Critical literacy is also often described as a result or characteristic of a **critical consciousness** (see **Ira Shor** [1992]). Freire began teaching his literacy methods in the 1960s to Brazilian peasants. His pedagogy encourages social and political action in relation to the students' needs and realities and encourages students to question dominant ideology and to analyze seemingly politically neutral structures and everyday concepts they may usually leave unexamined. With critical literacy, students understand the relationship between knowledge and power and the constructed nature of each; they understand that these constructions largely uphold dominant ideologies. Proponents of critical literacy value the knowledge, cultures, and experiences of the students, building on what they already know.

Freire's pedagogy has been adapted to the composition classroom. As opposed to "**cultural literacy**," critical literacy does not privilege dominant usages, meanings, forms, and accents. Instead, one practicing critical literacy would question why such meanings are given privilege in society and what is excluded by such privileging. In addition to questioning, the student would connect the questions and possible answers to his or her own situation. Through the development of critical consciousness, students come to see how language can be used as an instrument of oppression.

Generally, critical literacy has been applauded as a way to foster critical thinking and to teach rhetorical strategies in a social context; however, scholars have criticized the concept, especially its adaptation to American classrooms. Henry Giroux,* a strong proponent of critical literacy, claims in his 1992 article "Paulo Freire and the Politics of Postcolonialism" that Freire's literacy pedagogy loses political insight when transferred to the Western classroom. For Freire's critical literacy to remain effective, the instructor must recognize the historical and social situation from which it emerged. In contrast, conservative critics see no place for critical literacy in the classroom, arguing that a pedagogy based on critical literacy often intimidates students because of the instructor's overt political perspective and does not improve students' logic or writing ability. Seeking to reestablish the importance of this concept, **James Berlin** (1996), in proposing a cultural studies emphasis in English education, places Freire's critical literacy in a "postmodern frame," arguing that coupled with "postmodern theory," a critical literacy can better address the fragmentation of modern society (97). In composition studies, the term often appears as a key term in major publications and presentations in the late 1980s to the early 1990s.

(b) "At the core of [Freire's] notion of literacy is the insight that culture contains, not only a moment of domination, but also the possibility for the oppressed to produce, reinvent, and create the ideological and material tools they need to break through the myths and structures that prevent them from transforming an oppressive social reality" (Giroux, *Theory* 226).

"Habits of thought, reading, writing, and speaking which go beneath surface meaning, first impressions, dominant myths, official pronouncements, traditional clichés, received wisdom, and mere opinions, to understand the deep meaning, root causes, social context, ideology, and personal consequences of any action, event, object, process, organization, experience, text, subject matter, policy, mass media, or discourse" (Shor 129).

"the ability to interrogate, challenge, complicate, transform, redefine, and elaborate ostensibly neutral social and institutional facts. This literacy requires the capacity for dialectical thinking, by positing knowledge-in-language as an ongoing critique, in which conclusions lead to further questions, oppositions, and relationships" (Covino, *Magic* 25).

(c) "Increasingly, Freire's work has become the standard reference for engaging in what is often referred to as teaching for critical thinking, dialogical pedagogy, or critical literacy" (Giroux, "Paulo" 15).

"Critical literacy develops from engaging a negative hermeneutic with what the dominant ideology offers to students as models of success and reward and from encouraging a utopian recovery of cultural capital that has been excluded from academic canons" (Bizzell, "Marxist" 63).

"English studies refigured along the postmodern lines of social-epistemic rhetoric in the service of critical literacy would take the examination and teaching of reading and writing practices as its province" (Berlin, *Rhetorics* 104).

(d) James Berlin, **Ann E. Berthoff, Patricia Bizzell, Lil Brannon, William Covino**, Paulo Freire, Henry A. Giroux, **C. H. Knoblauch, Ira Shor**.

CRITICAL PEDAGOGY (see RADICAL PEDAGOGY)

CULTURAL LITERACY

(a) A term used by **E. D. Hirsch** and popularized in *Cultural Literacy: What Every American Needs to Know* (1987). (Hirsch developed the term earlier, in "Culture and Literacy" [1980], in a 1981 conference presentation and in two 1983 articles, "Reading, Writing, and Cultural Literacy" and "Cultural Literacy."). Education secretary William Bennett, who also popularized this concept, has argued for a similar restructuring of educational curricula based on a specific canon of knowledge. To be culturally literate, in Hirsch's use of the term, one should have at least some knowledge of a broad base of information that is commonly known by the general public. In his book, Hirsch makes a long list of items the culturally literate person should know, including authors, terms, and historical names and places.

The list has stirred controversy because it ignores information representative of women and other minorities. Many see it as an "elitist" form of literacy, valuing traditional canonical information while devaluing other forms of knowledge. Other composition scholars object to Hirsch's use of the term because they argue that it limits students' education to a mere absorption of knowledge and acceptance of the dominant culture, without the need for critical thinking (see, for example, Patrick Hartwell's article "Creating a Literate Environment in Freshman English: Why and How" [1987]).

Some scholars in composition studies have used the term in a broader context to refer to a multi- or popular cultural literacy or to the social nature of all literacy. In her 1988 article "Arguing About Literacy," **Patricia Bizzell** argues for a rhetorical view that recognizes the "cultural" in all literacies and that takes history and social context into consideration. In "Beyond Anti-Foundationalism to Rhetorical Authority: Problems Defining 'Cultural Literacy' " (1990), Bizzell agrees with Hirsch that a "shared knowledge" is needed; she disagrees, however, that this knowledge is stable or that it is easily definable (662). In this and later articles, Bizzell attempts to negotiate what would constitute a shared cultural literacy in our multicultural society. Many composition conference presentations, especially from the late 1980s to the early 1990s, called for a multicultural literacy. In composition studies, the term "cultural literacy" had been a focus in major conference presentations or publications, in the late 1980s to the early 1990s.

(b) "lies above the everyday levels of knowledge that everyone possesses and below the expert level of knowledge known only to specialists. It is that middle ground of cultural knowledge possessed by the 'common reader' " (Hirsch, *Cultural* 19).

"This concept suggests that all literacy is in fact cultural literacy—that is, that no symbol system in and of itself induces cognitive changes. A cultural context is necessary to invest the features of the system with meaning" (Bizzell, "Arguing" 144).

(c) "One reason why recent conservative attacks on teaching have met with success is that they have claimed to provide students access to power—usually in some form of 'cultural literacy'—that an emphasis on individual growth and expression cannot offer" (J. Harris, "After Dartmouth" 643).

"We should not be 'naive' about the power or the ingenuity of those in the school setting who want things to remain just as they are: advocates of a 'cultural literacy' . . . including the Department of Education, who want to use myths of monolithic culture and the American melting-pot to ensure the suppression of appeals for institutionally sanctioned diversity" (Knoblauch, "A Response" 182–83).

"It is the desperate character of our current national political life that dismays me when I contemplate the reaction of scholars in English studies to E. D. Hirsch's cultural literacy proposals, wrong-headed though these proposals are. It seems as if these scholars are denying my hope for the political consequences of a national discourse, denying their own vocation as intellectuals" (Bizzell, "Beyond" 663).

"the advocates of 'cultural literacy' . . . [claim] that student writing is thread-bare because students simply do not know enough about their culture to say anything beyond their own experience" (Connors, *Composition-Rhetoric* 327).

(d) William Bennett, Allan Bloom, E. D. Hirsch, Jr.

CURRENT-TRADITIONAL RHETORIC

(a) A term coined by Daniel Fogarty in *Roots for a New Rhetoric* (1959) and used to describe the "present-day traditional form" of Aristotelian rhetoric. According to Fogarty, current-traditional rhetoric emphasizes grammar, syntax, mechanics, and spelling. It also focuses on the **modes of discourse** (exposition, description, argumentation, and narration). **Richard Young** helped popularize the term in composition studies through his 1975 conference presentation and 1978 article "Paradigms and Problems: Needed Research in Rhetorical Invention." Young used the term to refer to the accepted philosophy of many writing programs before 1963, when, according to many scholars, the "**paradigm shifted**" to **process** theories of writing. The turn from current-traditional methods was in response to the realization that current pedagogical methods were not meeting students' needs. The term often refers to ineffectual pedagogy and an overemphasis on editing and on the final written product.

According to **James Berlin** (see especially *Rhetoric and Reality* [1987]), current-traditional rhetoric was appropriated into the American university system by Harvard and has been the dominant method of writing instruction in the twentieth century. **Albert Kitzhaber** contends that current-traditional rhetoric spread widely and quickly through the much-used textbooks of the "**big four**," **Adams Sherman Hill, Fred Newton Scott, Barrett Wendell, and John Franklin Genung**. The history of current-traditional rhetoric can be traced to eighteenth-century **Scottish common sense realism** and more specifically to the philosophies of **George Campbell, Hugh Blair**, and **Richard Whately**, who saw truth as existing in the external world, independently of the human mind. In Scottish realism, a strong emphasis is placed on "correct" style and "proper" usage and on polishing the written product instead of examining the writing process.

Current-traditional pedagogy has been criticized for denying the writer's voice and for doing little or nothing to improve students' writing. One of the strongest criticisms against the pedagogy is its neglect of **invention**. Most of the teacher's emphasis is on surface correctness and form. The five-paragraph theme is a current-traditional product, and in the classroom, the teacher represents a strict **authority** figure, the one who has the "right" answers. Many modern composition textbooks are criticized for relying on current-traditional thought. (See **Sharon Crowley's** 1986 article "The Current-Traditional Theory of Style: An Informal History" and Berlin and Robert Inkster's 1980 article "Current-Traditional Rhetoric: Paradigm and Practice.")

The term often stands for what is negative in composition studies and is used as a point of contrast to show how the field has progressed and to argue for process approaches to composing. It is also a part of James Berlin's taxonomy of four dominant pedagogical theories (see "Contemporary Composition: The Major Pedagogical Theories" [1982]). Berlin equates "current-traditional" with "**positivism**." Some scholars, however, have called for a closer examination of current-traditional rhetoric and thinkers. **Donald Stewart** (1979, 1985), for example, has shown the work of Fred Newton Scott in a new and more positive light. Similarly Berlin (1987) sees in Scott's work foreshadowings of **epistemic** rhetoric. **S. Michael Halloran** (1990) urges scholars to see the work of nineteenth- and early twentieth-century current-traditionalists in their historical context, and **Robert Connors** (1997) sees the term "current-traditional rhetoric" as problematic, since, he argues, the different views and approaches to rhetoric the term is used to describe are neither unified nor unchanging. In place of "current-traditional rhetoric," Connors encourages the use of the categories of "older" and "newer" forms of "composition-rhetoric." In composition studies, the term appears most often from 1980 to the mid 1990s.

(b) "The overt features, however, are obvious enough: the emphasis on the composed product rather than the composing process; the analysis of discourse into words, sentences, and paragraphs; the classification of discourse into description, narration, exposition and argument; the strong concern with usage . . . and with style . . . the preoccupation with the informal essay and the research paper; and so on" (R. Young, "Paradigms" 31).

"Its [the current traditional paradigm's] adherents believe that competent writers know what they are going to say before they begin to write. . . . They also believe that the composing process is linear. . . . Finally, they believe that teaching editing is teaching writing" (Hairston, "Winds" 78).

(c) "The philosophy of language preached by current-traditional textbooks is suited, at best, for quite restricted kinds of technical writing. At worst, it hinders students from using language as an exploratory or rhetorical medium" (Crowley, "Current-Traditional" 247–48).

"Once we abandon the current traditional rhetoric's notion of writing as a neutral, apolitical skill, we must recognize that discourse is inseparable from institutions, from organizational structures, from disciplinary and professional knowledge claims and interests, and from the day-to-day interaction of workers" (Herndl, "Teaching" 353).

"If not giants on whose shoulders we now stand, the <u>current-traditional</u> rhetoricians are nonetheless significant contributors to the tradition of writing instruction. Seen in the context of their time, their accomplishments are deserving of some attention and respect" (Halloran, "From Rhetoric" 178).

"In blaming <u>current-traditional</u> writing instruction for the hatred students felt toward writing and for their poor writing skills, we have almost defined ourselves as the 'saviors' of students—and of learning in general" (Payne 101).

(d) Aristotle, John Genung, Adams Sherman Hill, Fred Newton Scott, and Barrett Wendell (the "**big four**"), Alexander Bain, Hugh Blair, George Campbell, Richard Whatly; for critiques, see, for example, James Berlin, Sharon Crowley, Daniel Fogarty, Maxine Hairston, and Richard Young.

DARTMOUTH SEMINAR

(a) A three-week seminar held at Dartmouth College in Britain during August and September 1966 and fully titled the Dartmouth Anglo-American Conference on the Teaching and Learning of English. It is often credited for significantly contributing to the "**paradigm shift**" from product to **process** emphasis in writing instruction, as explained in **Maxine Hairston**'s 1982 article "The Winds of Change." The conference, funded by the Carnegie Corporation, was attended by fifty leading British and American teachers and scholars representing various English specialties, from linguistics and literature to rhetoric and writing. Specialists in other areas, such as psychology and education, served as consultants. Central to the seminar was the thematic question "What IS English?" Though not definitively answering this question, most participants concluded that student-oriented, **collaborative workshops** should replace traditional teacher-controlled, skills-oriented classrooms. An interdisciplinary and democratic approach to language learning and teaching was advocated, as was the importance of creativity in English education. Largely, the seminar's focus was on elementary and secondary schools; yet the findings have been applied to higher education. Two books resulted from the conference: John Dixon's *Growth Through English* and Herbert J. Muller's *The Uses of English*.

In composition studies, the Dartmouth seminar was important in signaling the move to process-centered, **expressionist** classrooms in which teachers encouraged students to write in **authentic voices** and to share in classroom **authority**. Influenced by Jean Piaget* and Lev Vygotsky,* the Dartmouth seminar also encouraged an interest in cognitive psychology. Although the conference has been widely praised, some critics feel the original question was not adequately answered or that the answers have not been sufficiently applied to composition classes (see, for example, Sharon Hamilton-Wieler, "Empty Echoes of Dartmouth" [1988]). Also, as composition studies began to adopt **social construc-tionist** theories, the methods upheld at Dartmouth came under scrutiny because of participants' reliance on and confidence in **expressive** theories of writing. As early as 1971, **Ann E. Berthoff** criticized the conference for focusing solely on expressive writing ("The Problem of Problem Solving"). Dartmouth, a key his-torical event in composition studies, was most discussed in the late 1960s and the 1970s.

(b) "A major event that encouraged the shift of attention to the process of writing . . . the participants de-emphasized the formal teaching of grammar and usage in the classroom and emphasized having children engage directly in the writing process in a non-prescriptive atmosphere" (Hairston, "Winds" 77).

(c) "While the Seminar was united in the essential value of literary experience . . . it was full of doubt and dismay about prevailing approaches to the teaching of literature, not only at school level. . . . There is a widespread and self-defeating refusal . . . to see that literature cannot be 'taught' by a direct approach, and that the teacher who weighs in with talk or lecture is more likely to kill a personal response than to support and develop it" (Dixon 58).

"Is the influence of Dartmouth waning? . . . Will the renewed emphasis on testing at all levels, the popular appeal of the Bloom-Hirsch call for cultural-heritage, information-transmission pedagogy, and the comfortable inertia of tradition divert us from 20 years of efforts to implement post-Dartmouth ped-agogical developments in our classrooms?" (Hamilton-Wieler, 41).

"[Ann] Berthoff's objection to the Dartmouth Conference is that it divided the use of language into two unrelated areas: communication and expression" (Berlin, *Rhetoric and Reality* 176).

"You may remember that the theme song of the Dartmouth Conference was, 'What *is* English?' That kind of questioning gets us nowhere; it is neither prag-matic nor scientific" (Berthoff, *Making* 74).

(d) Maxine Hairston, **Joseph Harris**; participants included **Wayne Booth, James Britton**, John Dixon, **Albert Kitzhaber, James Moffett**, Herbert Muller.

DIALOGIC / DIALOGUE

(a) A term often used to describe the language theory of Mikhail Bakhtin.* He develops his dialogic theory in his early works, but his most recognized discussion of dialogics is in his later *Problems of Dostoevsky's Poetics* (1963, translated in 1973), *Rabelais and His World* (1965, translated in 1968), and *The Dialogic Imagination* (1975, translated in 1981). According to Bakhtin, language acts are social and contextual acts, and, therefore, writing is not produced in a vacuum, but responds to and anticipates other voices in that conversation. For Bakhtin, the novel is the literary genre that best represents dialogics, as in the novel, multiple, diverse, and conflicting voices and forms of discourse interact.

Bakhtin contrasts dialogics with rhetoric, arguing that a dialogical view accepts and even requires contrasting views, whereas rhetoric insists on a "right" and "wrong." Dialogics includes connotations of activity, growth, and change and is made up of agreement and argument, questions and ridicule. Dominant ideology and subversion are two sides of dialogue. Users of language, texts, and words themselves are dialogic in that they interact with and respond to previous and future writers, speakers, texts and words.

In addition to Bakhtin, Paulo Freire* stresses the importance of "dialogue" to his liberatory pedagogy, encouraging students to take part in dialogic learning or in dialogue. Along with Bakhtin, Freire discourages a sole voice of **authority**. For Freire, dialogue should result in change—change of understanding and/or of social and political realities.

The concept of dialogics has been used to justify various composition pedagogies and theories. Some in composition, **Lisa Ede** and **Andrea Lunsford** (*Singular Texts / Plural Authors* [1990]), for example, have used Bakhtin's dialogics to support their view that all writing is in some way **collaborative**. Judith Goleman (1986) uses dialogics to argue for **ethnography** as a method of composition research. Don Bialostosky ("Liberal Education, Writing, and the Dialogic Self" [1991]) uses the concept to argue for a composition pedagogy that cultivates a recognition of various voices instead of a focus on only **academic discourse**.

Feminists often claim the term as an alternative to traditional, hierarchical rhetorics and ways of knowing (see, for example, Dale Bauer's *Feminist Dialogics: A Theory of Failed Community* [1988]). In contrast, **Robert Connors** attempts to problematize "dialogic, feminist, and 'subversive' " methods in the classroom because, he contends, they pose problems for male students ("Teaching and Learning as a Man" [1996]).

Additionally, advocates of **writing across the curriculum** use the term to encourage interaction among different disciplines and different literacies and between students and professors (see, for example, Catherine Blair Pastore's 1988 article "Opinion: Only One of the Voices: Dialogic Writing Across the Curriculum" and Marilyn Cooper's 1994 article "Dialogic Learning Across Disciplines"). Computers and advanced technology are also seen as tools leading to a more dialogic, interactive classroom. In composition studies, the term is most used from the late 1980s to the mid-1990s, not surprising since social theories of composing were growing in popularity during these years. Judith Goleman's 1986 article "The Dialogic Imagination: Something More Than We've Been Taught" is one of the first in composition studies to use dialogics as a key term.

(b) "the name for this social imbrication of voice and response" (Nealon 131).

"For dialogue (in the Bakhtinian sense) is a cooperative and constructive activity that leads to a new and heightened understanding of the issue at hand" (Halasek 68).

"Dialogue is communication that creates and recreates multiple understandings. It moves its participants along the learning curve to that uncomfortable place of relearning and unlearning. It can move people to wonderful new levels of knowledge . . . it can change things" (Wink 36, discussing the use of dialogue in Freire's critical pedagogy).

(c) "The word, breaking through to its own meaning and its own expression across an environment full of alien words and variously evaluating accents, harmonizing with some of the elements in this environment and striking a dissonance with others, is able, in this dialogized process, to shape its own stylistic profile and tone" (Bakhtin, *Dialogic* 277).

"Through much of his career [Bakhtin] defined the dialogic in contradistinction to a monologic rhetoric that aimed to determine its audience's responses and close off further discussion" (Bialostosky, "Antilogics" 86).

"The problem for male students is that many do not come to dialogic collaboration easily, or come to it at all, and if egalitarian, communitarian, consensus-based collaboration is part of a teacher's expectations of group work, male students will consistently disappoint" (Connors, "Teaching" 154).

"Dialogic writing necessarily evades the consistency, coherence, and blindness of an insistent 'thesis' " (Covino, "Defining" 120).

"It follows, then, that what we call consciousness is dialogic through and through, that the self is an event of language experience, and that neither consciousness nor emergent selfhood are able to attain the kind of crowning moment after which it may be said that this or that person is developmentally *finished*" (Farmer, "Voice" 308).

(d) Mikhail Bakhtin, Paulo Freire, advocates of collaborative and social theories of composition.

DISCOURSE COMMUNITY

(a) A term that implies a group who share similar ideas, attitudes, assumptions, and values, and whose language use is also defined by similar conventions. The community regulates what is and is not acceptable language use for its members. It is possible, and probable, to belong to different discourse communities. This does not, however, imply that one can pick and choose discourse community membership at will; one's social, economic, and professional position is often a defining factor in who belongs to which discourse community.

Some scholars, especially in the 1980s and early 1990s, have argued for a pedagogy based on the concept of discourse communities. **Patricia Bizzell**'s "Cognition, Convention, and Certainty: What We Need to Know About Writing" (1982) and **David Bartholomae**'s "Inventing the University" (1985) are two early articles influential in arguing for a pedagogy based on discourse conventions. Such a pedagogy focuses on the idea of community and the social nature of language and denies existence of transcendent truth or reality; proponents see "truth" as constituted in and by the language of a discourse community. The goal of such a pedagogy is to make evident the assumptions governing writing in different discourse communities. The teacher does not teach these conventions as "correct" or "preferable" but as conventions that the student will need to recognize to participate within a certain academic or professional community.

The concept of discourse community has been important in studies of writing in nonacademic settings as scholars explore how organizational context influences writing choices. In the classroom, many supporters of **writing across the curriculum** advocate studying and teaching discipline-specific discourse conventions because such an approach will allow the students to understand how language works in their discipline, to participate in the conversations, and even to change the conventions when they no longer suit their communities' needs. Critics of this pedagogy worry that students will be assimilated into an **academic discourse community** and forfeit their former community ties. Also, in the 1990s, scholars, including **Joseph Harris** and **Lester Faigley**, have critiqued the concept of community, pointing out that the term implies the exclusion of minority or dissenting voices. Gregory Clark (1998), recognizing ethical dilemmas implied by "community," proposes that composition scholars replace "metaphors of territory" with the "metaphor of travel." He suggests that we see students (as well as ourselves) not as residents (or aspiring residents) of discourse communities but as "travelers who encounter and assist each other as they journey separately across a common space" (17). As Clark explains, the goal of the writing instructor who is informed by the idea of travel would be to teach students to cross rhetorical boundaries as opposed to teaching a clearly defined set of discourse conventions (11). "Discourse community" is a key term in social theories of writing and has been often used from the mid-1980s to the late 1990s.

(b) "a social group that pursues its common purposes through linguistic activity that operates according to conventionalized norms of the sort that can be studied, learned and taught" (Crosswhite 4).

"The established discourse community that is the focus of most research is analogous to what Sartre calls a collective, a group that is not a community but rather a collection of individuals whose actions are regulated by the rules and structures of the group" (M. Cooper, "Why" 203).

(c) "Since any effort to assess writing skills necessarily makes certain assumptions about a writer's discourse community, the ultimate context for assessment must be the writer's discourse community and the communities in which that writer wishes to participate" (Faigley et al., *Assessing* 90).

"In contrast to [Lucille Parkinson] McCarthy's picture of an environment with clear boundaries between discourse communities, Joseph Harris argues that the distinctions among differing communities are not so definite" (Doheny-Farina, *Rhetoric* 295).

(d) David Bartholomae, **Carol Berkenkotter**, Patricia Bizzell, Lester Faigley, Joseph Harris.

DOUBLE-VOICEDNESS

(a) A term developed by Mikhail Bakhtin* in his collection of essays *The Dialogic Imagination* (published 1975, translated 1981). Bakhtin uses the term to describe the style of the novel and to differentiate it from that of poetry, which he called "single-voiced." Double-voicedness is the inclusion of another's words, or style of words, into the discourse without quotations or recognition that the words are not the author's. It is the intermingling of two or more different "languages" or voices that stand unreconciled in the text. Such discourse is what Bakhtin calls **dialogic**, and it recognizes the diversity and many layers of meaning found in language. In Bakhtin's theories, the author works with these multiple meanings and voices to create a work unique to the genre of the novel.

When applied to composition theory, the term refers to those essays in which different discourses are evident; for example, a double-voiced essay would be one in which resonances of both academic discourse and the language common to a particular social class or ethnic community are evident. As John Edlund (1988) points out, while the multiple voices are controlled by the novelist, they are not completely controlled by the student writer (61). Scholars also use the term "multi-voiced" to refer to this concept or to the *many* voices or discourses evident in a piece of writing. In composition studies, Bakhtin's work is most often referenced beginning in the late 1980s.

(b) "a transformation that Bakhtin describes as occurring when individuals are submerged in a diverse social and linguistic milieu, as part of the ongoing process of 'becoming' " (Ritchie, "Beginning" 168).

"It is important to illustrate the ways that Bakhtin allows us to analyze more clearly certain kinds of dialogical language use where the blurring of the elements is most clearly evidenced. Bakhtin calls such blurrings 'double-voiced' and they occur often, particularly in narratives where a narrator's (speaker's) language comes into a zone of dialogical contact with a character's (hero's)" (Schuster 535).

(c) "This double-voicedness makes its presence felt by the novelist in the living heteroglossia of language, and in the multi-languagedness surrounding and nourishing his own consciousness" (Bakhtin, *Dialogic* 326–27).

"The student text I discussed above contains clear examples of hybrid constructions and heteroglossia, the double-voiced discourse that Bakhtin attributes to the novel. In the student texts, however, the multiple voices are not entirely under the author's control" (Edlund 61).

(d) Mikhail Bakhtin, compositionists influenced by social theories of writing.

DOUBTING GAME

(a) A term developed by **Peter Elbow** in 1973 along with its companion and opposing term "**believing game**." "Doubting game" refers to meeting ideas and opinions of others with arguments and criticism instead of acceptance and provisional belief. The term is usually associated with conflict, competition, and masculinity. Generally, women are assumed to feel uncomfortable playing the doubting game, and proponents of **collaborative** learning often see it as disruptive of the collaborative process. In *Women's Ways of Knowing: The Development of Self, Voice, and Mind* (1986), Mary Field Belenky and her colleagues favor collaborative, cooperative learning and oppose such learning to Elbow's doubting game, or to competitive learning. However, not all critics agree that the doubting game is always negative. Elbow himself contends that the doubting game is powerful and important in the search for truth but that it must be "played well" and played alternatively with the believing game.

Some feminists have also questioned the negative connotations of the term and have, to some extent, redefined it. Influenced by poststructuralism and **social construction**, feminists have argued against **essentialist** views of "feminine" and "masculine." Such views are reflected in the reevaluation of conflict or disagreement in the classroom, as feminist scholars question whether "feminine" values of acceptance, patience, and nurturing always help women teachers and students and whether such qualities are essentially "feminine." Some find the doubting game a productive check on its opposite, the believing game. For example, **Susan Jarratt** ("Feminism and Composition: The Case for Conflict" [1991]), drawing on the work of bell hooks and Kathleen Wieler, sees the place for "productive conflict" in the classroom. Similarly, Marilyn Cooper suggests, in response to Mary Field Belenky and her co-authors' criticism of the "doubting game," that competition and collaboration can offer "productive checks" on each other.

(b) "seeks truth by indirection—by seeking error" (Elbow, *Writing Without* 148).

(c) "For entrance into the intellectual world, we tend to require willingness to play the doubting game. This would be all right if we also required willingness to play the believing game" (Elbow, *Writing Without* 175).

"The classic dormitory bull session, with students assailing their opponents' logic and attacking their evidence, seems to occur rarely among women, and teachers complain that women students are reluctant to engage in critical debate with peers in class, even when explicitly encouraged to do so. Women find it hard to see doubting as a 'game'; they tend to take it personally" (Belenky et al. 105).

"The problem with these equations ["doubting with competition and conflict and believing with collaboration and accord"] is that not only are women excluded in educational settings that depend on competitive practices, they are also excluded from reasoned critical discourse, which depends on the doubting game" (M. Cooper, "Dueling" 52).

(d) Peter Elbow, Mary Field Belenky, Blythe McVicker Clinchy, Nancy Rule Goldberger, Jill Mattuck Tarule, Susan Jarratt.

DRAMATISTIC PENTAD

(a) A concept developed by **Kenneth Burke** in *A Grammar of Motives* (first published in 1945) and further expanded and clarified in later work for critically analyzing the motives of all human action, including language use and thought. The method consists of five prompts or areas for question—act, agent, scene, agency, and purpose—and thus the method is called a pentad (although Burke later added a sixth term to the heuristic—attitude). In establishing the pentad, Burke draws on both Aristotle and medieval scholastics (Irmscher 113). The five terms are worded in language of drama and of action, themes of Burke's philosophies, and are intended for the analysis of literary texts as well as human relations. Basically, the dramatistic terms ask the questions what, who, where, when, how, and why. In the field of composition, **Joseph Comprone** and **William Irmscher** have discussed and developed the pentad. For the writing classroom, it is used mainly as a prewriting **heuristic** or an **invention** technique, although Burke states that his intention when developing the pentad was that critics would use it to determine what was happening in existing literary texts ("Questions" 332). The term appears most often in composition studies beginning in the late 1970s. Responding to composition studies' interest, Burke, in a 1978 *College, Composition, and Communication* article, explains his pentad within the context of composition.

(b) "The pentad is thus an analytical and heuristic device. Burke cautions that it can be used 'profoundly or trivially,' a reminder to those practitioners who choose to see in the pentad little more than an investigatory tool like the journalistic formula and overlook the potential of it as a logical method" (Irmscher 113).

"a heuristic for interrogating the immediate situation in order to impute motives for individual language acts" (M. Cooper, "Ecology" 368).

(c) "Act, Scene, Agent, Agency, Purpose. Although, over the centuries, men have shown great enterprise and inventiveness in pondering matters of human motivation, one can simplify the subject by this pentad of key terms, which are understandable almost at a glance" (Burke, *Grammar* xv).

"The five terms . . . become the 'pentad' for examining human motivation dramatistically, in terms of action and its ends" (Lindemann, *Rhetoric* 50).

"Kenneth Burke, however, whose pentad structure of act, agent, agency, purpose, and scene is a continual assertion of the importance of the various elements of the dramatic context of discourse, maintains the central importance of man as a symbolic act" (W. Horner, *Nineteenth* 174).

(d) Kenneth Burke.

ECOLOGICAL MODEL OF WRITING

(a) A term used in composition studies to indicate the need for a rhetoric that considers the broad context of the rhetorical situation. Richard M. Coe uses the term in his 1975 *CCC* article "Eco-Logic for the Composition Classroom," in which he argues for a rhetoric that emphasizes "wholeness" and "system inter-relations instead of analytic separations." Marilyn Cooper develops this meta-phor for composition in her article "The Ecology of Writing," which appeared in *College English* in April 1986. Cooper sees ecology, the study of the rela-tionship of an organism to other organisms and to its surroundings, as a helpful model for composition studies. She reacts against **cognitive process models** of writing that position the writer as solitary, untouched by the social situation in which he or she writes. Her model is based on the idea that texts are social activities and that these activities are shaped not only by the writer's immediate context but also by a larger social group of other writers and readers and by social systems, such as textual and cultural norms. Those writers and readers who recognize the larger context can possibly challenge contextual norms. In a 1993 national conference presentation, Coe uses the ecological metaphor in his discussion of teaching genre, arguing that genres need to be taught in relation to the context in which they develop and exist. Reflecting societal concerns, terms related to the environment drifted into composition studies' vocabulary, especially in the 1980s.

(b) "What I would like to propose is an ecological model of writing, whose fundamental tenet is that writing is an activity through which a person is con-tinually engaged with a variety of socially constituted systems" (Cooper, "Ecol-ogy" 367).

"Our traditional rhetoric reflects the logic which dominated Western science and culture from the early-seventeenth through the mid-twentieth centuries. That logic was precisely the opposite of an eco-logic: far from being designed for understanding wholeness, it was a set of methods for reducing wholes into com-ponent parts, which could then be arranged in order and analyzed individually" (Coe, "Eco-Logic" 232).

(c) "The ecological model usefully complicates the learning and teaching of writing because it reminds us of the social context in which all writers work" (Lindemann, "Three" 9).

"The 'ecological' or social or collaborative model focuses on writing in sit-uations in which authors actually *do* know their audiences and will, in fact, receive feedback from them during their writing process" (Fulkerson, "Com-position" 416).

(d) Richard M. Coe, Marilyn Cooper.

EGOCENTRISM

(a) A term used by cognitive-development psychologist Jean Piaget* in his studies of child logic and language use (*The Language and Thought of the Child*, originally published in 1926, and *The Child's Conception of Space* with B. Inhelder, originally published in 1956). Piaget divides the types of children's language into two groups: socialized and egocentric. In egocentric speech, children make no effort to adapt their talk to the needs of a listener; often the talk is about the children themselves. Piaget divides this type of speech into three categories: In *repetitive* speech, children repeat words and syllables for the mere enjoyment of hearing themselves speak, with no thought to a listener. In *monologue*, children "think out loud" with no attempt to address an **audience**. In *collective monologue*, children speak to someone, but this audience is not expected to understand or even respond. The presence of another serves only as a stimulus for the children to speak. Piaget uses the term *egocentrism* to describe the inability of the children exhibiting these three modes of speech to "de-center," to see beyond their own frame of reference and recognize the perspective of the receiver of their message. Russian psychologist Lev Vygotsky* calls this concept "inner speech" in opposition to "communicative speech" (*Thought and Language* 1962, originally published in 1934). The term has acquired negative connotations, though Piaget and Vygotsky describe it as a stage in the development of communication abilities.

While Piaget and Vygotsky focused their research on spoken communication, egocentrism has been adopted in composition studies in discussions of **cognitive processes** and audience awareness. **James Moffett**, in *Teaching the Universe of Discourse* (1968), claims that egocentrism has a part in ineffective written communication; and Barry Kroll, in "Cognitive Egocentrism and the Problem of Audience Awareness in Written Discourse" (1978), proposes and tests the hypothesis that egocentrism is more apparent in children's written communication than in their spoken communication because writing entails greater cognitive demands. He concludes that writers who are cognitively able to see beyond their own personal perspective are likely to exhibit audience awareness in written communication. This cognitive perspective moves audience analysis further from the study of the audience's demographic features toward the study of the writer's mental processes.

The concept of egocentrism was much discussed in composition studies in the late 1970s. In her influential work *Errors and Expectations* (1977), **Mina Shaughnessy** discusses the "egocentricity" of the beginning writer. Also in the late 1970s, **Linda Flower** introduces her term "**writer-based prose**." Flower fully developed and popularized the concept of egocentrism with her 1979 article "Writer-Based Prose: A Cognitive Basis for Problems in Writing," in which she argues that students' problems with writing could be linked to their lack of awareness of audience. She coined the term "writer-based" to refer to egocentric writing or writing that does not consider the reader's needs. By Flower's terminology, **reader-based prose** is more mature writing that meets the needs of the reader, and with the help of the instructor, students can turn their egocentric, writer-based prose into prose that is effective and reader-based. Others have also explained the problem that **basic**, or inexperienced, **writers** have in meeting their audience's needs as egocentric (see, for example, **Andrea Lunsford**'s 1979 article "Cognitive Development and the Basic Writer").

Recent research casts doubt on the role of egocentrism in these problems, questioning instead the nature of the writing task and the social context in which the writer writes. For example, James L. Collins and Michael M. Williamson (1984) propose that certain assignments may lead to egocentric writing. In his 1987 CCCC presentation, **Joseph Harris** argues from a social perspective that egocentric language does not indicate a cognitive failure on the writer's part but shows the difficulty in entering an unfamiliar **discourse community**. Recent social theorists point out that the concept of egocentrism implies that if the student would work harder and revise better, the writing problem could be remedied. In contrast, such theorists see writing "problems" in relation to social issues and contexts (see, for example, essays in **Theresa Enos'** 1987 edition *A Sourcebook for Basic Writing Teachers*). In composition studies, the term is often used in major journals and presentations beginning in the late 1970s through the early 1980s and then again in the late 1980s.

(b) "Ego-centric language is, as we have seen, the group made up by the first three of the categories we have enumerated—*repetition, monologue*, and *collective monologue*. All three have this in common that they consist of remarks that are not addressed to anyone, or not to anyone in particular, and that they evoke no reaction adapted to them on the part of anyone to whom they may chance to be addressed" (Piaget, *Language* 35).

"Even college-age students, who are presumably 'decentered' and relatively proficient oral communicators, may fail, when writing, to consider their readers' needs and expectations. Often this failure has been characterized as 'egocentricity' " (Kroll, "Rewriting" 121).

"the degree to which a person is unable to perceive the perspective and feelings of others" (Greenberg, "Research" 194).

(c) "It is clearly a natural, less cognitively demanding mode of thought and one which explains why people, who can express themselves in complex and highly intelligible modes, are often obscure. Egocentric expression happens to the best of us; it comes naturally" (Flower, "Writer-Based Prose" 22).

"Our studies lead to the conclusion that perhaps researchers (and teachers) evoke a tendency toward 'egocentric, context-dependent, dialogic' writing when they assign tasks that call for rather specialized writing that is simply too difficult for some writers to produce in isolation from necessary contexts" (Collins & Williamson 295).

"It is important to note that egocentrism does not imply selfishness; rather, it refers to a natural stage in a child's acquisition of communication skills" (Ede, "Audience" 145).

(d) Jean Piaget, basic writing theorists, cognitive development theorists.

ELABORATED CODE

(a) A term used by Basil Bernstein, a British educational sociologist, in *Class, Codes, and Control* (volume one was published in 1971, volume two in 1973,

and volume three in 1975) to describe a type of speaking or writing characterized by complicated sentence structure, a broad vocabulary, and context-
independence. According to Bernstein's research, working class children seldom
develop this code at home, whereas middle-class children do. He found that the
elaborated code is normally used by the middle classes, whose family life is
often "person-oriented" with emphasis on personal responsibility instead of on
strict authority structures. Thus when entering school, children with an elaborated code are at an advantage. They are able to work with syntactic abstractions
and varied sentence structures as well as to distance themselves from the words
they use and the context in and of which they speak. According to Bernstein,
students using this code will be receptive to loosely structured classroom techniques such as **collaborative** learning and **workshopping**. Bernstein defines the
"**restricted code**" in opposition to the elaborated.

In composition studies, the terms have been used to recommend a pedagogy
that teaches the elaborated code to those who have not learned it at home. In a
controversial article, John Rouse (1979) criticizes, based on Bernstein's codes,
the work of **Mina Shaughnessy**, arguing that her approach to **basic writing**
instruction harmfully "socializes" basic writers and "ignores" Bernstein's explanation of students' problems. Responding to Rouse, Gerald Graff* (1980) defends Shaughnessy, proposing that Rouse's pedagogical position may be harmful
to the students he hopes to "liberate." (See also Patricia Harkin's [1991] refu-
tation of Rouse's argument.) In "Class, Codes, and Composition: Basil Bernstein
and the Critique of Pedagogy" (1988), Myron Tuman links Bernstein's work to
composition studies' recent emphasis on acknowledging social and historical
factors that influence composition theory and pedagogy. Tuman argues that compositionists' dedication to nonauthoritarian, student-centered, **process** pedagogies may not be "liberating" for all students, but could actually be a form of
"domination" for those not socialized to thrive in "nontraditional" classrooms.

Though Bernstein's work does explain certain problems students have in writing classes, some scholars propose that the cause-and-effect relationship between
socioeconomics and language ability is not as simple as he suggests. For example, in "Reflections on Class and Language" (1982), **Richard Ohmann** argues that language choices are influenced by the specific context, which may
call either for a restricted code, an elaborated code, or a combination of the two.

(b) "a syntax which generates a large number of choices" (Bernstein 152).

"includes more adjectives, adverbs, prepositions, complex verbs. It facilitates
distinctions of all sorts, in particular logical ones . . . users distance themselves
more from the immediate situation and from the content of their talk, through
abstraction, through passives, through expressions of probability, through sup-
positions . . . through questions and refusals to commit themselves quickly to
definite interpretations of ambiguous experience" (Ohmann, "Reflections" 6).

(c) "Schools in the industrial society take people away from their familiar,
intimate places and require them to make their meanings plain to everyone, to
work with an elaborated code. Usually the middle-class child has learned those

speech forms and habits of mind needed for success in school and the outside world . . . but the lower-class child may not have been socialized in the same advantageous way" (Rouse 5).

"For Rouse, the elaborated code is the speech of alienated humanity in a fallen capitalist world; to teach it is therefore a form of oppression" (Graff, "Politics" 854).

"Partially in response to this criticism, Bernstein has gradually modified his claims, generally in the direction of a more complex (and less clear) correlation between socioeconomic class and the use of restricted and elaborated codes" (Fox 71).

(d) Basil Bernstein.

EMIC/ETIC

(a) Terms often used in discussions of case studies or **ethnographies**. In research, the term "emic" means an "insider's" point of view, or the point of view of those in the culture or environment being studied. In ethnographies and case studies, often the researcher may choose to study a culture by becoming a participant, rather than only an outside observer, in the culture in order to gain an "emic" perspective. A popular example in composition is the **teacher-researcher**, whose subject may be her or his own classroom. The term describes the role the researcher takes in relation to the subject of study, and it connotes an empathy and understanding of the subject of study. It is contrasted with the "etic" perspective, or the "outsider's" point of view. Researchers taking an etic approach do not participate in or attempt to become a part of the group they study. "Etic" can refer to the perspectives, preconceived notions, and expectations researchers bring to the research environment that without self-awareness might unintentionally cloud the study's results.

In composition studies, the terms "etic" and "emic" have been discussed in conjunction with descriptive research, most often in the late 1980s and 1990s as ethnography gained popularity as a method of composition research. During these years, many researchers have striven for contextual description and a critical awareness of their own "location" (cultural, political, gendered) in relation to the subject of study. By examining the etic attitudes and personal positions they bring to their study, researchers hope to gain access to a more emic perspective and thus to gain a deeper and more ethical insight into their subject. In the middle to late 1990s, however, researchers have shown concern over the potential for ethical breeches even in studies based on an emic perspective; for example, qualitative researchers must carefully weigh choices of self-representation and subject representation as they record for publication the results of their studies; also they must ethically handle what Thomas Newkirk (1996) calls the "bad news," a potentially embarrassing or insulting portrayal of the research subject ("Seduction" 3).

(b) "the insider's perspective and beliefs" (Zaharlick & Green 215, describing emic).

"outsider's perspective" (Zaharlick & Green 215, describing etic).

"At the root of most ethnographic research is the native's perspective (the emic perspective), usually accessible to ethnographers through fieldwork" (Moss 157).

"The journalist often writes from the outsider perspective, quoting insiders. The fieldworker must combine an outsider's point of view with an insider's perspective. Anthropologists use the term *emic* to mean the insider perspective and *etic* to refer to that of the outsider" (Chiseri-Strater & Sunstein 14).

(c) "Case study research . . . builds an 'emic' reconstruction of the respondents' constructions in contrast to an 'etic' one that would reinforce a positivist's *a priori* inquiries" (Bridwell-Bowles 106).

"One version of the argument in anthropology marches to the tune of emic and etic—the former emphasizing folk concepts and the latter stressing those of the ethnographer" (Agar 45).

"Research that begins from the emic perspective of a participant, rather than the etic perspective of the observer, raises its own forms of ethical and representational issues" (Ray, "Afterword" 292).

(d) ethnographers and other descriptive researchers.

ENGFISH

(a) A term coined by **Ken Macrorie** in 1970 to describe the "overdone," stilted, "dishonest" prose that Macrorie found students (and professors) to be writing on a regular basis. The reason for this lifeless language, he concluded, was the lack of respect teachers showed for students' own voices. **William E. Coles, Jr.,** uses the term "themewriting" to describe this same prose. To combat Engfish, Macrorie urged **freewriting** and "honesty" in writing. Though no one would object to Macrorie's critique of stiff, difficult prose, some critics, especially **social constructionists**, object to the concept of a true voice or the implication that one can write successfully only in a true voice—that writers cannot write in many and varied voices, depending on the context. "Engfish" has become a common term in composition studies since Macrorie popularized it in the 1970s. It stands for that which writing instructors hope to combat in the composition classroom.

(b) "the bloated, pretentious language I saw everywhere around me, in the students' themes, in the textbooks on writing, in the professors' and administrators' communications to each other. A feel-nothing, say-nothing language, dead like Latin, devoid of the rhythms of contemporary speech" (Macrorie, *Uptaught* 361).

"An individual style that avoids cliché, jargon, and stereotypes is preferable to pretentious or derivative language (Macrorie calls it 'Engfish')" (Lindemann, "Three" 8).

(c) "The sign of <u>Engfish</u> is not merely a big vocabulary; it is marked also by dishonest or empty use of words, either to mislead so that real truth may be hidden or to obfuscate so that the writer's ignorance won't show" (Crowley & Redman 280).

" 'Provocative' topics stimulate cant and cliché; they breed <u>Engfish</u>; they lead to debate, which is by no means dialectic" (Berthoff, "Is Teaching" 754).

"Macrorie's 'natural voice' versus 'institutional-<u>Engfish</u> voice' pair does not ring so 'true' anymore, now that natural voices seem themselves shot through with cultural conditionings" (Hill 108).

(d) Ken Macrorie.

ENGLISH COALITION CONFERENCE

(a) A three-week-long conference that took place in the summer of 1987 at Wye Plantation in Maryland. The purpose of the conference was to attempt a consensus about English education and its goals for the coming decades and to find solutions to lingering problems caused, for instance, by changing student populations and institutional environments. The theme of the conference was "Democracy through Language," which reiterated participants' view that for students to become better citizens, they must learn to analyze, question, reflect, and make meaning, instead of passively consuming knowledge handed down from authoritative sources.

Sixty English teachers (elementary, secondary, and university levels) participated in the conference, and these participants were selected by those organizations that made up the coalition—the College English Association, the Association of Departments of English, the College Language Association, the Modern Language Association, the **National Council of Teachers of English, (NCTE)** the **Conference on College Composition and Communication, (CCCC)**, the Conference of Secondary School English Department Chairs, and the Conference on English Education. The roots of the ECC can be traced to the 1982 MLA convention where the officers and staff members of a majority of the above organizations met and decided to form a coalition to address common concerns about education reform. The conference itself was fueled by an inability of the coalition to come to consensus on reform issues. The Andrew W. Mellon and Rockefeller foundations along with the Exxon Education Foundation and the National Endowment for the Humanities funded the conference.

As reported in **Richard Lloyd-Jones** and **Andrea Lunsford**'s edition of the official report of the conference (1987), **Peter Elbow**'s *What Is English?* (1990), and Julie Jensen's edition *Stories to Grow On: Demonstrations of Language Learning in K–8 Classrooms* (1989), conference participants agreed that English studies encompassed more than an emphasis on writing, language, and literature; for English also includes reading, speaking, and listening. Participants also saw benefits in integrating the students' knowledge of language gained from home and community with the language skills taught in school. They argued against tracking (the placement of students into hierarchical educational tiers) and for improved working conditions for teachers. Other items of consensus included agreement that students should be active learners, interacting with each other as well as with the teacher, and that students must become critical users and learners of language, able to reflect on their own use of language as well as on the way language is used in society. Also considered important was students' need to negotiate new information technology and to articulate their own views while also respecting and understanding diverse opinions. Participants drafted an additional list of resolutions pertaining to all subgroups and dealing with issues such as student assessment, the use of media in the classroom, and teacher professional development. Participants also endorsed the **Wyoming Conference Resolution**, recognizing the need to improve working conditions for many college writing instructors.

Criticisms of the conference include that of Daniel Mahala and Jody Swilky who in "Remapping the Geography of Service in English" (1997) fault conference participants for not adequately acknowledging the different cultural, economic, and social locations represented both at the conference itself and at the various institutions represented by the conference. For compositionists, the ECC has not seemed as influential nor as controversial as the widely recognized **Dartmouth Seminar**.

(b) "Unlike the Dartmouth Conference, which was attended primarily by college and university professors, the Coalition Conference brought together teachers from all levels of schooling" (Lloyd-Jones & Lunsford xix).

(c) "In short, the main conclusion of the conference may be that we see the same constructive and social activity as the central process at all levels of the profession in English. Inherent in the overarching emphasis on making meaning is the principle of getting the learner to be active, not passive: learning as hypothesis making, world building, experiential—and active, especially in the process of questioning and reflecting back on what one has been doing" (Elbow, *What* 19).

"The ECC attended only tangentially to the radically different politics of location in the lives of conference participants and their students. Its report develops a progressive understanding of 'theory' as a critical reflexivity about language, but rather than theorizing a terrain of competing needs, it positions theory as a kind of umbrella for English specialisms, an implicit justification for an accretive model of disciplinary change" (Mahala & Swilky 637).

"Accounts of the English Coalition Conference, which was called to establish our sense of self, agree that no such sense was forthcoming" (Moran 202).

(d) Phyllis Franklin (of MLA), Jack Maxwell (of NCTE); for further information, see Peter Elbow, Richard Lloyd-Jones and Andrea Lunsford, Julie Jensen.

ENVIRONMENTAL MODE OF INSTRUCTION

(a) A term developed by **George Hillocks, Jr.**, in his research during the early and mid-1980s and popularized in *Research on Written Composition: New Directions for Teaching* (1986). Hillocks' purpose was to examine recent empirical research in composition, extending **Richard Braddock, Richard Lloyd-Jones**, and Lowell Schoer's *Research in Written Composition* published in 1963. Hillocks analyzed approximately two thousand studies conducted from 1963 to 1982. He then conducted extensive meta-analysis on sixty studies from his analysis.

According to Hillocks' meta-analysis of experimental research, the environmental mode is the most effective mode of composition instruction, as opposed to three other categories of instruction, including the presentational, natural process, and individual modes. The environmental mode describes a teaching method in which lectures and teacher-led discussion are minimal, while group work and student interaction occupy most of the class time. Often the students' work serves as the topic of discussion. Though traditional lectures are not characteristic of this mode, the teacher does provide clear and specific objectives for each class. Ideally, the teacher offers some structure but does not stifle the students' own interests. Grammar is not emphasized in this method, though Hillocks sees work on the sentence level as useful.

Hillocks' work has been criticized and debated. An often-cited criticism is that of **Arthur Applebee** (1986), who questions the distinctions between Hillocks' modes of instruction, arguing that the environmental mode is simply a structured version of the **process** method of instruction. Alan Purves (1988) also expresses similar concern over Hillocks' labels and categorizations. Perhaps because of these problems with categorization, Hillocks' label of "environmental" writing has not caught on in composition studies, as have, for example, the **"current-traditional"** and **"expressive."** The environmental mode of instruction is mostly discussed in reference to Hillocks' work.

(b) "teaching that creates environments to induce and support active learning of complex strategies that students are not capable of using on their own" (Hillocks, *Teaching* 55).

"[pedagogical approaches] with specific objectives and which engage students in specifiable processes" (Newkirk, "Politics" 125).

(c) "Hillocks found that an environmental mode and a focus on inquiry were the most beneficial pedagogies for improving writing" (Smit, "Some Difficulties" 54).

"*Research on Written Communication* generally avoids the use of obvious metaphors, though it cannot entirely do so. Hillocks' favored mode of instruction, the 'environmental' mode, for instance, depends not only on the results of meta-analysis but also on the metaphoric implications of the term 'environmental' for its persuasive impact" (Ede, "Teaching Writing" 124).

(d) George Hillocks, Jr.

EPISTEMIC (see SOCIAL EPISTEMIC)

ESSENTIALISM (ANTI-ESSENTIALISM)

(a) A term used by Stephen Resnick and Richard Wolff in *Knowledge and Class: A Marxian Critique of Political Economy* (1987) to define the assumption that every object, being, or circumstance can be explained by determining the causes of the event or of the effect. The opposite of essentialism is anti-essentialism, the refusal to see a phenomenon as the result of only one or a few effects. An anti-essentialist will recognize the complexities and not reduce an event to the product of simple cause and effect. The meaning of the term is similar to that of Stanley Fish's term **"foundationalism"** except that "essentialism," according to Patricia Harkin (1991), connotes a less than innocent, possibly intentional, reductionism. In many uses, however, the term does appear to be used interchangeably with "foundationalism."

Harkin uses the term in her argument for a reevaluation of **practitioner's lore**. She argues against the tendency, especially in composition studies' embrace of theory, to discredit lore, proposing that it is "anti-essential," refusing to reduce complex situations to cut-and-dried, "scientific" cause-and-effect relations. The term is also used to refer to stereotypical definitions of "masculine" and "feminine"; many poststructuralists, **social constructionists**, and feminists argue that such assumptions (for example, that women are innately emotional) are grounded in essentialism. An anti-essentialist would see character traits as the result of many undefinable variables, including, but not limited to, culture, class, gender, and race.

In most cases, "essentialism" is the negative term, and anti-essentialism the positive. This is not always the case, however, as feminists, including Diana Fuss (1989) and Gayatri Chakravorty Spivak (1990), have proposed a positive or "strategic" use of essentialism. Fuss sees essentialism as a stage that disenfranchised groups go through in finding identity and in gaining political consciousness. For Spivak, essentialism is unavoidable in discourse; therefore, the critic's responsibility is to use essentialism strategically in critical analysis, always aware that the argument stands on an essentialist premise.

An application of Fuss and Spivak's ideas to the composition classroom is found, for example, in Donna Qualley's 1994 article in which she argues that one of her first-year composition students should begin her study of feminism from an essentialist perspective in order to form a collective feminist identity before recognizing the different kinds and views of feminism. In composition studies, the terms "essentialism" and "anti-essentialism" appear most frequently in the 1990s.

(b) "presumption . . . that any apparent complexity—a person, a relationship, a historical occurrence, and so forth—can be analyzed to reveal a simplicity lying at its core . . . the presumption that among the influences apparently producing any outcome, some can be shown to be inessential to its occurrence while others will be shown to be essential causes" (Resnick & Wolff 2–3).

"The foundationalism that for Fish is merely naive becomes for Resnick and Wolff an 'essentialism' that is reductive in a particularly dangerous way" (Harkin, "Postdisciplinary" 133).

(c) "In other words, when we stop talking about a split world—a world possessing an intrinsic nature set apart from an internal realm of mental states—and, instead, start talking about how we employ our vocabularies, we can get beyond essentialism and stop imagining that words possess a transcendental essence beyond the everyday pragmatic uses we give them" (Kent, "Talking Differently" 261).

"But it is not possible, within discourse, to escape essentializing somewhere. . . . In deconstructive critical practice, you have to be aware that you are going to essentialize anyway. So then strategically you can look at essentialisms, not as descriptions of the way things are, but as something that one must adopt to produce a critique of anything" (Spivak 51).

(d) Stephen Resnick and Richard Wolff, feminists, social constructionists.

ETHIC OF CARE

(a) A term made popular after social scientist Carol Gilligan used it in her influential book *In a Different Voice* (1982). By focusing her study on women, Gilligan reevaluates Lawrence Kohlberg's proposal of a moral hierarchy favoring men (1958, 1981). Kohlberg's six stages of moral development are based on his analysis over twenty years of eighty-four boys, yet he claims universality for his study. Subsequent studies indicated that those groups not included in Kohlberg's study, especially women, do not often reach what Kohlberg sees as the highest stage of moral maturity in which moral decisions are made based on abstract ideals of justice and rights.

In her study, Gilligan found that whereas men tend to make moral decisions according to a hierarchy of justice, or morality of rights, women often make such decisions based on the specific context and on relationships involved. Such moral decision making Gilligan calls an "ethic of care," and she claims that this perspective stems from women's traditional role as caregivers. Kohlberg's hierarchical stages of development, Gilligan argues, undervalue women's perspectives and the importance of care in moral decision making. Nell Noddings in *Caring: A Feminine Approach to Ethics and Moral Education* (1984) and Mary Field Belenky, Blythe McVicker Clinchy, Nancy Rule Goldberger, and Jill Mattuck Tarule in *Women's Ways of Knowing: The Development of Self, Voice, and Mind* (1986) further develop this idea.

Gilligan's alternative scheme of moral development has been welcomed as a model to inform composition courses. Informed by Gilligan's work, David Bleich, in *The Double Perspective* (1988), proposes that the **cognitive process** approach reflects an individual approach to language learning, not one that emphasizes relationships and context—elements of a "feminine" mode of thinking. As an alternative, Bleich argues for a social approach to language instruction. Especially in the mid-1980s and early 1990s, composition scholars have argued for additional assignments that do not reward only objectivity and linear narrative, but that value "feminine" perspectives and approaches and explore gender differences (see, for example, Pamela Annas' "Style as Politics: A Feminist Approach to the Teaching of Writing" [1985], **Elizabeth Flynn**'s "Composing as a Woman" [1988], and Catherine Lamb's "Beyond Argument in Feminist Composition" [1991]). Peter Mortensen and Gesa Kirsch (1993) propose a definition of classroom **authority** that is informed by an ethic of care. Later arguments, advanced by scholars including Susan V. Wall (1994), question this "feminine" approach to composition, cautioning that environment, not only gender, must be considered. In this line of thought, Eileen E. Schell (1998) urges a "feminist" ethic of care that recognizes classroom difference and conflict and that challenges social constructs and stereotypes of feminine caring.

(b) "Epitomized early on in Creon's battle with Antigone, men within the long tradition of Western rationality have often deemed moral decisions based in the value that one should not harm friends and family—Gilligan's "ethic of care"—as lacking in objectivity and compromised in refusing impartiality" (Swearingen 126).

"While an ethic of justice proceeds from the premise of equality—that everyone should be treated the same—an ethic of care rests on the premise of nonviolence—that no one should be hurt" (Gilligan 174).

(c) "Operating under the guidance of an ethic of caring, we are not likely to find abortion in general either right or wrong. We shall have to inquire into individual cases" (Noddings 87).

"An ethic of care, we argue, presents one possibility for rethinking notions of objectified, stable, autonomous authority" (Mortensen & Kirsch 557).

"Given the feminist contention over this concept, how can we exercise an ethic of care in feminist composition studies that simultaneously encourages caring relations and empowers those who care, both physically and economically? We can begin by thinking of care as a socially constructed interaction, not as a natural instinct or impulse that women possess" (Schell 80).

(d) Mary Belenky et al., Elizabeth Flynn, Gesa Kirsch and Peter Mortensen, Carol Gilligan, Nell Noddings, Eileen Schell.

ETHNOGRAPHY/ETHNOGRAPHERS

(a) A descriptive experimental method used in the social sciences, especially in anthropology, and derived from phenomenological theory in which the researcher studies a person or group of people in their own environment. Ethnography is a qualitative approach to research, as are case studies. Context is of extreme importance in obtaining valid and reliable results; therefore, the researcher goes to the subject instead of requiring the subject to come to the laboratory. In addition to the actual study, researchers produce an interpretative account of their observations, and, as in phenomenology, many different interpretations of an ethnographic account are common and even encouraged. A purpose of ethnographic study is to learn about another culture while gaining insight into one's own. Those who practice ethnography as a means of research are called ethnographers. Margaret Mead's studies offer examples of early ethnography, and the work of anthropologist Clifford Geertz,* especially *The Interpretation of Cultures* (1973), is integral to modern uses of ethnography and to composition studies' adoption of the method. Examples of ethnographic studies include **Shirley Brice Heath**'s study of working- and middle-class families in the Carolina Piedmont (*Ways with Words: Language, Life, and Work in Communities and Classrooms* [1983]), and Stephen Doheny-Farina's study of **collaborative writing** in a computer software company ("Writing in an Emerging Organization" [1986]).

Ethnography became important in composition studies beginning in the 1980s, with the field's emphasis on social theories of writing. Early articles on the subject include Martha King's 1978 "Research in Composition: A Need for Theory," in which she calls for more emphasis on context in composition research, and specifically for ethnographic research; in 1981, Kenneth Kantor, Dan Kirby, and Judith Goetz published "Research in Context: Ethnographic Studies in English Education," an influential article proposing the use of ethnography in English studies. For Kantor and his colleagues, ethnography was appropriate for research into language teaching and learning because of its emphasis on hypothesis generation, context, **thick description, participant-observation**, and the making of meaning. In the 1990s, however, Kantor and his colleagues' portrayal of ethnography has been criticized for failing to recognize ethical implications of ethnographic research. Discussions of such research in composition studies during the 1990s, especially the mid- to late 1990s, often encompasses issues such as the researcher's authority, values, and responsibilities to the subjects of the research. (See, for example, *Ethics and Representation in Qualitative Studies of Literacy* [1996], edited by Peter Mortensen and Gesa Kirsch.)

In addition to serving as a research method for composition scholars, ethnography can be a tool for composition students. Many argue that using ethnography as a research method in the classroom allows students **authority** over their work, possibly minimizing the student-teacher hierarchy. Others point out that such an approach stimulates students' interest in their topics. Additionally, advocates of ethnography in the classroom value the method's focus on the students' experiences and argue that it encourages personal **reflection** as well as social criticism. Some propose that an ethnographic approach should replace the traditional research paper. (For more discussion of how ethnography is incorporated into the classroom, see articles by Thomas Recchio [1991], William Wright [1991],

Wendy Bishop [1994], Patricia Roberts and Virginia Pompei Jones [1995], and Matthew Wilson [1995].)

Although introduced early, the term was used most often in composition scholarship from the late 1980s to the mid-1990s. The emphasis on ethnographic research in composition studies can be seen as a reaction to disillusionment with more "scientific" research, such as **protocol analysis**. Though very popular in the early 1980s, by the mid-1980s, protocol research was widely criticized for disrupting the natural environment of the subject studied and for drawing conclusions based on artificial context. In contrast to protocol research, ethnography attempts to maintain the natural environment of the research subject.

Problems with ethnographic studies include their context-dependence, which makes questionable the application of ethnographic results to general situations other than the particular one studied. Researchers also often have problems blending with the culture they are studying in a way that will not cause the subjects to change their normal behavior. (See also **emic/etic**, **thick description**, and **teacher-researcher**.)

(b) "Drawing on the theories and methods of educational sociology, anthropology, applied linguistics, and communications, ethnographers attempt to observe and describe phenomena in the contexts in which they actually occur" (Greenberg, "Research" 200).

"a qualitative research method that allows a researcher to gain a comprehensive view of the social interactions, behaviors, and beliefs of a community or social group. In other words, the goal of an ethnographer is to study, explore, and describe a group's culture" (Moss 155).

(c) "Doing ethnography is like trying to read (in the sense of 'construct a reading of') a manuscript—foreign, faded, full of ellipses, incoherencies, suspicious emendations, and tendentious commentaries, but written not in conventionalized graphs of sound but in transient examples of shaped behavior" (Geertz *Interpretation* 10).

"Ethnographic methodology in the 1970s and 1980s has been used to examine the immediate communities in which writers learn to write—the family and the classroom" (Faigley, "Competing" 536).

"One especially powerful way to have students reflect on their experience is through teaching methods of ethnography. . . . In short, the students experience research as a moving negotiation between what one once knew and what one is learning" (Roberts & Jones 538).

"If the other is the enabling condition of ethnographic research, I will argue, then an ethnography must be both an adequate account of the literate practices of others and accountable to those others" (P. Sullivan, "Ethnography" 98).

(d) Wendy Bishop, **Linda Brodkey**, Clifford Geertz, Shirley Brice Heath, **George Hillocks**; ethnographic studies have been done by researchers such as Elizabeth Chiseri-Strater, Stephen Doheny-Farina, **Donald Graves**, Kenneth Kantor, Dan Kirby and Judith Goetz, **Lee Odell** and **Dixie Goswami**, Carol Talbert.

ETIC (see EMIC)

EXPRESSIONISM (OR NEO-PLATONISM)

(a) A term used by **James Berlin** in "Contemporary Composition: The Major Pedagogical Theories" (1982) to describe one of four pedagogical theories he finds in the modern composition classroom. Those who hold this theory are called Expressionists. (Those who hold the other dominant pedagogical theories are labeled by Berlin as **neo-Aristotelians** or classicists, **positivists** or **current-traditionalists**, and **new rhetoricians**). He uses the term again in his 1988 article, "Rhetoric and Ideology in the Writing Class" as one of three rhetorics that influence current composition studies (the others are **cognitive** psychology and **social epistemic**). "Expressionism" and "neo-Platonism" are the terms that he uses to describe the pedagogical theory that arose in reaction to the current-traditional pedagogical theory. Expressionism, according to Berlin, can be traced to American transcendentalism and even back to Plato and has roots in romanticism and pragmatism. It gained widespread support after the **Dartmouth seminar**, where participants emphasized the advantages of writing instruction guided by an active, student-oriented philosophy. In the 1960s and 1970s, expressionism was associated with critique of the dominant culture. Often the terms "**expressive**" or "**expressivist**" are substituted for "expressionism" to indicate the same or similar concept as Berlin describes (see, for example, **Richard Fulkerson**'s "Composition Theory in the Eighties: Axiological Consensus and Paradigmatic Diversity" [1990]).

Expressionist or expressive theories of rhetoric emphasize the individual, and writing is seen as a creative art through which the self is discovered. This view implies that writing, as art, cannot be taught directly; therefore, the teacher cannot give explicit instruction in writing, but can create an inviting environment in which the student can learn. In the classroom, students often engage in dialogue with one another and the teacher about their writing. As Berlin points out, in engaging in class discussion, the students are attempting not to adapt their message to their **audience,** but to omit material that is not "true" or "authentic." A goal of many expressionists is to help students write in an **authentic voice**.

Although the emphasis on the individual is a defining factor of this rhetoric, it is also, according to Berlin, its greatest limitation in that the individual cannot create societal change in isolation. Berlin also maintains that in this rhetoric we see the roots of **process** views of writing. Berlin labels the work of **Peter Elbow, William Coles, Jr. Walker Gibson, Ken Macrorie**, and **Donald Murray** as recent examples of expressionist rhetoric, although others have criticized Berlin's expressionist category, claiming that it limits the work and goals of the above scholars (see, for example, Mark Wiley's "Writing in the American Grain" [1989]). In composition studies, the term itself is seen most often in discussions in the late 1980s to the mid-1990s. The philosophy it describes was most popular in the 1960s and 1970s, although in the middle to late 1990s, scholars have looked to this view with new interest.

(b) "the conviction that reality is a personal and private construct. For the expressionist, truth is always discovered within, through an internal glimpse, an examination of the private inner world" (Berlin, *Rhetoric and Reality* 145, describing the common epistemology of expressionistic approaches).

"Berlin grants that, unlike the Cognitive school, Expressionistic rhetoric embraces as one of its primary aims a critique of a dominant and corrupt society. Unfortunately, Berlin concludes, the Expressionists' epistemology is its own worst enemy, defining resistance in purely individual rather than collaborative and social terms" (Freisinger 257).

(c) "In the case of expressionists, for example, I distinguish those influenced by surrealism, from those influenced by group therapy techniques, from those concerned with overt political action inside and outside of the classroom, from those who wish to replace overt political action with a privatized politics of self-discovery" (Berlin, "Comment" 775).

"At the extreme, advocates of expressionism argue that students, when left alone, develop a 'natural,' even transcendent, voice" (Yancey ix).

(d) James Berlin, William Coles, Jr., Peter Elbow, Walker Gibson, Ken Macrorie, Donald Murray, **Donald C. Stewart**.

EXPRESSIVE WRITING (EXPRESSIVISM)

(a) A term used by **James Britton** in *The Development of Writing Abilities (11–18)* (1975) to describe one of three categories of writing functions; the other two are **transactional** and **poetic** writing, both of which, according to Britton, develop from expressive writing. He developed these terms based on the various forms of writing done by British secondary school children ages eleven to eighteen. In his study, Britton found that expressive writing was seldom, if ever, practiced in school; it accounted for 5.5 percent of writing done by each group of children studied. In Britton's definition, expressive writing is personal writing not intended for an external audience, but often used to explore ideas or feelings. Those writing expressively pay little attention to formal stylistic or grammatical constraints but write freely to verbalize personal thoughts and ideas. Proponents of expressive writing argue that this type of personal writing allows writers to explore and develop independent thoughts. A popular pedagogical use of expressive writing is the journal.

In "Competing Theories of Process: A Critique and a Proposal" (1986), **Lester Faigley** uses the term "expressive" to describe one of three major views on composing. (His other categories include the **cognitive** and the social.) Faigley finds the modern roots of this view in the "romantic" notions expressed in early composition research, such as that of D. Gordon Rohman and Albert Wlecke (1964). Romantic ideas of "good" writing found in expressive views include emphasis on integrity, spontaneity, and the abilities of the unconscious as well as on the separation of thinking and writing. Richard Fulkerson (1979) also lists "expressive" as one of his four categories of composition philosophies, and those who hold this philosophy are called "expressivists." (See **expressionist** for a similar concept, but describing **James Berlin**'s pedagogical taxonomy; often expressivist and expressionist are used interchangeably.)

Some teachers, including some composition teachers, are wary of using expressive writing in the classroom because they fear that in emphasizing personal, informal writing, teachers will neglect "basic" writing skills such as grammar. Also, expressive writing is difficult to evaluate, since students write about personal, sometimes sensitive, topics. More recent criticisms are that the expressive view ignores the writer's social context and does not recognize the poststructuralist concept of the self as shaped by historical, social, and economic factors (see, for example, Henry Giroux's *Theory and Resistance in Education: A Pedagogy for the Opposition* [1983]). Many critics of expressivism are **social constructionists** or **radical pedagogists** who prefer writing instruction that emphasizes cultural critique, with students learning to recognize the hierarchical and interested positions embedded in everyday discourse and institutions.

A recent trend in composition studies is the reevaluation of expressivism. Some feminists prefer the expressive emphasis on the personal and nonhierarchical. Others, however, argue that an expressive pedagogy may not always work for women and other minority teachers. A female teacher's nonhierarchical approach may serve to support societal stereotypes that question the validity of women authority figures, seeing women instead as caregivers and nurturers. Also, with female and minority **authority** often in question and hard-won, many such teachers experience classroom difficulty when parting with authority. (See **Susan Jarratt**'s "Feminism and Composition: The Case for Conflict [1991], Jill Eichhorn et al.'s "A Symposium on Feminist Experiences in the Composition Classroom" [1992], and Michelle Payne's "Rend(er)ing Women's Authority in the Writing Classroom" [1994].)

Advocates of **writing across the curriculum** such as **Art Young** and **Toby Fulwiler** (*Writing Across the Disciplines* [1986]) propose that expressive writing, as in journals and logs, should be an important ingredient of writing done in all classrooms regardless of discipline. Such writing, they argue, helps students learn the material and become comfortable with it as they make it their own through writing. Other scholars are now examining expressive theories in relation to social views. In 1990, the journal PRE/TEXT devoted an entire issue to expressive writing. In addition, Stephen M. Fishman and Lucille McCarthy (1992, 1995) explore the relationship between expressivism and social views of writing, and in 1994, Kathleen Blake Yancey edited an NCTE publication on voice, a central concern of expressivist pedagogy. Lad Tobin and Thomas Newkirk also published a 1994 collection (dedicated to James Britton) discussing the writing **process** movement, largely from an expressive point of view. Many who sanction a reemergence of expressive writing argue that social and expressive views of writing are not dichotomies. The term frequently appears in composition conversations beginning in the late 1970s, with most citations occurring in the late 1980s to the mid-1990s, as the term undergoes a reevaluation.

(b) "This form of writing is essentially written to oneself, as in diaries, journals and first-draft papers—or to trusted people very close to the writer, as in personal letters . . . [and it] often looks like speech written down and is usually characterized by first-person pronouns, informal style, and colloquial diction" (Fulwiler 24).

"The expressive approach, such as that popularized by Ken Macrorie, sees *language* primarily as the expression of the personal perceptions, feelings, and thoughts of the *writer*. . . . The primary goal of an expressive course in writing is the honest expressing of personal truths" (Dowst 67).

"writing that makes sense to the writer but has not yet been shaped in such a way that it makes sense to a reader" (Flynn, McCulley & Gratz 161).

(c) "At times, I am led to see the litany of gripes with expressivist practices from politically concerned theorists as emerging from their particular visions of revolutionary change in politics and culture, their implicit assumption that any change not accompanied by trumpet blasts and a comprehensive epistemology must be a mere pantomime of change" (O'Donnell 437).

"Where the social constructivists and cultural critics come together with the traditionalists, then, is in their criticism of expressivism and personal writing, and so that is where the critique of the writing process movement has been strongest" (Tobin, "Introduction" 6).

(d) James Britton, **William Coles, Jr., Peter Elbow**, Lester Faigley, Richard Fulkerson, Toby Fulwiler, **Walker Gibson, Stephen Tchudi (Judy)**, Ken Macrorie, James Miller, **James Moffett, Donald Murray, Donald C. Stewart**, Art Young.

FELT SENSE

(a) A term coined by philosopher Eugene Gendlin and explained in his book *Focusing* (1978). Felt sense describes a "fuzzy" impression or reaction writers experience when encountering certain words or contexts. These reactions are based on writers' past experiences that are in some way invoked by specific words or topics. The feelings serve as a vague inspiration and can be felt not only in the mind but in the body. As writers contemplate the "fuzzy" images and impressions the topic or word produces, they eventually capture the essence of the thought and are able to progress in their writing. In earlier work, Gendlin spoke of "felt meaning," urging teachers to pay more attention to this cognitive process. In composition studies, **Sondra Perl** is responsible for popularizing this concept in her studies of the **cognitive processes** of composing. In her 1980 article "Understanding Composing," Perl discusses felt sense as a **recursive** move and an integral part of a successful writing process.

(b) "the soft underbelly of thought . . . a kind of bodily awareness that . . . can be used as a tool . . . a bodily awareness that . . . encompasses everything you feel and know about a given subject at a given time"(Gendlin 35).

"a basic step in the process of composing that skilled writers rely on even when they are unaware of it and that less skilled writers can be taught. This process seems to rely on very careful attention to one's inner reflections and is often accompanied with bodily sensations" (Perl, "Understanding" 367).

(c) "as any teacher who has seriously tested journal writing knows, certain forces of popularly accessible 'evidence'—folk belief, anecdote, 'felt-sense,' qualitative observations, speculative analogies—assert themselves with greater force in the more open forum that journals should represent" (Mahala 785).

"Writers often have only a 'felt sense' of their intentions without ever articulating them, but they know how to use their unarticulated intentions to determine that something is amiss and to decide what to do about their problems" (Beach, "Demonstrating" 59–60).

(d) Eugene Gendlin, Sondra Perl.

FOUNDATIONALISM (ANTI-FOUNDATIONALISM)

(a) Terms used by Stanley Fish, borrowed from Richard Rorty.* Rorty develops the term "foundationalism" in *Philosophy and the Mirror of Nature* (1979), and Fish expands the usage of the term in his articles "Consequences" (1985) and "Anti-foundationalism, Theory Hope, and the Teaching of Composition" (1987). In composition studies, **Patricia Bizzell** popularized the term in "Foundationalism and Anti-Foundationalism in Composition Studies" (1986). Foundationalism describes the assumption that there is an objective truth, or absolute foundation, on which to base arguments and discourse. Such a foundation is not restricted to certain contexts but is considered universally valid. To Fish, any claim to know "the right way" is naive. Fish uses the term "anti-foundationalism" to describe the philosophies of various scholars, such as Richard Rorty, Thomas Kuhn,* Clifford Geertz,* and Jacques Derrida.* **Social constructionists** and poststructuralists consider themselves anti-foundationalists or nonfoundational, since they see knowledge and fact as historically and contextually situated, not as objective truth. Anti-foundationalists rely on **interpretive communities**, another of Fish's terms, to reach agreement, since there is no objective standard on which to agree.

Some scholars caution that social constructionists are approaching foundationalism because of their fervent belief in their own philosophy's "rightness" (see, for example, James Porter [1990]). Fish himself makes a similar point in his warning against "**theory hope**," asserting that many anti-foundationalists slip into foundationalism by assuming that anti-foundationalism allows access to the "truth," even if "truth" is interpreted to be an absence of truth. Another often-cited problem associated with anti-foundational philosophies is that they allow a critique of dominant ideologies but do not provide a method for change or improvement. Patricia Bizzell, in her 1990 article "Beyond Anti-Foundationalism to Rhetorical Authority," following the direction of some feminists and Marxists, sanctions a move away from anti-foundationalism in the classroom and encourages a rhetorical approach in which instructors make explicit their own beliefs and even attempt to persuade students to agree with them. Similarly, David Smit ("Hall of Mirrors: Antifoundationalist Theory and the Teaching of Writing" [1995]) questions the benefits of a purely anti-foundational approach, critiquing what he sees as composition studies' whole-hearted and unexamined acceptance of anti-foundationalism, urging a closer examination of this popular perspective, especially of how or even if it informs writing instruction. The terms "foundationalism" and "anti-foundationalism" appear frequently in composition's conversations beginning in the late 1980s.

(b) "By foundationalism I mean any attempt to ground inquiry and communication in something more firm and stable than mere belief or unexamined practice" (Fish, "Anti-Foundationalism" 65).

"Anti-foundationalism teaches that questions of fact, truth, correctness, validity, and clarity can neither be posed nor answered in reference to some extra-contextual, ahistorical, nonsituational reality, or rule, or law or value" (Fish, "Anti-Foundationalism" 67).

"For Stanley Fish, for instance, any sort of philosophical or ethical system which suggests that any kind of standard exists objectively is a form of 'foundationalism,' and foundationalism is always anti-rhetorical, formalist, and archaic" (Roberts & Jones 535).

(c) "The social constructionist alternative to this foundational cognitive assumption is nonfoundational. It assumes that there is no such thing as a universal foundation, ground, framework, or structure or knowledge" (Bruffee, "Social Construction" 774–75).

"If antifoundationalism is to have any relevance to composition and rhetoric, it must offer some convincing suggestions about how we ought to teach writing, suggestions which seem to be organic or integral to the theory" (Smit, "Hall" 41).

"Though these revisionists have accused traditional rhetoric historians (like Robert Connors) of foundationalism, their own position has itself become a foundation, privileged arbitrarily for its ironic posture" (J. Porter 200).

"In their deconstructive mode, the anti-foundationalist critics do point out the effect of historical circumstances on notions of the true and good which their opponents claim are outside time. . . . But once the ideological interest has been pointed out, the anti-foundationalists throw up their hands" (Bizzell, "Beyond Anti-Foundationalism" 667).

(d) Stanley Fish, Richard Rorty, social constructionists in composition studies, including Patricia Bizzell and **Kenneth Bruffee**.

FREEWRITING

(a) A term originating in the 1960s with **Ken Macrorie** and often used and popularized by **Peter Elbow** in the early 1970s. It describes a method of writing instruction in which students for short periods write nonstop about whatever comes to mind. According to its proponents, freewriting helps students become more comfortable and confident with writing and also helps them to think clearly and to see relationships between ideas that they would not otherwise see. The term can be used as a verb when referring to the activity of nonstop writing or as a noun when referring to the actual piece of writing produced. In the classroom, students often freewrite in journals, and, according to Elbow, the writing may be skimmed by the instructor but should not be graded. Freewriting is often used as a **heuristic** to help students think about topics for essays.

Although often used, freewriting has met with some theoretical opposition. Some, for instance, criticize the method for its lack of emphasis on stylistic and grammatical correctness. **George Hillocks** (1986) concludes that freewriting is not an effective method for teaching writing. Hillocks sees freewriting as a better pedagogical technique than grammar instruction, but worse than other instructional techniques. In 1991, Pat Belanoff, Peter Elbow, and Sheryl Fontaine published *Nothing Begins with N: New Investigations of Freewriting* with the purpose of providing theoretical validation of freewriting. In composition studies, the term appears in major journal publications and presentations most often between 1979 and 1993.

(b) "sometimes called 'automatic writing,' 'babbling,' or 'jabbering' exercises. The idea is simply to write for ten minutes. . . . Don't stop for anything. . . . Just put something down. The easiest thing is just to put down whatever is in your mind. The only requirement is that you never stop" (Elbow, *Writing Without* 3).

"It's writing the students do for themselves, not their teachers; and . . . it constitutes the kind of practice familiar to anyone (an athlete, for example, or a musician) who wants to perfect a skill" (Southwell 676).

(c) "Over the past fifteen or twenty years, freewriting has gradually become a staple in our profession, sometimes serving as the center around which a text or class is structured, sometimes taking a place alongside other writing heuristics or warm-ups taught to students" (Belanoff, Elbow, & Fontaine, *Nothing* xi–xii).

"By contrast [to grammatical drills], a classroom activity such as 'freewriting' assumes a different view of learning: that writers already possess grammatical competence, that the best way to improve writing performance is to keep the writer writing, and that pursuit of meanings is as important a growth incentive for unpracticed writers as it is for experienced writers" (Knoblauch & Brannon, *Rhetorical* 16).

"It is true that free writing became prominent in the late 1960s before process-oriented instruction itself became prominent. Nevertheless, today, writing freely in journals or learning logs is one staple of process-oriented instruction at all levels, however independent its origins might have been" (Stotsky, "Research" 95).

(d) Peter Elbow, Ken Macrorie, expressionists.

GARRISON APPROACH

(a) A popular tutorial method developed by Roger H. Garrison and used in composition classes. Garrison explains his conference teaching method in "One-to-One: Tutorial Instruction in Freshman Composition" (1974). In 1978, his method was tested and recommended by the Los Angeles Community College District. Garrison published *How a Writer Works*, based on the "Garrison method," in 1981.

In this method, students write many papers while meeting one-on-one with the teacher in a writer-editor or master-apprentice relationship. Students spend the majority of class time writing, not listening to lectures, doing exercises, or even reviewing peers' essays. At intervals of the writing process, students meet with the teacher for very short (approximately 5-to-10-minute) one-to-one conferences; each conference focuses on only one aspect of the student's writing. Garrison prioritizes five "operational skills" and recommends that during the conference the instructor focus only on the first until the student has mastered it and only then move on to the next skill. He recommends that the instructor first focus on global issues of content, then on the writer's point of view or stance toward the material, and third, on organization. After the student has mastered these areas, the instructor should then direct the student to focus on style and to edit the draft, looking at, for example, sentence structure and diction. The instructor should also advise the student to concentrate on mechanical correctness. The number of drafts a student writes for a certain assignment depends on how long it takes to "master" the operational skills.

The theoretical assumption behind this teaching method is that by writing often and by receiving immediate feedback from the teacher during different stages of the writing process, students will learn to correct and later avoid writing problems. Building on the conferencing techniques of **expressivists** such as **Peter Elbow**, Garrison attempts to eliminate traditional teacher **authority** from the classroom by recommending that no grade be given on early drafts and by fostering a view of the instructor as an "editor-helper."

Criticisms of the approach come from **social constructionists** who support **collaboration** among students instead of a strictly student-teacher relationship. Feminists, such as Carol Stanger ("The Sexual Politics of the One-to-One Tutorial Approach and Collaborative Learning" [1987]), oppose the method because, as Stanger argues, it is based on male values and hierarchical thinking. The term is most cited by composition scholars in the early 1980s.

(b) "The *most* effective teaching method is one-to-one: tutorial or editor-to-writer. The student brings his work-in-progress to the face-to-face session; and you, the teacher-editor, bring analytical reading, judgment, diagnosis, and suggestions for further action by the student. This kind of teaching is *creative* intervention in the student's work process, at times and in ways that can be most immediately useful to his understanding of what he is doing" (Garrison, "One" 69).

"based on the belief that the problem in teaching writing is to find ways to keep students writing all the time and to provide constant and almost immediate feedback for the writer from the instructor" (Stanger 34).

(c) "The one-to-one conference is the heart of the Garrison method; the three-to-seven minute conference creates a new relationship between teacher and student" (Simmons 224).

"A large-scale study in 1978 (performed by the Los Angeles Community-College District) indicated that Garrison-method students showed significantly greater gains in writing skills than did non-Garrison students" (M. Harris, "The Ins" 92).

"Students . . . often ask for more help from the teacher although the Garrison method claims to make the student less dependent. This is because the structure of the student-teacher relationship in the Garrison approach is the traditional hierarchical one" (Stanger 36).

(d) Roger H. Garrison.

GENERATIVE

(a) A term commonly used by and in reference to Paulo Freire's* **critical literacy** programs. The term is often combined with other words such as "generative word" and "generative theme" and refers to the use of words and concepts that are common to particular groups of students in their search for meaning and understanding that, according to Freire, education should foster. As explained by Barbara Bee (1981), when devising a literacy program in Brazil, Freire and his teaching team would study the community they would teach, noticing their daily activities and the words they often used. Freire would ask for community input in establishing a list of words, selected because of emotional value and phonetic representation of the language. These words served as the basis of the literacy classes as students engaged in critical discussion generated by the words and as they studied the words, breaking them apart and rearranging the letters and syllables to make other words (Bee 44). A generative word is one that encourages the freedom to experiment with language and leads to the creation of new words. This concept is important to the work of liberatory or **radical pedagogists** as well as to social theorists of language and literacy. Using this concept in the Western composition classroom, an instructor may invite students to participate in selecting course topics and may focus discussion or writing topics on subjects of interest and concern to the students, such as popular culture or university activities. Fully to encompass the meaning of the term, however, critical awareness should result from the use of "generative top-ics" in the classroom as, for example, students gain awareness of the political functions of mass media or of the university curriculum. Freire's work has been most influential in composition studies since the 1980s.

(b) "the names which represent what is important in their [students'] lives. These are the 'generative words': they are represented in visual form, they are discussed and renamed" (Berthoff, "Paulo" 317).

"Acting on the assumption that adults, and children too, can learn to read with easy words that are familiar and meaningful to them Freire and his literacy teams developed what he calls 'generative words' . . . meaning those words whose syllabic elements offered, through recombination, the creation of new words" (Bee 43–44).

"We are speaking of words which matter profoundly to the people and which, for just this reason, contain their own inherent catalytic power" (Kozol xiii).

(c) "Let us say, for example, that a group has the responsibility of coordi-nating a plan for adult education in a peasant area. . . . The plan includes a literacy campaign and a post-literacy phase. During the former stage, problem-posing education seeks out and investigates the 'generative word'; in the post-literacy stage, it seeks out and investigates the 'generative theme' " (Freire, *Pedagogy* 101).

"The students found their voices, enough to carry us through a ferocious hour, once I found a 'generative' theme, an issue generated from the problems of their own experience" (Shor 3).

(d) Ann E. Berthoff, Paulo Freire, **Ira Shor**.

GENERATIVE RHETORIC

(a) A term used by **Francis Christensen**, in the tradition of **generative-transformational grammar**, to describe his idea, based on structural linguistics, that the basic structure of the sentence and paragraph "generates" ideas (see especially Christensen's "A Generative Rhetoric of the Sentence" [1963] and "A Generative Rhetoric of the Paragraph" [1965]). The typical sentence, ac-cording to Christensen, is a "cumulative" sentence, which contains a sentence base and modifiers. His analysis of the paragraph is similar; he describes the paragraph as containing a core sentence with modifying sentences. Christensen likens the paragraph to a "macro-sentence," an assumption that has drawn some criticism (see, for example, **Alton Becker** and Paul Rodgers, Jr., in *CCC*'s "Symposium on the Paragraph" [1966]).

Christensen's goal is to establish a method for analyzing the levels of gen-eralization and modification in a piece of writing. He uses the concept "levels of structure" to encourage students to add more levels of description, details, and support to the sentences or paragraphs they have already constructed. These additions will create what he calls "textured" writing, writing that exhibits not only more words, but more thought than the original sentence or paragraph. As stated by Richard M. Coe, Christensen's central claim is that "increased subordination correlates, in general, with quality" (*Toward* 14); in other words, the more supporting detail and development, the more effective the piece of writing. Though Christensen's theory was much discussed and much practiced in composition classrooms, some in the 1970s called for more detailed studies of the benefits of generative rhetoric. **Lester Faigley** (1979), for one, attempted to respond to such calls and, through his research, concluded that generative rhetoric instruction had the potential to improve student writing. Christensen opposed his generative rhetoric to traditional **sentence-combining**, which often lacked rhetorical context. **James Moffett** (1968), however, faults Christensen's generative rhetoric because in classroom application, rhetorical context is often neglected. In spite of its early popularity, generative rhetoric was not widely discussed in the 1980s and 1990s. In composition studies, this concept was most visible in the 1960s and 1970s.

(b) "a technique that uses form to produce ideas" (R. Young, "Concepts" 136).

"Francis Christensen used the term 'generative' to suggest a rhetoric that progresses from a general topic or idea to a more specific and developed exposition" (De Beaugrande, "Generative" 240).

"Like sentence-combining, generative rhetoric takes as its goal the expansion of the student's syntactic repertoire.... Unlike sentence-combining, generative rhetoric accomplishes this goal by asking students to supply content in a rhetorical situation rather than by asking students to join short sentences in an a-rhetorical context" (Faigley, "Generative" 176).

(c) "The foundation, then, for a generative or productive rhetoric of the sentence is that composition is essentially a process of *addition*" (Christensen, *Notes* 4).

"Christensen wants us to teach sentence patterns not as sentence-combining exercises ... but as generative forms that will encourage students to invent more information, more specifics, which they will use to develop more texture, more depth, in their writing. Thus a dialectic is established between arrangement and invention" (Coe, *Toward* 68).

"Christensen's way of analyzing sentences ... is rather misleadingly called 'A Generative Rhetoric of the Sentence.' It is generative only in the technical sense of a deductive system, being derived from transformational theory as popularized by Paul Roberts (whose rendition is unacceptable to most transformationalists themselves), not in a psychological sense relating to actual sentence creation" (Moffett 174).

(d) Francis Christensen, Richard M. Coe, **Frank D'Angelo**.

GENERATIVE TRANSFORMATIONAL GRAMMAR (see TRANSFORMATIONAL GRAMMAR)

GOD-TERMS

(a) A term initially used by **Kenneth Burke** and then by **Richard Weaver** that describes the "ultimate" rhetorical terms of a society or a community, terms around which humans can build their lives with hope of finding "transcendence" or "unity." According to Burke, language use tends to culminate in an "ultimate" or "god-term." In Burke's philosophy, god-terms stand in the place of "God"; words and the concepts they invoke guide a community and provide its ultimate motives; they also uphold and stabilize ideology. God-terms influence all action, thought, and communication within a community. Examples of such terms include the names of various deities and certain sources of power such as money. These terms usually unite and stabilize the group through common identifications, but Burke warns that they can be potentially harmful and lead to divisions in society by justifying disputes such as war. In Burkean philosophy, god-terms are not static but change with time. Most uses of the term in composition studies are based on Burke's explanation of the term, which he continued to develop in his work after 1945 (Rueckert 129). Weaver developed the term in his 1953 book *The Ethics of Rhetoric* and 1963 article "Language Is Sermonic." Weaver sees "progress" as a likely but not necessarily healthy god-term for the society of his day (89). "God-term" is often used in composition conversations to warn against **essentialist** tendencies and limited perspectives; for example, Lad Tobin (1993) warns against the tendency to see **collaborative** learning in itself as a god-term or as an "ideal" pedagogy. In her controversial article "Diversity, Ideology, and Teaching Writing" (1992), **Maxine Hairston** voices her discomfort with the political turn in composition instruction and expresses concern that "multiculturalism" or "cultural diversity" may become "god-terms" or the ultimate purpose of first-year writing programs.

(b) "We are here talking about ultimate dialectical tendencies, having 'god,' or a 'god-term,' as the completion of the linguistic process. . . . We have enough area of agreement for our study of rhetoric if you but concede that, language being essentially a means of transcending brute objects, there is in it the 'temptation' to come upon an idea of 'God' as the *ultimate* transcendence" (Burke, *Rhetoric* 276).

"By 'god term' we mean that expression about which all other expressions are ranked as subordinate and serving dominations and powers. Its force imparts to others their lesser degree of force, and fixes the scale by which degrees of comparison are understood" (Weaver, *Ethics* 88).

"Science, Nature . . . Democracy, Communism, Capitalism, Money, Power, Peace, Truth, Justice . . . Allah, Brahma, Buddha, Christ, and, of course, God. When invoked by individual members of a culture (or society), they draw those

individuals, whatever their differences, into a cohesive group—a community"
(Sheard 299).

(c) "The crucial question, however, is . . . how one guards against their [the
terms 'multiculturalism' and 'cultural diversity'] becoming what Richard Weaver called 'god terms' that can be twisted to mean anything an ideologue wants
them to mean" (Hairston, "Diversity" 186).

"So powerful are god-terms that we alter our meanings of lower-level terms
so they are consistent with our god-terms" (R. Heath 106).

"Unfortunately, given the 'god term' status that collaboration currently enjoys,
we have done very little to separate the chaff from the wheat (or, as teachers
often worry when they assign collaborative projects, the waif from the cheat)"
(Tobin, *Writing* 130–31).

(d) Kenneth Burke, Richard Weaver.

HERMENEUTICS

(a) A term referring to principles and theories of interpretation, both textual
interpretation and human interpretation of the world. Regarding textual interpretation, it is the study of how one interprets unfamiliar discourse; it involves
identifying and interpreting important texts, focusing on various textual features,
and establishing principles of interpretation. Hermeneutics originally referred to
interpretation of biblical and legal theory but then was adapted to the general
humanities in the nineteenth century by Friedrich Schleiermacher and Wilhelm
Dilthey. Generally, Schleiermacher is credited with establishing modern hermeneutics and beginning the strong German influence in hermeneutical studies.

Martin Heidegger and Hans-Georg Gadamer are main figures in twentieth-
century hermeneutics, and their work advanced philosophical hermeneutics, with
emphasis on interpretation as a key concept in the study of Being. Gadamer and
Heidegger saw the importance of recognizing the interpreter's historical and
cultural position and the influence of this position on the interpretation. An
underlying assumption of philosophical hermeneutics is that our knowledge
about texts is colored by our individual context; therefore, truth about the texts
is never completely certain. Hermeneutics is a leading mode of inquiry in literary
studies (see, for example, **E. D. Hirsch** [1967] and Stanley Fish [1980]).

In *The Making of Knowledge in Composition* (1987), **Stephen North** states
that hermeneutical inquiry is rare in composition studies. He cites **James Kinneavy**'s 1971 *A Theory of Discourse* as one of the few examples at the time of
hermeneutical inquiry in composition. Kinneavy's work can be considered hermeneutic because he offers a "canon" and method of interpreting composition
texts. Composition's interest in hermeneutics has increased, however, with the
Journal of Advanced Composition and *Rhetoric Review* frequently publishing
articles on the subject. Hermeneutics has been most used in composition dis-

cussions beginning slowly in the late 1970s and then again in the mid-1980s to the mid-1990s.

Scholars have argued for the use of hermeneutics both in the classroom and in interpreting composition texts and composition history. For example, **Susan Miller**, in "The Student's Reader IS Always a Fiction" (1984), and Bruce Lawson, Susan Sterr Ryan, and **W. Ross Winterowd**, editors of *Encountering Student Texts* (1989), use a hermeneutical perspective to discuss how composition teachers read students' texts. James Kinneavy ("Process" 1987) applies the theories of Heidegger to what he sees as a limited view of the writing **process**, and Mariolina Salvatori (1988) proposes that the use of hermeneutical critique in the writing classroom will help increase students' critical understanding. Working from the theories of Gadamer, Heidegger, and Paul Ricoeur, Timothy Crusius (1991) defines a "hermeneutical rhetoric" that can be applied to composition pedagogy; similarly, Peter Sotirou ("Articulating" 1993) calls for a hermeneutic pedagogy in the writing classroom. Margaret Strain advises the use of hermeneutics in the historical analysis of composition as a discipline (see her 1993 article and 1994 CCCC presentation). Dilip Parameshwar Gaonkar (1997), however, questions the use of rhetoric as an interpretive tool, arguing that rhetoric's Aristotelian roots do not support such a use.

(b) "It has three major concerns:—(a) establishing a body of texts, usually called a canon, for interpretation; (b) the interpretation of those texts; and (c) generating theories about what constitutes a canon, how interpretation should proceed, and to what end" (North 116).

"broadly defined as the study of meanings and contexts" (Spellmeyer 9).

"an intense study of the processes by which humans understand and interpret the world" (Haswell 124).

(c) "Current thinking in hermeneutics and critical theory stresses that even perception (not just judgment) derives from communities of discourse" (Elbow, *Embracing* 220).

"A central assumption of hermeneutics is that there is no unmediated access to the extramental world, that what we perceive out there is always already preinterpreted, not only by the selectivity of our brain and senses but also by our culturally engendered expectations" (Crusius, *Teacher's* 161).

"The problems with which hermeneutics deal were initially defined within individual areas of study, especially theology and jurisprudence, and ultimately also the historical disciplines. But it was a deep insight of German Romanticism that understanding and interpretation not only come into play in what [Wilhelm] Dilthey later called 'expressions of life fixed in writing,' but they have to do with the general relationship of human beings to each other and to the world" (Gadamer 21).

"Even our culture appears to promote this hermeneutic impulse in rhetoric. . . . What does it tell us about a culture that it finds interpretive solace in rhetoric rather than in religion or in economics or in science?" (Gaonkar 25)

(d) Hans-Georg Gadamer, Ernesto Grasi, E. D. Hirsch, Martin Heidegger, James Kinneavy, Paul Ricoeur.

HETEROGLOSSIA

(a) A term used by Mikhail Bakhtin,* especially in his collection of four essays *The Dialogic Imagination* (translated in 1981), to refer to the many voices that influence language. For Bakhtin, all language use constitutes a social inter-action; an utterance is never individualized, but reflects input from various other past and future speakers and is also influenced by the specific historical and cultural context of the discourse situation. Heteroglossia implies that no word is ever "pure," but is marked by its previous uses and changes in relation to its context; heteroglossia is both **dialogic** and **double-voiced**. Initially, Bakhtin used the term "heteroglossia" to describe the socially diverse speech in novels, but in later writings, he applied the concept to language in general.

The term, as well as references to all of Bakhtin's work, appears often in composition studies beginning in the late 1980s. Bakhtin's terms and theories have frequently been used to advocate a **social constructionist** and **collabora-tive** approach to writing. **Lisa Ede** and **Andrea Lunsford** (1990), for example, use Bakhtin's theories and concept of heteroglossia to promote a collaborative theory of pedagogy and writing, and **Lester Faigley** (1986) draws from Bakhtin to support his social view of the composing **process**. Helen Rothschild Ewald (1993) warns against using Bakhtinian terminology too loosely, however, as she makes clear that though Bakhtin's work has been useful for composition schol-ars, the same terms, including "heteroglossia," "dialogics," and "**carnival**," are used at times to promote different and sometimes conflicting philosophical, po-litical, and pedagogical positions.

(b) "the term he [Bakhtin] uses to denote the meeting of individual utterance and the broader social context present in every word" (Selzer 173).

"In short, all writing is intensely sociohistorical, and, in this sense, is by nature collaborative. *Heteroglossia*, or many-voicedness, accounts for individual di-versity within this collaborative enterprise. An individual's voice resounds, in-deed can only sound, as one voice among many" (Ewald, "Writing" 332).

(c) "The prose writer witnesses as well the unfolding of social heteroglossia surrounding the object, the Tower-of-Babel mixing of languages that goes on around any object" (Bakhtin, *Dialogic* 278).

"Unlike the traditional composition teacher, Bakhtin describes a good prose writer as a person who welcomes the heteroglossia of language. He would prob-ably view the composition teacher's effort to still the heteroglossia of language as humorous, if not totally impossible" (Mack 163).

(d) Mikhail Bakhtin, social theorists of composition.

HEURISTIC

(a) A general term naming a prewriting or **invention** technique, derived from Aristotle's *topoi*, in which the writer contemplates a set of questions with the idea that the questions will lead to a topic or to a deeper understanding of a topic already selected. The questions have no 'right' or 'wrong' answer but are intended to stimulate the writer's thinking and memory and lead the writer to find connections between previously unassociated objects or ideas. As **Richard Young** explains in "Recent Developments in Rhetorical Invention" (1987), the term "heuristic" comes to composition studies from the fields of cognitive psychology, artificial intelligence, and, before these, logic. **Peter Elbow** and **Ken Macrorie**'s **freewriting**, **Kenneth Burke**'s **dramatistic pentad**, and Richard Young, **Alton Becker**, and **Kenneth Pike**'s **tagmemics** are examples of popular heuristics used in composition classrooms. Various scholars, **Ann E. Berthoff**, for example, have observed that words themselves are heuristics, since one word leads to another and then to another as phrases are made into sentences and sentences into paragraphs.

Heuristics have been a popular and controversial topic of conversation in composition studies since the 1960s. The major composition journals focused heavily on heuristics in the 1970s and early 1980s. (**Richard Leo Enos** has prepared a bibliography of research on heuristic procedures conducted between 1970 and 1980; see *Rhetoric Society Quarterly*, issue 1, 1982). **Janice Lauer** was an early proponent of heuristics in the classroom and of bringing heuristic procedures into composition studies from other disciplines, especially from psychology. Lauer and Berthoff entered into a well-known debate on heuristics in the early 1970s, beginning with Lauer's 1970 "Heuristics and Composition." Berthoff responded in 1971 with "The Problem of Problem Solving." Lauer continued the discussion in the May 1972 issue of *CCC*, and again, Berthoff issued her counterstatement in the December 1972 issue. Among other objections, Berthoff argues that a possible problem with heuristics is that they may become conventionalized and rule-governed to the point that creativity and free-thinking are stifled.

(b) "a systematic way of moving toward satisfactory control of an ambiguous or problematic situation, but not to a single correct solution" (Berlin & Inkster 3).

"All problem-solving procedures rely on some kind of 'heuristic,' a term deriving from a Greek root meaning 'to discover.' . . . A heuristic may be a set of questions or analytical categories which help define the issues involved in a problem" (Foster 20).

(c) "How might we approach instruction in thinking? One strategy, teaching the use of heuristics, can make students aware of their own thought process" (Gleason 65).

"Given the recognition of modern rhetoric that discourse is implicitly heuristic, that it enables and articulates new knowledge, composing, written and otherwise, is the most important activity going on in schools" (Knoblauch & Brannon, *Rhetorical* 109).

"I would like to argue for pluralism in our thinking. Those working seriously on <u>heuristics</u> are dealing with studies in psychology, philosophy, mathematics, and rhetoric as they must, since this is where the important theoretical work is being done" (Lauer, "Response" 210).

"It is language itself that is the indispensable <u>heuristic</u>. It is language that enables us to know that we know that, and to know how to know how" (Berthoff, *Making* 57).

(**d**) Aristotle, Ann E. Berthoff, Richard Leo Enos, Janice Lauer.

HOLISTIC EVALUATION

(**a**) A method of evaluating students' papers developed by the Educational Testing Service and often used to determine placement or in large-scale testing. Often, holistic grading is conducted by a group of teachers or graders who evaluate a batch of student essays, together reading each essay quickly and focusing on its overall quality, and then giving a score. Typically, the graders make their judgments based on criteria or a guide that they formulate before they begin grading. To increase objectivity, teachers should also undergo instruction before participating in group holistic grading. Ideally, raters are assumed to be approaching the papers from a similar frame of reference.

An advantage to holistic grading is that readers can evaluate many papers in a short span of time because they do not comment on or correct the students' work. Advocates of this method also propose that it makes grading more objective, since students' names do not appear on the papers and since the rater may not have had the student in a class, and thus is not influenced by factors that are not directly related to the student's writing performance. **Charles Cooper** has strongly advocated holistic scoring (see especially his 1977 article "Holistic Evaluation of Writing").

Critics of the method have questioned its validity and reliability, arguing that holistic ratings are swayed by superficial factors such as length and appearance of an essay, that holistic ratings cannot be generalized beyond the group that designed the criteria for judgment, and that the agreed-upon criteria can limit the readers' views on the merits of the writing they are evaluating. (See, for example, Charney [1984], **Faigley** [1985], Huot [1990], and **Elbow** [1993 & 1996].) Holistic grading may also be problematic because if used throughout a semester and not only for placement, students do not receive in-depth instructor feedback on their work. Even if used only in placement exams, holistic grading can be faulted because it is part of a system that expects students to produce effective writing without regard to rhetorical context (see especially **Sharon Crowley**, "A Personal Essay on Freshman English" [1991]). In response to some of the problems associated with holistic evaluation, Peter Elbow (1996) advocates "minimal" or "bottom line" holistic scoring in which essays are not given a numerical score but are often scored simply as either "satisfactory" or "unsatisfactory." "Holistic evaluation" frequently appears in composition conversation beginning in the 1970s, but it is most discussed from the mid-1980s to the early 1990s.

(b) "a quick, impressionistic qualitative procedure for sorting or ranking samples of writing" (Charney, "Validity" 67).

"Later, essays came to be rated according to judges' general impressions of overall quality, a procedure that is called holistic evaluation. . . . Often overlooked, however, is the fact that holistic evaluations yield nothing more than relative, impressionistic judgments that cannot give detailed information about writing abilities" (Faigley et al., *Assessing* 205).

"For holistic evaluation, the rater assigns a single rank or score to a piece of writing, either grouping it with other graded pieces or scoring it on the basis of a set scale" (Lauer & Asher 130).

(c) "When papers are graded holistically, we assume that their rhetorical effectiveness lies in the combination of features at every level of the discourse, that the whole is greater than the sum of its parts" (Lindemann, *Rhetoric* 201–2).

"It is disconcerting to find holistic scores, which are supposed to be a *qualitative* measure, so directly predictable by such mundane quantitative measures as the length of the sample, the number of errors and the number of unusual vocabulary items" (Charney, "Validity" 75).

"Mass holistic reading sessions are little more than discursive gangbangs" (Crowley, "Personal" 170).

(d) Charles R. Cooper, Educational Testing Service, Lester Faigley, **Sarah Washauer Freedman, Richard Lloyd-Jones**, Miles Myers, **Lee Odell, Edward White**.

IDENTIFICATION

(a) A term that **Kenneth Burke** develops in his 1950 *Rhetoric of Motives* and suggests should at least complement "persuasion" as the key rhetorical term. **Richard Weaver**, influenced by Burke, also uses the concept in his rhetorical theory. According to Burke, the use of "identification" as a key rhetorical term allows recognition of rhetorical "motives" in discourse where they may not be expected. Burke shows limitations of the concept "persuasion," arguing that "persuasion" does not explain the formation or cohesion of social groups and classes, nor does it explain the rhetorical power that is part of "mysticism" or "courtship." Identification accounts for the willingness of the audience to listen with an open mind to the speaker or writer's message. Simply put, the writer uses rhetorical skill to urge the audience to *identify* with her; common ground is implied. Identification refers to that rhetorical process by which humans encourage and maintain social unity. But, as Burke explains, the concept of identification necessarily implies division, because if society was not initially fragmented, there would be no need for women and men to seek or to foster identification with others (*Rhetoric* 23–25). Identification can be reached through "consubstantiality"; Burke adapts this term from Christian theology in which it refers to the paradox of Christ as both human and divine and thus to the unity of God the Father and God the Son. Burke uses "consubstantiality" to explain how humans, while different, unify through shared ideologies and how through identification, humans join forces while remaining separate. In rhetoric and composition studies, many scholars see the replacement of persuasion with identification as a characteristic of the **new rhetoric**.

In regards to the composition classroom, the term is used in discussions of **audience**, community, and discourse analysis. For example, Dale Bauer (1990) uses Burke's concept of identification to further her radical, feminist pedagogy. Her use of identification is largely centered on the division that identification implies as she emphasizes differences between her political stance and that of her students, calling for students to identify with her as a representative of feminist politics. She reads their **resistance** as evidence of progress toward "realistic" identification. In contrast, Virginia Anderson (1997), while recommending a pedagogy based on identification, focuses instead on making "a strong conjecture argument that can serve as a shared starting point with skeptical listeners" (209). Anderson proposes that teachers "identify" with their audience, the students.

(b) "Rhetoric can be visualized as altogether a process of making this kind of <u>identification</u>. The process is simply that of merging something we would like to see taken as true with something that it believed to be true, of something we would like to get accepted with something that is accepted" (Weaver, *Ethics* 144).

"*Identification* means to suggest more powerfully than *persuasion* the workings of rhetorical discourse in everyday language. Burke examines the ways in which the terms used to create identification work to include the members of a group in a common ideology, while at the same time they exclude alternate terms, other groups, and competing ideologies" (Bizzell & Herzberg, *Rhetorical* 990).

"To achieve <u>identification</u> . . . is to articulate an area of shared experience, imagery, and value; it is to define my world in such a way that the other can enter into that world with me" (Halloran, "On the End" 626).

(c) "<u>Identification</u> ranges from the politician who, addressing an audience of farmers, says, 'I was a farm boy myself,' through the mysteries of social status, to the mystic's devout <u>identification</u> with the source of all being" (Burke, *Rhetoric* xiv).

"There is a natural uniformity of emotional response among human beings, and that uniformity constitutes the grounds for the establishment of the kind of <u>identification</u> that Burke says is necessary for communication" (Corbett, "John Locke's" 428).

"In sum, radical compositionists often fail to incorporate important lessons of rhetorical theory as they construct their relationships with students. They especially devalue identification" (V. Anderson, "Confrontational" 208–9).

(d) Kenneth Burke.

INCUBATION

(a) A term referring to that stage in problem solving in which the mind works unconsciously to solve the problem. It is thought to be an important stage in both the writing and creativity processes, occurring unconsciously, after the writer has actively worked on a project and then put it aside for a while. According to H. Poincaré (1914), who conducted his work on how discovery is achieved in mathematics, there are four stages in problem solving: preparation, incubation, illumination, and verification. These stages are also discussed in Graham Wallas' *The Art of Thought* (1926) and in Michael Polanyi's* 1958 *Personal Knowledge*, in which Polanyi also cites Wolfgang Kohler's (1927) studies on the stages of problem solving in chimpanzees. **James Britton** and his co-authors (1975) also use the term in describing three stages in writing: preparation, incubation, and articulation. In composition studies, the term is used in discussions of the writing **process**, especially from the mid-1970s to the early 1980s when **cognitive process theories** were at a peak of popularity.

(b) "that curious persistence of heuristic tension through long periods of time, during which the problem is not consciously entertained" (Polanyi, *Personal* 122).

(c) "While it is clear that incubation plays an important and little-understood role in writing of all kinds, we might speculate that in much poetic writing incubation does duty also for the earlier stage, preparation" (Britton, "Composing" 23).

"If we are to optimize writing conditions for our students, we must include incubation in our instruction on composing processes, urging students to take breaks when writing" (Anderson et al. 34).

"Given the chance to observe a writer's processes over time, we can see incubation at work. The flashes of discovery that follow periods of incubation (even brief ones) are unexpected, powerful, and catalytic" (Berkenkotter, "Decisions" 163).

(d) James Britton, cognitivists, H. Poincaré, Michael Polanyi.

INNER-DIRECTED/OUTER-DIRECTED

(a) Terms developed by **Patricia Bizzell** in her 1982 *PRE/TEXT* article "Cognition, Convention, and Certainty: What We Need to Know about Writing." She uses the terms to describe the two "theoretical camps" she sees as comprising composition studies. She uses the term "inner-directed" to critique the **cognitive process** view of composing, a view, according to Bizzell, that sees language use as independent of social context. **Linda Flower** and **John Hayes** are often associated with inner-directed theory because of their reliance on scientific methodology with roots in cognitive psychology and their focus on the individual writer. Their work suggests that the same mental processes may be involved in all writing situations, regardless of the context or purpose of writing.

Outer-directed theorists view writing and thinking as intimately tied to the social context in which these activities occur. Following this theory, teachers would discuss language as related to **discourse communities**. Also, the outer-directed camp is defined by its ability to recognize the provisionality of **knowledge**, as based on context. Often, Bizzell's terms are used to argue for a social view of writing instruction, a view that gained much popularity in the mid-1980s and came to dominate composition theory by the late 1980s. Some scholars, however, question whether composition studies must take an either/or perspective, arguing instead that both social and cognitive views are relevant (see **cognitive process theory**).

(b) "One theoretical camp sees writing as primarily <u>inner-directed</u>, and so is more interested in the structure of language-learning and thinking processes in their earliest state, prior to social influence. The other main theoretical camp sees writing as primarily <u>outer-directed</u>, and so is more interested in the social processes whereby language-learning and thinking capacities are shaped and used in particular communities" (Bizzell, "Cognition" 215).

"Theorists who support context-dependent models of writing instruction are said to have a 'social,' '<u>outer-directed</u>,' or 'local knowledge' perspective, whereas those who support more broadly applicable models are said to have a 'cognitive,' '<u>inner-directed</u>,' or 'general knowledge' perspective" (Foertsch 361).

(c) "In rejecting the cognitivist 'quest for certainty' that looks for 'one universal model of the composing process' [citing "Cognition" 235], Bizzell recommends that we balance the work of this '<u>inner-directed</u>' school with that of the more social '<u>outer-directed</u>' one, itself honoring context and community" (Hill 186).

"In the research of Kenneth Bruffee, Karen Burke LeFevre, and James Berlin, for example, the model of social construction of knowledge is presented as a clear political, philosophical, and mutually exclusive alternative to the invention of truth by an individual writer. Patricia Bizzell summarizes this split by arguing that all composition research is either '<u>inner-directed</u>' or '<u>outer-directed</u>' " (Tobin, *Writing* 97).

(d) Patricia Bizzell.

INTERNALLY PERSUASIVE WORD

(a) A term used by Mikhail Bakhtin* in *The Dialogic Imagination* (first published in 1975; translated in 1981) to describe a word or a discourse that invites interaction and examination instead of demanding unquestioned acceptance. The word is similar to the words of the receiver (or audience) and not overly intimidating or imposing. Unlike the **authoritative word**, which is untouchable and daunting, the receiver feels comfortable to develop and to use productively the internally persuasive word. In the composition classroom, many **process** teachers hope to foster an environment that encourages internally persuasive discourse. As proposed in social, **collaborative**, process, and feminist theories, students learn, not by repeating authoritative discourse of the instructor, but by questioning and interacting with the material and with each other (see also authoritative word and **dialogic**).

(b) "half-ours, half someone else's. Its creativity and productivity consist precisely in the fact that such a word awakens new and independent words . . . [it] does not remain in an isolated and static condition. It is not so much interpreted by us as it is . . . developed, applied to new material, new conditions" (Bakhtin, *Dialogic* 345).

"What Bakhtin calls *internally persuasive discourse* is discourse that ranges freely among other discourses, that may be creatively recontextualized and that is capable of engaging other discourses in dialogue" (Farmer, "Voice" 307).

(c)"When a person populates the ideas of others with his or her own 'life-world' experiences, Bakhtin tells us that the 'externally authoritative' word becomes 'internally persuasive' and that individual becomes the 'author' of his or her own perspective" (Qualley & Chiseri-Strater 114).

"Normally, a portion of the teacher's discourse is internally persuasive to most students. If this were not the case, teaching would be an impossible and useless activity" (Edlund 62).

(d) Mikhail Bakhtin, social constructionists, process theorists, feminists.

INTERPRETIVE COMMUNITIES

(a) A term borrowed from literary criticism and popularized in composition studies in discussions of **social construction** and **collaboration**. Literary critic Stanley Fish developed the term in the 1970s and early 1980s and used it to explain why different people have similar interpretations of the same text. Interpretive communities are made of people who share "interpretive strategies" or learned methods of interpreting texts; and thus, similar readings of texts occur not because of any stability in the text but because of shared methods of interpretation.

Kenneth Bruffee and other proponents of collaborative learning and social constructionism use and adapt this term for the composition classroom to support their argument that knowledge is made through social interactions and maintained by community agreement. **Elaine Maimon** (1986) uses the term in her discussion of and rationale for **writing across the curriculum** programs. Other critics with similar scholarly beliefs see problems with the way Fish uses the term because, they argue, he does not recognize the inequalities that exist within such communities. Interpretive communities, according to critics such as **Susan Jarratt** ("Feminism and Composition" 1991), are defined by powerful voices that often marginalize and silence other voices. Similarly Reed Way Dasenbrock (1991) questions the term's blindness to difference, and David Smit (1995) also offers a critique of the term, urging scholars in composition studies to examine the field's unproblematic acceptance of **anti-foundational** theories and to evaluate anti-foundational philosophy's value for the teaching of writing. Often in composition conversations, the term **"discourse community"** is used to broaden the scope of Fish's concept. The term is discussed frequently in composition studies from the mid-1980s to the early 1990s.

(b) "Interpretive communities are made up of those who share interpretive strategies not for reading (in the conventional sense) but for writing texts, for constituting their properties and assigning their intentions. In other words, these strategies exist prior to the act of reading and therefore determine the shape of what is read rather than, as is usually assumed, the other way around" (Fish, "Interpreting" 115).

"Stanley Fish completes the argument by saying that these 'interpretive communities' are the source of our thought and of the 'meanings' we produce through the use and manipulation of symbolic structures, chiefly language . . . [and] that interpretive communities may also be in large measure the source of what we regard as our very selves" (Bruffee, "Collaborative" 640–41).

(c) "This useful concept helps us, for example, to see why we as composition teachers tend to respond to student writing the way we do: our interpretive community has a set of coherent and powerful assumptions and strategies for approaching (Fish would say writing) student texts" (White, "Post-structural" 193).

"Scholars in literary theory, such as Gerald Graff and Kathleen McCormick, have pointed out the difficulties of relying on interpretive communities as a basis for a theory of knowledge: such a concept does not sufficiently distinguish between the kinds of strategies that people may use in understanding; nor does it explain how individuals within a community acquire these strategies or how they may move from community to community and develop new strategies" (Smit, "Hall" 36).

"What is wrong with Fish's interpretive community model of interpretation, the notion that readers write texts, is, finally, that it is a hermeneutics of identity. . . . [W]e understand a text by making it like us" (Dasenbrock, "Do" 16–17).

(d) Kenneth Bruffee, proponents of collaborative learning, Stanley Fish, social constructionists.

INVENTING THE UNIVERSITY

(a) A term coined by **David Bartholomae** in his 1985 article of the same name. The term describes attempts by students, especially new students or **basic**

writers, to write successfully in the university by imitating the prose style and vocabulary of more experienced academic writers. To "invent the university," students must place themselves in an assumed position of privilege and speak in the voice of the (English, math, science, . . .) scholar whom they may aspire to be but have not yet become. Inexperienced writers, according to Bartholomae, should attempt to use **academic discourse** with which they are not yet fully familiar or comfortable; but other critics argue that students should speak in their own voices, not the voice of someone else. Also, Bartholomae's pedagogy is critiqued for requiring students to imitate dominant discourses without having the opportunity or encouragement to change them. **Victor Vitanza** (1991) and Susan V. Wall and Nicholas Coles (1991) similarly argue that such a pedagogy unquestioningly accepts the power positions and exclusions implied in academic discourse. Bartholomae's term and article greatly encouraged a composition pedagogy that would introduce students to academic discourse. This idea was widely debated, especially in the late 1980s and early to mid-1990s.

(b) "assembling and mimicking its [the university's] language while finding some compromise between idiosyncrasy, a personal history, on the one hand, and the requirements of convention, the history of a discipline, on the other" (Bartholomae, "Inventing" 135).

"founding one's self on the modes of university discourse" (Vitanza 157).

(c) "Every time a student sits down to write for us, he has to invent the university for the occasion—invent the university, that is, or a branch of it, like history or anthropology or economics or English" (Bartholomae, "Inventing" 134).

"Advanced literacy requires learners to adopt a stance that will allow them to see and to change their relationship to language, including the language of the academy; but the language of the academy itself will have to be redefined as multiple and changeable if we and our students are to have a hand in 'inventing' it" (Wall & Coles 243).

"And so here, too, the learning of a new discourse seems to rest, at least in part, on a kind of mystical leap of mind. Somehow the student must 'invent the university,' appropriate a way of speaking and writing belonging to others" (J. Harris, "Idea" 17).

(d) David Bartholomae.

INVENTION

(a) In classical rhetoric, the first of the five arts (invention, arrangement, style, memory, delivery) that comprise rhetoric. Invention's purpose in classical rhetoric is to help the speaker find an effective and persuasive angle from which to approach a subject. Through invention, the speaker considers the best method of persuasion and formulates persuasive appeals, often with the use of **heuristics.**

Scholars in contemporary composition and rhetoric have shown great interest in the history of invention (see, for example, **Winifred Bryan Horner**'s and **Richard Young**'s bibliographies and George Kennedy's, James Murphy's, **James Berlin**'s, and **Sharon Crowley**'s historical treatment of invention). Though scholars interpret the history of invention differently, most agree that the concept of invention lost its classical importance with the growth of Christianity because knowledge was assumed to be absolute and needed no generation through logic. In the sixteenth century, Peter Ramus separated invention (along with arrangement) from rhetoric, leaving rhetoric only with stylistic concerns, a popular view until the seventeenth century when Francis Bacon helped (along with the neo-Ciceronians) restore invention to rhetoric though changing the meaning slightly in relation to science. For Bacon, invention in science means a discovery of something new, whereas in rhetoric it means a recollection based on scientific knowledge. Late eighteenth- and early nineteenth-century rhetoricians **Hugh Blair, George Campbell**, and **Richard Whately** were largely responsible for excluding invention from nineteenth century rhetoric. In the nineteenth century, the dominant view held that through close observation and scientific methods one could obtain pure knowledge and that this knowledge need only be recorded. Classical invention, then, as an art of discovery was not needed, and style became a main concern of rhetoricians. This view persisted into the twentieth century, and is evident in the "**current-traditional**" approach of many composition instructors. Because of the **positivist** assumption that the writer merely recorded reality, invention was not integral to this school of thought. When **process** theories became widely accepted in the study of composition, the idea of invention again gained theoretical support and became a popular topic of study.

In modern composition and rhetoric, invention is discussed in relation to the writing process. Writing instructors often encourage invention in the classroom through the use of heuristics to aid in discovery of a topic and in problem solving. Invention is also seen as a way not only of discovering meaning but of creating meaning. In composition theory, depending on the theoretical inclinations of the person using the term, invention can be encouraged through a formal technique, such as Richard Young, **Alton Becker**, and **Kenneth Pike**'s **tagmemic** system or **Kenneth Burke**'s **dramatistic pentad**; invention can also be prompted through nonstructured, expressive means, such as **freewriting**. Karen Burke LeFevre's influential *Invention as a Social Act* (1987) has been important in positioning invention not only as an individual activity but as a social and collaborative action.

(b) "Invention . . . is designed to help one discover valid or seemingly valid arguments in support of a proposition" (R. Young, "Invention" 9).

"serves as little more than a general rubric under which contributions from a variety of methodological perspectives can be loosely gathered; and which, for one reason or another, a particular commentator thinks are relevant to the generation of things to write about. What the term will actually mean in any given contribution . . . will depend on its methodological source" (North 339).

(c) "Invention proper had no place in the foundations of [current-traditional] rhetoric. [Adams Sherman] Hill tied the composing process up into three neat graphic bundles—words, sentences, and paragraphs. Invention came down to the making of choices between correct and incorrect renderings" (Crowley, *Methodological* 142).

"It is, however, the canon of invention that gives rhetoric its substance; without it, rhetoric merely arranges, clothes, and dispatches the arguments and observations other disciplines have discovered. Without invention, rhetoric is not an epistemic activity, and as such it can never hold anything but a secondary place in the English department" (Pullman 369).

"*Invention* does not belong solely to the rhetorician; it is a way of becoming in all of the arts and sciences" (Corder, "Rhetoric" 19).

(d) Aristotle, Francis Bacon, **Alton Becker**, **Ann E. Berthoff**, Kenneth Burke, Cicero, **William A. Covino, Sharon Crowley**, John Franklin Genung, **William Irmscher, Janice Lauer, Richard Larson**, Karen Burke LeFevre, Kenneth Pike, Quintilian, Peter Ramus, **Richard Weaver**, Richard Young.

KNOWLEDGE (AS SOCIALLY CONSTRUCTED)

(a) A term referring to socially constructed concepts. In **social constructionist** philosophy, knowledge is not based on "objective fact" but is considered a social construct. In other words, all knowledge is generated by interaction within social communities and through the communities' **conversations** and is made known through the communities' language. Thomas Kuhn* uses this concept in his 1962 book *The Structure of Scientific Revolutions* to discuss what he sees as the nonobjective, but social, knowledge of the scientific community. Studies such as that of Bruno Latour and Steve Woolgar (*Laboratory Life: The Social Construction of Scientific Fact* [1979]) have supported Kuhn's hypothesis that scientific conclusions are based not on "fact" but on community **consensus**. Richard Rorty* adapted Kuhn's ideas in his 1979 *Philosophy and the Mirror of Nature* to apply to knowledge in general. Left-wing critics, such as Greg Myers (1986) argue that through the dominant classes' knowledge-making conversation, minority voices are not heard and that therefore in society knowledge is not fairly distributed.

(b) "a dialectical interplay of investigator, discourse community, and material world, with language as the agent of mediation" (Berlin, *Rhetoric and Reality* 176).

"To say that knowledge is indeterminate is to say that there is no fixed and certain point of reference against which we can measure truth. If there is no such referent, then knowledge must be a made thing, an artifact. . . . Knowledge is generated by communities of knowledgeable peers" (Bruffee, "Peer" 11).

"Knowledge in a discipline is seen not as discovered, but as agreed upon—as socially justified belief, created through the ongoing 'conversation' (written as well as oral) of those in the field" (McLeod, "Writing" 5).

(c) "As an alternative to a seemingly disinterested view of knowledge, Bruffee turns to social construction theory—to social practice and language—as a way to account for the construction of knowledge" (Greene 157).

"We have learned from Kuhn, Fish, Rorty, and others to locate the authority of knowledge not in subject matter, the cumulative results of research and scholarship, but in disciplinary matrices, in the discursive practices of interpretive communities, in the conversations and professional self-images of English teachers, literary critics, philosophers, engineers, chemists, sociologists, and so on" (Trimbur, "Really Useful" 23).

"If we turn a blind eye to social factors we are likely merely to perpetuate the provision of different kinds of knowledge for the rich and the poor" (Myers, "Reality" 167).

(d) **Charles Bazerman, Kenneth Bruffee**, Thomas Kuhn, Bruno Latour and Steve Woolgar, Richard Rorty, and other social constructionists.

LORE

(a) A term coined by **Stephen North** in *The Making of Knowledge in Composition: Portrait of an Emerging Field* (1987). He uses the term to name beliefs and practices of composition **practitioners**, especially those beliefs that are not solidly grounded in theory or proved by experimental research. ("Practitioner" is North's term for those composition teachers who teach heavy loads and seldom have time for research or for keeping up with the latest theories). According to North, anything that apparently works in the classroom becomes a part of this body of knowledge. Also, once something is a part of lore, it cannot be easily dropped. Lore is usually passed on by word of mouth, and when it is written down, it is usually found in **current-traditional** textbooks, teachers' guides, lesson plans, syllabi, and handouts. North does not use the term negatively, but uses it to represent often valuable, experience-based knowledge.

In other uses, however, lore is negative and usually refers to an insubstantial body of knowledge with no scientific or theoretical backing. According to many composition scholars, the use of lore in the classroom is one cause of students' problems because lore often represents contradictory theories used simultaneously, which can lead to confusion and frustration. North locates the roots of resistance to lore in the call for a scientific and theoretical approach to composition that swept the field in the 1970s.

From a poststructuralist perspective, Patricia Harkin urges the validation of lore as a producer of **knowledge**. She celebrates lore as "non-disciplinary" or "post-disciplinary" and argues that the multifaceted aspects of lore, its many influences and lack of attention to disciplinary boundaries, do not detract from its usefulness but, instead, increase its value, making it "**anti-essential**." (For more on Harkin's use of "lore," see "Bringing Lore to Light" [1989], "The Postdisciplinary Politics of Lore" [1991], and her 1994 CCCC conference presentation "Research as Lore.") Questioning Harkin's emphasis on lore, **W. Ross Winterowd** [1998] contends that while composition instructors may not actually teach theory to first-year composition students, teachers should be versed in theoretical knowledge in order to support and explain their practice adequately. The term "lore" has been most used during the late 1980s to mid-1990s, often in conversations on the politics of composition as a field.

(**b**) "the accumulated body of traditions, practices, and beliefs in terms of which Practitioners understand how writing is done, learned, and taught" (North 22).

"experience-based knowledge . . . a cumulative assortment of anecdotal information about writing and writers which is passed from teacher to teacher on an ad hoc basis. . . . It is knowledge gained in bits and pieces—often incomplete and frequently self-contradictory—but flexible enough to adapt to changing situations in the classroom" (Pemberton 161).

(**c**) "A goodly portion of composition at the post-secondary level is taught by an underclass of faculty, a cadre of part-time, temporary teachers who are often trained in literature and whose knowledge of composition consists only of what Stephen North calls 'lore' " (McLeod, "Pygmalion" 380).

"I'm suggesting that we think of teaching as a site or moment when we are free to bracket disciplinary procedures, to do what needs to be done without worrying about meeting disciplinary standards of knowledge productions. I'm asking my audience to join me in bringing lore to light" (Harkin, "Bringing Lore" 66).

"A composition teacher unaware of such [theoretical] influence needs to lay aside the red pencil and raise his or her eyes from the stack of themes, to look into and behind the practices inherited from personal experience, lore, and composition textbooks" (Winterowd, *English* 222).

(**d**) Patricia Harkin, Stephen M. North.

MODES OF DISCOURSE

(**a**) A term, sometimes called "forms" of discourse, that refers to the classification of discourse into four categories: narration, description, exposition, and argument. The modes are faulted for relying on faculty and associationist psychology. Faculty psychology assumes the mind is governed by the "faculties" of understanding, imagination, passion, or will. Associationist psychology contends that we know the world through the grouping, or association, of ideas, which follows basic "laws" and order. Thus early proponents of the modes of discourse assumed that one should choose a form of discourse according to the "faculty" to be influenced and based on laws of association. Such psychology influenced eighteenth century Scottish rhetoricians, who then influenced nineteenth-century American textbook authors (for further explanation see **James Berlin**'s *Writing Instruction in Nineteenth-century American Colleges* [1984] and **Frank D'Angelo**'s "Nineteenth Century Forms/Modes of Discourse: A Critical Inquiry" [1984]).

As explained by **Robert Connors** in "The Rise and Fall of the Modes of Discourse" (1981), the "modes of discourse," with roots in the rhetoric of **George Campbell**, can be traced to Samuel Newman's 1827 text *A Practical System of Rhetoric* and later to Henry Day's 1850 text *Elements of the Art of Rhetoric*. The modes, however, gained popularity with the publication of **Alexander Bain**'s 1866 text *English Composition and Rhetoric*. From the late nineteenth century to the 1950s, the modes of discourse informed the majority of writing courses. Connors (1997) attributes the acceptance of Bain's modes of discourse largely to the educational culture of the late nineteenth century as the student population increased, as curricula broadened, and as large universities replaced small religious colleges. In response to larger classes and a more diverse student body, composition classes began to emphasize mechanics and form. In the late nineteenth century, the textbooks by the **big four** (**John Genung, Adams Sherman Hill, Fred Newton Scott**, and **Barrett Wendell**), which relied on the modes, reinforced the modes' popularity.

Connors attributes the fall of the modes of discourse largely to the rise of interest beginning in the 1930s in "thesis texts," texts based on one main concept, and in expository writing, which was emphasized to the neglect of the other modes. Also, Connors explains, new theories of writing began to emerge that challenged the modes. Similarly, **S. Michael Halloran** (1990) credits the rise of professionalism beginning in the late nineteenth century with the neglect of description and narration ("From Rhetoric" 168). Whereas Connors contends that the modes are not dominant features of modern composition instruction, other scholars in response to Connors' article have argued that Connors understates the influence of the modes. For example, **Sharon Crowley**, in a 1984 "Counterstatement," sees lingering influences of the modes. Similarly, **Richard Larson** claims, in a 1984 article, that evidence of the modes in contemporary composition persists.

A focus on the modes of discourse is often seen as a defining characteristic of **current-traditional rhetoric**. In the light of current composition theory, problems with the modes of discourse as a guiding principle of composition pedagogy are numerous. For example, Sharon Crowley (1984) faults the modes for focusing only on text and writer, ignoring the **audience**, and thus being "arhetorical" (90); Kathleen Welch (1987) criticizes "traditional" writing texts for relying on the modes as well as on the classical canons. Such categorization, she argues, ignores current theory and takes the "energy" and interest from composition instruction. (Welch does, however, state that at the time of her research, she sees evidence of change in textbook production, citing as examples the work of **Linda Flower, Peter Elbow**, and Rise Axelrod and **Charles Coo-**

per in *The St. Martin's Guide to Writing*.) Similarly, **Susan Miller** (1991) sees the divorce of writing instruction from actual writing situations students may encounter as a result of the focus on modes of discourse. Though theoretically out of favor, the modes persevere in composition practice because they offer a convenient method for organizing writing and writing instruction in the first-year composition classroom. Often used in the nineteenth century, this concept again became much-cited during the 1980s as compositionists became increasingly interested in the histories of the discipline.

(b) "the most influential classification scheme of the last hundred years" (Connors, "Rise" 444).

"exposition, description, narration and argumentation—EDNA for short" (Crowley, "Response" 88).

(c) "As far as I can determine, the classification of the nineteenth-century forms/modes of discourse into description, narration, exposition, and argumentation was an attempt to establish some kind of order among a bewildering number of the kinds of discourse that developed during the nineteenth century" (D'Angelo 32).

"Stripped of their theoretical validity and much of their practical usefulness, the modes of discourse cling to a shadowy half-life in the attic of composition legends" (Connors, *Composition-Rhetoric* 253).

"Traditional writing texts . . . cut off language from any of its intrinsic interest with their taxonomic imperative and their failure to connect to anything, much less to a student writer's life. The categories of the diluted classical canons, the modes, and the excerpts that accompany them in these traditional textbooks arise from nowhere and they go nowhere" (K. Welch, "Ideology" 277).

"The modes therefore assimilate composing into spiritual rather than functional aims, 'ideals' like those that were established for literary study. . . . They divorce writing from the mundane—or active—reasons that students will write, just as increasingly aesthetic views of literature have substituted formalist for rhetorical categories of analysis" (Miller, *Textual* 61).

(d) Alexander Bain, George Campbell, Robert Connors, Frank D'Angelo, Adams Sherman Hill.

MULTI-VOICED (see DOUBLE-VOICED)

NATIONAL WRITING PROJECT (BAY AREA WRITING PROJECT)

(a) An outgrowth of the Bay Area Writing Project, which was started by James Gray in the early 1970s at the University of California at Berkeley. The underlying philosophies of the National Writing Project (NWP) are that writers are themselves the best teachers of writing and that teachers are the best teachers of other teachers. The NWP has sites throughout the United States and in Canada, England, and Australia; the sites are affiliated with colleges and universities. Each summer NWP directors at each site organize and direct an institute in which high school teachers of writing meet to discuss composition theories and what has and has not worked for them in the classroom. Participants also take time to write. The program encourages collegial involvement and sharing from all participants. As well as the intensive summer seminars, the project sites offer in-service workshops during the school year. In 1976, the project was adopted as a model for the state, and in 1977, the National Endowment for the Humanities (NEH) funded the project for national extensions—thus the National Writing Project. **James Berlin** applauds the NWP for helping fill the "leadership vacuum" caused by lack of government support of education ("Writing" 215), and **Stephen North** credits the NWP for establishing equal relations among **practitioners**, researchers, and theorists. **Susan Miller** (1991), in contrast, questions the NWP's focus on writing-as-process, proposing that "**process**" is too limited a "content" area for teachers of writing; instead, according to Miller, more emphasis should be placed on historical and cultural systems in relation to writing.

(b) "a teachers-teaching-teachers effort" (North 373).

"The National Writing Project, a public school/university partnership, evolved from its inception in 1973 by James Gray as the Bay Area Writing Project" (Bratcher & Stroble 67).

(c) "But one program sympathetic to [James] Britton's approach achieved national prominence and influenced cross-curricular writing instruction in secondary and higher education: the Bay Area Writing Project (BAWP)" (Russell, *Writing* 280).

"Commonly, after NWP institutes (usually held on university campuses) teachers return to implement strategies in their own classrooms and conduct workshops within their individual schools and districts" (Pritchard & Marshall 260).

"In one of the most prominent offshoots of process theory, for instance, the National Writing Project that engages high-school teachers in every state, process has even further been made the only content that teachers, not students, must learn" (Miller, *Textual* 119).

"It should also be noted that the NWP has no hard party line insofar as theory is concerned. It can, however, best be characterized as student-centered and expressive in its orientation" (Berlin, "Writing" 215).

(d) James Gray.

NCTE

(a) Initials that stand for the National Council of Teachers of English, an organization dedicated to curricular studies and improvements in the grades kindergarten through college. Founded in 1911, this organization is the parent organization of the Conference on College Composition and Communication (CCCC), as well as of the Conference on English Education and the Conference on English Leadership. The NCTE was founded largely in response to the Modern Language Association's (MLA) focus on literature to the neglect of pedagogy and to the conservative rhetorical view of many educators who emphasized "proper" form, mechanical correctness, and "great" literature. As Myron Tuman explains (1986), founding members of NCTE championed an expanded view of literacy and combated the attempts by private Eastern schools to establish a narrow college preparatory curriculum (346) (see also J. N. Hook [1979]). **Fred Newton Scott** served as NCTE's first president.

The organization's first journal was the *English Journal*, published continually since 1912, mainly for high school teachers. NCTE also offers twelve other publications: journals include *College English, Language Arts, Teaching English in the Two-Year College, Research in the Teaching of English, Primary Voices K–6*, and *Voices from the Middle*. Newsletters include *Notes Plus, School Talk, The Quarterly Review of Doublespeak*, and *The SLATE* (Support for the Learning and Teaching of English) *Newsletter*. Annually, NCTE publishes *Ideas Plus*, a collection of teaching strategies.

In 1914, speech teachers broke from NCTE to form their own professional organization, now called the Speech Communication Association. Recently, NCTE has been criticized for losing its early enthusiasm, for becoming too bureaucratic, for lacking a clear institutional purpose, and for diminished outspokenness in regard to human rights, politics, and classroom activity (see Alan Purves [1984], George Henry [1984], and Elisabeth McPherson [1984]). NCTE is often credited, however, for historically supporting minority groups' rights.

(b) "an agency for improving the teaching of English at all educational levels, even if its main focus initially was secondary school instruction" (Berlin, *Rhetoric and Reality* 35).

"The Council is now a large bureaucratic organization. It has developed a set of rules and procedures for doing everything and for doing nothing" (Purves, "NCTE" 694).

(c) "Much of the fundamental difference in philosophy between the MLA and the NCTE—between, on the one hand, an emphasis on English as rigorous research into certain privileged, literary texts and, on the other hand, an emphasis on English as an emancipatory pedagogic practice designed to give all students the power to create and comprehend expressive language—can be explained by the fact that pupil enrollment in secondary schools increased ninefold in the three decades separating the founding of the two organizations" (Tuman, "Astor" 341).

"That courageous little band of teachers, mostly from third-rate colleges, who in 1911 formed the NCTE, were hardly aware of what they were setting in motion when in radical dissent they broke from the MLA (Henry 668).

(d) Founding members include Harry Kendall Bassett, Emma J. Breck, Percival Chubb, John M. Clapp, James F. Hosic, Clarence Kingsley, Edwin Miller, Theodore Mitchell, Fred Newton Scott.

NEO-ARISTOTELIAN

(a) A term that describes a modern philosophy or approach to rhetoric based on "traditional," Aristotelian rhetoric. Characteristics of this view include emphasis on types of discourse (forensic, deliberative, epideictic), classification of proofs (logical, emotional, ethical), and canons of rhetoric (**invention**, arrangement, style, memory, delivery). Attention to and emphasis on persuading the audience is also characteristic of this approach. An Aristotelian view of rhetoric was influential in the early years of composition studies, as exemplified by the popularity of **Edward Corbett**'s *Classical Rhetoric for the Modern Student* (1965).

Rhetorician Edwin Black uses the term "neo-Aristotelians" in *Rhetorical Criticism: A Study of Method* (1965) for his classification of approaches to rhetorical criticism. Black contends that this view had then dominated rhetorical thought and urges its critique. He faults the neo-Aristotelian approach for a narrow view of context and a limited view of how discourse can influence the audience as well as the speaker or writer. In 1982, **James Berlin** uses the term in "Contemporary Composition: The Major Pedagogical Theories." According to Berlin, neo-Aristotelianism is one of four pedagogical theories found in the modern composition classroom. The categories include neo-Aristotelianism or classicism, **positivism** or **current-traditionalism**, neo-Platonism or **expressionism**, and **new rhetoric**. Neo-Aristotelian rhetoric, in Berlin's usage, would necessarily involve an emphasis on rationality and logic, through which "truth" can be known. Accordingly, in this view, language is an unproblematic tool used to come to truth and to persuade others of this truth. Berlin, preferring the new rhetorical approach, indicates that by 1982, the neo-Aristotelian view was not widely held, with many who professed an Aristotelian view actually practicing current-traditional rhetoric.

A more favorable view of neo-Aristotelians is found in "The Revival of Rhetoric in America" (1984). In this article, **Robert Connors, Lisa Ede**, and **Andrea Lunsford** credit the "Chicago Neo-Aristotelians" (or Chicago Formalists) with participating in the reintroduction of classical rhetoric in the mid-1900s, thus broadening the view of English composition beyond a **current-traditional** emphasis on style and "correctness." Members of this group, as defined by Connors, Ede, and Lunsford, include scholars from the University of Chicago such as Richard McKeon, Ronald Crane, **Richard Weaver, Edward Corbett, Wayne Booth**, and P. Albert Duhamel. To this list, Berlin (1990) adds Henry Sams.

A feminist critique of neo-Aristotelian rhetoric comes from **Elizabeth Flynn**. In her 1991 article "Composition Studies from a Feminist Perspective," Flynn classifies **I. A. Richards**, Richard Weaver, **Stephen Toulmin, Chaim Perelman**, and **Kenneth Burke** as neo-Aristotelians and argues that their approach to rhetoric is from a "male point of view" (144). Hierarchy is implied in a neo-Aristotelian approach, a concept that many feminists critique and deconstruct. Some, however, argue that Aristotle's rhetoric and influence on rhetoric cannot simply be forgotten (see, for example, John Poulakos' "Aristotle's Voice, Our Ears" [1996]).

(b) "Contemporary rhetoricians, especially neo-Aristotelians, ground their conceptions of what communication is in the categories and concepts of classical rhetoric, the rhetoric of public debate, a realm traditionally reserved for men" (Flynn, "Composition Studies" 144).

"Under the intellectual leadership of Richard McKeon and Ronald S. Crane, this group used ancient poetic theory, in particular Aristotle's *Poetics*, to launch formalist attacks on the arhetorical, a prioristic work of the New Critics" (Connors, Ede, & Lunsford 9).

(c) "the neo-Aristotelian critics tend, on the whole, to take a restricted view of context, their tendency being to comprehend the rhetorical discourse as tactically designed to achieve certain results with a specific audience on a specific occasion" (Black 39).

"If composition studies lost a great deal from the neo-Aristotelians, it stands to gain nothing from the anti-Aristotelians" (Poulakos 297).

(d) Wayne Booth, Kenneth Burke, Edward Corbett, Ronald Crane, P. Albert Duhamel, Richard McKeon, I. A. Richards, Chaim Perelman, Stephen Toulmin, Richard Weaver; critics include Edwin Black, James Berlin, Elizabeth Flynn.

NEW RHETORIC

(a) A broad term that is probably better conceptualized in plural, as the "new rhetorics." Often, the term is used to describe current approaches to rhetoric, including **cognitive process** theories, **expressivism, social constructionism**, and feminism—approaches that reacted against **current-traditional rhetoric**. In most accounts, the new rhetoric benefits from a multidisciplinary perspective, drawing knowledge from fields such as social science, psychology, and linguistics. The term implies a new look and reconceptualization of classical rhetoric in light of twentieth-century needs and perspectives. (See, for example, *Essays on Classical Rhetoric and Modern Discourse* (1984), in which editors **Robert Connors, Lisa Ede**, and **Andrea Lunsford** clarify connections between classical and "new" rhetorics.)

Additionally, the term describes an approach to rhetoric usually dated in the late 1950s. **I. A. Richards** and **Kenneth Burke** are often credited as leaders of the new rhetoric; **Chaim Perelman, Stephen Toulmin**, and **Francis Christensen** also were early contributors to this approach. According to **Richard Ohmann** ("In Lieu of a New Rhetoric" [1964]), new rhetorics (and he does use the plural) are not concerned only with persuasion but with other forms of discourse. Also, old rhetoric, Ohmann states, presents the rhetor as possessor of "truth" or the "right" answer, whereas new rhetorics depict truth as ever-changing and even shaped by the rhetorical process. In the 1950s and 1960s, composition studies was heavily influenced by "new rhetoric," with emphasis on **invention, audience** awareness, and style.

Chaim Perelman, with Lucie Olbrechts-Tyteca, claim to have introduced the concept of new rhetoric in 1949 with their influential work *The New Rhetoric: A Treatise on Argumentation* (translated in 1969). (Perelman, *The New Rhetoric and the Humanities* 31). In their use, this new rhetoric is related to dialectical reasoning, which Aristotle separated from analytics. Perelman and Olbrechts-Tyteca argue that rhetoric should be seen as an addition to formal logic, thus linking rhetoric and philosophy. In the new rhetoric, context and audience, or the social situation of which the discourse is a part, are important factors. Nelson J. Smith III, however, explains in his 1969 *CCC* article "Logic for the New Rhetoric," that the term "new rhetoric" comes from Kenneth Burke's *A Rhetoric of Motives* (1950) and from a **CCCC** presentation delivered by Kenneth Burke entitled "Rhetoric—Old and New" (published in 1951). And according to Smith's reading of Burke, a major characteristic of new rhetoric is post-Freudian psychology that allows more advanced analysis of and **identification** with an audience (305).

James Berlin also initially labeled as "new rhetoric" his "epistemic" rhetoric in the 1982 article "Contemporary Composition: The Major Pedagogical Theories." Some scholars have even questioned whether the new rhetoric is really new (Schwartz [1966], for example). However, in two edited collections, while recognizing multiple meanings of the term, **Theresa Enos** and Stuart C. Brown (1993, 1994) attempt to define the "new rhetorics." The term has been a part of composition studies' vocabulary since the beginning of the field.

(b) "When we speak of the *new rhetoric* we are referring not to any unified, codified system that has developed in recent years, but rather to the roots of a new system that we find in the work of the General Semanticists, of the cultural anthropologists, or the behavioral scientists, of those interested in stylistics, and of men like I. A. Richards, Kenneth Burke, Marshall McLuhan, and Kenneth Pike" (Corbett, "New Look" 63).

"We [Perelman and L. Olbrechts-Tyteca] called this new, or revived, branch of study, devoted to the analysis of informal reasoning, *The New Rhetoric*" (Perelman, *New Rhetoric and the Humanities* 9).

"The difference between the 'old' rhetoric and the 'new' rhetoric may be summed up in this manner: whereas the key term for the 'old' rhetoric was *persuasion* and its stress was upon deliberate design, the key term for the 'new' rhetoric is *identification* and this may include partially 'unconscious' factors in its appeal" (Nichols 101).

(c) "The newness of any 'new' rhetoric will have validity only if that rhetoric is an integral part of the vital and lively tradition of 'old' rhetoric. So it seems to me, there is little gained but novelty in identifying our contemporary attempts at communication as a 'new' rhetoric, except as the term 'new' is analogous" (Schwartz 216).

"But if *the* new rhetoric has yet to appear, there is no shortage of new ideas about rhetoric: even the briefest survey of definitions and positions uncovers a somewhat bewildering variety" (Ohmann, "In Lieu" 299).

"The projection of a new rhetoric will have to consider the broadening of its aim and scope to include the many other language situations besides that formal and one-to-many situation of the classical orator" (Fogarty 131).

(d) James Berlin, Kenneth Burke, Francis Christensen, **Albert Kitzhaber**, Chaim Perelman, Lucie Olbrechts-Tyteca, I. A. Richards.

NORMAL DISCOURSE (ABNORMAL DISCOURSE)

(a) Richard Rorty's* expanded version of Thomas Kuhn's* term "normal science," which Kuhn developed in *The Structure of Scientific Revolutions* (1970). Rorty uses the term in *Philosophy and the Mirror of Nature* (1979) to refer to the common everyday discourse used within a community holding similar values and attitudes.

In composition studies, **Kenneth Bruffee** develops the term in his argument for **collaborative** writing, contending that collaboration in the classroom provides a setting in which students can "practice" normal discourse. In "Collaborative Learning and the 'Conversation of Mankind' " (1984), Bruffee explains normal discourse as persuasive or informative writing directed to one's community of peers, a group whose knowledge, assumptions, and values are similar to the writer's. Normal discourse does not challenge the basic beliefs, or **paradigms**, of the community but is **conversation** that supports or furthers existing community knowledge. According to Bruffee, normal discourse should be the content of most composition courses because to know the normal discourse of a community is a requirement of membership in that community. Admittance to an academic or professional community is often the goal of university students, and to indicate competence and knowledge of a certain field, students must have a strong grasp of the community's normal discourse.

In Rorty's and Bruffee's use of the term, normal discourse upholds common beliefs and assumptions instead of challenging them as does the opposing term "abnormal discourse." Rorty also adapts the term "abnormal discourse" from Thomas Kuhn's term "abnormal science," using it to refer to a disruption in the normal activities, beliefs, and behaviors of a **discourse community**. For Rorty, the term describes a dissension or break from accepted thought in which the dissenter is considered either crazy or a genius. Although "abnormal" often carries a negative connotation, Rorty does not use the term negatively but, rather, very positively because in his view such discourse has the potential to refresh, challenge, and even revolutionize the established order of normal discourse. For

Bruffee, abnormal discourse is also a part of **collaborative learning**, and the interaction of normal and abnormal discourses models the way **knowledge** is socially constructed and maintained. Unlike normal discourse, however, abnormal discourse cannot be taught.

Rorty's and Bruffee's applications of the terms normal and abnormal discourse have been challenged by left-wing critics, especially in the late 1980s and early 1990s, as composition scholars began to problematize the **social constructionist** notion of community and to emphasize the political context of writing. Critics of early applications of "normal" and "abnormal" discourse include **John Trimbur** (1989), David Smit (1989), and John Schilb (1991). The general argument of such critics is that Rorty's and Bruffee's use of the terms is naive in ignoring the political and social implications of normal discourse. Some suggest that instead of teaching students to imitate normal and abnormal discourse, teachers should encourage students to question and challenge accepted behaviors. To such critics, abnormal discourse represents power struggles within a community that determine what behaviors and ideas are and are not validated (see also **consensus**). Objecting to Rorty's terms "normal" and "abnormal," anthropologist Clifford Geertz* (1983) offers instead the terms "standard" and "nonstandard" discourse. Geertz disagrees with the "pathological" nuances of Rorty's terms as well as to the "dichotomous dualisms" the terms imply (222–23).

(b) "[Normal discourse is] that which is conducted within an agreed upon set of conventions about what counts as a relevant contribution, what counts as answering a question, what counts as having a good argument for the answer of a good criticism of it" (Rorty 320).

"Knowledge-generating discourse . . . [that] occurs between coherent communities or within communities when consensus no longer exists . . . [it] sniffs out stale, unproductive knowledge and challenges its authority" (Bruffee, "Collaborative" 647–48, describing abnormal discourse).

(c) "The normal discourse of many of our academic and professional communities is a disgrace. This is a point which has been made repeatedly over the past forty years by professional writers who are appalled at academic jargon" (D. Stewart, "Collaborative" 67–68).

"Abnormal discourse, from this perspective, is neither as romantic nor as pragmatic as Rorty makes it out to be. Rather it offers a way to analyze the strategic moves by which discourse communities legitimize their own conversation by marginalizing others" (Trimbur, "Consensus" 609).

(d) Kenneth Bruffee, Richard Rorty, social constructionists, advocates of collaborative learning.

OPPOSITION

(a) A term used by **radical pedagogists** such as Paulo Freire,* Henry Giroux,* and Stanley Aronowitz to describe a disruption in the educational process that is a reaction to an oppressive political system but that does not lead to a change in that system. Oppositional behavior is similar to **"resistance"** except that in the case of opposition, the defiance is not effective in bringing change, usually because it is an isolated rebellion and is carried out without critical awareness of the dominant culture and its hegemonic tools. However, according to Aronowitz and Giroux, all oppositional behavior should be analyzed to see if it represents a form of resistance; the radical educator should be careful to differentiate opposition from resistance, to distinguish futile rebellion from potentially liberating and reflective behavior (see *Education Still Under Siege* [1993]). In composition studies, the term is used to explain disruptions in the educational process, often in relation to student response to academic conventions. For example, when a student fails to follow an assignment or attempts to verbally interrupt class, an instructor may question whether the student's actions are motivated by a sense of rebellion against the educational system and the inequality of power inherent in educational institutions. This instructor would attempt to analyze the behavior as either opposition or resistance. If the behavior is determined to be **reflective** and politically motivated (thus resistance), the instructor would help the student see potential change. If the behavior is opposition, potential for change is not a likely outcome. The term is most used in composition studies beginning in the late 1980s to the mid-1990s.

   (b) "When deliberate subversions of routine occur in isolation and without much reflection, they constitute what Giroux terms "opposition"—essentially futile, or even self-destructive, defiance" (Bizzell, "Marxist" 61).

   "movement against the dominant ideology, but it does not move toward anything else, and because it does not lead to a transformation of any kind, it serves ultimately only to reinforce the dominant ideology" (Chase, "Accommodation" 15).

   (c) "The assumptions that surround reading and literature study in English account for some of the contradictions students experience in literature study and, thus, for their opposition and resistance" (Ritchie, "Resistance" 122).

   "As I noted earlier, students' behavior and discourses often show a mixture of oppositional and accommodative tendencies which need to be critically unpacked for their hidden values and implications" (Canagarajah 193).

   (d) Radical pedagogists including Paulo Freire, Henry Giroux, **Ira Shor**.

PARADIGM

   (a) A term popularized by Thomas Kuhn* in *The Structure of Scientific Revolutions* (1970) and used to refer to the way **knowledge** is made and maintained in scientific communities. Kuhn uses the term to refer to the commonly held beliefs of a scientific community and to the examples or models that constitute knowledge in that community. **Richard Young** is often credited for popularizing the term in composition studies largely through his 1978 article "Paradigms and Problems: Needed Research in Rhetorical Invention," in which he urges composition's turn from the ineffective **current-traditional** paradigm to one that emphasizes **process, invention**, and meeting students' needs. In their 1980 article "Current-Traditional Rhetoric: Paradigm and Practice," **James Berlin** and Robert Inkster further develop Young's concept of paradigms in composition, and **Maxine Hairston** claims a new paradigm for composition studies in her 1982 article "The Winds of Change: Thomas Kuhn and the Revolution in the Teaching of Writing." (See **paradigm shift**.) Scholars in composition have since adopted the term and use it to refer to shared beliefs about the teaching of writing.

Although the term is commonly used by writing teachers and researchers, some critics argue that the original meaning of Kuhn's term is often distorted when applied to composition studies. Thomas E. Blom, for instance, argues in his 1984 response to Hairston's 1982 article that Hairston's use of Kuhn's term "paradigm" is inaccurate, since Kuhn states that "paradigm" can be applied only to hard sciences. Similarly, in 1993, **Richard Larson** calls Hairston's use of the term paradigm "incautious," claiming that the "world views" in composition had not radically changed as they would in a true scientific revolution ("Competing" 283). In composition studies, the term "paradigm" has often been a key concept in presentations at significant conferences and in articles. The term was most used from the late 1970s to the mid-1990s.

(b) "A paradigm is what the members of a scientific community share, *and*, conversely, a scientific community consists of men who share a paradigm" (Kuhn 176)

"A paradigm determines, among other things, what is included in the discipline and what is excluded from it, what is taught and not taught, what problems are regarded as important and unimportant, and, by implication, what research is regarded as valuable in developing the discipline" (R. Young, "Paradigms" 29).

"a set of tacit assumptions which has determined how [practitioners] define and carry out their activities in research and teaching" (Berlin & Inkster 1).

(c) "Kuhn argues that a paradigm is established, even in the natural sciences, not because of compelling empirical evidence, but because of a rhetorical process that delimits the shared language of the intellectual community governed by the paradigm" (Bizzell, "Thomas Kuhn" 764).

"The truth is that rhetoric has never had more than a broad consensus; rhetorical thought is normally paradigmless and conflictual. . . . We must come to terms somehow with what we have—a field that will never have the degree of internal coherence of those guided by paradigms" (Crusius, *Discourse* 106).

(d) James Berlin, **Robert Connors**, Maxine Hairston, Robert Inkster, Thomas Kuhn, Richard Young.

PARADIGM SHIFT

(a) A term first developed by philosopher of science Thomas Kuhn* in *The Structure of Scientific Revolutions* (1970) and initially used in the field of composition to refer to the transition from **current-traditional** theories and teaching methods to **process** theories and teaching methods. Kuhn explains that a shift in paradigms occurs when old solutions no longer satisfy current problems and when theories thus change. Those in composition argue that because current-traditional rhetoric could not meet educational and social needs, there was a paradigm shift during the 1960s to the process approach. Two early and influential uses of the concept of paradigm shift in composition studies are **Richard Young**'s in "Paradigms and Problems: Needed Research in Rhetorical Invention" (1978) and **Maxine Hairston**'s in "The Winds of Change: Thomas Kuhn and the Revolution in the Teaching of Writing" (1982).

Whereas many influential composition scholars support the idea of this product-process paradigm shift in composition studies, others see little or no basis for this claim. For example, **Stephen North**, in his 1987 text *The Making of Knowledge in Composition*, argues that the product-to-process paradigm shift is better seen as a power play, or, in North's words, an "intermethodological struggle for power" (321). Others argue that actual teaching practices have not substantially changed from those in the product "paradigm." (See, for example, **Robert Connors**' 1983 article "Composition Studies and Science," Sharon Hamilton-Wieler's 1988 article "Empty Echoes of Dartmouth: Dissonance Between the Rhetoric and the Reality," and **Susan Miller**'s 1991 *Textual Carnivals: The Politics of Composition* as well as her 1992 conference presentation "The Disciplinary Processing of Writing-as-Process.") In contrast, some scholars point to a second paradigm shift in composition studies—from the often-unpoliticized process theories to reliance on highly politicized postmodern philosophies and theories. In this shift, Hairston, largely because of her 1992 article "Diversity, Ideology, and Teaching Writing," is seen as resisting change instead of initiating it.

The term "paradigm shift" is often evoked by composition scholars to explain or to argue for changes in pedagogy, theory, or research. It also justifies the disciplinary status of composition studies. Some, however, disagree with such frequent use of the term and question what exactly constitutes a paradigm shift. For example, in his 1993 article "Competing Paradigms for Research and Evaluation in the Teaching of English," **Richard Larson** cautions against improper use of the term. He claims that what Hairston was noting in her popular 1982 article was not a paradigm shift but a "shift of attention" in the composition community (284). Similarly, **Sharon Crowley** (1996) proposes that the changes in composition scholarship in the 1960s and 1970s do not signal a paradigm shift as, she argues, process pedagogy requires no new epistemology. What did occur, according to Crowley, was a change in "professional identity" as composition began to disciplinize (72–73).

(b) "one of those breaks from a tradition-bound period Kuhn sees when he looks at the histories of many intellectual activities" (Bizzell, "Thomas Kuhn" 766).

"The replacement of one conceptual model by another" (Hairston, "Winds" 77).

(c) "For the last few years, Richard Young's and Maxine Hairston's accounts of the process movement as a Kuhnian paradigm shift have served as justifications for disciplinary status" (Faigley, "Competing" 527).

"To the question of whether a paradigm shift has actually occurred, we must answer 'not quite.' A realistic history of writing suggests that 'process' is serviceable mainly as an affective improvement in the classroom and as a way of granting composition a qualified academic legitimacy. Viewed from both historical and theoretical contexts, however, process theory has not yet provided an accurate or even a very historically different theory of contemporary writing" (Miller, *Textual* 107–8).

"If composition studies did not undergo a paradigm shift in the 1960s and 1970s, what did happen? What was it that felt so revolutionary then? . . . I will hazard that what changed was our professional identity" (Crowley, "Around" 72).

"[Maxine] Hairston, who herself participated in an earlier paradigm shift from writing product to writing process in the seventies and early eighties, now finds her place threatened by this new paradigm shift to postmodern inquiry, which is overtly political and highly theoretical" (Graham & Goubil-Gambrell 103).

(d) Maxine Hairston, Thomas Kuhn, Richard Young.

PARALOGY

(a) A term that describes what accounts for the unpredictable decisions we make in communication. These decisions are paralogic in that they do not follow a set of rules or logic. Whereas language is rule-bound, decisions one makes in communicative action do not follow a formal logic; they cannot be predicted or mapped by theory. Thomas Kent (1989, 1993) explains the concept of paralogy through the notion of guesswork in that we can only guess how our communications are interpreted and can only guess that we have achieved the intended interpretation of another's communication. Unlike semiotics or linguistics, paralogics does not study the systematic aspects of language; instead, it focuses on language use and on the act of using language to communicate in practical activities. In critical theory, Jean-François Lyotard is a key figure in the discussion of paralogy. In the late 1980s and early 1990s, **Victor Vitanza** and Thomas Kent began to advance the discussion of paralogy in composition studies and rhetoric. Applied to the field of composition, the concept suggests that areas of discourse analysis and production cannot be reduced to formulas, processes, or systematic concepts.

(b) "As the etymological origin of the term suggests, paralogy means 'beyond logic' in that it accounts for the attribute of language-in-use that defies reduction to a codifiable process or to a system of logical relations" (Kent, *Paralogic* 3).

"Paralogy is an attempt not only to make the weaker argument the stronger but also to favor a radical heterogeneity of discourses over either the favored protocol of One or the homogeneity of the Many" (Vitanza 147).

(c) "If writing is taught, Vitanza argues, it should be taught as a 'nondiscipline' with 'postpedagogy' or 'paralogic pedagogy' " (Faigley, "Street" 226).

"In admitting that the production and reception of discourse are paralogical endeavors that defy our attempts to reduce them to some kind of framework theory such as a cognitive process model or a system of social conventions, we are not forced, however, to accept the essentialist claim that communicative interactions like writing and reading constitute quasi-mystical activities that lie outside our abilities to understand them" (Kent, *Paralogic* 16).

"[Jacques] Derrida argues and [Donald] Davidson suggests that language possesses a paralogical dimension, a dimension that, in any conventional sense, refutes formalization, codification, and systemization" (Kent, "Beyond" 503).

(d) Thomas Kent, Jean-François Lyotard, Victor Vitanza.

PARTICIPANT OBSERVER

(a) A major practice in **ethnographic** research in which the **ethnographer** acts as both an insider and an outsider of the community that is being studied. As an insider, the ethnographer is also a part of the study and thus acknowledges his or her own perspectives and perceptions. An example of participant observation common in composition studies is the **teacher-researcher**. Instructors practice ethnography in their classroom, using their students as subjects of study—as part of the class, the teacher is a participant, yet also the researcher, the observer. In this role, the researcher attempts to minimize her presence as "observer" and to minimize her influence on that being investigated. The term appears most frequently in composition scholarship beginning in the 1980s, when ethnography also began to gain popularity as a research method in composition.

(b) "Participant/observers enter a community on supposedly equal footing with the indigenous population, categories and measures emerge from the experience, and no one attempts to generalize—the goal is thick description of a unique interaction" (Charney, "Empiricism" 581).

"In this role, researchers interact with participants only to establish themselves as an acceptable presence to the participants and to clarify the data collected" (Doheny-Farina & Odell 513).

(c) "Three major ethnographic techniques were used in this study. The first involved acting as a <u>participant-observer</u> in the class itself, recording events in the form of field notes" (Kantor, "Classroom" 77).

"<u>Participant observation</u> . . . allows researchers to reflect critically on their own subject position, both as researchers and as authors, in the twin sites of study—in the field and on the page" (P. Sullivan, "Feminism" 57).

(**d**) ethnographers, teacher-researchers.

POETIC WRITING

(**a**) According to **James Britton** and his colleagues, one of three categories of writing done by British school children. Discussions of these categories can be found in Britton's 1971 article "What's the Use? A Schematic Account of Language Functions" and in the study conducted by Britton, Tony Burgess, Nancy Martin, and Alex McLeod entitled *The Development of Writing Abilities (11–18)*, published in 1975. The study focused on the writing of British school children and classified this writing into three categories: **transactional, expressive**, and poetic. According to Britton, writing begins as expressive and then can be shaped into either transactional or poetic. Poetic writing is often referred to as creative writing, and the product of such writing is considered a work of art. When engaged in poetic writing, the writer, according to Britton, takes on a "spectator" role, meaning that the writer is not writing to get something done, but to observe, to shape past events, or to think about present ones. In Britton's study, poetic writing accounted for 18 percent of the writing done by the children studied. Britton argues, however, that more poetic writing should be done in the classroom, not to produce works of art, but to allow students to use their imagination to explore educational subject matter from a different perspective and to relate it to personal feelings and personal experience. **Art Young** (see, for example, "Considering Values: The Poetic Function of Language" [1982]) and **Toby Fulwiler** (see, for example, "The Argument for Writing Across the Curriculum" [1986]) have argued the benefits of using poetic writing in **writing across the curriculum**, also pointing out that such writing should not be graded. Poetic writing was most discussed in composition studies in the 1980s.

(**b**) "is akin to what we call 'creative writing' in this country; . . . deal[s] with 'larger' not 'literal' kinds of truth. Nor is . . . governed by any stringent rules or formulas, as the work of Joyce, Faulkner, e.e. cummings and many others will attest" (Fulwiler 21).

"a verbal object, an artifact in words, a work of art: its organization is not on the principle of efficiency as a means, but on the coherence and unity achieved when every part is appropriate to each other and to the whole design" (Britton, "Composing Processes" 20).

(**c**) "James Britton, in particular, has stressed the importance of <u>poetic writing</u>, to use his term, in encouraging students to explore their own feelings and values in conjunction with new learning experiences" (Gorman, Gorman, & Young 139).

"Consciously and frequently using poetic language will not make us all Shakespeare, but it will give us better opportunities for uniting theory and practice, reason and imagination, knowledge and action" (A. Young, "Considering" 95).

(d) James Britton, Toby Fulwiler, Art Young.

PORTFOLIO EVALUATION

(a) A method of instruction and evaluation in composition studies in which students often turn in a variety of writing, exhibiting their ability to write in different genres and toward different **audiences**. Portfolio grading is frequently adopted by instructors who are disillusioned with conventional forms of evaluation, which may seem to rely on false writing conditions. Portfolio evaluation can be used wide-scale as a method of placement testing or for exit examinations as a replacement for or in addition to standardized tests. It can also be used for evaluation in individual writing classes. The work that makes up the student writer's portfolio is accumulated over time, usually during the course of the semester. If the portfolio is used for entrance or placement purposes, then the writing might, for instance, represent a student's high school career.

In a portfolio grading system, students select what they consider their best or most interesting work to revise (and revise) and finally to submit in the portfolio. Ideally, the teacher does not grade drafts of the papers but instead offers advice that will help the student improve as a writer. When used in an individual classroom, the instructor decides when to assign grades. Some do so at midterm, some grade throughout the semester, and some give grades only at the end of term. Proponents of portfolio grading see it as a fair way of evaluation, since students are given ample time to revise and since this method of grading is consistent with the **process** of writing. A much-cited benefit of this method is the emphasis placed on revision and process writing. Also, some see this method as lessening the role of teacher as **authority**, instead casting the instructor in the role of mentor or coach with the goal of helping students improve their selected essays. Grading, they argue, is not the central emphasis of a portfolio-based classroom, and this argument is strengthened when a panel of teachers, not only the course instructor, is responsible for evaluating the portfolio. Another argument for the method is that a portfolio system may give students a stronger sense of control over their own work, since they select for evaluation what they see as their best writing, and the reflection encouraged by this system of selection is often revealed through the preface or cover letter students turn in with their portfolio. (See **reflective**.)

Critics of the method contend that while grading is delayed in the portfolio method, it is not eliminated, and that students are still aware that their work will be judged, probably by the teacher. Another problem with the method may be that some students will find the responsibility of accumulating a final portfolio intimidating (see especially Nancy Baker, 1993). Karen Greenberg [1998] also recognizes that portfolio grading substantially adds to the writing instructor's workload. Used as early as the 1970s, portfolio evaluation gained popularity in the early 1990s and continues to be used and discussed into the late 1990s. Multiple books have been published on the subject; in 1992, CCCC hosted a roundtable session on portfolios, and in 1993, the *Journal of Teaching Writing* dedicated a volume to the topic.

(b) "A portfolio (which can be broadly defined as a collection of student writing compiled over a period of time) represents a range of the student's writing ability in a variety of genres" (Baker 155).

"Although there are dozens of portfolio systems, almost all ask students to submit a number of different pieces for a final single grade; most ask students to play a role in choosing the work to be evaluated; and some ask students to play a significant role in that evaluation" (Tobin, *Writing* 67).

"The procedure, portfolio evaluation, incorporates what we know about how students develop as writers by emphasizing process, multiple drafting, and collaborative learning. In addition, portfolio evaluation encourages instructors to become respondents to student writing rather than error-seeking proof-readers" (Burnham 126).

(c) "Portfolio assessment takes the stance of an *invitation*: 'Can you show us your best work, so we can see what you know and what you can do—not just what you do not know and cannot do?' " (Elbow, Foreword xvi).

"While these practices [entrance exams, exit exams, tests of proficiency, tests of learned skills] are currently being challenged by the portfolio movement, they still see widespread use because they have become embedded within the university and our pedagogy" (L. Anderson, 25).

"It [portfolio assessment] is rooted in the same positivist paradigm as other forms of writing assessment, a paradigm requiring pre-specified, decontextualized assignments and standardized conditions for the production of the writing (for the sake of comparability). . . . it imposes an inordinate amount of extra (and usually uncompensated) work, and it undermines [the instructor's] authority to evaluate students' writing" (Greenberg, "Grading" 276).

(d) Pat Belanoff, Marcia Dickson, **Peter Elbow, Edward White**, Kathleen Blake Yancey.

POSITIVIST (POSITIVISM)

(a) A term now often used to critique methods of research, usually scientific research. The term indicates the assumption that truth and reality exist in the external world and can be objectively observed. Regarding writing instruction, this view proposes that objectively observed reality can be transmitted through writing. Positivism rejects the importance of context, thus proposing generalized and universal theories that supposedly represent the one and only correct world view. The best-known positivistic rhetoric in the field of composition is **current-traditional rhetoric**, which is based on the premise that reality is knowable and that good writers are those who clearly and accurately transcribe reality onto paper. In discussions of scientific or empirical research, a positivist perspective would assume that the researcher could objectively observe and report his or her findings and that the researcher's presence would not necessarily affect the subject or the outcome of the study.

Compositionists use the term to critique scientific research methods as well as current-traditional rhetoric. For example, Elliot Mishler's 1979 article "Meaning in Context: Is There Any Other Kind?" and **Janet Emig**'s 1982 article "Inquiry Paradigms and Writing" critique positivism and empirical research and have been influential in composition circles. **Ethnography, teacher-research**, and feminist research methods are challenges to positivist inquiry. Recently, however, scholars are cautioning against assuming too close an association between positivism and empiricism. For example, in "Taking Criticism Seriously" (1993), **John Hayes** questions whether empirical studies in composition have been positivist, proposing that positivists may be "an imaginary foe invented for the familiar rhetorical purpose of *name calling*" (313). In a 1996 article ("Reconsidering Behaviorist Composition Pedagogies: Positivism, Empiricism, and the Paradox of Postmodernism"), David Wallace argues against the assumption that all empirical work is positivist. According to Wallace, the neglect of empirical work is detrimental to composition studies, and a solution would be to combine empirical methods with a postmodern perspective. Similarly, Davida Charney (1996) argues that empiricism has its place in composition and technical writing research and criticizes the tendency of some composition scholars to "demonize" scientific approaches. The debate surrounding empiricism is ongoing as seen by the response to and critiques of Charney's article (see especially the December 1997 issue of *College Composition and Communication*). The term appears most often in composition conversations from the mid-1980s to the mid-1990s.

(b) "assumes that reality is located in an empirically verifiable material world which it is the duty of a writer to represent as accurately as possible" (Berlin, *Rhetoric and Reality* x).

"a naive misconception of scientific method—what is sometimes called 'scientism.' Positivists believe that empirical tests yield true facts and that's that; they do not understand that scientists test hypotheses. Underlying all positivist methods and models is a notion of language as, alternately, a set of slots into which we cram or pour our meanings or a veil that must be torn asunder to reveal reality directly" (Berthoff, *Making* 62).

(c) "Inquiry governed by a positivistic gaze is also often identified as 'conventional inquiry'; classical research; empirical research; experimental research; pure research; or, simply, globally, and, of course, mistakenly, as The Scientific Method" (Emig, "Inquiry" 65–66).

"If there is a villain to be unmasked, it is not empirical science, given the proper sense of the term 'empirical,' but rather the positivistic understanding of empiricism. . . . Positivism, not empirical science, is responsible for that erroneous belief in an absolute objectivity which gives rise to artificial hierarchies of knowledge" (Knoblauch & Brannon, "Knowing" 21).

"My hope is that as information about the nature and history of empirical inquiry becomes more readily available, we can get beyond positivist bashing and onto something more productive" (Hayes, "Taking Criticism" 314).

(d) current-traditionalists, scientists (according to some critics).

PRACTITIONERS

(a) **Stephen North**'s label for those composition specialists whose work is mainly in the classroom. North developed the term in his 1987 book *The Making of Knowledge in Composition*. Practitioners' knowledge, according to North, is called "**lore**." As stated by North, practitioner knowledge and study are largely based on "informed intuition and trial and error" (45). Traditionally, practitioners have not been as highly respected as the composition specialists that North labels "researchers" and "scholars." In his defining and analysis of the types of composition specialists, North's stated purpose is to validate the knowledge of practitioners; however, North's definition and usage of the term has been criticized for simplifying what teachers do and what they know. (See especially Elizabeth Rankin's "Taking Practitioner Inquiry Seriously: An Argument with Stephen North" [1990].) In *The Making of Knowledge in Composition*, North provides a list of well-known names that he claims fit the definition of practitioner; the list includes, but is not limited to, **Walker Gibson, Ken Macrorie, Richard Braddock, Donald Murray, Mina Shaughnessy, Elaine Maimon, Peter Elbow**, and **Toby Fulwiler**. Though "practitioner" has been used often in composition to refer to those in the classroom, North's definition helped open discussion on academic values and priorities related to the three activities: composition practice, research, and writing theory.

(b) "Practitioners are regarded essentially as technicians: Scholars and especially Researchers *make* knowledge; Practitioners apply it" (North 21).

"writing teachers who are in the classroom, doing their work, while the new field of composition studies defines itself around them" (R. Murphy 75).

(c) "Practitioners apply the research and knowledge, creating in their application a different, but also respectable, body of knowledge which Stephen North refers to as 'lore' " (Tirrell et al. 167).

"Unlike the consciousness-raising groups of the women's movement in the early seventies, we offer these accounts not as sharing for sharing's sake, as confessional, as the celebration of any and all narratives, or as a simple exchange of practitioner's lore. Rather, our teaching narratives serve to reclaim and construct us as women with agency in the composition classroom and academy" (Eichhorn et al. 297–98).

(d) Stephen North.

PRAXIS

(a) A term used by Aristotle to mean "practical" knowledge or "practice" as separate from strictly "theoretical" knowledge; Aristotle favors the theoretical, or "theoria." Additionally, the term has been developed in Marxist thought to describe an action taken by someone, often together with others, to improve present reality and life conditions. In this second sense, before action is taken, the potential actor or actors must gain a theoretical perspective or the ability to reflect critically upon the present situation. The next step is taking action that changes reality. Praxis, therefore, does not exclude theory. The term implies a productive mix of practice and theoretical knowledge. Paulo Freire* adapts this concept to education and proposes that praxis results from two occurrences: when action and reflection combine to create the "authentic" or "true word" and when this true discourse leads to action that transforms reality. For Freire, praxis is an integral part of education. The term "praxis" is used often in composition conversations, and not only by Freirians and Marxists; feminists and social theorists of writing also use the term. "Praxis" appears most frequently in composition studies in the late 1980s through the mid-1990s.

(b) "the action and reflection of men upon their world in order to transform it" (Freire, *Pedagogy* 66).

"Praxis is the constant reciprocity of our theory and our practice. Theory building and critical reflection inform our practice and our action, and our practice and action inform our theory building and critical reflection" (Wink 48).

(c) "Freire has applied his concept of 'praxis' with dramatic results to the circumstances of teachers and students in classrooms concerned with literacy, helping the disenfranchised in particular to assert their power to name and transform the world" (Knoblauch, "Rhetorical" 125).

"If our research is centered on a politics of location it demands an extra measure of responsibility and accountability on our part. It requires using research as 'praxis' to help those who participate with us in research to understand and change their situation, to help those who have been marginalized to speak for themselves" (Kirsch & Ritchie 25).

(d) Aristotle, Paulo Freire, Marxists, feminists, radical educators.

PRIMARY TRAIT SCORING

(a) A method of writing evaluation developed in 1974 by the National Assessment of Educational Progress; **Richard Lloyd-Jones**, with Carl H. Klaus, developed this form of evaluation for the National Assessment. As Lloyd-Jones explains, the assessment method was a result of a meeting of the Commission on Composition in the early 1970s. The Commission was created by **NCTE** to examine changes in the field of composition, and as a result of its study, the

Commission rejected existing methods of assessment ("Right" [1992]). Primary trait scoring is a form of **holistic evaluation** in which the criteria used for assessment are more thoroughly and specifically defined. This method of evaluation is designed so that each piece of writing is evaluated according to the specific writing situation, to the writer's main goal, and to the specific form of discourse represented in the assignment. According to **Edward M. White** (1986), the creators of primary trait scoring consulted rhetorical theory and history to construct an evaluation method that would reflect an understanding of the goals of writing and that would effectively assess these goals (143). For example, in evaluating a persuasive piece of writing, the scorer would focus only on certain criteria designated as essential for that particular persuasive assignment, including the specified audience and purpose. Other issues, such as mechanics, may not play a part in the evaluation. Primary trait scoring differs from **analytic scoring** in that raters assume that a generic scale cannot be applied to all essays, even of the same genre, but that new criteria must be designated for each assignment.

Because of its limited scope and specificity, this method of scoring can be helpful in responding to students' drafts and in encouraging and shaping revision. While recognizing benefits of primary trait scoring, **Lee Odell** (1993) notes possible problems surrounding this method. For example, Odell warns that testing agencies have used the name "primary trait" to identify scoring methods that seemingly are not backed by current theory. Also, the large-scale testing environment in which this method is often used does not allow students and teachers to select criteria for evaluation. Odell also faults the evaluation method for ignoring social and institutional contexts of writing and for neglecting the wide range of writing strategies (299–300). Primary trait scoring is most discussed in composition studies from the late 1970s to the early 1990s.

(**b**) "The 'primary trait' system . . . suggests that we judge writing with criteria tailored to specific writing tasks rather than apply a general standard of 'good' writing" (Gere, "Writing Well" 260).

"As originally conceived, primary-trait scoring is designed to assess a writer's ability to produce written texts for particular audiences and purposes. Scoring is based on characteristics in students' responses to specific tasks" (Faigley, "Performative Assessment" 177).

(**c**) "The great advantage of primary trait scoring is that it adds the option of a narrow focus to holistic scoring and thus allows teachers to fit such methods of assigning and responding to student work into their curricula. In simple terms, the primary trait theory supports every teacher's knowledge that we cannot do everything at once, nor need we try" (White, *Teaching* 144).

"Holistic scoring systems . . . are intended to produce a rating of the compositions rather than to provide advice and assistance to the student-writer. Analytic scales and primary trait analysis are more likely to generate information about specific elements in a composition, and thus to provide information for the student" (Probst 76).

"Primary trait scoring thus involves a lot of hard thinking about rhetorical situations and some judgment calls about what is, in fact, *the* most important demand of the writing task" (Brown 127).

(**d**) **Lester Faigley**, Richard Lloyd-Jones, Edward White.

PROBLEM-POSING EDUCATION

(**a**) A term coined by Paulo Freire* in his popular *Pedagogy of the Oppressed* (1968). Freire uses the term to describe an effective and "liberating" approach to education. The goals of problem-posing education are to encourage students to think critically and to challenge them to consider the problems that this thinking exposes. Students are encouraged to be active learners, to be creative, and to achieve a realistic recognition of their surroundings so that they can respond appropriately. This type of education helps students see education as relevant to them and to their own situation, instead of as a collection of foreign and unattainable "facts." They do not simply memorize information, but instead, participate in dialogue with each other and with the teacher. In true problem-posing education, the disparity between the teacher's knowledge and power and the students' apparent lack of these qualities is resolved as both teacher and student take part in the learning process; in Freire's words, teacher and student are "co-investigators." Freire explains that this form of education allows men and women to become fully human and is in direct opposition to the oppressive educational philosophy that he calls the "**banking**" **approach** to education, in which students passively await "deposits" of knowledge from the teacher. Ideally, the result of problem-posing education is action; once students have critically questioned and analyzed the problems (cultural, social) that this pedagogy exposes, they work to solve the problems. In composition studies, the term appears most frequently in the 1980s.

(**b**) "education in which students and teachers participate, through dialogue, as free subjects in the ceaseless reconstituting of their social reality" (Knoblauch, "Some Observations" 51).

"Problem-posing teaching begins with the students' presentation of their own experience, what Freire calls the student's 'thematic universe.' The teacher's task is to present the students' situation back to them as a problem. Students then need to understand the situation again, this time actively participating in a dialogue with another person" (Fox 38).

(**c**) "Problem-posing education does not and cannot serve the interests of the oppressor" (Freire, *Pedagogy* 74).

"Themes and words from daily life are strong resources for problem-posing. The turn toward student language and perceptions makes this pedagogy a *situated* model of learning. . . . The problem-posing teacher situates learning in the themes, knowledge, cultures, conditions, and idioms of students" (Shor 44).

"the classroom community becomes a 'problem posing' environment in which meanings must be exchanged—made and shared—with other members of the community so that the full impact of one's own words can be fully felt" (Onore 232).

(d) Paulo Freire, Henry Giroux,* **Ira Shor**.

PROCESS (WRITING-AS-A-PROCESS MOVEMENT)

(a) A movement in composition studies in which the focus of pedagogy, theory, and research became, not the final product of a writing assignment, but the process of composing. Scholars accept that this process is **recursive** and that the stages include prewriting, drafting, revising, and editing. **Donald Murray** is often credited with coining the phrase "teach writing as a process not product" through his 1972 article, likewise named. **Janet Emig**'s case study using **protocol** analysis reported in her book *The Composing Processes of Twelfth Graders* (1971) is an important work in the shift to the process movement, as is **James Britton** and his colleagues' *The Development of Writing Abilities (11–18)*. **Maxine Hairston** is also seen as a key figure in the "**paradigm shift**" in composition from emphasis on product to process.

Many scholars see this "shift" as a reaction to the **current-traditional** or product approach. The process view places emphasis on writing **workshops**, revision, dialogue, **audience**, and interaction among students and instructors as opposed to a traditional lecture-oriented classroom. Scholars have located the roots of the process movement in the 1960s and early 1970s, times of political radicalism, and such politics can be seen in liberal methods and goals of the movement and of many of its teachers. The movement corresponded with rejection of traditional **authority** figures, and many teachers began to emphasize content over form and grammar and to urge students to take authority over their own writing. This theory is put into practice in the classroom through methods including workshops, **collaboration**, student-teacher conferences, peer critique, multiple drafts, and emphasis on critical thinking. Most composition textbooks have adopted this perspective, showing students how to take their papers through each step in the process. Within the process movement there exist several views commonly divided into three categories: **cognitive, expressive/expressionist**, and social.

Beginning in the 1980s, critics began to question the basis and results of the process movement. The cognitive and expressive views, which held the most prominence in the early years of the movement, have been criticized for not placing enough importance on the writers' "situatedness," the cultural and political context, and for not recognizing the political significance of certain written products (see, for example, **Susan Miller**'s *Textual Carnivals* [1991]). Also, a concern is that by focusing on the writing process, the written product has been neglected, to students' detriment, since they will ultimately be expected to provide and be responsible for a final product. In response to such concerns, the field is reevaluating all three approaches to the process movement and attempting to integrate process and product into composition theory and pedagogy. Some scholars propose that in the 1990s composition studies has moved from a process to a "post-process" focus with the emphasis on pedagogical and theoretical examination of culture, race, class, and gender.

(b) "The writing process itself can be divided into three stages: *prewriting, writing, and rewriting. . . .* It is not a rigid lock-step process, but most writers most of the time pass through these three stages" (Murray, 90).

"But most of all [the process movement] has come to mean a critique (or even outright rejection) of traditional, product-driven, rules-based, correctness-obsessed writing instruction" (Tobin, "Introduction" 5).

"For the purpose of this study, the term 'writing process' refers to the practice of requiring students to produce multiple drafts of each assignment with revisions based on the feedback given by their instructors and classmates" (Baker 155–56).

(c) "Teachers themselves promote this narrow and inhibiting view of perfection by ignoring all stages of the writing process except the last, where formal correctness becomes important, and by confronting students with models of good writing by well-known writers without ever mentioning the messy process that leads to clarity" (Shaughnessy, *Errors* 79).

"Almost from the beginning, teachers of writing as process and later researchers of composing were divided into competing camps, but it was not until the later 1980s that expressions of general disillusionment with writing as process began to be heard" (Faigley, *Fragments* 68).

"The transformation of my teaching mirrored, and was influenced by, a movement in writing theory and pedagogy away from the cognitive and individualist sets of assumptions that initially fueled the process movement, towards a social model of writing" (Fox 2).

" 'Process'—as in 'the process movement' and in 'process texts'—is a slippery term, with no universally accepted definition that I know of" (Belanoff, 411).

(d) Arthur Applebee, Carol Berkenkotter, James Britton, **William Coles, Jr., Joseph Comprone, Charles R. Cooper**, Janet Emig, **Peter Elbow, Lester Faigley, Linda Flower, Donald Graves, John Hayes**, Maxine Hairston, Donald Murray, **Lee Odell, Sondra Perl, Nancy Sommers, Richard Young**.

PROGRESSIVE EDUCATION

(a) An outgrowth from the Progressive era—a time in which Americans began to question nineteenth-century individualism and to look more carefully at social reform. Scholars date this period from the late 1890s to the time of American involvement in World War I. The influence and work of progressive education, however, continued beyond World War I, especially through the establishment of the Progressive Education Association in 1918–1919. (See Robert Church [1976] for a more detailed analysis of the education movement's connection with the political and social reform movement.) Progressive education is often associated with the educational philosophies of John Dewey* and is seen as having roots in the work of Jean-Jacques Rousseau. Other leading figures of the early progressive education movement include Jane Addams and William Kilpatrick, a follower of Dewey.

What has been called progressive education has changed throughout the century, but in general, it is associated with social reform through education and emphasis on "child-centered" education as well as educational experimentation and the role of scientific method in education. Barry Kroll ("Developmental" [1980]) cites Freudianism and **expressionism** as major influences on progressive education, or as it was often called, "new education." Additionally, early and/ or liberal progressivists incorporated Dewey's belief that education should combine individual growth and development with social and community improvement. Dewey argued that the school, community, and home should not be isolated, but should all work together to educate children for academic success and democratic participation. According to Dewey, education should foster connections between scholastic subjects and the students' daily life. Schools were to emphasize democracy and to move away from elitist notions, such as the traditional literary canon. A "general education" was emphasized, moving beyond the emphasis on technical education and economic security. After World War I, proponents of progressive education attempted to use science, mainly social and behavioral, to improve education.

Progressive education has been viewed differently by liberals and conservatives. Liberal progressive reformers embraced educational reform that encouraged growth of smaller, local communities, the embracing of cultural difference, and nonelitist views—such views as those held by Dewey and Addams. Especially after World War I, progressive conservatives gained influence, saw community in larger terms than did the liberals, and attempted to establish centralized control of education. Such a move was supported by big business and those who advocated schools as a place where students learned, among other things, respect for **authority** and industrious work habits; education was seen as a means to train workers, not as a means for individual and social development (see Church for further discussion).

Scholars are somewhat divided as to the cause of the decline of the progressive education movement. Kroll (1980) claims that the progressive education movement was unified until after World War I, when it fragmented. Some commentators on progressive education find it most influential between the two world wars (see, for example, Christian O. Weber). Kenneth Kantor ("Creative" [1975]) sees it as most influential in the 1930s and coming under criticism for "permissiveness" in the 1940s and 1950s. Most scholars agree that the experience of World War II led to a popular reembracing of conservatism that carried over to views of education, thus halting the progress of experimental educational strategies. As **Arthur Applebee** (1974) points out, progressive education came under attack during the 1960s, especially for increased pragmatism, empiricism, and an overly broad conception of "general education" (*Tradition* 174–75). Contemporary composition studies has looked to progressive education for its emphasis on child-centered education, its use of psychology, and its focus on social reform—all concerns of modern composition scholars. Scholars have also drawn on Dewey in establishing service-learning courses that encourage community outreach through writing. Service-learning reflects Dewey's ideal of community and school interaction. Through their recent work, Lucille McCarthy and Stephen Fishman have helped rekindle interest in Dewey's progressive ideas for education. Additionally, scholars, including James Marshall ("Of What" [1994]), have begun to take a closer look at progressive education in order to recognize the parallels between the writing-as-a-**process** movement and progressivism and to learn from the failures and accomplishments of this earlier movement.

(b) "Progressive education was an extension of political progressivism, the optimistic faith in the possibility that all institutions could be reshaped to better serve society, making it healthier, more prosperous, and happier" (Berlin, *Rhetoric and Reality* 58).

"Deweyan progressivism, therefore, originated as a self-conscious attempt to make schooling socially responsive: oriented towards a social future rather than a cultural past. Its goal was to provide the skills, knowledge, and social attitudes required for urbanized commercial and industrial society" (Castell & Luke 166).

(c) "The Progressive movement revived Rousseau's ideal of linking citizenship and individual education by treating the principles of democracy as a ground for a consistent view of personal development and social responsibility" (Herzberg, "Composition" 110).

"The search for a new function and a new method was begun in the rhetoric and enthusiasm that marked the Progressive Era in education, and if the leaders of NCTE were only occasionally themselves comfortable in the company of the leaders of the progressive movement, preferring in general a more moderate and subject-oriented position, they were buoyed by the optimism and sense of mission that pervaded the movement as a whole" (Applebee, *Tradition* 131).

"By virtually ignoring Dewey and the progressive movement in developing our own theory and practice, we have not only failed to exploit a rich resource, but we also have missed an opportunity to study how a movement similar to our own, but larger and more comprehensive, fared in making the kinds of changes in schools we hope to make" (Marshall, "Of What" 53).

(d) John Dewey.

PROTOCOL ANALYSIS / PROTOCOL

(a) Terms borrowed from cognitive psychology. Protocol analysis is a research tool in which researchers ask writers to verbalize their thoughts as they

compose, usually in front of a tape recorder. A protocol is the text that results
from the study and, ideally, represents what the writer thought as she wrote.
The researcher analyzes the protocol with the goal of uncovering information
about the composing process. David Dobrin credits Carnegie-Mellon for developing the model for protocol analysis, explaining that the initial reason for the
method was to improve the problem-solving capabilities of computers by having
them follow human methods ("Protocols Once More" [1986]). **Linda Flower**
and **John Hayes** introduced protocol analysis to the field of composition studies,
and they used it to develop a **cognitive model** of the writing **process** in their
1981 article "A Cognitive Process Theory of Writing." The protocol research
method was widely used in composition studies during the early and mid-1980s.

Protocol analysis and Flower and Hayes' use of it has been questioned by
other composition scholars. **Lester Faigley** and Stephen Witte express uncertainty about what can be learned from protocol analysis because of the artificial
writing situation ("Analyzing Revision" [1981]). The most notable critique of
protocol analysis is Marilyn Cooper and Michael Holzman's 1983 article "Talking about Protocols," in which the authors argue that protocols are unreliable
and invalid. Cooper and Holzman question the narrow scope of the protocols
("Do these people never fantasize about, say, lunch?") and the applicability of
the theories derived from the analysis to normal writing situations. They see a
strong probability that speaking aloud while writing influences and changes the
writing process. In his 1986 article, David Dobrin agrees with Cooper and Holzman's objections and cites more of his own. He dismisses protocol analysis
because it makes "implausible" assumptions about the writing process: that it is
a problem-solving process, that it consists of ordered steps, and that other cognitive processes do not interrupt the writing process (723). Recent composition
research acknowledges that the writing situation in protocol analysis is unnat-
ural, and thus claims based on protocol analysis must take this context into
account.

(b) "To collect a protocol, we give writers a problem . . . and then ask them
to compose out loud near an unobtrusive tape recorder. We ask them to work
on the task as they normally would—thinking, jotting notes, and writing—except that they must think out loud" (Flower & Hayes, "Cognitive" 368).

"The transcript of this session . . . is called a protocol. As a research tool, a
protocol is extraordinarily rich in data and, together with the writer's notes and
manuscript, it gives us a very detailed picture of the writer's composing process"
(Flower & Hayes, "Cognitive" 368).

"Protocols, far from being 'extraordinarily rich in data' are exceedingly im-
poverished sources of information on what writers are thinking about" (Cooper
& Holzman 286).

(c) "Analyzing a protocol is like following the tracks of a porpoise,
which occasionally reveals itself by breaking the surface of the sea" (Hayes &
Flower 9).

"The protocols of skilled writers document the ways in which they make a mental sketch of their audience and choose the type of discourse which best fits their representation" (Berkenkotter, "Understanding" 392).

"Protocols, then, are limited to what people can articulate, and by what they are asked to articulate. Protocol-based research also is limited by the degree to which protocol transcripts are summarized" (Brand 439).

"If, in other words, after reflecting on your own mental processes, you think that your fantasies about lunch might affect your writing, then you shouldn't believe that protocol analysis gives any special evidence" (Dobrin 723).

(d) **Carol Berkenkotter**, Linda Flower, John Hayes, **Sondra Perl**, cognitivists; critics include Marilyn Cooper, David Dobrin, Lester Faigley, Michael Holzman, Stephen Witte.

RADICAL PEDAGOGY

(a) A term sometimes used interchangeably with "critical pedagogy," "critical teaching," or "liberatory teaching" and associated with Marxist theories and the literacy programs of Paulo Freire.* Such a pedagogy attempts to expose that traditional education is not politically neutral, but privileges the elite. Critical thinking is a main emphasis in this pedagogy, as it aims to guide students to critical analysis of dominant culture and ideology. Students are urged to probe common sense assumptions and social structures in order to understand their historical production and the interests that they serve. Radical pedagogy serves as a critique of **positivism**, which presents a static view of the world and of knowledge that requires no critical thought, but only a passive acceptance of the status quo (see **banking education**). Traditional education's emphasis on standard English and correct grammar and form are also critiqued by radical pedagogists as methods of oppression and control (see, for example, John Rouse's "The Politics of Composition" [1979]). The goal of most radical pedagogy is political resistance and change. Recently, Virginia Anderson (1997) has questioned the effectiveness of some radical teachers' methods. While agreeing with their goals, she proposes that student **resistance** is not always productive and urges teachers to foster **identification** with students. Following up on Anderson's article, Derek Soles (1998) questions the role of radical pedagogy in the writing classroom, asserting that the teacher's goal should be to improve students' writing, not to change their political views. He claims that though a radical perspective seems almost commonplace in composition theory, "[m]any writing teachers and students simply do not share these beliefs" (268). In reply, Anderson (1998) proposes that because of the relationship between writing and thinking, teachers cannot help students improve their writing without also changing their views. Anderson also recognizes that the label "radical" is broad and can encompass a variety of teaching practices. The term is most widely discussed in composition studies during the late 1980s and 1990s. (See also **critical consciousness** and **critical literacy**.)

(b) "[Radical pedagogy] must somehow get them [students] outside their own repressive consciousness, allowing them to lift themselves up by their bootstraps" (Paine 558).

"[Proponents believe that] the conception of good writing that guides the standard composition course is little more than the rhetorical and grammatical complement of capitalism, that forcing students to write by conventional models is a form of bureaucratic or managerial social control, that the very encouragement of analytical modes of writing and thinking plays into the hands of our technocratic masters" (Graff, "Politics" 851).

(c) "radical pedagogy needs to be informed by a passionate faith in the necessity of struggling to create a better world. In other words, radical pedagogy needs a vision—one that celebrates not what is but what could be . . . it means appropriating the critical impulse so as to lay bare the distinction between reality and the conditions that conceal its possibilities" (Giroux, *Theory and Resistance* 242).

"The task of radical theory, especially in the case of radical educational theory, is to see Marxism not as a doctrine valid for all times under all historical conditions, but as a critical 'way of seeing' " (Aronowitz & Giroux 112).

"My sense that we often gloss over these fundamental processes through which we might create identification leads me to a final question: with whom, exactly, do radical scholars really want to identify?" (V. Anderson, "Confrontational" 212).

(d) Virginia Anderson, Stanley Aronowitz, Dale Bauer, **James Berlin, Patricia Bizzell, Lil Brannon**, Paulo Freire, Henry Giroux,* bell hooks, **Susan Jarratt, C. H. Knoblauch, Ira Shor**.

READER-BASED PROSE

(a) A type of writing defined by **Linda Flower** in her article "Writer-Based Prose: A Cognitive Basis for Problems in Writing" (1979). Flower describes this prose as that which is written by experienced writers who can put themselves in the place of the **audience** to see how they will respond to the text. According to Flower, this type of prose constitutes "good" writing. It is written with the audience in mind, is revised appropriately, and thus is a piece of successful communication. Flower uses this term in contrast to her term "**writer-based**" **prose**, writing that does not meet the audience's needs.

Flower's term comes out of a **cognitive** view of composition, and thus is often criticized by those whose views reflect **expressive** or social theories. For example, in a 1987 conference presentation, **Joseph Harris**, speaking from a social perspective, redefines reader-based prose as an exclusive, privileged discourse, which many students are not prepared to enter. **Peter Elbow** also modifies the definition of reader-based prose in his 1987 article "Closing My Eyes as I Speak: An Argument for Ignoring Audience." He makes an argument based on expressivist views that personal writing at times can be better than that written with the audience in mind (see discussion of this article under "writer-based prose"). The term appears most frequently in major composition journals and conferences in the early 1980s and again in the late 1980s as scholars adapt it to social views of writing.

(b) "In contrast [to writer-based prose], Reader-Based prose is a deliberate attempt to communicate something to a reader. To do that it creates a shared language and shared context between writer and reader. It also offers the reader an issue-centered rhetorical structure rather than a replay of the writer's discovery process" (Flower, "Writer-Based" 20).

"In reader-based prose . . . writers shape their discourse to create a shared context and language between themselves and the reader" (L. Perelman, "Context" 477).

(c) "Writer-Based prose needs to be revised into Reader-Based prose, but it can be effective as a 'medium for thinking' " (M. Harris, "Composing" 102).

"I go further now and argue that ignoring audience can lead to better writing—immediately. In effect, writer-based prose can be *better* than reader-based prose" (Elbow, "Closing" 54).

(d) Linda Flower.

REAL VOICE (see AUTHENTIC VOICE)

RECIPE SWAPPING

(a) A term used by **Ann E. Berthoff** in a 1979 presentation, later published in *The Making of Meaning* (1981). The term refers to the practices of those composition teachers who neglect to apply theory to their classrooms. The term has negative connotations because though Berthoff sees the necessity for practicality in the classroom and understands teachers' reluctance to follow abstract principles, she also sees the need for composition theory to serve as a guidepost and justification for classroom action. Berthoff sees recipe swapping, practice not backed by theory, as an unproductive and potentially detrimental classroom convention.

(b) "the result of rejecting theory" (Berthoff, *Making* 4).

(c) "[Berthoff] writes frequently about 'recipe swapping' which seems to be her version of what Practitioners, left alone or at their typical worst, might do. . . . 'Recipe swapping' thus sounds as if it might be her account of lore and its production, but one can't be sure" (North 334–35).

"Although it is not my purpose to hold up an assignment for others to imitate—I am reminded of Ann Berthoff's wry observation about writing teachers swapping recipes—I would assume that any ideas springing from the following

examples will be naturally altered when they are applied in different contexts"
(Minock 502).

"We English teachers are given to recipe swapping—and that can be hazard-
ous" (Berthoff, *Making* 33).

(d) Ann E. Berthoff.

RECURSIVE

(a) A term adopted from mathematics that explains the accepted "order" of
the writing **process**, which is, in effect, not ordered; prewriting, writing, revising, and editing occur throughout the writing process at various stages. This
term entered the composition conversation with the emphasis on **cognitive process** theories. It became a key term in scholarly conversation during the early
and mid-1980s with influential studies on the processes of writing such as those
by **Sondra Perl** ("Understanding Composing" [1980]) and **Nancy Sommers**
("Revision Strategies of Student Writers and Experienced Adult Writers" [orig-
inally published in 1980]). **Linda Flower** and **John Hayes** are often associated
with the concept because of their 1981 article "A Cognitive Process Theory of
Writing." In this article, they claim that the recursiveness of their cognitive
process model differentiates it from the linear stage models of writing. Earlier
writing models had portrayed a strictly ordered sequence of writing activities
which is now considered an outdated way of classifying the writing process.

(b) "The term refers to the fact that writers can engage in any act of composing—finding ideas, thinking about ways of organizing them, imagining ways
of expressing them—at any time during their writing and often perform these
acts many times while writing" (Larson, "Competing" 284).

"We have advocated the idea that writing is a recursive process, that throughout the process of writing, writers return to substrands of the overall process,
or subroutines . . . [and] writers use these to keep the process moving forward"
(Perl, "Understanding" 305).

(c) "The experienced writers see their revision process as a recursive process—a process with significant recurring activities—with different levels of
attention and different agenda for each cycle" (Sommers 127).

"While it is established practice today to speak of the composing process as
a recursive activity involving prewriting, writing, and rewriting, it is not difficult
to see the writer-reality-audience-language relationship as underlying each of
these three stages" (Berlin, "Contemporary" 47).

"The outcome of the Emig monograph [*The Composing Processes of Twelfth
Graders*] was more than significant, for it convinced many teachers to focus on
the process of composition, not the product, and provided the basis for a model
that became virtually doctrinal: prewriting, writing, and rewriting recursively"
(Winterowd, *English* 4).

(d) **Carol Berkenkotter, Ann E. Berthoff, Janet Emig**, Linda Flower, John
Hayes, Sondra Perl, Nancy Sommers.

REFLECTIVE

(a) A term that is often combined with others—such as reflective practice, reflective thought, and reflective writing. The term comes primarily from educational theory and refers to thinking focused on solving problems, improving situations, or coming to terms with and making connections between the real and ideal, or the past, present, and future. It refers to one's awareness of one's own thought processes, whether in relation to writing, teaching, or other forms of problem solving.

The concept was developed by John Dewey.* (See especially *How We Think* [1910].) For Dewey, an education should foster reflective thinking as opposed to "mere thinking" and to the more traditional emphasis on memorization and recitation. In recent educational theory, Donald A. Schön, who builds on the work of Dewey, is credited with popularizing the concept. (See especially *The Reflective Practitioner: How Professionals Think in Action* [1983] and *Educating the Reflective Practitioner: Toward a New Design for Teaching and Learning in the Professions* [1987].) Schön argues against professional education that values only "systematic" or scientific knowledge at the expense of knowledge gained by "reflection-in-action," claiming that students need more than technical knowledge to enter their profession as prepared practitioners, since often the problems they will face are not "textbook" cases, but are complex and unique. In his later work, he proposes a new design for professional education based on the ideals of "reflective practicums" and teachers as coaches.

The term is often used in reference to teacher education and development, as experts now encourage teachers toward "reflective practice." Used in this way, the term refers to teachers' critical thinking about their practices in the classroom as well as their interrelations with students. A reflective practice connotes professional growth and development as teachers carefully consider what has worked in their classrooms and what has not and as they analyze and theorize the reasons for their successes and failures in their particular context.

In composition studies, the term is often found in conversations about the training of new teachers and about professional development. For example, in teaching practicums, some graduate teaching assistants keep a teaching journal as a requirement. Such a journal, supporters propose, allows new teaching assistants the opportunity to make connections between the material studied in the practicum and the reality of the classroom in which they teach. (As Sarah Liggett [1997] argues, however, the teaching journal should not be put away after the practicum ends, as it is helpful for writing teachers at all levels in their careers.) Graduate teaching assistants are also encouraged to reflect critically on classroom practice through the text *Scenarios for Teaching Writing: Contexts for Discussion and Reflective Practice* (Anson et al. [1993]), which represents various classroom scenarios, encouraging new teachers to reflect on and discuss possible courses of action. Building on Schön's work, **George Hillocks, Jr.**, in *Teaching Writing as Reflective Practice* (1995), encourages a reflective practice for both new and seasoned writing instructors that examines composition theory as well as informs it.

In addition to teacher education and development, reflective thinking is urged for students in the writing classroom. A standard feature of a writing **portfolio** is the reflective letter of self-evaluation. As Alice Horning (1997) argues, such reflective writing allows students a greater awareness of their own writing strategies and processes while fostering a more productive relationship between students and teachers, as teachers can gain insight into students' attitudes and thoughts about writing and can better respond to students' concerns about their development as writers. Additionally, reflection, through journal writing and class discussion, is an important part of service-learning composition classes. In relation to reflective writing in the service-learning classroom, Chris Anson (1997) reminds instructors that reflection does not occur automatically but that reflective journal entries result from instructor guidance, encouragement, and response. Anson encourages the development of a journal-writing genre for service-learning separate from the journals used in other composition courses that better enables reflection. **Collaborative learning** is also largely thought to encourage reflective thought as students must articulate and at times defend their ideas to their classmates. (Lorraine Higgins, **Linda Flower**, and Joseph Petraglia, however, have asserted that collaboration does not necessarily result in reflection [1992].)

"Reflective" is a key term in discussions of teaching students to develop critical thinking skills. It is associated with development of **critical consciousness** and thus with the work of liberatory pedagogists such as Paulo Freire* and Henry Giroux.* The term is most used in composition studies beginning in the mid-1980s. By 1996 the concept was so widely discussed that the **NCTE** annual conference was entitled "Learning and Literacies: Reflecting on Reflection, Self-Assessment, and External Assessment."

(b) "True, reflective attention, . . . always involves judging, reasoning, deliberation; it means that the child has a question of his own and is actively engaged in seeking and selecting relevant material with which to answer it, considering the bearings and relations of this material—the kind of solution it calls for" (Dewey, *School* 148–49).

"When teachers reason about choices, plan in light of those reasons, implement those plans, examine their impact on students, and revise and reformulate reasons and plans in light of all that experience, that conjunction constitutes theory-driven teaching. Such teachers are engaged in reflective practice and inquiry" (Hillocks, *Teaching* 36–37).

(c) "I shall assemble the outlines of a theory of the reflective practicum as a vehicle for education in artistry—a response to the predicament of professional schools increasingly aware of the need to prepare students for competence in the indeterminate zones of practice" (Schön, *Educating* 21).

"Reflective practice is a key catalyst in the transformation from GTA to Writing Instructor" (Liggett 1).

"Many composition teachers now assume that collaboration in its many forms ... provides an ideal context for fostering <u>reflective thinking</u>. Teachers assign these activities hoping they will help students reflect on their own ideas and writing processes" (Higgins et al. 53).

"Instead of adopting common practices for journal writing in standard, self-contained composition classes, we need to create a genre of the academic journal for service-learning courses that deliberately, creatively, and effectively brings the concept of <u>reflection</u> into sharp focus" (Anson 170).

(d) Chris Anson, John Dewey, George Hillocks, Jr., **Louise Weatherbee Phelps**, Donald Schön.

RESISTANCE

(a) A term that is part of the conversation of various disciplines including critical theory, psychoanalysis, and composition studies. In composition studies, it is most often used in the context of **radical pedagogy**, poststructuralist discourse, and cultural studies. Scholars use the term to describe the reactions of some students who are asked to scrutinize cultural assumptions and societal power structures. In radical or liberatory pedagogy, "resistance" is used in reference to the literacy practices of Henry Giroux* and Paulo Freire* and describes disruptive behavior within the educational system that has a productive political purpose of critiquing the dominant social order. Resistance can take many forms, as for instance a student's refusal to respond to an assignment. In these terms, such behavior is not futile defiance (see **opposition**), but brings about further action to resist and reform unjust political systems.

The term often surfaces in discussions of the composition classroom as an avenue for students to explore and confront difference—especially of gender, race, and class. In this context, scholars often report on student resistance, their anger and hostility, when faced with ideologies that oppose their own. Such emotion is viewed as a useful and necessary part of the educational process. For example, in "Writing Passionately: Student Resistance to Feminist Readings," Janice Wolff (1991) discusses the angry responses of some first-year composition students when confronted with feminist readings that challenged their beliefs. Wolff concludes that such student reaction can be educationally productive if countered by "teacherly resistance" that encourages students to write about and explore their initial resistances. Similarly exploring resistance in the classroom, Angelletta Gourdine (1991) argues that resistance must be a part of the response of African-American students to the socialization of the composition classroom. Urging a productive use of student resistance in the classroom, Victor Villanueva (1991) asks students to reflect on their own resistance, and Beth Daniell and **Art Young** (1993) encourage writing teachers to help students "learn to resist effectively," citing a connection between students' critique of educational **authority** and critical thinking (232).

Professional writers also show signs of resistance; in this context, writers may choose to resist the discourse conventions of their professional community. As Gesa Kirsch has shown (1993), women in the academy often resist the formality and impersonality of traditional **academic discourses**, favoring instead a way of writing that reaches a broader **audience** and that involves **collaboration**. Looking also at resistance to professional discourse conventions, Carl Herndl (1993, 1996) studies writing in nonacademic settings and notes ways that professionals resist institutional expectations.

Scholars sometimes use the term in connection with psychoanalysis, drawing largely on the work of Sigmund Freud and Jacques Lacan. For example, Patrick McGee (1987) and Ann Murphy (1989) make connections between a patient's resistance to therapy in psychoanalysis and a composition student's resistance to writing and teaching. (For further discussion of resistance in a Freudian context, see *College English*, October & November 1987, a double-issue dedicated to psychoanalysis and pedagogy.) In this context, Shoshana Felman's work on psychoanalysis and education (1982) has also been influential in composition studies. "Resistance" becomes a prominent term in the field of composition beginning in the late 1980s.

(b) "Resistance is not only a way of saying 'no' to the dominant culture, but a way of saying 'yes' to an alternative vision of the culture which is more truly democratic in nature. An act of resistance must be seen as an act of refusal which holds within it a critique of the dominant culture because it works to do, or present, something as an alternative" (Chase, "Perhaps" 31).

"Resistance is more than willful ignorance or dysfunctional behavior. Instead, it is a means by which people respond to the constraints of social and educational structures" (Ritchie, "Resistance" 118).

"Resistance can be defined as those games or strategies, ranging from fun to deadly seriousness, played by those with little or no power against those with power; the point of resistance is to diffuse authority, to thwart the plans of the bosses" (Daniell & Young 224–25).

(c) "In other words, resistance must have a revealing function, one that contains a critique of domination and provides theoretical opportunities for self-reflection and for struggle in the interest of self-emancipation and social emancipation" (Giroux, *Theory & Resistance* 109).

"Borrowing from Henry Giroux's adaptation of resistance theory, students are asked to consider in their writing the degrees to which they can or do resist, oppose or accommodate conflicts" (Villanueva 259).

"Every instance of student misbehavior—scrawled writing on an assignment, failure to complete an assignment, fighting, taking drugs, absenteeism—cannot be interpreted as evidence of resistance. The analysis of resistance as a phenomenon must be more judicious to be persuasive, Giroux argues" (Erickson 220).

(d) Paulo Freire, Henry Giroux, **Ira Shor**, radical pedagogists, proponents of cultural studies, feminists.

RESTRICTED CODE

(a) A term used by Basil Bernstein, a British educational sociologist, in *Class, Codes, and Control* (volume one [1971], volume two [1973], and volume three [1975]). Bernstein researched the influence of class on working- and middle-class school children and found a correlation between socioeconomic class and language use. According to Bernstein, the restricted code is used mainly by working-class children whose families are organized around strict authority figures and systems that are not to be questioned. The code itself is characterized by simple sentence structures, specific contexts, communal responses, and concrete, not abstract, discussion. Bernstein argues that children using this code are often more comfortable and perhaps learn more in classrooms with strong **authority** figures emphasizing drills and specific grading scales. It is opposed to the **elaborated code**.

(b) "a syntax with few choices" (Bernstein 1:152).

"[The codes] realize context-dependent principles and meanings. The principles and meanings are embedded in local contexts, in local social relationships, practices, activities. To this extent they are relatively strongly related to a specific material base" (Bernstein 1:193–94).

(c) "For if Bernstein and [Claus] Mueller are right, those who have available only a restricted code can do little more than passively observe the shaping of the future" (Ohmann, "Reflections" 8).

"Those who can only teach their children a restricted code belong to a social class far removed from the major decision-making areas of the social structure, they have limited access to those specialized roles that require and teach an elaborated code" (Rouse 8).

"Equally clearly, the child who has only the restricted code figures to be a loser in the competitive world after schooling, a world rigged for those whose less communal, middle-class childhood has forced them to master the elaborated code" (Graff, "Politics" 853).

(d) Basil Bernstein.

ROGERIAN RHETORIC

(a) A form of rhetoric, sometimes referred to as "empathetic," derived from a method of psychotherapy developed by Carl Rogers* in the 1950s and early 1960s. His 1951 paper "Communication: Its Blocking and Its Facilitation" is often cited as the most influential application of his theories to rhetoric (Lunsford, "Aristotelian" 147). Rogers' theories are based on the premise that communication is often hindered because the participants in a communication act feel threatened. His techniques were initially used by therapists who would continually restate the patient's perspective with the purpose of fully understanding it. According to this perspective, a writer or speaker should attempt to objectively understand the opposition's case and values.

Richard Young, Alton Becker, and **Kenneth Pike** adapted Rogerian ideas to writing theory in their 1970 text *Rhetoric: Discovery and Change*, and Rogerian concepts influence their well-known **tagmemic heuristic. Maxine Hairston** was also influential in introducing Rogers' methods to the writing classroom through her 1974 text *A Contemporary Rhetoric* and through her 1976 **CCCC** conference presentation and article "Carl Rogers's Alternative to Traditional Rhetoric." Many see Rogerian rhetoric as a more inclusive, less combative alternative to Aristotelian rhetoric. (**Andrea Lunsford** disagrees with this opposition, however, in her 1979 article "Aristotelian vs. Rogerian Rhetoric: A Reassessment.") The Rogerian method is most often used to teach argument but can also be applied to all aspects of the composition classroom, including class discussion and responding to students' papers.

Some critics argue that this method incorrectly assumes that we can speak of a subject without being influenced by personal biases or past experiences. **James (Jim) Corder** proposes limits to the Rogerian approach, explaining that at times, threat cannot be eliminated (see "Argument as Emergence, Rhetoric as Love," originally published in 1985). In contrast, **Lisa Ede**, in her 1983 CCCC presentation and 1984 article, questions whether Rogerian rhetoric is really Rogerian. She faults Young, Becker, and Pike for distorting Rogers' principles into steps for argument with emphasis on an "opponent" and "winner," terms that contradict Rogers' nonevaluative perspective.

Feminists are divided on the method: some see Rogerian argument as feminist and beneficial because it appears less antagonistic than traditional Aristotelian argument. Others argue that when used by women, this type of argument reinforces the "feminine" stereotype, since historically women are viewed as non-confrontational and understanding (see especially Catherine E. Lamb's 1991 article "Beyond Argument in Feminist Composition" and Phyllis Lassner's 1990 article "Feminist Responses to Rogerian Argument"). In composition studies, the concept appears most between the late 1970s and the mid-1980s.

(b) "The primary goal of this rhetorical strategy is to reduce the reader's sense of threat so that he is able to consider alternatives to his own beliefs. The goal is thus not to work one's will on others but to establish and maintain communication as an end in itself" (Young, Becker, & Pike 8).

"Unlike Aristotelian rhetoric, which assumes an adversarial relationship between speaker and listener and strives for speaker control, Rogerian argument, based on the patient-client therapy of Carl Rogers, seeks conversion through mutual acceptance and understanding" (Ewald, "Implied" 168).

(c) "Rogerian theory is predicated on the existence of a non-evaluative language with which the therapist (or rhetor) can restate the client's (or audience's) views in a non-threatening manner" (Brent 458).

"My experience using Rogerian argument and teaching it to my students, is that it is feminine rather than feminist. . . . Rogerian argument has always felt too much like giving in" (Lamb 17).

(d) Alton Becker, James Corder, (some) feminists, Maxine Hairston, Kenneth Pike, Carl Rogers, Richard Young.

SCOTTISH COMMON SENSE REALISM

(a) A school of thought that influenced writing instruction and rhetorical theory in American universities, beginning in the early nineteenth century. Many composition texts written in the late nineteenth century were influenced by this philosophy; thus, the reach of this view of writing was broad. This philosophy greatly influenced the rhetorical treatises of **George Campbell** and **Hugh Blair**, who shaped the field of rhetoric and writing instruction in the nineteenth century. As **Winifred Bryan Horner** (*Nineteenth-Century Scottish Rhetoric* [1993]) explains, most scholars credit Francis Hutcheson (1694–1746) with founding the school of thought, and Thomas Reid did much to articulate the philosophy in the eighteenth century.

According to the tenet's of Scottish Common Sense Realism, reality can be objectively observed through sensory perception. Emphasis is on personal observation because language and social factors can distort the "truth." The world is readily observable to all who look, and nothing other than "proper observation" is required, not even logic. Because reality is transparent, to communicate, the writer or speaker must only use the "correct" word, which responds to the external world. Such philosophy does not recognize a difference between the word and that which is described. This view of language supported the idea of scientific objectivity, and its influence is felt today in the tendency to see scientific prose as "objective" and nonpersuasive (see David Russell's *Writing in the Academic Disciplines* [1991]).

Scottish Common Sense Realism is also seen to foster the belletristic emphasis of composition courses in the nineteenth and twentieth centuries. The concept of taste is a major ingredient in the Scottish Common Sense philosophy, especially in the work of Hugh Blair and George Campbell, as they argue that along with one's sensory perceptions comes an innate sense of order and beauty, which must be cultivated. This aspect of the philosophy continues to influence today's composition classes and texts that place importance on literary and personal writing, metaphors and analogies, and strong authorial voice. (See Horner for a more detailed explanation; see also **current-traditional rhetoric**.)

(b) "Scottish Common Sense Realism locates reality in two discrete realms, the spiritual and the material, and posits a set of separate and likewise discrete mental faculties constituted so as to apprehend each" (Berlin, *Writing* 6).

"In summation, the Scottish commonsense philosophy proceeded on the premise that the human mind could be studied by observation" (W. Horner, *Nineteenth* 30).

(c) "The naive view of language as transparent recorder of thought or physical reality grew up with the scientific method in the eighteenth and nineteenth centuries. It underlay the <u>Scottish Common Sense</u> rhetorical theory of Hugh Blair and George Campbell, which Americans imported in the early nineteenth century" (Russell 10).

"<u>Common Sense Realism</u> denies the value of the deductive method—syllogistic reasoning—in arriving at knowledge. Truth is instead discovered through induction alone" (Berlin, "Contemporary" 51).

(d) Hugh Blair, George Campbell, Winifred Bryan Horner, Francis Hutcheson, Thomas Reid, Adam Smith, **Richard Whately**.

SENTENCE-COMBINING

(a) An activity used in composition courses with the intention of expanding or combining "kernel" or simple sentences into complex sentences. The underlying idea behind a sentence-combining pedagogy is that "mature" or successful writers create complex, embedded sentences. Sentence-combining stems from Noam Chomsky's **transformational-generative grammar**, which views long, complex sentences as a combination of short core sentences. (Shirley Rose [1983] argues, however, that sentence-combining was in use long before Chomsky's advocation of it.) Kellogg Hunt's studies in the 1960s and early 1970s were integral in fostering interest and faith in sentence-combining, as his studies indicated that through sentence-combining activities, students learned to increase the **T-unit** length of their sentences, and thus, according to Hunt, the maturity of their writing. John Mellon, influenced by Hunt's work, was an influential advocate of sentence-combining, as argued in his 1969 book *Transformational Sentence Combining*; building on Mellon, **Frank O'Hare** furthered the study of sentence combining in his 1973 work *Sentence-Combining: Improving Student Writing Without Formal Grammar Instruction*.

In the classroom, sentence-combining is often practiced by drills in which students are given several "kernel" sentences and instructed to combine them into one complex sentence. At its peak, sentence-combining was seen by some as a cure-all, with complex sentences alone indicating a writer's competence. Another danger of a sentence-combining pedagogy is that complex sentences can be seen as a good in themselves, regardless of whether a complex form will better communicate the information in a certain rhetorical situation (see, for example, **Mina Shaughnessy**'s *Errors and Expectations* [1977] and Robert De Beaugrande's "Sentence Combining and Discourse Processing" [1985]). Others, including **Lester Faigley** ("Names in Search of a Concept" [1980]), argue that the T-unit, which is normally used to measure the success of sentence-combining exercises, is not an adequate indicator of the success or failure of a sentence-combining pedagogy because measures such as T-units or clause lengths do not prove anything about a writer's ability to respond effectively to a rhetorical situation.

By 1983, Michael Holzman concludes that "the main influence of the hard-line sentence combiners has passed" ("Scientism and Sentence Combining"). In the 1980s, however, some scholars attempted to situate sentence-combining within the current academic context. For example, in their 1985 collection *Sentence Combining: A Rhetorical Perspective*, Donald Daiker, Andrew Kerek, and Max Morenberg contend that though not as popular as it once was, sentence-combining is still in use in composition classrooms, still of interest to practitioners and scholars, and still pedagogically important. Contributors to this collection reexamine sentence-combining in relation to **process** and rhetorical theories of composing. From the 1960s to the mid-1980s, much was written about sentence-combining. In the 1990s, articles and presentations surface occasionally about the topic, and sentence-combining exercises can still be found in handbooks, but the discussion has certainly slowed.

(**b**) "In that it is governed by certain 'rules,' sentence-combining is much like a game. The point of the game is to produce one sentence (not two or three) from the given kernel sentences" (Graves, "Levels" 228).

"We can formulate three of the most crucial presuppositions of the sentence-combining enterprise: 1. The maturity and quality of one's writing are meaningfully dependent on the relative syntactic complexity of the sentences. 2. Student writing is inadequate because the sentences are not sufficiently elaborated syntactically. 3. Explicit training in the combining of sentences will carry over to one's normal writing skills" (De Beaugrande, "Sentence" 63).

(**c**) "Perhaps the strongest contribution of sentence combining to writing pedagogy is its substitution of a creative, sentence-*building* activity for the sentence-*repairing* drills traditional to writing texts" (Foster 67).

"Despite the lack of a coherent theory or rationale, despite some overly unqualified and overgeneralized claims about its benefits, sentence combining as a classroom methodology is enjoying continued vitality and adaptability—and this in the face of dramatic developments in the teaching of writing that could have left it hopelessly behind" (Daiker, Kerek, & Morenberg xiii).

(**d**) Noam Chomsky, Donald Daiker, Kellogg Hunt, Andrew Kerek, John C. Mellon, Max Morenberg, Frank O'Hare.

SOCIAL CONSTRUCTION

(**a**) A theory that has a philosophical base in the works of Thomas Kuhn* and Richard Rorty,* especially in their works *The Structure of Scientific Revolutions* (1962) and *Philosophy and the Mirror of Nature* (1979), respectively. Social constructionists are known for being **anti-foundational**, meaning that they view **knowledge** not as objective facts but as community-produced and maintained through **conversation** and **consensus**. Therefore, "truth" is defined only as community agreement on a matter, which can change through persuasion. Language is key to this philosophy as individuals cannot gain an unmediated view of the world, but both see and construct the world through language. Greatly influential in composition studies, this view has also been called "new pragmatism" or "dialogism."

The discussion of social construction in scientific circles has been controversial in that social construction requires a break from the traditional **positivistic** view that scientific knowledge is objective, divorced from concerns of rhetoric and persuasion. In contrast, social constructionists argue that scientific truths are arrived at through rhetorical negotiation in the scientific community. For example, Bruno Latour and Steve Woolgar (*Laboratory Life: The Social Construction of Scientific Facts* [1979]) conducted an **ethnographic** study of biochemical research and traced what they saw as the social construction of a scientific "fact" by studying the negotiations and inscriptive practices in a Pasteur Institute lab. They demonstrated that the process of "fact construction" is not as well ordered as scientists' reconstructions in publications suggest, instead entailing negotiation, confrontation, and persuasion. Latour and Woolgar argue that scientific "facts" should be seen in relation to the circumstances of their production. Other influential research on the social construction of knowledge in scientific communication includes K. D. Knorr-Cetina's 1981 *The Manufacture of Knowledge: An Essay on the Constructivist and Contextual Nature of Science*, **Charles Bazerman**'s 1983 "Scientific Writing as a Social Act," and Greg Myers' 1985 article "The Social Construction of Two Biologists' Proposals" and 1990 *Writing Biology.*

Kenneth Bruffee has been important in popularizing and developing the social constructionist perspective in composition studies, especially in relation to **collaborative** learning. In "Writing and Reading as Collaborative or Social Acts" (1983), based on the work of Thomas Kuhn, Richard Rorty, Stanley Fish, and Lev Vygotsky,* Bruffee argues that reading and writing are inherently social, contrary to the traditional view that they are solitary, individual acts. As Bruffee explains, writing is influenced by the writer's larger social context. Therefore, learning to write involves participating in the negotiation of meaning as a member of a **discourse community**, and collaborative learning mirrors the negotiation of knowledge described by social constructionists. In "Collaborative Learning and the 'Conversation of Mankind' " (1984), Bruffee further develops his social constructionist argument for collaboration, advising the use of pedagogical techniques such as writing **workshops** and peer tutors. (See also Bruffee's "Social Construction, Language, and the Authority of Knowledge: A Bibliographical Essay" [1986] and *Collaborative Learning: Higher Education, Interdependence, and the Authority of Knowledge* [1993].)

In addition, and sometimes complementary to collaborative learning, social constructionist philosophy is used to support a discourse community model of composition instruction. The underlying idea behind such a pedagogy is that to be successful communicators, students must understand the assumptions and expectations about communication held by their respective discourse communities (or by those they hope to join). Social constructionists find fault in **ex-**

pressionist and **cognitive** theories and pedagogies because, they argue, these theories focus too heavily on the individual. In the case of expressionism, they see too much emphasis on finding the individual's **"authentic voice"** without acknowledging the role of community and context, and in the case of cognitivism, on the individual's thought processes without considering how the social context affects the writer.

Social constructionist theories are also used in discussions of literacy and feminism. For example, **Patricia Bizzell**, in "Arguing about Literacy," (1988) supports a social constructionist view of literacy, one in which the definition of what constitutes literacy is arrived at collaboratively (as opposed to **E. D. Hirsch**, who seems to define literacy in relation to Western classical thought). Feminists use such theories to point out **essentialist** definitions of the "masculine" and "feminine," arguing that traditional gender roles are socially constructed.

Critics of social constructionism, such as Thomas Kent, often point out that the theory can lead to total relativism, as knowledge and meaning can be defined by individual communities. Others criticize its omission of the human agent, arguing against the replacement of individual voices with communal consensus (see, for example, **Donald Stewart**'s "Collaborative Learning and Composition: Boon or Bane?" [1988] and "Cognitive Psychologists, Social Constructionists, and Three Nineteenth-Century Advocates of Authentic Voice" [1992]). Some Marxists, feminists, and radical theorists fault social construction, especially Bruffee's articulation of it, for requiring and even celebrating a **consensus** that ignores marginal voices. **James Berlin** (*Rhetorics* [1996]) finds fault in social construction for omitting a full critique of economic and political institutions and existing power structures. According to Berlin, social constructionist views have failed to relinquish the idea that individuals can act freely, overcoming social and material limitations; he advocates instead a **social-epistemic rhetoric** (*Rhetorics* 80).

Largely through the influence of Kent, some in composition are beginning to look at the work of analytic philosopher Donald Davidson as an alternative to some of the problems seen in social constructionism. Davidson disagrees with the concept of **discourse communities**, arguing against the concept of discourse conventions and asserting that language is not "shared" but that each individual has his or her own "theory" of language. For Davidson, writing, or other discourse production, is interpretation, a **hermeneutical** act, and he calls his theory of interpretation "radical interpretation." This theory posits that when we communicate, we assume that those with whom we communicate hold similar beliefs to our own until proven otherwise. Once we see evidence to the contrary, we then improvise, creating a "passing theory" that allows communication. (For further discussion of Davidson's philosophy, see also Reed Way Dasenbrock [1991] and Kevin J. Porter [1998].)

In composition studies, the term "social construction" is most discussed beginning in the mid-1980s, with much popularity in the late 1980s and early

1990s, although problems with the application of social constructionism to composition, including problems resulting from a broad use of the term, began to surface in the 1980s.

(b) 'Social construction' assumes that the matrix of thought is not the individual self but some community of knowledgeable peers and the vernacular language of that community. That is, social construction understands knowledge and the authority of knowledge as community-generated, community-maintaining symbolic artifacts" (Bruffee, "Social Construction" 777).

"According to social constructionists, we manufacture our subjectivity through the social conventions we share with fellow human beings. We are who we are because of our position within a particular cultural domain or discourse community" (Kent, *Paralogic* 101).

(c) "Composition's social constructionists have also worked to disturb the discipline's harmonious image of the writing process as natural, asocial, and apolitical; they stress that no classroom and no piece of writing can ever be free from the problematic encounter between an individual and society" (N. Welch 148).

"However, the fact of social construction (its inability to escape a certain metaphysics or absolutism—the fact that it *is* a fact) seems to open up more questions than it answers" (Nealon 143).

"The social constructionist lives in a world in which people lose their identities in collaborative uses of language—in business, science, technology" (Stewart, "Cognitive" 283).

"It is surprising, given the current popularity of deconstruction and social construction theories, that so little attention has been paid to conceptualizations of power itself as socially constructed" (Hubbuch 42).

(d) Charles Bazerman, Patricia Bizzell, Kenneth Bruffee, Stanley Fish, Clifford Geertz,* Thomas Kuhn, Greg Myers, Richard Rorty, Lev Vygotsky.

SOCIAL EPISTEMIC

(a) One of three categories of current rhetorics named by **James Berlin** in his 1988 article "Rhetoric and Ideology in the Writing Class." This category corresponds to other social views of rhetoric and combines a **social constructionist** philosophy with views of **radical** scholars such as **Ira Shor** and Henry Giroux.* "Social epistemic" implies political awareness and concern for social reform. Berlin favors the social epistemic view over the other two classifications in his rhetorical taxonomy, **"cognitivist"** and **"expressionist,"** that he named as current in the 1988 article.

In developing the term, Berlin adds to his earlier category of "epistemic" rhetoric, adapted from Robert L. Scott's 1967 article "On Viewing Rhetoric as Epistemic." In *Rhetoric and Reality* (1987), Berlin sees "epistemic" as one of the three major **"transactional"** rhetorical approaches from 1960 to 1975. Berlin defines "epistemic" as a "**new rhetoric**," and in both "epistemic" and "social epistemic" rhetoric, all language is seen as a product of a specific time and place, with meaning always changing as a result of interaction of the writer, the **discourse community** and the social, political, material, and historical context in which the discourse takes place. **Knowledge** is found in the dialectic among the writer, community, and context. From a social epistemic view, language is the key in this dialectic, since knowledge is gained only through language. Berlin differentiates his two categories by defining social epistemic rhetoric as political, maintaining that it includes a critique of dominant society. The term "social epistemic" mostly appears as a key concept in major articles and presentations in the early 1990s, and is at times used interchangeably with **social constructionism** although Berlin differentiates these two terms, explaining in *Rhetoric, Poetics, and Cultures* (1996) that social-epistemic rhetoric has roots in social constructionism but reflects and responds to postmodernist issues.

(**b**) "Social-epistemic rhetoric views knowledge as an arena of ideological conflict: there are no arguments from transcendent truth since all arguments arise in ideology. It thus inevitably supports economic, social, political, and cultural democracy" (Berlin, "Rhetoric and Ideology" 489).

"Social-epistemic rhetoric is the study and critique of signifying practices in their relation to subject formation within the framework of economic, social, and political conditions" (Berlin, *Rhetorics* 77).

(**c**) "The 'contest' between expressivist and social epistemic rhetoricians masks larger concerns: the place of the irrational, the unconscious, and the affective in subject formation as well as the role of the hypermasculine critic in these schema" (Langstraat 10).

"I agree with the social-epistemic rhetoricians that we think in language, so that—in the logic of this argument—if we change the *way* students write, change their language, we also change *what* they think, what it is possible for them to think. If form is the shape of content, content is the shape of form" (L. Anderson 25).

"Berlin distinguishes theories that cater to the isolated individual—the romantic and cognitivist—from 'social-epistemic' theories of rhetoricians and compositionists who stress the engagement of the writer with an audience of real men and women in a real historical situation" (Killingsworth 36).

(**d**) James Berlin, radical pedagogists, social constructionists; epistemic rhetoric is often associated with **Alton Becker, Ann E. Berthoff, Richard Ohmann, Kenneth Pike, Richard Young, W. Ross Winterowd**.

SOLITARY AUTHOR

(**a**) A term used by Marilyn M. Cooper in her article "The Ecology of Writing," which appeared in *College English* in April 1986. It describes the "ideal" writer projected by the **cognitive process** model, which Cooper argues, ignores the complex social contexts that influence writers and their writing. "Solitary authors" do not see their writing as a part of an ongoing conversation about their topic, but as a text—a finished product. According to Cooper, many writing classes are shaped by this image, though others escape it through pedagogical tools such as **collaborative** writing, open discussion, "real-world" writing, and group editing. Along with Cooper, other scholars in the middle and late 1980s critiqued the notion of writing as a solitary act. For example, **Linda Brodkey**, in "Modernism and the Scene(s) of Writing" (1987), suggests "revising" the scene of writing to incorporate the social, political, and historical contexts of writing. The concept is important in composition studies because it supports social theories and pedagogies of writing while positioning the cognitive and **expressive** views as insufficient because of their apparent focus on the individual.

(b) "The solitary author works alone, within the privacy of his own mind. He uses free writing exercises and heuristics to find out what he knows about a subject and to find something he wants to say to others; he uses his analytic skills to discover a purpose, to imagine an audience, to decide on strategies, to organize content; and he simulates how his text will be read by reading it over himself, making the final revisions necessary to assure its success when he abandons it to the world of which he is not a part" (M. Cooper, "Ecology" 366).

(c) "Indeed, the notion of the solitary author whose main goal is the discovery and communication of personal meaning ignores the institutional context of classroom writing and the consequent attitudes students bring to it" (L. Perelman, "Context" 471).

"When I picture writing, I often see a solitary writer alone in a cold garret working into the small hours of the morning by the thin light of a candle. It seems a curious image to conjure, for I am absent from this scene in which the writer is an Author and the writing is Literature. In fact it is not my scene at all" (Brodkey, "Modernism" 396).

"In 'Modernism and the Scene(s) of Writing,' . . . Linda Brodkey demonstrates how the suppressed metaphor of the scene of writing—that of 'a solitary writer alone in a garret working into the small hours of the morning' (396)—has influenced the teaching of writing" (Ede, "Teaching" 124).

(d) Linda Brodkey, Marilyn M. Cooper.

SPEECH ACT THEORY

(a) A theory originating with J. L. Austin in his 1955 William James lectures on philosophy of language at Harvard. The lectures were published in 1962 and entitled *How to Do Things with Words*. John Searle further developed Austin's ideas, especially in *Speech Acts: An Essay in the Philosophy of Language* (1969). Searle concluded that language itself is a form of action, that language *does* things; it does not simply *report* or *describe*. Austin called language that "does" something "performative," in contrast to "constative" language, which does not aim to get something done, but describes or makes a statement. Eventually, however, he came to see all language as performative. An often-cited example of the performative aspect of speech is the statement "I do" at a wedding ceremony. Speech acts are divided into three categories: the locutionary (or the propositional), the illocutionary, and the perlocutionary. A locutionary act is a proposition; it refers to the act of the speaker as he or she speaks; an illocutionary act refers to that which is performed by the speaker in making the proposition (a threat, a question, an order), and a perlocutionary act refers to how the speech affects or influences the listener (intimidating, puzzling, impressing). In literary studies, reader-response theorists, including Stanley Fish, have used speech act theory to interpret literary texts, and scholars, including **Richard Ohmann**, have encouraged the use of speech act theory in analysis of literary style. Ohmann focuses on the illocutionary act, analyzing choices made by writers as they attempted to accomplish the perlocutionary act, or attempted to create the desired effect on the reader. These choices, Ohmann proposes, are stylistically important. (See especially "Speech, Action, and Style" [1971] and "Instrumental Style: Notes on the Theory of Speech as Action" [1972].)

In composition studies, such literary analysis can be adapted to the study of student texts and prose models. Additionally, speech act theory can be used in discussions of the writing **process**, audience awareness, voice, and text interpretation. For example, Susan Mallet (1985) uses speech act theory to help student writers see themselves as "co-communicants" with their audience, and Kim Lovejoy (1987) applies speech act theory to the teaching of revision. **Winifred Bryan Horner** (1979), however, suggests the use of "text act" in place of "speech act" when referring to written compositions. Focusing on composition theory, Paul Beauvais (1986, 1989) encourages a redefinition of "metadiscourse" in the context of speech act theory, and Reed Way Dasenbrock (1987) proposes speech act theory as a "point of departure" for a new rhetoric (292). For Dasenbrock, speech act theory as explained by Austin offers positive options for a **new rhetoric**, as opposed to classical rhetoric with its focus on persuasion and tropes—a focus, Dasenbrock claims, that holds negative connotations. Speech act theory is most frequently discussed in composition during the 1970s and then again in the late 1980s and early 1990s.

(b) "The theory of speech acts starts with the assumption that the minimal unit of human communication is not a sentence or other expression, but rather the performance of certain kinds of acts, such as making statements, asking questions, giving orders, describing, explaining, apologizing, thanking, congratulating, etc." (Searle, Kiefer, & Bierwisch vii).

(c) "Speech act theory, then, reintroduces the concept of speaker/writer with intentions and hearer/reader with idiosyncratic responses into the study of style. Style once again becomes the concern of rhetoric proper" (Winterowd, "Linguistics" 215).

"Finally, if, by explicitly expressing our teaching in terms of speech-act theory, we discover our students' expectations of informative speech and show the written corollaries of each one, we will acknowledge that they are trying to do the right things, that we agree with their aims, and that we can help them 'translate' their communicative aims from one context to another" (Mallet 133–34).

"What I hope to show is that Austin's work with speech acts ... gives us a point of departure for the construction of a new rhetoric that conserves the essentials of a rhetorical vision of language, defends that rhetorical view against the traditional attacks on it, yet is also free of several aspects of classical rhetoric that are now outmoded" (Dasenbrock, "Austin" 292).

(d) J. L. Austin, Paul Grice, Winifred Bryan Horner, Richard Ohmann, Mary Louise Pratt, John Searle, **W. Ross Winterowd**.

T-UNITS

(a) An abbreviation for "minimum terminable units." Kellogg Hunt first used the term in his book *Grammatical Structures Written at Three Grade Levels* (1965) to describe a method of measuring syntactic maturity. A T-unit contains an independent or main clause along with subordinate clauses and clause modifiers. Grammatically, a T-unit is a sentence and can be punctuated as a single sentence, but a sentence may contain more than one T-unit. Judging from the results of his studies conducted in the 1960s, Hunt claimed that mature writers produce sentences with longer T-units. This claim led writing teachers to increase their emphasis on **sentence-combining** exercises, with the hope of teaching students to increase their T-unit length and thus to produce more sophisticated writing.

In more recent studies, however, Hunt's hypothesis has been questioned and nearly invalidated as critics argue that "good" writing should not be defined based on the length of clauses but on other variables, such as the writer's response to a specific writing situation. In studies published in the late 1970s and early 1980s, scholars argue that readers, even teachers, do not see a relation between increased clause length and better writing (see especially Ellen Nold and **Sarah Washauer Freedman**'s "An Analysis of Readers' Responses to Essays" [1977], Murray F. Stewart and Cary H. Grobe's "Syntactic Maturity and Mechanics of Writing" [1979], **Joseph Williams**' "Defining Complexity" [1979], and **Lester Faigley**'s "Names in Search of a Concept: Maturity, Fluency, Complexity, and Growth in Written Syntax" [1980]). In composition studies, the term "T-unit" was most used in the late 1970s and early 1980s.

(b) "a single main clause (or independent clause, if you prefer) plus whatever other subordinate clauses or nonclauses are attached to, or embedded within, that one main clause. Put more briefly, a T-unit is a single main clause plus whatever else goes with it" (Hunt 93).

"an independent clause along with any subordinate structures attached to or embedded in it" (Sloan 447).

(c) "The reason for defining a T-unit, as distinguished from a sentence, is simply that the T-unit turns out, empirically, to be a useful concept in describing some of the changes that occur in the syntax of the sentences produced by schoolchildren as they grow older" (Hunt 93).

"The coinage of the term was one of Hunt's most important contributions to composition research. The 't-unit' became the composition research equivalent of such linguistic terms as the 'morpheme' or the 'quarks' of theoretical physics" (Holzman 76).

(d) Kellogg Hunt.

TACIT KNOWLEDGE

(a) A term used by scientist, chemist, and philosopher Michael Polanyi* in *Personal Knowledge* (1958) and further explained and developed in later books such as *The Tacit Dimension* (1966). Thomas Kuhn* adopted Polanyi's term in *The Structure of Scientific Revolutions* (1962); both Kuhn and Polanyi argue that much of scientific knowledge is gained through experience and cannot be completely or specifically expressed. Tacit knowledge, also called "personal knowledge," refers to a type of unconscious knowledge acquired not by learning rules but by practice and by following examples. This knowledge is unarticulated and underlies our articulated forms of knowledge. Polanyi contrasts his theories of knowledge with the common desire in science for detachment and "pure" objectivity in research. In tacit knowledge, solutions are found by making connections between current problems and previous ones that have already been solved.

In composition studies, **Janet Emig** uses the term to argue for cross-disciplinary approaches to writing pedagogy and to provide a list of scholars she sees as "promising new ancestors" for composition studies ("The Tacit Tradition" [1980]). Scholars, including **Patricia Bizzell** ("Thomas Kuhn, Scientism, and English Studies" [1979]) and **Kenneth Bruffee** ("Writing and Reading as Collaborative or Social Acts" [1983]), often use the term to discuss Thomas Kuhn's theories of the **social construction** and of the rhetorical or social nature of **knowledge**. In relation to writing instruction, the term suggests the futility of teaching writing by teaching rules and emphasizes the unconscious knowledge that writers (and teachers) bring to the rhetorical situation, the research site, or to the classroom. The concept of tacit knowledge encourages teachers to build on the knowledge that students already have about the writing **process**. Polanyi's concept of tacit knowledge appears most often in composition conversations during the 1980s, with a 1981 double issue of *PRE/TEXT* devoted to Polanyi, largely to his concept of the "tacit."

(b) "is learned by doing science rather than by acquiring rules for doing it" (Kuhn 191).

" 'Tacit knowledge' in this case is thinking in metaphors or exemplars, the

capacity novice scientists gain through doing textbook problems, the capacity
to see that a problem is like one they have done before" (Bruffee, "Writing"
163).

(c) "The declared aim of modern science is to establish a strictly detached,
objective knowledge. . . . But suppose that <u>tacit</u> thought forms an indispensable
part of all knowledge, then the ideal of eliminating all personal elements of
knowledge would, in effect, aim at the destruction of all knowledge" (Polanyi,
Tacit 20).

"To make the notion of <u>tacit knowledge</u> either into a recipe for learning or
into a set of requirements for a 'good' pedagogy is to exempt it from its own
insight" (Fish, "Anti-foundationalism" 77).

"One reason for the inevitability of a multi-disciplinary approach for research into writing and other linguistic functioning is that the scholars of our
<u>tacit</u> tradition, within their own histories as thinkers and doers, are multi-
disciplinarians" (Emig, "Tacit" 155).

(d) Thomas Kuhn, Michael Polanyi.

TAGMEMIC INVENTION

(a) Tagmemics is a linguistic theory developed in the 1950s by **Kenneth Pike**
that has as a fundamental characteristic the thorough exploration of a situation,
problem, or point of view before one draws conclusions. It is based on two sets
of concepts: the first is the often-cited triad of "particle, wave, field," a concept
drawn from physics that views the world as a group of particles caught in
dynamic relationships. The second concept on which tagmemics is based, also
a triad, is "contrast, variation, distribution," coming from structural linguistics.
These two triads are to be analyzed against each other to allow new perspectives
to surface.

Tagmemic theory provides a **heuristic**, which is the main contribution of
tagmemic theory to composition. Pike developed this heuristic in his 1964 article
"A Linguistic Contribution to Composition" and in his 1970 textbook, co-written
with **Alton Becker** and **Richard Young**, *Rhetoric: Discovery and Change*. The
heuristic is intended for use in composition classes to help writers closely examine a situation from the three perspectives of particle, wave, and field. According to Pike, when we view the world from the perspective of particles, we
see objects as single and individual units. From the perspective of waves, we
see a dynamic world with many parts, and from the field perspective, we see
the relationships between the objects and sets of objects in our world. As Pike
explains, these three perspectives are needed to examine language use, and, for
a comprehensive analysis, all three ways of seeing should be applied to a piece
of writing.

In composition textbooks, the grid, in different forms, is used as a method of
invention, for generating content for writing assignments. The theory and heu-

ristic have been criticized for making "universal" claims about the structure of human thought and knowledge and for being difficult to understand (see, for example, James Kinney's "Tagmemic Rhetoric: A Reconsideration" and "Classifying Heuristics" [1978–79] and **Donald Stewart**'s "Composition Textbooks and the Assault on Tradition" [1978]). Though the heuristic is still used in some composition textbooks, tagmemics is not the focus of theoretical discussion it was in the 1960s and even into the early 1980s.

(b) "not just a theory of language but a general theory about the structure of all purposive human behavior" (Kinney, "Tagmemic" 141).

"conceives of invention as essentially a problem-solving activity, the problems being of two sorts: those arising in one's own experience of the world and those arising out of a need to change others" (R. Young, "Paradigms" 39).

(c) "Although we customarily consider a subject from only one point of view, tagmemic invention forces us to shift mental gears to see it differently" (Lindemann, *Rhetoric* 88).

"The core of Young's work was a new art of rhetorical invention based on tagmemic linguistics and a defense of its adequacy and usefulness" (Lauer & Asher 5).

(d) Alton Becker, Kenneth Pike, Richard Young.

TALK-WRITE PEDAGOGY

(a) A writing pedagogy developed by Robert Zoellner that was presented in the January 1969 issue of *College English*. **Richard Ohmann**, the journal editor at the time, devoted the entire month's issue to Zoellner's monograph "Talk-Write: A Behavioral Pedagogy for Composition," which was met with harsh criticism. The method is based on behavioral psychology, specifically operational conditioning, and influenced by the work of B. F. Skinner. Zoellner developed the model after noticing that intelligent students who could express themselves effectively in speech could not do the same in writing.

The talk-write model is often seen as an alternative to the **cognitive model** of composing. Zoellner disagrees with cognitive approaches to writing because they locate problems with writing in relation to mental development. He opposes the "think-write" metaphor of writing and describes his method as based on the "paradigm of responsive man" as opposed to the "paradigm of mentalistic man." Through these two terms, he takes issue with pedagogies based on the "inner" self or the mind, as traditionally defined. Instead he proposes that a person's observable behavior constitutes what is normally thought of as the "mind." Therefore, the talk-write model gives attention to students' observable behaviors which, Zoellner proposes, can be changed and manipulated.

Zoellner's pedagogy is a radical one. According to Gary Hatch and Margaret Walters ("Robert Zoellner's Talk-Write Pedagogy" [1993]), Zoellner was one of the first to discuss writing as a **process** instead of a finished product. In the classroom, he advocated the elimination of desks and chairs, favoring easels with large notepads or blackboards at which students could stand and write. Zoellner's model also relied on the interaction of students with teachers and with other students, anticipating recent discussions of writing as a social activity. The object of the model is that the students clarify what they want to say through speech, receive immediate reaction from the teacher and other students, and write and rewrite the words spoken until the audience indicates that the communication is effective.

Zoellner's ideas were very much discussed in 1969 and the early 1970s. The May 1969 issue of *College English* was devoted to the discussion, and more responses were published in November 1969. The response was largely negative, with critics citing problems with Zoellner's own writing style (which is at times characterized by much psychological jargon) and simply disagreeing that writing problems could be addressed without addressing mental activities. Another criticism is that the student would become overly dependent on the teacher, thus not really learning to write, but reacting to prompts (see Lynn Z. and Martin Bloom [1969]). Others, however, found the talk-write method useful in the classroom. For example, in the 1972 article "Talk-Write Composition: A Theoretical Model for Proposing the Use of Speech to Improve Writing," Terry Radcliffe discusses an experiment that indicates talking about ideas is an effective "prewriting" strategy.

Beginning in the early to mid-1980s, the talk-write method experienced a reexamination. Richard VanDeWeghe (1983), for example, proposes a "write-talk-write" model to help improve student writing, and George Douglas Meyers, in a 1985 article, argues for adapting Zoellner's model to the business writing classroom. In *Rhetoric and Reality* (1987), **James Berlin** credits Zoellner (along with Lynn and Martin Bloom, who also fostered a behavioristic approach to composition, though different from Zoellner's) for encouraging talk about writing as a process and for showing the benefits of teacher intervention during the writing process (145). With his 1996 article "Reconsidering Behaviorist Composition Pedagogies: Positivism, Empiricism, and the Paradox of Postmodernism," David Wallace also credits behaviorist approaches such as Zoellner's for their part in ushering in the process movement. Gary Layne Hatch also encouraged a reexamination of Zoellner's pedagogy, emphasizing the social, **collaborative**, and process approaches the method offers (see, for example, his 1991 CCCC presentation "Reviving the Rodential Model for Composition: Robert Zoellner's Alternative to Flower and Hayes" and his 1993 article "Robert Zoellner's Talk-Write Pedagogy," co-authored with Margaret Bennett Walters).

(b) "In Zoellner's <u>talk-write</u> proposal, response began with individual students' needs, and both students and teachers actively contributed to learning. The teacher or peer became a coach, listening (or reading) first and then helping students to shape their discourse" (Wallace 107–8).

"The <u>talk-write pedagogy</u> suggests a reversal in how we treat writing problems. Instead of teaching students how to think, <u>talk-write</u> assumes that students are mentally competent and focuses instead on the physical manipulation of language through speaking and writing" (Hatch & Walters 338).

(c) "[The talk-write school] attempted to get students to draw upon the 'natural resources' of speaking as they began to write" (Freisinger 249).

"With talk-write, writing becomes public. Each student is a model of the writing act for others, and students can walk around, reading and commenting on others' work" (Wixon & Wixon 132).

(d) Robert Zoellner.

TEACHER-RESEARCHER

(a) A term first used in the 1960s by Lawrence Stenhouse, a British educator, to identify the movement toward the active engagement of teachers in the making of **knowledge** in their field. This movement has its roots in England, and the initial emphasis of the movement was on elementary and high school teachers and on their conducting research studies in the classroom. Currently the term implies, not necessarily scientific experiment, but the importance of teachers making their experiences in the classroom known and part of the professional conversation. This movement recognizes the value of teachers' observations and stories of classroom experiences; it calls on them to make closer observations and to share information with others. Often, teacher-research relies on **ethnographic** research methods. Some see teacher-research as a way to narrow the split between theory and practice.

In America, **Mina Shaughnessy** and **Lee Odell** called for teacher-conducted classroom research, both in 1976 articles, "Diving In: An Introduction to Basic Writing" and "The Classroom Teacher as Researcher," respectively. **Ann E. Berthoff, Shirley Brice Heath**, Miles Myers, and **Janet Emig** also began championing teacher-research in composition studies during the late 1970s and early 1980s. Since this time, support for teacher-research has grown, with more research being done on and by teacher-researchers.

(b) "This approach pairs the roles of teacher and researcher in a cooperative search for answers to questions raised by the teacher about what is happening in the classroom and why" (S. Heath, "A Lot" 42).

"This grassroots movement began by seeking to empower the pre-higher education teacher who conducts research in the classroom through a system of notes, observations, teaching and learning logs, etc., thereby contributing to and shaping developing theory and practice in the field of composition" (Grego 228).

(c) "The initiation of the teacher as Researcher could be the ritual burning of all instructors' manuals, and the students could ceremoniously toss on the bonfire their study guides and their yellow felt marking pens" (Berthoff, *Making* 35).

"Because the teacher-researcher movement is still in its early stages, and because it is most influential among K–12 teachers who do not always publish their findings, its epistemology and methodology have not been fully articulated" (Ray, *Practice* xi).

"The aim of the <u>teacher-researcher</u> is not to create educational laws (as is sometimes done in the physical sciences) in order to predict and explain teacher and learning. Instead, the <u>teacher-researcher</u> attempts to make visible the experience of teachers and children acting in the world" (Burton 227).

(d) Ann E. Berthoff, **Lil Brannon**, Glenda Bissex and Richard Bullock, **James Britton**, Janet Emig, **Anne Ruggles Gere, Dixie Goswami**, Shirley Brice Heath, **C. H. Knoblauch, Ken Macrorie**, Miles Myers, Peter Stillman.

TERMINISTIC SCREENS

(a) A term used by Kenneth Burke, primarily in *Language as Symbolic Action* (1966). Loosely, this concept implies that our world view is formed by our backgrounds and individual contexts. Our experiences, beliefs, values, and prejudices shape the way we see particular subjects. According to Burke, our reality is shaped by the "terms" or symbols we use; our language serves as screens or filters through which we see the world. Our view cannot be pure, but is shaped even by the language we use; thus no one can speak or write with complete objectivity. In composition studies, the concept foreshadows **social constructionist** and poststructuralist views that emphasize the importance of language in the making of **knowledge**. The term illustrates the need to recognize multiple "truths" and to be aware of how one's subject position shapes one's writing, learning, researching, theorizing, and teaching. The term is also used by composition scholars in discussing issues of historiography. For example, **Robert Connors** (1991) recognizes the inevitability of terministic screens in writing composition histories, but he still encourages scholars to avoid "totalizing perspectives" that may limit scholarly interpretation ("Writing" 68). Similarly, Robin Varnum (1992) argues that **current-traditional rhetoric** serves as a terministic screen that prevents composition historians from examining the early developments in the field, choosing instead to begin historical research of composition studies in the 1960s with the contemporary professionalization of the field. To limit the range of historical research, Varnum proposes, is to unnecessarily restrict our view of contemporary composition studies. To check such limitations, Beth Daniell (1994) proposes that intellectuals examine their theories for terministic screens, asking questions about the theory's limitations and about possible effects theoretical application may have outside the scholar's intentions.

(b) "a perspective formulated in a symbolic language, to be taken as *a* not *the* perspective on the world" (Comprone 337).

"They frame and limit our existence. They constitute the categories through which we experience the social structures that often seem so determining" (Gusfield 36).

(c) "We must use <u>terministic screens</u>, since we can't say anything without the use of terms; whatever terms we use, they necessarily constitute a corresponding kind of screen; and any such screen necessarily directs the attention to one field rather than another" (Burke, *Language* 50).

"Every ideology is another 'terministic screen,' and as such has no choice but to represent only one particular, narrow approach to 'reality' " (Hassett 475).

"I once critiqued James Berlin for filtering his research effort through powerful terministic screens. . . . Berlin's reply was that such screens are inevitable in any research project, and that since objectivity is impossible . . . all a historian can do is try to be aware of the terministic screens that exist for him or her" (Connors, "Writing" 66).

"Compositionists, as I will argue, either consciously or unconsciously adopt the terministic screens of their hegemonic English-department brethren, the literarists, and the most acceptable terminology in literary studies at the present time is that of deconstruction" (Winterowd, *English* 205).

(d) Kenneth Burke.

THEME-WRITING (see ENGFISH)

THEORY HOPE

(a) A term used by literary critic Stanley Fish that names the desire for a convenient, foolproof problem-solving theory and the certainty that such a theory can exist. In composition studies, the term is often associated with **foundationalists** who are convinced that their method is *the* correct one. Yet as some have pointed out, **anti-foundationalists** can also fall prey to theory hope by privileging their beliefs as methods of objective judgment. For example, **Victor Vitanza** (1991) contends that social theorists in composition studies have failed to interrogate their "will to knowledge and power" ("Three" 143) and thus are victims of theory hope (as well as of what Vitanza calls "pedagogy hope"). In composition studies, the term has been used especially in the early to mid-1990s as composition scholars have become more reflective and more cautious of the pedagogical consequences resulting from the rise of critical theory and of the professional dangers of sanctioning one theory of composing to the neglect of other views, both new and old.

(b) "the belief that whatever a theory sanctions us to do is surely correct, whatever we learn under its aegis surely true, and whatever results we get using its methods are surely valid" (Bruffee, "Social Construction" 782).

"Fish refers rather sarcastically to 'theory hope,' the belief that theory can help us out of the hall of mirrors" (Smit, "Hall" 50).

(c) "Theory has become, for the field of composition, the will to unified theory . . . it has become 'theory hope' " (Vitanza 160).

"We cannot connect a theory of writing with a theory of reading with a theory of communication with a theory of ethics, etc. to produce a metatheory that solves all of the problems we have always had by revealing the ground upon which we have always stood. To believe in the possibility of such a transhistorical metatheory is a logical error Stanley Fish calls 'theory hope' " (Harkin, "Bringing Lore" 62).

(d) Stanley Fish.

THICK DESCRIPTION

(a) A term initially used by Gilbert Ryle but often associated with anthropologist Clifford Geertz* and **ethnographic** studies. Geertz develops the term in *The Interpretation of Cultures* (1973). Thick description is a type of complex description that goes beyond basic assumptions and attempts to see both a broad and detailed picture of the issue or community explored. Such a description involves **triangulation**, looking at something from several different perspectives in an attempt to achieve a full (or thick) description. Thick description is an essential element of ethnography. For ethnographers, the context of the study is of utmost importance, and as they attempt a thick description, they strive to acknowledge and to record multiple elements of their context in order to expose as many implications of a cultural act as possible. To gain such a description, the researcher must become immersed in the culture studied, becoming a **participant-observer**. Thick description works against **"context-stripping"** or the assumption that the setting of the study is unimportant, or minimally important.

Problems can occur as ethnographers begin to record their research results. Questions arise surrounding the "best" or "fairest" way to write the thick description. For example, where in the text should the author position him or herself? How much of the narrative should the author occupy? What are the researcher's rights in speaking for the subject of study? What are the subject's rights and needs? Even, is there enough information or too much and is it "representative"? In composition studies, these questions have been widely debated, mainly in the late 1980s and 1990s. (See, for example, **Janice Lauer** and J. William Asher [1988], Peter Mortensen and Gesa Kirsch [1996].)

(b) "Ethnography is thick description. What the ethnographer is in fact faced with . . . is a multiplicity of complex conceptual structures, many of them superimposed upon or knotted into one another, which are at once strange, irregular, and inexplicit, and which he must contrive somehow first to grasp and then to render" (Geertz, *Interpretation* 10).

"At the heart of ethnographic inquiry, then, is the concern for discovering and elaborating upon specific features of context. This priority calls for what Geertz (1973) has termed 'thick description,' the concrete and careful account of particular events. . . . In effect, this is the language of literature" (Kantor, Kirby, & Goetz 296).

"an approach set against the practices of 'universalizing' the concept of culture, practices which ignore the 'piled up structures of inference and implication' that complicate social life." (Covino, *Art* 126).

(c) "Case study research . . . provides 'thick description' or triangulated data . . . thus improving the likelihood that the reader can see implications for new settings" (Bridwell-Bowles 106).

"Whereas ethnography relies on thick descriptions based on exhaustive observations usually conducted over a long period of time, ethnomethodology often works with a small slice of life" (Brandt 318).

(d) Clifford Geertz, ethnographers.

THIRD WAY

(a) The name that **Ken Macrorie** gives to what he sees as the most beneficial pedagogical method. Macrorie developed the term in his 1970 text *Uptaught*. As he describes it, the "first way" involves the teacher's handing out material and requiring students to repeat what they have memorized on tests. This method connotes tedious memorization and learning completely divorced from the students' lives and interests. The "second way" of teaching is opposite of the first in that the teacher provides no structure, direction, or set requirements. A few students may succeed in this environment, but most will not. Macrorie's "third way" is student-centered and provides both freedom and structure. Teachers take the students seriously as learners and scholars, and the teacher "shares" power with the students in order to allow students to explore their own interests in their writing. A goal for this pedagogy is to help students find and increase their "power." As do most **expressivist** pedagogies, this method emphasizes personal writing and the valuing of students' feelings and observations. This way of teaching also downplays the **authority** of grades and of teachers, often allowing students to give their own grades. Peer review and "publication" of student work are features of such a classroom.

By the late 1970s, expressivist methods, while still somewhat popular, were also widely criticized. For example, in "*Uptaught* Rethought—Coming Back from the 'Knockout' " (1978), James Vopat criticizes the third way's emphasis on the individual student at the expense of using writing to help students locate themselves in the wider context of society.

(b) "In the Third Way, which I stumbled onto, students operate with freedom and discipline. They are given real choices and encouraged to learn the way of experts" (Macrorie, *Uptaught* 27).

"This Way involves a course structured in such a manner that students can go their own way with their writing, with minimal fear of grading reprisal, at the same time that Macrorie as the teacher assumes that both he and they will bring disciplined thinking to that writing" (Hill 110).

(c) "Supporters of Macrorie's experiential Third Way . . . insist that students must start with what they know and that they can eventually learn to deal with the broader issues of life" (Nudelman & Schlosser 497).

"After three years and a few hundred students, I realized that there was something basically wrong with the Third Way and the student-centered approach to the teaching of writing which it defined. I reluctantly came to understand that: It is not sufficient that students tell the truth about their feelings. It is not altogether a good thing to know one's students deeply" (Vopat 42).

"Freedom and discipline, the essence of the Third Way, became the philosophy supporting two textbooks: *Writing to Be Read* (1968; rev. 2nd ed. Rochelle Park, NJ: Hayden, 1976) and *Telling Writing* (Rochelle Park, NJ: Hayden, 1970; revised in 1976, the third edition appearing in 1980)" (Lindemann, "Ken Macrorie" 362).

(d) Ken Macrorie.

TOULMIN MODEL OF ARGUMENT

(a) A model of argument created by British logician **Stephen Toulmin** in his 1958 work *The Uses of Argument*. Toulmin departs from traditional methods of analytical argumentation and in his model identifies six parts of rhetorical argument. Three of these parts, according to Toulmin, are mandatory for a developed argument: claim, data, and warrant. The claim is the issue in dispute or the "conclusion" of an argument; the data, or evidence, support the claim; and the warrant indicates the relation between the claim and the data and moves the argument from the data to the claim. The other three parts of Toulmin's model, which may or may not be a part of an argument, include the qualifier, reservation (or rebuttal), and backing (or support) for the warrant; these elements of argument are used to qualify the argument or adapt it to a specific audience. The qualifier acknowledges the probabilities surrounding the claim, and the reservation indicates instances when the claim may not apply. The backing or support, as stated above, strengthens the warrant.

Though criticized by logicians, this model has been widely adopted by speech departments, beginning in the 1960s with Wayne Brockriede and **Douglas Ehninger**'s article "Toulmin on Argument: An Interpretation and Application," which appeared in the *Quarterly Journal of Speech* in 1960. In a 1978 *CCC* article, Charles W. Kneupper introduced the model to a composition audience. Toulmin's method now appears in many composition textbooks and is used in composition and speech classes to teach argumentative and persuasive discourse. Toulmin created the model in support of his view that probabilistic argument is not inferior to formal logic in creating truth (which he sees as **socially constructed**). The model of argument does not differentiate between inductive and deductive logic since Toulmin created it as an alternative to traditional syllogistic logic.

(b) As described by Toulmin, an argument is *movement* from accepted *data*, through a *warrant*, to a *claim* (Brockriede & Ehninger 242).

"Toulmin logic, like traditional logic, is a tool for analyzing existing arguments, rather than a system for creating them" (Fulkerson, "Technical" 446).

(c) "A coherent essay could result from the development of each functional element of the Toulmin model in the kernel argument and from tying the interrelated claims together in a conclusion" (Kneupper 239).

"My many conversations with teachers of writing indicate that if any formal system of logic has replaced the scholastic logic of the syllogism in the modern composition classroom, it is symbolic logic of the claim/data/warrant system devised by Stephen Toulmin" (Corbett, "John Locke's" 429).

"The weakness of Toulmin's system is fuzziness in the definitions of some key components and in the guidelines for relating them in logically sound ways" (Fairbanks 104).

(d) Wayne Brockriede, Douglas Ehninger, Richard Fulkerson, Charles Kneupper, Stephen Toulmin.

TRANSACTIONAL RHETORIC/THEORY

(a) A term used by **James Berlin** in *Rhetoric and Reality: Writing Instruction in American Colleges, 1900–1985* (1987) to describe one of the major rhetorical theories of the twentieth century. Berlin's other two categories are (1) "objective" rhetoric, which is based on **positivist** thought and is represented by Robert Zoellner's behavioralist "**talk-write**" method of composition instruction and (2) "subjective" rhetoric, which is characterized by a belief that truth is found internally and thus cannot be taught; it is represented by **expressionists** including **Ken Macrorie, Peter Elbow,** and **William Coles, Jr**. Transactional rhetoric, according to Berlin, is based on an epistemology "that sees truth as arising out of the interaction of the elements of the rhetorical situation" (15). In the modern writing classroom, Berlin sees three predominant forms of transactional rhetoric: classical, **cognitive,** and **epistemic**. As Berlin explains, the classical view was most prevalent in the 1950s and 1960s and is associated with the work of **Edward P. J. Corbett**; the cognitive approach surfaced in the 1960s and 1970s and is represented by scholars such as **Janet Emig** and **Janice Lauer**. Epistemic rhetoric has roots in the early twentieth century, Berlin explains, but gained strength in the 1960s and 1970s and is seen in the work of composition scholars including **Ann Berthoff, Richard Ohmann, Kenneth Pike, Alton Becker,** and **Richard Young**. The term was most discussed in the late 1980s and has been criticized for its broad scope.

(b) "Transactional rhetoric . . . discovers reality in the interaction of the features of the rhetorical process itself—in the interaction of material reality, writer, audience, and language" (Berlin, *Rhetoric and Reality* 155).

"Transactional-epistemicism, which Berlin identified in *Rhetoric and Reality* (1987), is a catch-all for a broad range of theorists marked only by agreement that at least some knowledge is socially created through discourse" (Fulkerson, "Composition" 421).

(c) "*Epistemic rhetoric*, the third subcategory in Berlin's third category of transactional rhetoric, holds that all knowledge comes about through rhetorical action in a community" (Winterowd, *English* 5).

"In *Rhetoric and Reality*, James Berlin portrays the development of writing instruction in this century as a conflict of epistemologies: objective or positivistic theories, subjective or expressionistic theories, and transactional or rhetorical theories" (S. Clark 103).

(d) James Berlin.

TRANSACTIONAL WRITING

(a) One of three categories of writing that, according to **James Britton** and his colleagues, is done by British school children. Discussions of these categories can be found in Britton's 1971 article "What's the Use? A Schematic Account of Language Functions" and in the study conducted by Britton, Tony Burgess, Nancy Martin, and Alex McLeod entitled *The Development of Writing Abilities (11–18)*, published in 1975. (The other categories of writing are **poetic** and **expressive**.) Transactional writing is writing that informs or persuades and includes assignments such as book reports, lab reports, and essay tests. It is the type of writing often done on the job. Transactional writing explains and indicates what the writer already knows about a topic; it illustrates concern with formal properties such as style and grammar, since the writing is usually prepared for an audience, usually a teacher or employer. When writing transactional prose, the writer takes on what Britton calls the "participant" role, as opposed to the "spectator" role. Both transactional and poetic writing, according to Britton and his colleagues, stem from expressive writing. From their study, Britton and his colleagues conclude that 63 percent of the children's writing was transactional.

With transactional writing commonly used in the classroom, some scholars argue that exclusive use of this style robs students of learning and discovery that can be gained from poetic and expressive writing. Britton and his colleagues are among those supporting the increase of poetic and expressive writing in school curriculums; however, some scholars argue that poetic and expressive writing do little to exercise critical thinking abilities. Those in favor of **discourse community** pedagogy often prefer the emphasis on transactional writing in the classroom because, they argue, this form prepares writers for participation in their academic or professional discourse community.

(b) "aims to inform, persuade or instruct an audience in clear, conventional, concise prose" (Fulwiler 23).

"communicates information in which already held values are either implied or explicitly stated" (Gorman, Gorman & Young 139).

(c) "They [students] say they are tired of courses that deny them their own reactions, and they equate the conventionality of transactional language with the petty tyranny of the schoolroom" (Lloyd-Jones, "A Balanced" 131).

"Hence James Britton, and his American followers such as Lil Brannon and C. H. Knoblauch, would provide many opportunities in school for 'expressive' speaking and writing in the students' home dialects as important ways of learning prior to, or perhaps instead of, practice in 'transactional' language using the Standard dialect" (Bizzell, "What Happens" 295).

(d) James Britton.

TRANSFORMATIONAL GRAMMAR
(GENERATIVE-TRANSFORMATIONAL GRAMMAR)

(a) A theory of grammar first presented in Noam Chomsky's *Syntactic Structures* (1957) and further developed and modified in Chomsky's later work, especially in *Aspects of the Theory of Syntax* (1965). Other linguists, as well, have modified Chomsky's theories. While other linguistic models, such as structural linguistics, focus on describing surface features of speech and writing, Chomsky's theory proposes that language is a mental system and that speech (writing) is the product of the system. The primary object of study is the mind, and language is the means through which it is studied. As a result, the transformational-generative model aims to provide logical answers to questions about issues related to language acquisition, use, and choices. As John Viertel (1964) explains, an emphasis on generative grammar was made possible by advances in logic and mathematics, especially by the theory of recursive systems.

Generative grammar attempts to provide systematic descriptions of language and to account for how speakers understand and create sentences that they have not previously heard spoken or seen written. According to Chomsky, language users intuitively grasp a set of rules that underlie their dominant language. Whereas the rules are finite, the sentences that result from them are not. Such a grammar, he claims, can be used to explain structures of different languages because there is, he proposes, a universal element to language structure.

A generative grammar is one concerned with creative aspects of language use, with the ways speakers "generate" language. The "transformational" aspect of Chomsky's concept proposes that superficial differences between surface sentences can be explained as the result of rule-governed changes in structure. For example, this model accounts for human ability to recognize the underlying relationships between sentences such as the following:

> John saw a cat.
> A cat was seen by John.
> What did John see?

In Aspects of the Theory of Syntax, Chomsky introduced the terms "deep structure" and "surface structure" to name the two levels of syntactic representation.

As explained by Chomsky, a deep structure determines the sentence's semantic interpretation; a surface structure determines the phonetic interpretation (*Aspects* 16). The deep structure is generated by phrase-structure rules while the surface structure is derived from the deep structure by the means of transformational rules. In Chomsky's words, "One major function of the transformational rules is to convert an abstract deep structure that expresses the content of a sentence into a fairly concrete surface structure that indicates its form" (*Aspects* 136).

The transformational generative model has been used in composition studies for the study and analysis of style and in composition teaching to encourage **sentence-combining**. Pedagogies based on transformational grammar frequently focus on the sentence as the key to stylistic analysis. (See, for example, **Richard Ohmann**'s "Generative Grammars and the Concept of Literary Style" [1964], in which he argues that transformational grammar holds great promise for stylistic analysis.) Beginning with a "kernel" sentence, writers-speakers add to, or transform, a simple sentence into a more complex one, and advocates of this model propose that insight into the ingredients of distinct writing styles can be found by studying kernel sentences and their transformations. Principles of generative-transformational grammar underlie the work of such advocates of sentence-combining as Donald Daiker, Andrew Kerek, and Max Morenberg. Additionally, John Mellon, in *Transformational Sentence-Combining* (1969), argues for the study of transformational grammar based on the claim that it helps students write "mature" sentences, and **Frank O'Hare** (1973) proposes that the tenets of transformational grammar would allow student writing to improve. A common question regarding sentence-combining and grammatical instruction is whether or not students should learn the formal system of grammar itself. O'Hare, supported by the work of other scholars including **James Moffett** (1968), answers that whereas teachers should be guided by the philosophy of this model, students could benefit without learning the formal system itself. A representative critique of generative-transformational grammar comes from John Viertel (1964), who points out that Chomsky's systematic theory does not account for "human" or contextual influences on language acquisition and use. The concept was most discussed in composition studies during the 1960s and 1970s as compositionists looked to linguistics for techniques to improve student writing.

(b) "By a generative grammar I mean simply a system of rules that in some explicit and well-defined way assigns structural descriptions to sentences. . . . Any interesting generative grammar will be dealing, for the most part, with mental processes that are far beyond the level of actual or even potential consciousness" (Chomsky, *Aspects* 8).

"Generative-transformational theory suggests that we transform sentences intuitively by adding to, deleting from, or rearranging kernel sentences" (Lindemann, *Rhetoric* 133).

"Thus transformation grammar is a model which may ultimately yield a full and ordered inventory of the vastly complicated sequence of choices at the command of anybody who wishes to say something. If style is choice, then transformation grammar is, I take it, the grammatical model that so far most fully maps out the system and range of this choice" (Enkvist 51).

(c) "If, as seems likely to happen, generative grammars with transformational rules help the linguist or critic to explicate convincingly the elusive but persistent notion of style, that achievement will stand as one more piece of evidence in favor of such grammars" (Ohmann, "Generative" 160).

"Transformational grammar proposed a model of language that suggested a system of steps by which shorter stretches of language are changed into longer stretches of language. In short, transformational grammar offered a view of processes for composing language" (Larson, "Language" 217).

"Transformational theory has rendered a service by inspiring people such as [John] Mellon and [Francis] Christensen to devise sentence-combining tasks, but since transformational theory itself merely reflects syntactic options confronting people when they discourse, sentence-combining may operate powerfully throughout the curriculum without referring to the theory that describes it" (Moffett 181).

(d) Noam Chomsky, Kellogg Hunt, Frank O'Hare, Richard Ohmann.

TRIANGULATION

(a) A method used by **ethnographers** to verify their research results and ensure that their data and results are valid. This check requires that the research is diversified. The ethnographer must use various avenues of observation and gain multiple perspectives over a long period of time; such rigorous observation and attention to detail leads to a **thick description**, the goal of the ethnographer. In "Ethnographic Research on Writing: Assumptions and Methodology" (1985), Stephen Doheny-Farina and **Lee Odell** discuss three types of triangulation. In theoretical triangulation, the researchers must use various theoretical interpretations in analyzing their data. In investigative triangulation, a team of researchers analyzes and collects the data, and in methodological triangulation, the researchers use multiple methods in gaining information from multiple sources. The term is used most often in composition studies in discussions of ethnographic research.

(b) "In much the same way that ethnographers cross-check data collected on the scene—from informants, activities, and artifacts—they are expected to discipline themselves, by cross-checking their own inferences against the data. This procedure, known as *triangulation*, is the keystone of analytical ethnography" (Brodkey, "Writing" 31).

"This combining of multiple sources of data is called *triangulation*, an important feature of good ethnographic research" (Lauer & Asher 42).

(c) "Ethnographers must be careful to actually listen to and see the community, rely on informants, and draw conclusions from actual data collected during the study. . . . Triangulation is one of the keys to success here" (Moss 167–68).

"They [ethnographers] have also tried to triangulate their observations of one event from the perspective of two of the participants in that event, perhaps describing, for example, a wedding from the standpoint of the bride and the groom's mother, as well as from the researcher's own point of view" (J. Johnson 103).

"The triangulation of data sources and collection techniques contributed to internal validity" (Kantor, "Classroom" 80).

(d) ethnographers.

WAC (see WRITING ACROSS THE CURRICULUM)

WORKSHOP

(a) A term usually referring to a classroom method of teaching writing based on active learning, involving class members as well as teachers. Writing workshops were recommended as teaching methods at the **Dartmouth Seminar** and are components of writing-as-**process** pedagogy, standing in sharp contrast to the traditional lecture approach to teaching. The workshop also reflects composition studies' interest and confidence in **collaborative** methods of writing instruction. In the classroom, a workshop can take different forms; for example, students can work in small groups or the workshop can encompass the class as a whole. Generally, emphasis is on peer review and revisions of essays, with the object being that students receive feedback not only from instructors but also from an **audience** of their peers. This concept is based on the premise that by presenting their work to a diverse audience, the writers will gain a clearer understanding of how to adapt their message to different communication situations. Also, a workshop environment may distribute classroom **authority**, blurring a strict teacher-student hierarchy by positioning students as active, contributing members of the class. During class time, while students participate in group discussion, the teacher can work with individual students or participate in the groups when needed. Ideally, the teacher is not inactive during workshops but carefully monitors the discussions to make sure they are moving smoothly and productively.

As theories of composition have changed, so has our view of the writing workshop. During the 1970s, when **Peter Elbow** and other **expressionists** encouraged adoption of workshop models, scholars saw in this method of teaching opportunities for equality, for sharing of power, and for development of voice. During the mid-1980s, the writing workshop was often seen in relation to **discourse communities**, as arenas where students worked to "make **knowledge**," to reach **consensus**, and to gain familiarity with **academic discourse** conventions. Also in the 1980s, especially the mid-1980s, scholars emphasized the benefits of a computerized classroom in fostering a workshop environment. In

the late 1980s and 1990s, the workshop holds possibilities for political awareness and change through dialogue, and even through confrontation with difference. In all uses, the term refers to activity and reflects the philosophy that
students learn to write by writing. "Workshop" is also used in discussing teacher
training for **writing across the curriculum**. The term became a major com-
ponent of composition conversations in the 1970s and was most widely discussed in the early 1990s.

(b) "A 'workshop' method, with individuals working with each other in
groups of changing pattern, properly begins quite early on in primary or elementary school. It ought to develop fairly smoothly, though with new situations,
into the secondary school" (Dixon 98).

"[Workshops] attempt to prepare students for genuine intellectual activity
rather than provide them with dry-run academic exercises. They emphasize the
development of individual epistemologies and individual voices within, but not
subsumed by, the academic community" (Ritchie, "Beginning" 153).

"The writing workshop depends on a style of response which differs altogether from that of traditional instruction because its concern is not merely to
elicit writing in order to judge it, but to sustain writing through successive
revisions in pursuit of richer insights and concurrently the maturation of competence" (Knoblauch & Brannon, *Rhetorical* 122).

(c) "A workshop allows people to explore and clarify writers' roles more or
less normally: by interacting as writers with other writers, in a structured, relatively safe, but pluralistic context" (Brooke 112).

"Classes should comprise small workshop groups in which all members are
active participants, apprentice-writers who are 'exercising their competence' as
they learn how to write well" (Lunsford, "Cognitive" 41).

"Current composition theorists agree, in principle anyway, on the importance
of dialogic discussions in which all students have a right to speak up and speak
out, along with the value of writing workshops and revisions that incorporate
the writer's resultant insights" (Bloom, 364).

(d) **Lil Brannon**, Robert E. Brooke, **Peter Elbow, Toby Fulwiler, Donald
Graves, C. H. Knoblauch, Donald Murray**, Joy Ritchie, **W. Ross Winterowd**.

WRITER-BASED PROSE

(a) A type of prose described by **Linda Flower** in her 1979 article "Writer-
Based Prose: A Cognitive Basis for Problems in Writing." The term refers to
writing that still needs revision and is not ready to be read by anyone except
the author. Flower, basing her work on that of Jean Piaget* and Lev Vygotsky,*
compares this prose to **egocentric** or inner speech. She concludes that writer-
based prose is often seen as "bad" because it is not organized for an audience;
instead, it reflects the writer's natural thought process and is difficult for the
reader to decipher. In Flower's terminology, instructors should help students

transform their work from "writer-based" to **"reader-based"** prose, which is written or revised with the audience in mind. In doing this, instructors should realize that writer-based prose has an underlying logic and form, with information organized often as survey or narrative, forms of writing that are "easier" for the writer than more complex analysis. In revising a writer-based draft to reader-based prose, the student needs instruction in developing ideas, making causal connections, and organizing information effectively. According to Flower, writer-based prose is a good starting point for teaching more demanding, audience-oriented rhetorical techniques.

Some critics, especially those who work with **basic writers**, argue that this concept oversimplifies the problems students have with writing and unfairly places the blame on students themselves by implying that the problem lies in their lack of effort and revision. Others contend that writer-based prose is not always "bad." In some **expressionist** classrooms, writing for oneself is encouraged as a method toward self-discovery. For example, in "Closing My Eyes as I Speak: An Argument for Ignoring Audience" (1987), **Peter Elbow** argues that an initial focus on writer-based prose can lead to a better final paper because the writer can initially avoid intimidation by the audience and, in writer-based prose, explore and become more familiar with the topic before shaping it for the reader. In some cases, Elbow argues, writer-based prose is better than reader-based, even as the final draft. In making this claim, Elbow questions Flower's assumption that writing for an audience shows greater cognitive maturity than does writing for oneself. Similarly, in *Getting Restless: Rethinking Revision in Writing Instruction* (1997) Nancy Welch challenges what she sees as composition's unquestioned privileging of writer-based prose, grounding her position in Bakhtinian and psychoanalytic theory.

The term comes out of the **cognitive** school of thought, and criticism of the concept, or early use of it, reflects arguments that more is involved in the writing process than the individual's cognitive processes. "Writer-based prose" appears most often in major journals and conference presentations in the early 1980s and again beginning in the late 1980s.

(b) "In *function*, Writer-Based prose is a verbal expression written by a writer to himself and for himself. It is the record and the working of his own verbal thought. In its *structure*, Writer-Based prose reflects the associative, narrative path of the writer's own confrontation with her subject. In its *language*, it reveals her use of privately loaded terms and shifting but unexpressed contexts for her statements" (Flower, "Writer-Based" 20).

"writing that makes sense to the writer but has not yet been shaped in such a way that it makes sense to a reader" (Flynn, McCulley, & Gratz 161).

(c) "The displacements forced upon students entering the discourses of the academy are examined in detail by David Bartholomae, who observes that basic writing students are not so much trapped in a 'writer-based prose' of personal language as they are aware of the privileged discourses of the university but unable to control these discourses" (Faigley, *Fragments* 34).

"Linda Flower has much to offer with these concepts [writer and reader-based prose] but I am convinced that her work is used to explain away remedial writers as a most egocentric group who cannot seem to escape their antisocial position in writer-based prose" (Mack 157)

"To celebrate writer-based prose is to risk the charge of *romanticism*: just warbling one's woodnotes wild" (Elbow, "Closing" 55).

"Views that revision always involves a desirable movement from 'writer-based' to 'reader-based' prose, a 'narrowing of focus,' an assurance that each sentence 'supports' a central thesis, creating a 'unified and coherent whole'— these views, lifted from their connection to the projects of modernism and formalism, and from their underpinnings in American ego psychology, are left unexamined and unquestioned" (N. Welch 26).

(d) Linda Flower.

WRITING ACROSS THE CURRICULUM (WAC)

(a) A term usually used to describe programs that aim to distribute responsibility for improving students' writing throughout the university (or elementary and secondary) curriculum. According to **Patricia Bizzell** and **Bruce Herzberg**, the roots of writing across the curriculum can be located in the findings of **James Britton** and his colleagues of the University of London Institute of Education ("Writing" 340). As Daniel Mahala (1991) explains, in Britain writing across the curriculum was a focus of secondary education, whereas in America the program began on university campuses. **Lee Odell** also sees roots of writing across the curriculum's writing-to-learn emphasis in the work of **Janet Emig** ("Process").

The philosophy behind such programs is that for students' writing to improve, students must write continuously in all classes, not just in English classes. These programs often include a focus on **writing to learn** and attempt to change the widely held view (outside of the English department) that writing is an elementary skill that can be improved with grammar and spelling drills. Instead, WAC directors emphasize that writing is a complex intellectual activity.

WAC programs vary, often using **workshops** to inform those in disciplines outside English about writing theory and pedagogy. Some WAC programs include the requirement of writing courses, at both upper and lower levels, in all disciplines and the establishment of multidisciplinary writing courses. Some programs offer first-year writing courses, but later in the student's career require an upper-level writing course in the student's major.

Throughout WAC history, debate has been ongoing about the program's purposes, its location within the university, and even its name. WAC programs reflect current trends in composition studies' theoretical focus. In the early years of WAC, emphasis was on encouraging students to go beyond **transactional writing** in the classroom, as instructors encouraged **expressionist** and even **poetic** writing in classrooms of various disciplines. During the 1980s, WAC participants often focused on teaching students the conventions of their respective

discourse communities. Daniel Mahala (1991) defines two dominant views of writing across the curriculum in America: formalism and expressivism. For Mahala, **Elaine Maimon** represents the formalist view, which emphasizes traditional academic literacy. **Toby Fulwiler**, according to Mahala, represents the American expressive approach to writing across the curriculum, with an emphasis on journal writing and a more "eclectic" approach to WAC pedagogy. (Mahala criticizes both approaches as "conservative," arguing that to the detriment of writing across the curriculum, in order to maintain institutional support, most WAC programs fail to embrace current theories that recognize difference and conflict.)

Uncertainty has also surrounded the location of WAC programs in the university system. Some propose that writing across the curriculum should be based in English departments, with those departments furnishing instructors for all WAC courses; others question the validity of English instructors teaching writing in various disciplines without awareness of their academic and professional communities' expectations and conventions of writing and language. This issue is discussed, for example, in *College English* (April 1988) where Louise Smith argues that WAC programs should be housed in English departments because English instructors have more thorough knowledge of rhetorical and composition theory. In contrast, Catherine Blaire Pastore proposes that the administration and teaching of WAC programs should be divided equally among departments, that it should be a **"dialogic"** effort. Recently, Barbara Walvoord (1996) has cautioned against the splits within the WAC movement, with different types of programs separating themselves from the WAC title and taking on different labels such as "Writing in the Disciplines" or "Language Across the Curriculum" (67). (See, for example, Margaret Eldred's interview [1995] with Charles Bazerman, who advocates the title "Writing in the Disciplines" instead of "WAC.")

Writing across the curriculum has been a topic of composition conversation since the 1970s, with presumably the first WAC workshop held at Central College in Pella, Iowa, in 1970 (see Barbara Walvoord [1996], David Russell [1991]). Writing across the curriculum has been most discussed in the middle to late 1980s as the program spread widely to many diverse university and college campuses.

(b) "Writing across the curriculum may be defined, then, as a comprehensive program that transforms the curriculum, encouraging writing to learn and learning to write in all disciplines" (McLeod, "Writing" 5).

"Realizing that literacy was not the sole province of English departments . . . these institutions have established programs that renewed the crucial link between learning to write and learning in general. Instead of inventing a purpose for writing, these types of courses, variously called 'writing across the curriculum,' or 'co-registered writing,' build upon already existing motivation" (L. Perelman, "Approaches" 72–73).

" 'Writing across the curriculum' has come to mean three things to writing teachers in America. It denotes, first, a theory of the function of writing in learning; second, a pedagogy to encourage particular uses of writing in learning; and third, a program that applies the pedagogy in a particular school" (Bizzell & Herzberg, "Writing" 340).

(c) "Writing-Across-the-Curriculum Programs aim to transform pedagogical practices in all disciplines, even those where patriarchal attitudes toward authority are most deeply rooted" (Flynn, "Composing" 424).

"No matter how successful the faculty workshops are in inculcating writing-to-learn strategies in the teaching of a few faculty from disciplines outside the humanities, permanent success in the WAC movement will be established only when writing faculty and those from other disciplines meet half way, creating a curricular and pedagogical dialogue that is based on and reinforced by research" (Jones & Comprone 61).

"One model of writing across the curriculum involves a writer's learning to operate within the accepted practices of a discourse community: a biology major is supposed to learn to write like a biologist" (Fulkerson, "Composition" 417).

(d) Charles Bazerman, James Britton, **Joseph Comprone**, Toby Fulwiler, **Anne Ruggles Gere, Anne Herrington, James Kinneavy**, Susan McLeod, Elaine Maimon, Nancy Martin, Lee Odell, David Russell, **Stephen Tchudi**, Barbara Walvoord, **Art Young**.

WRITING TO LEARN

(a) A term that explains the use of writing to encourage and facilitate critical thinking, dialogue, discovery, and engagement with course content. Writing to learn is often a part of discussions of **writing across the curriculum**, and it often serves as a rationale for these programs through the claim that students in all academic disciplines can gain a better understanding of course content by writing about it. Proponents argue that writing does not serve only to reflect what a student knows, but is itself a unique mode of learning as it serves as a **heuristic** for in-depth thought and exploration of a particular topic. When using writing as a method of learning, emphasis should not be on superficial correctness of form, but on fostering comprehension and allowing students to become more comfortable with the academic material by engaging with it, and by writing about it, often informally. Some proponents of writing to learn use journals, writing notebooks, and/or short (3-to-5-minute) exploratory or responsive writings at the beginning or end of the class period. Such assignments encourage **reflection** or what **James Britton** calls **expressive** and **poetic** writing.

The roots of writing to learn are often traced to James Britton and the London Project. Britton and his colleagues concluded that students practiced mostly **transactional** writing, without having many opportunities to write for purposes other than to relay information (see *The Development of Writing Abilities (11–18)* [1975]). **Janet Emig**'s study of the writing **process**, especially her work documented in "Writing as a Mode of Learning" (1977), is often cited as early composition work that supported and fostered interest in a write-to-learn philosophy. Similarly, **Ann Berthoff**, in *The Making of Meaning* (1981), is influential in establishing the connection between thinking and writing.

Though many scholars in composition studies as well as in fields such as cognitive psychology agree that writing and learning are linked, scholars have begun to call for a closer examination of the proposed benefits of writing to learn. Some researchers see the need for a more critical and in-depth look into how writing and learning are connected, questioning the lack of empirical evidence to support writing-to-learn claims (see, for example, **Arthur Applebee** [1984], Judith Langer [1986], and John Ackerman [1993]). Gary Schumacher and Jane Gradwohl Nash (1991) turn to cognitive psychology in their attempt to clear up "confusion" surrounding proposed benefits and limitations of writing to learn. And still others have qualified the benefits of writing as a mode of learning, proposing that the type of writing assigned, in addition to other classroom factors, such as student task interpretation, play a role in the effectiveness of writing as a learning tool (see, for example, James Marshall [1987], Langer and Applebee [1987], and Ann Penrose [1992]). The term itself became widely used beginning in the early 1980s.

(b) "This approach assumes that writing is not only a way of showing what one has learned but is itself a mode of learning" (McLeod, "Writing" 4).

"The phrase 'writing to learn' was in part an attempt by WAC leaders to give a more accurate picture of the workshops' focus on learning, not just on grammar. It was in part an attempt to woo those faculty who were more interested in their students' learning than in writing as they perceived it" (Walvoord, "Future" 63).

(c) "In this revised model of writing-to-learn-across-the-curriculum, the teacher's concern changes from dispensing knowledge to stimulating conceptual involvement and investigation in order to encourage the growth of students' intellectual capacities" (Knoblauch & Brannon, "Writing" 471).

"The 'writing as learning' approach implies that students do have something to say and that the process of writing provides at once the way for them to discover and communicate it" (**Herrington**, "Writing" 379).

"The distinction between the kinds of learning is important in understanding writing-to-learn. . . . It is possible that this difference in the conceptualization of learning may partially underlie the somewhat confusing pattern of research which has been reported in the writing-to-learn work" (Schumacher & Nash 74).

(d) Arthur Applebee, Ann E. Berthoff, James Britton, Janet Emig, **Toby Fulwiler, Anne Ruggles Gere,** Anne Herrington, Judith Langer, proponents of Writing Across the Curriculum.

WYOMING CONFERENCE RESOLUTION

(a) A resolution that documents the profession's dissatisfaction with the institutional inequality that exists in most university English departments between the composition faculty and the literature faculty. The resolution makes suggestions for reform and also calls upon the Executive Committee of the **Conference on College Composition and Communication (CCCC)** to (1) establish professional standards regarding salary and working conditions for postsecondary writing teachers after consultation with such teachers; (2) establish grievance procedures for those subjected to unfair working conditions; and (3) establish a method for censuring institutions and departments that do not comply with the professional standards. Those attending the Wyoming Conference on English in June 1986, in Laramie, Wyoming, proposed the resolution. Their proposal was the result, in part, of their reaction to the Association of Departments of English (ADE) statistics cited by **James Slevin**, which showed the trend in English departments, despite the growth in both graduate and undergraduate English programs, to hire part-time faculty members instead of establishing tenure-track positions. A draft of the resolution was given to the CCCC and was voted on, and endorsed, at the 1987 conference in Atlanta. The CCCC Executive Committee responded to the adoption with the development of two committees: the Wyoming Task Force and the CCCC Committee on Professional Standards for Quality Education, with James Slevin as committee chair. A statement of standards was drawn up, endorsed by the CCCC Executive Committee, and published in draft form in the February 1989 *CCC*. The final draft of the statement of standards was adopted as CCCC policy and published in the October 1989 *CCC* under the title "Statement of Principles and Standards for the Postsecondary Teaching of Writing."

This final "institutionalized" form of the resolution has been criticized for neglecting the intent of the original document to improve material conditions of nontenured and part-time writing instructors. The initial resolution called for the CCCC Executive Committee to censure institutions not supporting the standards, but the Committee concluded that it could not censure institutions, hoping instead to win support for proposed changes. Also, the final draft called for the transformation of nontenured positions to tenured positions, and Jeanne Gunner (1993), along with other part-time English instructors, has interpreted this to mean that part-time and nontenured instructors would not gain improved working conditions, but would lose their jobs and be replaced by instructors "from the composition/rhetoric scholarly establishment" (117). Gunner argues that the final draft "silenc[es] . . . the group that inspired the original document" (108). Another criticism of the outcome of the resolution comes from James Sledd. In his article "Why the Wyoming Resolution Had to Be Emasculated: A History of Quixotism" (1991), Sledd faults the Committee on Professional Standards along with the CCCC for, among other things, minimizing the importance of teaching in favor of research and publication, which, in effect, minimizes the contribution of many part-time and nontenured writing instructors. (For further discussion of the "Statement of Principles and Standards for the Postsecondary Teaching of Writing," see the October 1991 issue of *CCC* and Eileen E. Schell's *Gypsy Academics and Mother-Teachers* [1998].)

(b) "It is worth recalling that the <u>Wyoming Conference Resolution</u> intended to establish means for supporting initiatives at post-secondary institutions of higher learning" (CCCC Committee on Professional Standards 65).

"The <u>Wyoming Conference Resolution</u>, reported on in the March 1987 issue of *College English*, expresses the collective frustration of composition faculty over the powerlessness they experience daily in their departments" (Olson & Moxley 51).

(c) "The profession has responded to the plight of instructors with the now-famous <u>Wyoming Resolution</u> and the resulting 'Statement of Principles and Standards for the Postsecondary Teaching of Writing.' While the statement has been met with some skepticism and much criticism of its practicality (Merrill et al.), it does provide for the first time a public declaration that our most serious professional problem must be addressed at an institutional level" (McLeod, "Pygmalion" 381).

"The <u>Resolution</u> also raises a gender issue, since most part-time and graduate teachers of writing are women, while most full-time, permanent, ranking faculty are men" (Crowley, "Personal" 169).

"The CCCC has been seduced by what might be called 'MLA values,' as the CCCC committee's recasting of the language and intentions of the <u>Wyoming Resolution</u> so painfully reveals" (Gunner 119).

(d) Sharon Crowley, Frank Lentricchia, Linda R. Robertson, James Slevin.

Appendix: Scholars Outside Composition Studies Who Have Influenced the Field

The following list includes those scholars outside the field of composition studies whose work has greatly affected our discipline. In the entries, we give a brief explanation of the scholars' work and how this work has influenced composition theory and practice.

Mikhail Bakhtin Russian linguist, literary critic, and philosopher of language whose most influential scholarship was produced in the early to middle twentieth century. Bakhtin's writings were not widely available in the West until the late 1960s when his dissertation *Rabelais and His World* (1965) was published. Bakhtin views language as active and vital, made of multiple voices and multiple meanings. Central to Bakhtin's theories is his concept of **dialogics**, which situates utterances in social and historical context, positioned in response to and in anticipation of other utterances; language is not individual and isolated, but communal and contextual. Bakhtin faults "single-voiced" or authoritative texts in favor of **heteroglossia** or of **double-voiced discourse**. He values texts in which multiple voices or discourses interact and mingle to create meaning, and for Bakhtin, the novel is the literary genre that best illustrates the interplay of different voices. Bakhtin's work has been welcomed by structuralist and poststructuralist thinkers in various disciplines.

Although Bakhtin has contrasted rhetoric with his dialogic view of language, rhetoricians and composition scholars see his work as complementary to modern rhetorical scholarship. Practically every area of composition studies has been influenced by Bakhtin's work; for example, his theories are used to argue for **collaborative learning, writing across the curriculum** programs, feminist classrooms, writing **workshops**, journals, writing centers, and **ethnographic** methods of research. Composition scholars use Bakhtin's work to develop theories of voice in writing and to apply such theories in the writing classroom. Bakhtin's influential works include *The Dialogic Imagination* (first published in 1975, translated in 1981), *Problems of Dostoevsky's Poetics* (1963, translated 1973), *Rabelais and His World* (1965, translated 1968), and *Speech Genres and Other Late Essays* (1979, translated 1986).

Jerome Bruner   American psychologist integral to the development of cognitive psychology. His work deals with cognitive development, curriculum development, and narrative theory. Bruner's work posits an intertwined relationship between language and learning, showing that language acquisition is necessary for achieving high levels of cognitive development. He also champions the use of cognitive development psychology in curriculum design. Drawing on Jean Piaget, Bruner views learning as a process that progresses based on students' age and the level of cognitive maturity appropriate for that age. Bruner advocates a "spiral curriculum" that gradually introduces material to students based on their cognitive development. Additionally, Bruner advocates active learning and the role of writing in achieving advanced cognitive functions. Writing is important for learning, Bruner contends, because it is abstract in relation to oral communication.

Bruner's cognitive psychology has influenced twentieth-century rhetoric and composition studies. In composition, **cognitive process theories**, informed by Bruner and Piaget, have strongly shaped the way we view the writing process and thus the practice of contemporary composition instruction. For example, scholars including **James Britton** and **Janet Emig** have drawn on Bruner's work for their theories of composing processes and in developing insight into the connections between writing and thinking. **James Berlin** (1987) credits Bruner as a source of **process** models of composing. Scholars who share an **epistemic** view of language have drawn on his work that develops the relationship between language and knowledge, showing that one's language use shapes one's conceptualization of the world, of the self, and of knowledge in general. Such a view posits a very important role for writing instruction. Also, Bruner's ideas can be seen in modern student-centered composition classrooms where students write instead of listening to lectures about writing and where they practice **writing-to-learn** activities. Influential works include *The Process of Education* (1960), *Toward a Theory of Instruction* (1966), *Actual Minds, Possible Worlds* (1986), and *Acts of Meaning* (1990).

Jacques Derrida   French philosopher who is a leading thinker of the post-structuralist movement. His work has affected many disciplines, largely through his critical method "deconstruction." Derrida's work gained recognition in the 1960s primarily through his presentation at a structuralist conference in 1966 at Johns Hopkins University entitled "Structure, Sign, and Play in the Discourse of the Human Sciences." His critique of structuralist thought resulted in "deconstruction," both a theory of textual interpretation and a theory of discourse. In literary theory, deconstruction has been compared to new criticism because both emphasize a close reading of literary texts; yet deconstruction does not attempt closure as does new criticism, but recognizes the indeterminacy of meaning and insists on fragmentation and instability of texts. For Derrida, "text" is a key word; he contends that "there is nothing outside of the text" (*Grammatology* 158). In his view, language is the creator of the human subject; we know and are known through language. Another key concept in Derrida's work is "différance," taken from two French words meaning "to differ" and "to defer." Following the structuralist thought of Ferdinand de Saussure, Derrida uses the term to imply that language makes meaning through its relational differences. Yet breaking from structuralist thought, Derrida's term also implies that meaning is always deferred; a stable meaning is never attained. His work is a radical critique of traditional Western metaphysics in that he challenges dualistic thinking, arguing that binary opposition (good/bad, masculine/feminine, white/black) leads to hierarchical thinking, with one side of the opposition valued above the other. Derrida finds fault with this thinking, showing that these pairs are not naturally opposites but are defined by each other and are thus valued only relationally. Derrida's work is boldly **anti-essentialist** and **nonfoundational**, and partly because of this stance, Derrida's theories have been criticized for leading to nonproductive relativism.

In spite of such criticism, many compositionists have welcomed the importance that Derrida places on language as a creator of meaning as well as his anti-foundational stance. Also, his critique of binary thought encourages the examination of traditional oppositions, such as teacher/student, teacher/researcher, and theory/practice, that inform composition studies. In general, deconstruction has encouraged compositionists to examine the concepts with which we have become comfortable and accept as "common sense." Scholars have applied deconstruction to the work of other composition scholars and to the growth of the discipline of composition studies. **Sharon Crowley** and **Jasper Neel** have been influential in introducing Derrida's work to composition studies, although Neel (1995) also cautions against a composition curriculum based on deconstruction. Other works by Derrida include *Of Grammatology* (1967) and *Writing and Difference* (1967).

John Dewey American philosopher, critic, and educational theorist who is a leading philosopher of pragmatism and of the **Progressive Education Movement**. His writings and influence are wide in scope. Dewey focuses on the place of the individual in a democratic society, and in his work on education encourages preparing the student as a productive and integral member of his or her community. For Dewey, the school is involved not only in building the child's intellect but also in shaping his or her character and moral development. He emphasizes the relationship between education and the community, calling for community involvement in education as well as the school's participation in the community. Dewey's proposed system of education would foster well-rounded individuals through teaching methods that are anti-authoritarian and that encourage active student participation. In his educational methods, practical, hands-on experience is coupled with formal, theoretical training.

In composition studies, Dewey's work supports and offers guidelines for today's student-centered and participatory classrooms. His focus on the relation of community and school gives support to composition's interest first in the concept of community and in the tendency to see the classroom and the academy in terms of community. This focus also provides guidance for service-learning composition programs. Dewey's encouragement of **reflective** and critical thinking also widely informs contemporary composition theory and practice. **Janet Emig**, in her article "The Tacit Tradition," acknowledges the broad influence of Dewey on composition studies, and the work of Stephen Fishman and Lucille McCarthy has encouraged a new look at Dewey's work in relation to the composition classroom. Dewey's influential works include *The School and Society* (1899), *Experience and Nature* (1925), *The Quest for Certainty* (1929), and *How We Think* (1933).

Terry Eagleton   British cultural materialist, Marxist literary critic, and linguistic-rhetorical theorist. Eagleton's Marxism is influenced by the work of his teacher Raymond Williams and by critics including Louis Althusser, Pierre Machey, and Walter Benjamin. Eagleton's best-known work is *Literary Theory: An Introduction* (1983, 1997), in which he provides explanations of major literary theories and gives a historical look at the development of English studies. Eagleton's later works encourage political action and social change as results of textual studies.

Eagleton's *Literary Theory* has been important to scholars in composition studies. Many draw on the narrative of English studies' historical development presented in the first chapter entitled "The Rise of English." Eagleton sees the growth of English studies in the nineteenth century as a result of the decline of religion; he exposes the role of literary studies as a "civilizing" force and as a tool for a cohesive national identity. Because of this latter function, Eagleton argues, after the horrors of World War II, literary studies became a subject for the upper classes.

Additionally, in *Literary Theory* Eagleton champions a return to a rhetorical focus in literary studies. He is interested in the study of what effects discourses produce and how they produce such effects. Drawing on Michel Foucault, Eagleton encourages a view of "literature" as "a name which people give from time to time for different reasons to certain kinds of writing within a whole field of . . . 'discursive practices' " (178). With such a focus on discourse as opposed to 'literature,' the scope of study in English departments would broaden. This rhetorical focus is, of course, of interest to composition scholars, whose field has historically placed second to literary studies and, more recently, to literary criticism. Many composition scholars also draw on Eagleton's political view of rhetoric. Benefiting from Eagleton's historical study, his questioning of elitist notions of literature, and his encouragement of a rhetorical criticism, some compositionists, however, have criticized Eagleton's neglect of composition instruction in his history of the English department. Eagleton's major works include *Marxism and Literary Criticism* (1976), *Criticism and Ideology: A Study in Marxist Literary Theory* (1976), *Against the Grain: Selected Essays, 1975–85* (1986), *The Ideology of the Aesthetic* (1990), *The Significance of Theory* (1990), and *Ideology: An Introduction* (1991).

Michel Foucault French intellectual whose work focuses on the history of ideas and discourse theory. He was a student of Marxist philosopher Louis Althusser and was also influenced by Friedrich Nietzsche. For Foucault, discourse is the key to understanding the history of thought as well as the structure of societies and of human interactions. Discourse represents, in a Foucauldian sense, statements or texts that are shaped by common beliefs, values, and intentions. Such a discourse is not static, but an "event." Foucault's theories present an understanding of society as a complex field in which various discourses compete for power. In his work, Foucault traces historically what comes to be seen as "knowledge," aiming to show how discourse creates systems of "truth" in response to specific historical contexts. He maintains that "knowledge," that which seems common sense, is constructed to fit certain historical needs, most often the needs of the powerful. He illustrates how concepts such as madness, illness, and issues of sexuality are defined differently depending on the historical context and how such definitions and categories are used to establish and then to suppress deviance. Through his historical studies of social institutions, including legal and medical, Foucault concludes that knowledge and power are inseparable.

In composition studies, Foucault's work on discourse theory and his insight into power relations have been broadly influential. Composition scholars' interest in Foucault's work may stem from the field's historical awareness of **authority** and power relations in the classroom and in the academy itself. Foucault's analysis of power is applicable to composition's multicultural emphasis, to the growing interest in cultural studies, and to feminist scholarship and practice. Some have drawn on Foucault's concept of discourse to devise writing curricula and to encourage the influence of composition as a discipline; composition historians, such as **Victor Vitanza**, have drawn on Foucault's historiography. Additionally, important for composition studies is Foucault's contention that textual studies not be limited to what is normally considered literature but be applied to various modes of discourse. Important works include *The Order of Things: An Archaeology of the Human Sciences* (translated 1970), *Madness and Civilization* (translated 1971), *The Archaeology of Knowledge* (translated 1972), *Discipline and Punish: The Birth of the Prison* (translated 1979), and *The History of Sexuality* (translated 1980).

Paulo Freire Brazilian educator whose Marxist theories and practices of literacy instruction stemming from his work with Brazilian peasants have been adopted and adapted for the American classroom. He is a leader of what is called critical, **radical**, or liberatory pedagogy. Freire emphasizes an education that builds on students' own knowledge and their material and social conditions, and he encourages education that makes a change in the political reality of the students' lives. For Freire, reality can be transformed, and literacy, a **critical literacy**, is a key to power and action for social change. In his popular *Pedagogy of the Oppressed*, Freire lays out his critique of "**banking**" education, education that requires students only to listen and to repeat, showing it as a tool for oppression. Instead, he advocates **problem-posing** education, which, he argues, can lead to liberation through **dialogue** and the development of **critical consciousness**.

Composition studies is informed by many of Freire's concepts, such as critical consciousness and problem-posing education. Compositionists, especially in the late 1980s and early 1990s, have embraced Freire's liberatory agenda for education. Many see the writing classroom as the ideal setting for challenging students' assumptions about the dominant ideology, for subverting the banking model of education, and for encouraging social action. Those advocating a cultural studies approach to composition may draw on Freire's work encouraging the analysis of power structures embedded in popular culture as well as in the selection of subject matter from students' daily lives. Scholars developing Freire's work for the North American classroom include Stanley Aronowitz, Henry Giroux, **Ira Shor**, and **Ann E. Berthoff**. Freire's works that have influenced composition studies include *Pedagogy of the Oppressed* (1968), *Education for Critical Consciousness* (1973), *Learning to Question* (with Antonio Faundez, 1989), and *Literacy: Reading the Word and the World* (with Donaldo Macedo, 1987).

Henry Louis Gates, Jr. American literary scholar and leading critic and theorist of African-American literature and culture. He is known for his recovery of texts by black Americans and for his poststructuralist approach to African-American literature. In 1983, Gates reprinted *Our Nig* (1859), the first known novel by a black woman. He edits the *Schomberg Library of Nineteenth-Century Black Women's Writings*. In *Figures in Black: Words, Signs, and the Racial Self* (1987), Gates studies the application of dominant poststructuralist methods to black literature. In *The Signifying Monkey: Towards a Theory of Afro-American Literature* (1988), he explores the black vernacular tradition through the works of leading African-American writers. In more recent work, Gates examines controversies over the literary canon, arguing for multicultural perspectives. Gates argues for multiculturalism not only in the literature classroom but throughout the educational system as a method of countering problems of ethnocentrism in American education.

Gates' work on language theory, focusing on black vernacular, has been important in the composition classroom and in theoretical studies of linguistic difference in relation to literacy and writing instruction. His advocacy of multiculturalism supports the views of many compositionists and of composition programs that use the writing classroom as a means of revealing inequalities in dominant institutions and of encouraging broader understanding of difference. Also important is Gates' concept of "signifying," which refers to the African-American text that draws on oral tradition along with white and black cultural traditions. Such a text is a complex and "multi-voiced" form of discourse, a form of text that many composition instructors value in the classroom and experiment with in their own scholarly writing. Compositionists draw also on his book *Loose Canons: Notes on the Culture Wars* (1992).

Clifford Geertz American cultural anthropologist who is known for his innovative work in **ethnography** and his study of cultures based on methods of interpretation. In his well-known *Interpretation of Cultures* (1973), Geertz encourages anthropologists to treat cultural events as texts, and he advocates a "close reading" of these cultural texts as well as of the writings of other anthropologists. From his emphasis on a "close reading," Geertz defines "**thick description**" as a key to ethnographic research. For Geertz, researchers cannot provide "the" view of their subject, but must be aware of multiple meanings and attempt to avoid limiting and narrow views of a culture. Geertz is often labeled a **social constructionist**, as he proposes that the meanings of research are *made*, largely through the written narrative, and not *discovered*. Geertz contends that ethnographic scholarship is itself rhetorical and has called attention to the importance of writing research.

Today, much research theory and practice in the field of composition studies is informed by Geertz's work. The ways we view the "culture" of the writing classroom and the culture of the academy have been influenced by Geertz's methods. Compositionists draw on Geertz's insistence that research is not objective and that the researcher necessarily interferes with the study's setting and cannot be a pure observer. Also important are his observations on the role of context in limiting and shaping research. Compositionists are interested additionally in Geertz's focus on the rhetoric of ethnographic research. In the 1990s, composition researchers continue to build on Geertz's work, focusing on the "location" of the researcher and the ethics of ethnography. In addition to *The Interpretation of Cultures*, Geertz's *Local Knowledge* (1983) has been influential in composition studies.

Henry Giroux American educational theorist and social critic whose work, drawing on the liberatory pedagogy of Paulo Freire, calls for educational change. Seeing educational institutions as reinforcing the class structure of the workplace, Giroux, as a radical educator, argues for educational reform based on Marxist and poststructuralist ideals. Resisting conservative influences on education, his goal is a curriculum that fosters a **critical consciousness** through a

critical literacy that enables students to gain awareness of unequal power structures and the role of language in such structures. This awareness, according to Giroux, results in political and social change. In his work, he advocates educational reform that fosters a radical democracy, and with this goal, he supports a cultural studies curriculum and multicultural education.

In composition studies, Giroux's work has been influential especially with the political focus of writing instruction and theory in the late 1980s and 1990s. Leading scholars have drawn on Giroux's work in establishing a democratic emphasis for the writing classroom. For example, **James Berlin** bases his **social epistemic rhetoric** on Giroux's **radical pedagogy**, and many scholars have drawn on the concepts of **resistance** and **opposition** in explaining classroom dynamics. Understandably, composition scholars are interested in Giroux's focus on language's role in upholding dominant ideology and his call for critical analysis of discourse in order to expose and to understand power structures. Scholars also refer to Giroux when instituting a cultural studies focus in the composition classroom. Influential works include *Theory and Resistance in Education* (1983) and *Schooling and the Struggle for Public Life: Critical Pedagogy in the Modern Age* (1988).

Gerald Graff   American critical theorist and literary scholar whose work is influenced by a Marxist tradition. Graff's *Professing Literature: An Institutional History* (1987) is an often-cited account of the growth of English as a field. For Graff, the field has failed to confront differing views within English departments, and thus comes his well-known advice to "teach the conflicts." He proposes a "conflict model" of education that teaches disparities in the field of literary and cultural studies and encourages students to critically examine cultural constructs and practices in order to become aware of power structures in society. He encourages an awareness of how educational institutions contribute to the formation of subjectivity.

Graff's conflict model supports the practices of some **radical** compositionists who disagree with the theoretical emphasis on **consensus**, arguing that such a focus silences minority voices. His work supports what has been called the "political turn" in composition studies. Composition scholars draw on Graff's *Professing Literature: An Institutional History* (1987) while at the same time criticizing it for ignoring the growth of writing instruction as a discipline. Other works important for composition studies include *Literature Against Itself: Literary Ideas in Modern Society* (1979), "The Politics of Composition: A Reply to John Rouse" (1980, *College English*), and *Beyond the Culture Wars: How Teaching the Conflicts Can Revitalize American Education* (1992).

Thomas Kuhn   American philosopher and historian of science whose work on the **social construction** of scientific **knowledge** and the concept of **paradigms** has been influential in many disciplines. In *The Structure of Scientific Revolutions*, first published in 1962, Kuhn argues that scientific knowledge changes in a revolutionary, not evolutionary, manner, as one paradigm replaces the other. A paradigm will stand as knowledge in a scientific **community** until it is challenged by a paradigm that better solves the problem or answers unanswered questions. Then the **paradigm shifts** as the old solutions are replaced by new solutions that take on the status of "knowledge." Such knowledge is maintained by a communitywide **consensus**.

Rhetoricians and composition scholars find Kuhn's theories of great interest because of the role that persuasion plays in the creation and maintenance of community-generated knowledge. The determination, then, of a profession's definition of knowledge is rhetorical, and such a view points to a privileged position for language study. Also, the theory coincides with many composition scholars' view of rhetoric as epistemic—as knowledge creating. With the widespread acceptance of social constructionist views in composition studies, compositionists have built theories and practices upon the ideas of knowledge as constructed and as community maintained. Also, the concepts "paradigm" and "paradigm shift" are now common terminology in composition studies, used primarily to describe the move from product, or **current-traditional**, teaching to **process** teaching. Kuhn's ideas were popularized in composition studies partly by **Patricia Bizzell**'s 1979 article "Thomas Kuhn, Scientism, and English Studies" and by **Maxine Hairston**'s popular 1982 article "The Winds of Change: Thomas Kuhn and the Revolution in the Teaching of Writing." In several works, including "Collaborative Learning and the 'Conversation of Mankind' " (1984), **Kenneth Bruffee** also promotes Kuhn's theories, especially in relation to **collaborative learning**.

William Labov   American sociolinguist who is known largely for his work on dialect and language varieties. Labov's sociolinguistic approach has been influential, as has his concern with the relation of language style and usage to social-class structures. His work focuses largely on speech communities in the New York City area. Labov outlines the influence of socioeconomics and social context on language variation, focusing on educational and theoretical implications of his work on nonstandard English. His studies of oral narratives, mostly of black street children, help explain how events are transformed into narrative and indicate the complexity of such oral structure. His work has been important in establishing that speakers and writers using nonstandard English are not using language "incorrectly" but are following a separate set of linguistic rules.

Composition scholars have drawn on Labov's studies, showing that nonstandard English is neither illogical nor a signal of verbal deficiency. Labov's theories are important for teachers and theorists of **basic writing** and of English as a Second Language. His work furthers composition's interest in the relationship between language use and class, culture, and gender. Basil Bernstein, a British educational sociologist, has expanded Labov's work, and Bernstein's studies have also influenced contemporary composition studies largely through the connections made between class structure and language learning and use (see **elaborated** and **restricted codes**). Labov's major works include *The Social Stratification of English in New York City* (1966), "The Logic of Nonstandard English" in *Linguistics and the Teaching of Standard English to Speakers of Other Languages or Dialects* (1969), "The Place of Linguistic Research in American Society" in *Linguistics in the 1970's* (1970), *The Study of Nonstandard English* (1970), *Language in the Inner City: Studies in the Black English Vernacular* (1972), and *Sociolinguistic Patterns* (1972).

Jean Piaget Swiss cognitive development psychologist known for his research on the development of cognitive functions and his proposed four "stages" of cognitive development. His research centers on the study of children's intellectual development and proposes that all children go through similar stages of cognitive growth independent of their cultural context, gradually growing out of an initial **egocentricity**. Piaget has studied the relation of the environment to learning and has introduced the concepts of assimilation and accommodation to illustrate how context shapes knowledge. For Piaget, language supports the development of logical thought. Other psychologists have followed Piaget in developing schemes of cognitive development. William Perry has offered a scale of cognitive development for adolescents, and Lawrence Kohlberg has proposed stages of moral development. Such scales have been used for curriculum development (although uncritical use of these scales has been criticized, especially by feminists and social theorists).

In composition studies, Piaget's work has greatly influenced the development of **cognitive process theories** of composing. **James Moffett**, for example, has drawn on Piaget's ideas to offer a method of writing instruction based on students' cognitive development (*Teaching the Universe of Discourse* [1968]). **Arthur Applebee** (1974) and **James Berlin** (1987) credit Piaget's theories with influencing the important **Dartmouth Conference**. His concept of egocentrism has been important to discussions of **audience** awareness, revision, and **basic writing**. Some scholars see lack of audience awareness in an essay as evidence of a writer's egocentrism; others, however, argue that such a view lays blame on the writer. Piaget's theories of development are used to devise and respond to writing assignments. Important works include *The Child's Conception of the World* (1926), *The Language and Thought of the Child* (1926), *The Origins of Intelligence in Children* (1936), and *The Early Growth of Logic in the Child* (1958).

Michael Polanyi Hungarian scientist, chemist, and philosopher who in the 1930s emigrated to Britain. Polanyi's theory of "personal knowledge" or **tacit knowledge** is prominent in various disciplines and refers to a type of unconscious knowledge acquired by practice and by following examples. Polanyi faults societies' reliance on science for "truth," emphasizing instead the role of persuasion in scientific communities and encouraging more reliance on "personal knowledge." Thomas Kuhn has developed Polanyi's theories of knowledge in his work with scientific knowledge. In his later writings, Polanyi is interested in rhetorical concerns, especially those related to the persuasive power of political ideologies such as Nazism and Marxism.

Rhetoricians and compositionists often draw on Polanyi's philosophical work, predominantly for his theories regarding the social nature of persuasion, **knowledge**, and language in general. In composition studies, his concept of tacit knowledge is often used to support social views of writing instruction. Some also draw on Polanyi to justify personal writing assignments, and others use his concept of **incubation** in describing the role of the unconscious in the writing **process**. Important works include *Personal Knowledge* (1958), *The Tacit Dimension* (1966), and *Knowing and Being* (1969).

Carl Rogers   American psychotherapist and originator of "client-centered" or "non-directive" therapy. In his work, Rogers emphasizes the elimination of threat and judgment in the client-therapist relationship, encouraging instead an environment of acceptance, agreement, and trust. Rogers stresses the importance of clients' feelings and of establishing understanding in order to achieve optimal results. Also important is the sense of control the client possesses over the direction of the therapy.

Richard Young, Alton Becker, Kenneth Pike, and **Maxine Hairston** are often credited with introducing Rogers' work to composition studies in the 1970s. Rogers' theories and practices are grouped under the broad heading of **Rogerian rhetoric**, sometimes also called empathic theories, and were used initially in the composition classroom to teach argument. The reach of Rogerian rhetoric, however, has extended beyond argument to the writing classroom in general. Many compositionists have welcomed Rogers' emphasis on empathic listening, his insistence on nondirective authority figures, and his desire to understand multiple perspectives. His 1951 paper "Communication: Its Blocking and Its Facilitation" is often used by composition scholars in translating Rogers' theories to the classroom.

Richard Rorty   American philosopher, often considered a "new pragmatist," who is influenced by John Dewey, William James, and Martin Heidegger but also by poststructuralist theories. Rorty, generalizing Thomas Kuhn's claim that scientific knowledge is socially constructed, argues that all **knowledge** is socially constructed. He rejects the traditional assumption that language is used to report an objective reality; instead, Rorty contends that language and knowledge of reality cannot be separated because knowledge is, not a discovered "truth" or objective recognition of reality, but a "socially justified belief." For Rorty, knowledge is known, maintained, and even overthrown by **conversation** within communities. **Normal discourse** maintains knowledge through consensus; **abnormal discourse** challenges conventional knowledge through a breakdown of consensus. Rorty values such a breakdown as it leads to questioning, exploration of ideas, and possibly to a new concept of knowledge. Critiquing his own discipline, philosophy, Rorty argues that philosophy is not a privileged avenue to "truth" or understanding but one among other methods of inquiry differentiated by its conventions of communication. Such a view of professional disciplines, according to Rorty, can allow far-reaching and more inclusive conversation. Rorty's critique of philosophy has encouraged other academics to examine the assumptions underpinning their individual disciplines. Also important is Rorty's concept of edification, his social view of the development of selfhood in relation to one's historical context and social circumstance.

Rorty's **nonfoundational** thought has influenced composition theory and practice, supporting and furthering **social constructionist** theories of composing. Rorty's view that knowledge is social and community-generated often serves as support for **collaborative** pedagogies. While his philosophy has been actively applied to the composition classroom and to education in general, Rorty (1990) expresses doubt about the relevance of philosophy to education. In a well-known interview by Gary Olson in *JAC* (1989), Rorty exhibits reservations regarding established goals and practices of composition studies and seems bewildered with the way compositionists have applied his theories. For composition, *Philosophy and the Mirror of Nature* (1979) stands as Rorty's most influential work.

Louise Rosenblatt   American literary scholar who has been credited as an originator of reader-response criticism. Her work, however, was not widely recognized until the 1950s and 1960s. In her 1938 *Literature as Exploration*, Rosenblatt counters the then popular New Critics by placing importance on the reader's response or reaction to a text as opposed to basing critical interpretation solely on the text itself. She acknowledges the rhetorical nature of the literary text, seeing it as possessing a persuasive function, and contends that texts do not contain only one meaning. Her book was a response to the method of literary instruction that proposed teaching "the" interpretation of a literary work. Instead, Rosenblatt encouraged a method of instruction that invited students to think, discuss, and question. Her work emphasizes the need for active reading, and thus she develops a "transactional" approach to reading, an approach that accounts for the reader's existing knowledge. In her teaching, Rosenblatt encourages students to make connections between their personal experiences and what they read, allowing them insight into the work's persuasive structure. She acknowledges the influence of John Dewey's work on perception on her own transactional theory of reading; Dewey views perception as a creative action, not, as commonly assumed, a passive response. Rosenblatt has been active in both MLA and **NCTE** and has encouraged a synthesis of theory and pedagogy.

In composition studies, Rosenblatt's focus on the interaction between text and the reader has been influential, particularly through the connection between literature and rhetoric and through the shift in attention to the **audience** of a piece of writing. Importantly for composition studies, Rosenblatt recognizes that readers do not innocently encounter texts, but bring much "baggage" (such as past experience, preconceived notions) to the reading experience and thus to the meaning made from this experience; this view posits students as makers of meaning and thus encourages value and recognition of the knowledge that students bring to the classroom. Scholars have also drawn on Rosenblatt's transactional theory for assessment of student writing. Rosenblatt has contributed to edited collections of composition scholarship; her second book, *The Reader, the Text, and the Poem: The Transactional Theory of the Literary Work* (1978), has also been influential in composition studies.

Lev Semyonovich Vygotsky   Soviet psychologist known for his theories of cognitive development and his views on the relationship between language and thought. Influenced by Marxism, he emphasizes the influence of social factors on cognitive development. His most influential work, *Thought and Language* (1934), focuses on the inner life of children and the process of their socialization. Vygotsky differs from Jean Piaget, who argues for individualistic principles as key to higher cognitive development; for example, Piaget proposes that in children, **egocentric** speech "matures" into socialized speech. Vygotsky instead places more emphasis on social factors that could lead to higher development, seeing social speech as an early point of development that then splits into "communicative" speech, which is still "social," and "inner" or egocentric speech. He focuses on the sociocultural context for learning.

Vygotsky's work has influenced contemporary research and practice in composition studies. His theories have also influenced studies in literacy acquisition and instruction. Scholars agree that Vygotsky's theories influenced the **Dartmouth Conference** (Applebee 1974, Berlin 1987). Vygotsky explains cognitive growth as a process, contributing to **process** theories of composing. **James Moffett** has also drawn on Vygotsky's ideas to offer a method of writing instruction based on students' cognitive development (*Teaching the Universe of Discourse* [1968]). Vygotsky's work has informed **cognitive** theorists, including **Janet Emig** and **Sondra Perl**, as well as social theorists. For example, Vygotsky's emphasis on the child's "social" speech has influenced social theorists including **Patricia Bizzell** and proponents of **collaborative learning** such as **Kenneth Bruffee**. Composition scholars draw on Vygotsky's theories of the relationship between thought and language and his claim that writing is helpful in obtaining higher mental functions such as analysis and synthesis—a view reflected in **writing-to-learn** activities and theories. Also important is Vygotsky's claim that speech and writing represent different psychological processes; this view frees writing from the assumption that it is merely speech in a different form, thus supporting the need for different instruction, research, and theory in the areas of speech and written communication. Other influential work includes *Mind in Society: The Development of Higher Psychological Processes* (1978).

Works Cited

Ackerman, John. "The Promise of Writing to Learn." *WC* 10 (1993): 334–70.

Agar, Michael H. *Speaking of Ethnography*. Beverly Hills: Sage Publications, 1986.

Allen, Michael. "Writing Away from Fear: Mina Shaughnessy and the Uses of Authority." *CE* 41 (1980): 857–67.

Anderson, Larry. "Time and Writing: Institutional Forces and the Shape of Writing Pedagogy." *WI* 14 (1994): 25–37.

Anderson, Virginia. "Confrontational Teaching and Rhetorical Practice." *CCC* 48 (1997): 197–214.

———. "Instrumentalism and Dreaming." *CCC* 49 (1998): 270–74.

Anderson, Worth, Cynthia Best, Alycia Black, John Hurst, Brandt Miller, and Susan Miller. "Cross-Curricular Underlife: A Collaborative Report on Ways with Academic Words" *CCC* 41 (1990): 11–36.

Annas, Pamela. "Style as Politics: A Feminist Approach to the Teaching of Writing." *CE* 47 (1985): 360–71.

Anson, Chris. "On Reflection: The Role of Logs and Journals in Service-Learning Courses." *Writing the Community: Concepts and Models for Service-Learning in Composition*. Ed. Linda Adler-Kassner, Robert Crooks, and Ann Watters. Washington, D.C.: American Association for Higher Education, 1997. 167–80.

Anson, Chris, Joan Graham, David Jolliffe, Nancy Shapiro and Carolyn Smith. *Scenarios for Teaching Writing: Contexts for Discussion and Reflective Practice*. Urbana, IL: NCTE, 1993.

Applebee, Arthur. "Problems in Process Approaches: Toward a Reconceptualization of Process Instruction." *The Teaching of Writing*. Ed. Anthony Petrosky and David Bartholomae. Chicago: University of Chicago Press, 1986.

———. *Tradition and Reform in the Teaching of English: A History*. Urbana, IL: NCTE, 1974.

———. "Writing and Reasoning." *Review of Educational Research*. 54 (1984): 577–96.

Aronowitz, Stanley, and Henry Giroux. *Education Still Under Siege*. 2nd ed. Westport, CT: Bergin & Garvey. 1993.

Austin, J. L. *How to Do Things with Words*. 2nd ed. Ed. J. O. Urmson and Marina Sbisa. Cambridge: Harvard University Press, 1975.

Bain, Alexander. *English Composition and Rhetoric: A Manual*. London: Longmans, 1866.

Baker, Nancy Westrich. "The Effect of Portfolio-Based Instruction on Composition Students' Final Examination Scores, Course Grades, and Attitudes Toward Writing." *RTE* 27 (1993): 155–74.

Bakhtin, Mikhail. *The Dialogic Imagination*. Ed. Michael Holquist. Trans. C. Emerson and M Holquist. Austin: University of Texas Press, 1981.

———. *Problems of Dostoevsky's Poetics*. Ed. and trans. Caryl Emerson. Minneapolis: University of Minnesota Press, 1984.

———. *Rabelais and His World*. Trans. Helene Iswolsky. Cambridge: MIT Press, 1968.

Bartholomae, David. "Freshman English, Composition, and CCCC." *CCC* 40 (1989): 38–50.

———. "Inventing the University." *When a Writer Can't Write*. Ed. Mike Rose. New York: Guilford Press, 1985. 134–65.

———. "The Tidy House: Basic Writing in the American Curriculum." *JBW* 12 (1993). 4–21.

Bauer, Dale M. *Feminist Dialogics: A Theory of Failed Community*. Albany: State University of New York Press, 1988.

———. "The Other 'F' Word: The Feminist in the Classroom." *CE* 52 (1990): 385–96.

Bazerman, Charles. "Scientific Writing as a Social Act: A Review of the Literature of the Sociology of Science." *New Essays in Technical & Scientific Communication: Research, Theory and Practice*. Ed. Paul V. Anderson, R. John Brockman, and Carolyn R. Miller. Farmingdale, NY: Baywood, 1983. 156–84.

Beach, Richard. "Demonstrating Techniques for Assessing Writing in the Writing Conference" *CCC* 37 (1986): 56–65.

———. "Evaluating Writing to Learn: Responding to Journals." *Encountering Student Texts: Interpretive Issues in Reading Student Writing*. Ed. Bruce Lawson, Susan Sterr Ryan, and W. Ross Winterowd. Urbana, IL: NCTE, 1989. 183–98.

Beauvais, Paul. "Metadiscourse in Context: A Speech Act Model of Illocutionary Content." CCCC Annual Convention. New Orleans, LA. 13–15 March 1986.

———. "A Speech Act Theory of Metadiscourse." *WC* 6 (1989): 11–30.

Becker, A. L., Paul Rodgers, Jr., et al. "Symposium on the Paragraph." *CCC* 17 (1966): 60–87.

Bee, Barbara. "The Politics of Literacy." *Literacy and Revolution, The Pedagogy of Paulo Freire*. Ed. Robert Mackie. New York: Continuum, 1981. 39–56.

Belanoff, Pat. "Optimism, Writing, Teaching." *CCC* 48 (1997): 410–14.

Belanoff, Pat, Peter Elbow, and Sheryl Fontaine, eds. *Nothing Begins with N: New Investigations of Freewriting*. Carbondale: Southern Illinois University Press, 1991.

Belenky, Mary Field, Blythe McVicker Clinchy, Nancy Rule Goldberger, and Jill Mattuck Tarule. *Women's Ways of Knowing: The Development of Self, Voice, and Mind*. New York: Basic Books, 1986.

Berkenkotter, Carol. "Decisions and Revisions: The Planning Strategies of a Publishing Writer." *CCC* 34 (1983): 156–68.

————. "Paradigm Debates, Turf Wars, and the Conduct of Sociocognitive Inquiry in Composition." *CCC* 42 (1991): 151–69.

————. "Student Writers and Their Sense of Authority Over Texts." *CCC* 35 (1984): 312–19.

————. "Understanding a Writer's Awareness of Audience." *CCC* 32 (1981): 388–99.

Berlin, James A. "Comment and Response." *CE* 51 (1989): 770–77.

————. "Contemporary Composition: The Major Pedagogical Theories." *CE* 44 (1982). 765–77. Rpt. in *The Writing Teacher's Sourcebook.* Ed. Gary Tate and Edward P. J. Corbett. 2nd ed. New York: Oxford University Press, 1988. 47–59.

————. "Freirean Pedagogy in the U.S.: A Response." *(Inter)Views, Cross-Disciplinary Perspectives on Rhetoric and Literacy.* Ed. Gary A. Olson and Irene Gale. Carbondale: Southern Illinois University Press, 1991. 169–76.

————. "Rhetoric and Ideology in the Writing Class." *CE* 50 (1988) 477–94.

————. *Rhetoric and Reality: Writing Instruction in American Colleges, 1900–1985.* Carbondale: Southern Illinois University Press, 1987.

————. *Rhetoric, Poetics, and Cultures: Refiguring College English Studies.* Urbana, IL: NCTE, 1996.

————. *Writing Instruction in Nineteenth-Century American Colleges.* Carbondale: Southern Illinois University Press, 1984.

————. "Writing Instruction in School and College English, 1890–1985." *A Short History of Writing Instruction: From Ancient Greece to Twentieth-Century America.* Ed. James J. Murphy. Davis, CA: Hermagoras Press, 1990. 183–220.

Berlin, James A., and Robert Inkster. "Current-Traditional Rhetoric: Paradigm and Practice." *FEN* 8 (1980): 1–14.

Bernstein, Basil. *Class, Codes, and Control.* 3 vols. London: Routledge and Kegan Paul, 1971–1975. Rpt. vol 1. New York: Schocken, 1975.

Berthoff, Ann E. "Is Teaching Still Possible? Writing, Meaning, and Higher Order Reasoning." *CE* 46 (1984): 743–55.

————. *The Making of Meaning.* Montclair, NJ: Boynton/Cook, 1981.

————. "Paulo Freire's Liberation Pedagogy." *Rhetoric and Composition: A Sourcebook for Teachers and Writers.* 3rd ed. Ed. Richard L. Graves. Portsmouth, NH: Boynton/Cook, 1990. 314–21.

————. "The Problem of Problem Solving." *CCC* 22 (1971): 237–42.

————. "Reading the World . . . Reading the Word: Paulo Freire's Pedagogy of Knowing." *Only Connect: Uniting Reading and Writing.* Ed. Thomas Newkirk. Upper Montclair, NJ: Boynton/Cook, 1986. 119–30.

————. "Response to Janice Lauer." *CCC* 23 (1972): 414–15.

————. "The Teacher as REsearcher." California Association of Teachers of English Conference. San Diego, 1979. Rpt. in *Reclaiming the Classroom, Teacher Research as an Agency for Change.* Ed. Dixie Goswami and Peter Stillman. Upper Montclair, NJ: Boynton/Cook, 1987. 28–38.

Bialostosky, Don. "Antilogics, Dialogics, and Sophistic Social Psychology: Michael Billig's Reinvention of Bakhtin from Protagorean Rhetoric." *Rhetoric, Sophistry, Pragmatism.* Ed. Steven Mailloux. Cambridge: Cambridge University Press, 1995. 82–93.

————. "Liberal Education, Writing, and the Dialogic Self." *Contending with Words: Composition and Rhetoric in a Postmodern Age.* Ed. Patricia Harkin and John Schilb. New York: MLA, 1991. 11–22.

Birnbaum, June Cannell, and Janet Emig. "Case Study." *Handbook of Research on Teaching the English Language Arts*. Ed. James Flood et al. New York: Macmillan, 1991. 195–204.

Bishop, Wendy. "The Perils, Pleasures, and Process of Ethnographic Writing Research." *Taking Stock: The Writing Process Movement in the 90s*. Ed. Lad Tobin and Thomas Newkirk. Portsmouth, NH: Boynton/Cook, 1994. 261–79.

Bizzell, Patricia. "Arguing About Literacy." *CE* 50 (1988): 141–53.

———. "Beyond Anti-Foundationalism to Rhetorical Authority: Problems Defining 'Cultural Literacy.' " *CE* 52 (1990): 661–75.

———. "Cognition, Convention, and Certainty: What We Need to Know About Writing." *PRE/TEXT* 3 (fall 1982): 213–43.

———. "College Composition: An Initiation into the Academic Discourse Community." *Curriculum Inquiry* 12 (1982): 191–207.

———. " 'Contact Zones' and English Studies." *CE* 56 (1994): 163–69.

———. "The Ethos of Academic Discourse." *CCC* 29 (1978): 351–55.

———. "Foundationalism and Anti-Foundationalism in Composition Studies." *PRE/TEXT* 7 (1986) 37–56.

———. "Marxist Ideas in Composition Studies." *Contending with Words: Composition and Rhetoric in a Postmodern Age*. Ed. Patricia Harkin and John Schilb. New York MLA, 1991. 52–68.

———. "Power, Authority, and Critical Pedagogy." *JBW* 10 (1991): 54–70.

———. "Thomas Kuhn, Scientism, and English Studies." *CE* 40 (1979): 764–71

———. "What Happens When Basic Writers Come to College." *CCC* 37 (1986): 294–301.

Bizzell, Patricia, and Bruce Herzberg. *The Bedford Bibliography for Teachers of Writing*. 4th ed. Boston: Bedford Books of St. Martin's Press, 1996.

———. "Writing Across the Curriculum: A Bibliographic Essay." *The Territory of Language: Linguistics, Stylistics, and the Teaching of Composition*. Ed. Donald McQuade. Carbondale: Southern Illinois University Press, 1986. 340–52.

———, eds. *The Rhetorical Tradition: Readings from Classical Times to the Present*. Boston: Bedford Books, 1990.

Black, Edwin. *Rhetorical Criticism: A Study in Method*. New York: Macmillan, 1965.

Bleich, David. *The Double Perspective: Language, Literacy, and Social Relations*. New York: Oxford University Press, 1988.

Blom, Thomas. "Counterstatement: Response to Maxine Hairston, The Winds of Change: Thomas Kuhn and the Revolution in the Teaching of Writing." *CCC* 35 (1984): 489–94.

Bloom, Lynn Z. "Why I (Used to) Hate to Give Grades." *CCC* 48 (1997): 360–71.

Bloom, Lynn Z., and Martin Bloom. "But Will They Answer? A Critical Review of One Behavioral Attempt to Call the Creative Spirits." *CE* 31 (1969): 199–208.

Booth, Wayne, C. "The Rhetorical Stance." *CCC* 14 (1963): 139–45. Rpt. in *The Writing Teacher's Sourcebook*. 2nd ed. Ed. Gary Tate and Edward P. J. Corbett. New York: Oxford University Press, 1988. 151–57.

Braddock, Richard, Richard Lloyd-Jones, and Lowell Schoer. *Research in Written Composition*. Urbana, IL: NCTE, 1963.

Brand, Alice. "The Why of Cognition." *CCC* 36 (1987): 436–43.

Brandt, Deborah. "The Cognitive as the Social: An Ethnomethodological Approach to Writing Process Research." *WC* 9 (1992): 315–55.

Bratcher, Suzanne, and Elizabeth J. Stroble. "Determining the Progression from Comfort to Confidence: A Longitudinal Evaluation of a National Writing Project Site Based on Multiple Data Sources." *RTE* 28 (1994): 66–88.

Brent, Doug. "Young, Becker, and Pike's Rogerian Rhetoric: A Twenty-Year Reassessment." *CE* 53 (1991): 452–66.

Bridwell-Bowles, Lillian. "Research in Composition: Issues and Methods." *An Introduction to Composition Studies.* Ed. Erika Lindemann and Gary Tate. New York: Oxford University Press, 1991. 94–117.

Britton, James. "The Composing Processes and the Functions of Writing." *Research on Composing: Points of Departure.* Ed. Charles Cooper and Lee Odell. Urbana, IL: NCTE, 1978. 13–28.

———. "What's the Use? A Schematic Account of Language Functions." *EdRev* 23 (1971): 205–19.

Britton, James, and Tony Burgess, Nancy Martin, and Alex McLeod. *The Development of Writing Abilities (11–18).* London: Macmillan Education, 1975.

Brockriede, Wayne, and Douglas Ehninger. "Toulmin on Argument: An Interpretation and Application." *QJS* 46 (1960): 44–53. Rpt. in *Contemporary Theories of Rhetoric: Selected Readings.* Ed. Richard L. Johannesen. New York: Harper & Row, 1971. 241–55.

Brodkey, Linda. "Modernism and the Scene(s) of Writing." *CE* 49 (1987): 396–418.

———. "Writing Ethnographic Narratives." *WC* 4 (1987): 25–50.

Brooke, Robert E. *Writing and Sense of Self: Identity Negotiations in Writing Workshops.* Urbana, IL: NCTE, 1991.

Brown, Rexford. "Evaluation and Learning." *The Teaching of Writing: Eighty-fifth Yearbook of the National Society for the Study of Education.* Ed. Anthony Petrosky and David Bartholomae. Chicago: University of Chicago Press, 1986. 114–30.

Bruffee, Kenneth A. "Collaborative Learning and the 'Conversation of Mankind.' " *CE* 46 (1984): 635–52.

———. *Collaborative Learning: Higher Education, Interdependence, and the Authority of Knowledge.* Baltimore: Johns Hopkins University Press, 1993.

———. "Peer Tutoring and the 'Conversation of Mankind.' " *Writing Centers: Theory and Administration.* Urbana, IL: NCTE, 1984. 3–15.

———. "Social Construction, Language, and the Authority of Knowledge: A Bibliographical Essay." *CE* 48 (1986): 773–90.

———. "Writing and Reading as Collaborative or Social Acts." *The Writer's Mind: Writing as a Mode of Thinking.* Ed. Janice N. Hayes et al. Urbana, IL: NCTE, 1983. 159–69.

Burke, Kenneth. *A Grammar of Motives.* Berkeley: University of California Press, 1969.

———. *Language as Symbolic Action: Essays on Life, Literature, and Method.* Berkeley: University of California Press, 1966.

———. *A Rhetoric of Motives.* Rpt. Berkeley: University of California Press, 1969.

———. "Rhetoric—Old and New." *JGenEd* 5 (1951): 202–9.

———. "Questions and Answers About the Pentad." *CCC* 29 (1978): 330–35.

Burnham, Christopher C. "Portfolio Evaluation: Room to Breathe and Grow." *Training the New Teacher of College Composition.* Ed. Charles Bridges. Urbana, IL: NCTE, 1986. 125–38.

Burton, Fredrick R. "Teacher-Researcher Projects: An Elementary School Teacher's Perspective." *Handbook of Research on Teaching the English Language Arts*. Ed. James Flood et al. New York: Macmillan, 1991. 226–30.

CCCC Committee on Professional Standards for Quality Education. "CCCC Initiatives on the Wyoming Conference Resolution: A Draft Report." *CCC* 40 (1989): 61–72.

Canagarajah, Suresh A. "Safe Houses in the Contact Zone: Coping Strategies of African American Students in the Academy." *CCC* 48 (1997): 173–96.

Castell, Suzanne de, and Allan Luke. "Defining Literacy in North American Schools." *Perspectives on Literacy*. Ed. Eugene Kintgen, Barry Kroll, and Mike Rose. Carbondale: Southern Illinois University Press, 1988. 159–74.

Caywood, Cynthia L., and Gillian R. Overing, eds. *Teaching Writing, Pedagogy, Gender and Equity*. Albany: State University of New York Press, 1987.

Charney, Davida. "Empiricism Is Not a Four-Letter Word." *CCC* 47 (1996): 567–93.

———. "The Validity of Using Holistic Scoring to Evaluate Writing: A Critical Overview." *RTE* 18 (1984): 65–81.

Chase, Geoffrey. "Accommodation, Resistance, and the Politics of Student Writing." *CCC* 39 (1988): 13–22.

———. "Perhaps We Need Just to Say Yes." *JEd* 172 (1990): 29–37.

Chiseri-Strater, Elizabeth, and Bonnie Stone Sunstein. *Fieldworking: Reading and Writing Research*. Upper Saddle River, NJ: Prentice Hall, 1997.

Chomsky, Noam. *Aspects of the Theory of Syntax*. Cambridge: MIT Press, 1965.

———. *Syntactic Structures*. The Hague: Mouton, 1957.

Christensen, Francis. "A Generative Rhetoric of the Paragraph." *CCC* 16 (1965): 144–56.

———. "A Generative Rhetoric of the Sentence." *CCC* 14 (1963): 155–61.

———. *Notes Toward a New Rhetoric*. New York: Harper & Row, 1967.

Church, Robert L. *Education in the United States: An Interpretive History*. New York: Free Press, 1976

Clark, Gregory. "Writing as Travel, or Rhetoric on the Road." *CCC* 49 (1998): 9–23.

Clark, Irene L. "Portfolio Evaluation, Collaboration, and Writing Centers." *CCC* 44 (1993): 515–24.

Clark, Suzanne. "Rhetoric, Social Construction, and Gender: Is It Bad to Be Sentimental?" *Writing Theory and Critical Theory*. Ed. John Clifford and John Schilb. New York: MLA, 1994. 96–108.

Coe, Richard M. "Eco-Logic for the Composition Classroom." *CCC* 26 (1975): 232–37.

———. " 'Prophesying After the Event': The Archeology and Ecology of Genre." CCCC Annual Meeting. San Diego. 31 March–3 April 1993.

———. *Toward a Grammar of Passages*. Carbondale: Southern Illinois University Press, 1988.

Coles, William, Jr. *The Plural I: Teaching Writing*. New York: Holt, 1978.

Collins, James L., and Michael M. Williamson. "Assigned Rhetorical Context and Semantic Abbreviation in Writing." *New Directions in Composition Research*. Ed. Richard Beach and Lillian S. Bridwell. New York: Guilford Press, 1984. 285–96.

Comprone, Joseph. "Kenneth Burke and the Teaching of Writing." *CCC* 29 (1978): 336–40.

Connors, Robert J. "Composition Studies and Science." *CE* 45 (1983): 1–20.

————. *Composition-Rhetoric: Backgrounds, Theory, and Pedagogy.* Pittsburgh: University of Pittsburgh Press, 1997.

————. "Grammar in American College Composition: An Historical Overview." *The Territory of Language: Linguistics, Stylistics, and the Teaching of Composition.* Ed. Donald McQuade. Carbondale: Southern Illinois University Press, 1986. 3–22.

————. "Overwork/Underpay: Labor and Status of Composition Teachers Since 1880." *RR* 9 (1990): 108–25.

————. "The Rise and Fall of the Modes of Discourse." *CCC* 32 (1981): 444–55.

————. "Teaching and Learning as a Man." *CE* 58 (1996): 137–57.

————. "Writing the History of Our Discipline." *An Introduction to Composition Studies.* Ed. Erika Lindemann and Gary Tate. New York: Oxford University Press, 1991. 49–71.

Conners, Robert J., Lisa Ede, and Andrea Lunsford. "The Revival of Rhetoric in America." *Essays on Classical Rhetoric and Modern Discourse.* Ed. Robert J. Connors et al. Carbondale: Southern Illinois University Press, 1984. 1–15.

Cooper, Charles. "Holistic Evaluation of Writing." *Evaluating Writing: Describing, Measuring, Judging.* Ed. Charles Cooper and Lee Odell. Urbana, IL: NCTE, 1977. 3–32.

Cooper, Marilyn M. "Dialogic Learning Across Disciplines." *JAC* 14 (1994): 531–46.

————. "Dueling with Dualism: A Response to Interviews with Mary Field Belenky and Gayatri Chakravorty Spivak." *(Inter)Views: Cross-Disciplinary Perspectives on Rhetoric and Literacy.* Ed. Gary Olson and Irene Gale. Carbondale: Southern Illinois University Press, 1991. 51–57.

————. "The Ecology of Writing." *CE* 48 (1986): 364–75.

————. "Why Are We Talking About Discourse Communities?: Or, Foundationalism Rears Its Ugly Head Once More." *Writing as a Social Action.* Ed. Marilyn Cooper and Michael Holzman. Portsmouth, NH: Boynton/Cook, 1989. 202–20.

Cooper, Marilyn M., and Michael Holzman. "Talking About Protocols." *CCC* 34 (1983): 284–93.

Cooper, Marilyn M., and Cynthia Selfe. "Computer Conferences and Learning: Authority, Resistance, and Internally Persuasive Discourse." *CE* 52 (1990): 847–69.

Corbett, Edward P. J. *Classical Rhetoric for the Modern Student.* 3rd ed. (1st ed. 1965) New York: Oxford University Press, 1990.

————. "John Locke's Contributions to Rhetoric." *CCC* 32 (1981): 423–33.

————. "A New Look at Old Rhetoric." *Rhetoric: Theories for Application.* Ed. Robert Gorrell. Urbana, IL: NCTE, 1967. Rpt. in *Selected Essays of Edward P. J. Corbett.* Dallas: Southern Methodist University Press, 1989. 63–72.

————. "What Is Being Revived?" *CCC* 18 (1967): 166–72. Rpt. in *Selected Essays of Edward P. J. Corbett.* Ed. Robert Connors. Dallas: Southern Methodist University Press, 1989. 48–60.

Corder, James W. "Argument as Emergence, Rhetoric as Love." *RR* 4 (1985): 16–32. Rpt. *Professing the New Rhetorics.* Ed. Theresa Enos and Stuart C. Brown. Englewood Cliffs, NJ: Prentice Hall, 1994. 413–28.

————. "Outhouses, Weather Changes, and the Return to Basics in English Education." *CE* 38 (1977): 474–82.

————. "Rhetoric and Literary Study: Some Lines of Inquiry." *CCC* 32 (1981): 13–20.

Covino, William A. *The Art of Wondering: A Revisionist Return to the History of Rhetoric*. Portsmouth, NH: Heinemann, Boynton/Cook, 1988.

———. "Defining Advanced Composition: Contributions from the History of Rhetoric." *JAC* 8 (1988): 113–22.

———. *Magic, Rhetoric, and Literacy*. Albany: SUNY Press, 1994.

Cowan, Elizabeth Wooten. "Fractions Make My Head Hurt." *CE* 38 (1977): 460–654.

Crosswhite, James. "The Dissatisfactions of Rhetoric: Philosophy and Politics in the Teaching of Writing." *RSQ* 21 (1991): 1–16.

Crowley, Sharon. "Around 1971: Current-Traditional Rhetoric and Process Models of Composing." *Composition in the Twenty-First Century, Crisis and Change*. Ed. Lynn Z. Bloom, Donald A. Daiker, and Edward M. White. Carbondale: Southern Illinois University Press, 1996. 64–74.

———. "The Current-Traditional Theory of Style: An Informal History." *RSQ* 16 (1986): 233–50.

———. *The Methodological Memory*. Carbondale: Southern Illinois University Press, 1990.

———. "A Personal Essay on Freshman English." *PRE/TEXT* 12 (1991): 156–76.

———. "Response to Robert J. Connors, The Rise and Fall of the Modes of Discourse." *CCC* 35 (1984): 88–91.

Crowley, Sharon, and George Redman. "Why Teach Writing?" *CCC* 26 (1975): 279–81.

Crusius, Timothy W. *Discourse: A Critique and Synthesis of Major Theories*. New York: MLA, 1989.

———. *A Teacher's Introduction to Philosophical Hermeneutics*. Urbana, IL: NCTE, 1991.

Daiker, Donald A., Andrew Kerek, and Max Morenberg, eds. *Sentence Combining: A Rhetorical Perspective*. Carbondale: Southern Illinois University Press, 1985.

D'Angelo, Frank. "Nineteenth Century Forms/Modes of Discourse: A Critical Inquiry." *CCC* 35 (1984): 31–42.

Daniell, Beth. "Theory, Theory Talk, and Composition." *Writing Theory and Critical Theory*. Ed. John Clifford and John Schilb. New York: MLA, 1994. 127–40.

Daniell, Beth, and Art Young. "Resisting Writing / Resisting Writing Teachers." *The Subject Is Writing: Essays by Teachers and Students*. Ed. Wendy Bishop. Portsmouth, NH: Boynton/Cook, 1993. 223–34.

Dasenbrock, Reed Way. "Do We Write the Text We Read?" *CE* 53 (1991): 7–18.

———. "J. L. Austin and the Articulation of a New Rhetoric." *CCC* 38 (1987): 291–305.

Day, Henry N. *Elements of the Art of Rhetoric*. New York: A. S. Barnes and Co., 1850.

De Beaugrande, Robert. "Generative Stylistics: Between Grammar and Rhetoric." *CCC* 28 (1977): 240–46.

———. "Sentence Combining and Discourse Processing: In Search of a General Theory." *Sentence Combining: A Rhetorical Perspective*. Ed. Donald A. Daiker, Andrew Kerek, and Max Morenberg. Carbondale: Southern Illinois University Press, 1985. 61–75.

Dewey, John. *How We Think*. Boston: Heath and Co., 1910.

———. *The School and Society*. Chicago: University of Chicago Press, 1915.

Dixon, John. *Growth Through English*. Reading, England: National Association for the Teaching of English, 1967.

Dobrin, David N. "Protocols Once More." *CE* 48 (1986): 713–25.

Doheny-Farina, Stephen. *Rhetoric, Innovation, Technology: Case Studies of Technical Communication in Technology Transfers.* Cambridge: MIT Press, 1992.

———. "Writing in an Emerging Organization: An Ethnographic Study." *WC* 3 (1986): 158–85.

Doheny-Farina, Stephen, and Lee Odell. "Ethnographic Research on Writing: Assumptions and Methodology." *Writing in Nonacademic Settings.* Ed. Lee Odell and Dixie Goswami. New York: Guilford Press, 1985. 503–35.

Donelson, Ken. " 'The Jackson Twins' and the Basics (vs.) Linguistics and NCTE." *CCC* 28 (1977): 170–73.

Dowst, Kenneth. "The Epistemic Approach: Writing, Knowing, and Learning." *Eight Approaches to Teaching Composition.* Ed. Timothy R. Donovan and Ben W. McClelland. Urbana, IL: NCTE, 1980. 65–85.

Ede, Lisa. "Audience: An Introduction to Research." *CCC* 35 (1984): 140–54.

———. "Is Rogerian Rhetoric Really Rogerian?" CCCC Annual Convention. Detroit, MI. 17–19 March 1983.

———. "Is Rogerian Rhetoric Really Rogerian?" *RR* 3 (1984): 40–48.

———. "Teaching Writing." *An Introduction to Composition Studies.* Ed. Erika Lindemann and Gary Tate. New York: Oxford University Press, 1991. 118–34.

Ede, Lisa, and Andrea Lunsford. "Audience Addressed/Audience Invoked: The Role of Audience in Composition Theory and Pedagogy." *CCC* 35 (1984): 155–71. Rpt. in *Teaching with the Bedford Guide for College Writers.* 4th ed. Vol. 2. Background Readings. Ed. Shirley Morahan. Boston: Bedford Books, 1996. 100–114.

———. *Singular Texts / Plural Authors: Perspectives on Collaborative Writing.* Carbondale: Southern Illinois University Press, 1990.

Edlund, John R. "Bakhtin and the Social Reality of Language Acquisition." *WI* 7 (1988): 56–67.

Eichhorn, Jill, Sara Farris, Karen Hayes, Adriana Hernandez, Susan Jarratt, and Karen Powers-Stubbs. "A Symposium on Feminist Experiences in the Composition Classroom." *CCC* 42 (1992): 297–322.

Elbow, Peter. "Closing My Eyes as I Speak: An Argument for Ignoring Audience." *CE* 49 (1987): 50–69. Rpt. in *The Bedford Guide for College Writers.* Vol. 2. Ed. X. J. Kennedy et al. Boston: Bedford Books, 1996. 114–32.

———. *Embracing Contraries.* New York: Oxford University Press, 1986.

———. Foreword. *Portfolios: Process and Product.* Ed. Pat Belanoff and Marcia Dickson. Portsmouth, NH: Boynton/Cook, 1991. ix–xvi.

———. "Ranking, Evaluating, and Liking: Sorting Out Three Forms of Judgment." *CE* 55 (1993): 187–206.

———. "Reflections on Academic Discourse: How It Relates to Freshmen and Colleagues." *CE* 53 (1991): 135–55.

———. *What Is English?* New York: MLA, 1990.

———. "Writing Assessment in the 21st Century: A Utopian View." *Composition in the Twenty-First Century: Crisis and Change.* Ed. Lynn Z. Bloom, Donald A. Daiker, and Edward M. White. Carbondale: Southern Illinois University Press, 1996. 83–100.

———. *Writing with Power: Techniques for Mastering the Writing Process.* New York: Oxford University Press, 1981.

———. *Writing Without Teachers.* New York: Oxford University Press, 1973.

Eldred, Margaret. "Writing Is Motivated Participation: An Interview with Charles Bazerman." *WE* 6 (1995): 7–20.

Emig, Janet. *The Composing Processes of Twelfth Graders.* Urbana, IL: NCTE, 1971.

———. "Inquiry Paradigms and Writing." *CCC* 33 (1982): 64–75.

———. "The Tacit Tradition: The Inevitability of a Multi-Disciplinary Approach to Writing Research." *Reinventing the Rhetorical Tradition.* Ed. Aviva Freedman and Ian Pringle. Conway, AR: L & S Books, for the Canadian Council Teachers of English, 1980. Rpt. in *The Web of Meaning: Essays on Writing, Teaching, Learning and Thinking.* Ed. Dixie Goswami and Maureen Butler. Upper Montclair, NJ: Boynton/Cook, 1983. 145–56.

———. "Writing as a Mode of Learning." *CCC* 28 (1977): 122–27.

Enkvist, Nils Erik. "On the Place of Style in Some Linguistic Theories." *Literary Style: A Symposium.* Ed. Seymour Chatman. London: Oxford University Press, 1971. 47–61.

Enos, Richard Leo, et al. "Heuristic Procedures and the Composing Process: A Selected Bibliography." *RSQ* Special Issue No. 1 (1982): 1–59.

Enos, Theresa, ed. *A Sourcebook for Basic Writing Teachers.* New York: Random House, 1987.

Enos, Theresa, and Stuart C. Brown, eds. *Defining the New Rhetorics.* Newbury Park; CA: Sage Publications, 1993.

———, eds. *Professing the New Rhetorics.* Englewood Cliffs, NJ: Blair Press, 1994.

Erickson, Frederick. "School Literacy, Reasoning, and Civility: An Anthropologist's Perspective." *Perspectives on Literacy.* Ed. Eugene Kintgen, Barry Kroll, and Mike Rose. Carbondale: Southern Illinois University Press, 1988. 205–26.

Ewald, Helen Rothschild. "The Implied Reader in Persuasive Discourse." *JAC* 8 (1988): 167–78.

———. "Writing for Answerability: Bakhtin and Composition Studies." *CCC* 44 (1993): 331–48.

Faigley, Lester. "Competing Theories of Process: A Critique and a Proposal." *CE* 48 (1986): 527–42.

———. *Fragments of Rationality: Postmodernity and the Subject of Composition.* Pittsburgh: University of Pittsburgh Press, 1992.

———. "Generative Rhetoric as a Way of Increasing Syntactic Fluency." *CCC* 30 (1979): 176–81.

———. "Judging Writing, Judging Selves." *CCC* 40 (1989): 395–412.

———. "Names in Search of a Concept: Maturity, Fluency, Complexity, and Growth in Written Syntax." *CCC* 31 (1980): 291–300.

———. "Performative Assessment of Writing Skills." *Sentence Combining: A Rhetorical Perspective.* Ed. Donald A. Daiker, Andrew Kerek, and Max Morenberg. Carbondale: Southern Illinois University Press, 1985. 175–86.

———. "Street Fights over the Impossibility of Theory: A Report of a Seminar." *Writing Theory and Critical Theory.* Ed. John Clifford and John Schilb. New York: MLA, 1994. 212–235.

Faigley, Lester, Roger D. Cherry, David Jolliffe, and Anna Skinner. *Assessing Writers' Knowledge and Processes of Composing.* Norwood, NJ: Ablex, 1985.

Faigley, Lester, and Stephen Witte. "Analyzing Revision." *CCC* 32 (1981): 400–414.

Fairbanks, A. Harris. "The Pedagogical Failure of Toulmin's Logic." *WI* 12 (1993): 103–14.

Farmer, Frank. "Dialogue and Critique: Bakhtin and the Cultural Studies Writing Class-room." *CCC* 49 (1998): 186–207.

———. "Voice Reprised: Three Etudes for a Dialogic Understanding." *RR* 13 (spring 1995): 304–20.

Felman, Shoshana, ed. *Literature and Psychoanalysis: The Question of Reading Other-wise*. Baltimore: Johns Hopkins University Press, 1982.

Fish, Stanley E. "Anti-Foundationalism, Theory Hope, and the Teaching of Composi-tion." *The Current in Criticism*. Ed. Clayton Koelb and Virgil Lokke. West La-fayette, IN: Purdue University Press, 1987. 65–79.

———. "Consequences." *CritI* 11 (1985): 433–58.

———. *Doing What Comes Naturally: Change, Rhetoric, and the Practice of Theory in Literary and Legal Studies*. Durham, NC: Duke University Press, 1989.

———. "Interpreting the Variorum." *Contemporary Literary Criticism: Literary and Cultural Studies*. 2nd ed. Ed. Robert Con Davis and Ronald Schleifer. New York: Longman, 1989. 101–17.

———. *Is There a Text in This Class? The Authority of Interpretive Communities*. Cam-bridge, MA: Harvard University Press, 1980.

Fishman, Stephen M., and Lucille Parkinson McCarthy. "Community in the Expressivist Classroom: Juggling Liberal and Communitarian Visions." *CE* 57 (1995): 62–81.

———. "Is Expressivism Dead? Reconsidering Its Romantic Roots and Its Relation to Social Constructionism." *CE* 54 (1992): 647–61.

Flower, Linda. "Cognition, Context, and Theory Building." *CCC* 40 (1989): 282–311.

———. "Writer-Based Prose: A Cognitive Basis for Problems in Writing." *CE* 41 (1979): 19–37.

Flower, Linda, and John Hayes. "A Cognitive Process Theory of Writing." *CCC* 32 (1981): 365–87.

———. "Problem Solving Strategies and the Writing Process." *CE* 39 (1977): 449–61.

Flynn, Elizabeth A. "Composing as a Woman." *CCC* 39 (1988): 423–35.

———. "Composition Studies from a Feminist Perspective." *The Politics of Writing Instruction*. Ed. Richard Bullock and John Trimbur. Portsmouth, NH: Heinemann, Boynton/Cook, 1991. 137–54.

———. "Feminism and Scientism." *CCC* 46 (1995): 353–68.

Flynn, Elizabeth A., George McCulley, and Ronald Gratz. "Writing in Biology: Effects of Peer Critiquing and Analysis of Models on the Quality of Biology Laboratory Reports." *Writing Across the Disciplines*: Research into Practice. Ed. Art Young and Toby Fulwiler. Upper Montclair, NJ: Boynton/Cook, 1986. 160–75.

Foertsch, Julie. "Where Cognitive Psychology Applies." *WC* 12 (1995): 360–83.

Fogarty, Daniel. *Roots for a New Rhetoric*. New York: Teachers College, Columbia University Press, 1959.

Fort, Keith. "Form, Authority, and the Critical Essay." *CE* 32 (1971): 629–39.

Foster, David. *A Primer for Writing Teachers: Theories, Theorists, Issues, Problems*. Upper Montclair, NJ: Boynton/Cook, 1983.

Fox, Thomas. *The Social Uses of Writing, Politics and Pedagogy*, Norwood, NJ: Ablex, 1990.

Freire, Paulo. *Education for Critical Consciousness*. New York: Seabury Press, 1973.

———. *Pedagogy of the Oppressed*. 1968. Trans. Myra Bergman Ramos. New York: Herder & Herder, 1971.

Freisinger, Randall R. "Voicing the Self: Toward a Pedagogy of Resistance in a Modern

Age." *Voices on Voice: Perspectives, Definitions, Inquiry.* Ed. Kathleen Blake Yancey. Urbana, IL: NCTE, 1994. 242–74.

Fulkerson, Richard. "Composition Theory in the Eighties: Axiological Consensus and Paradigmatic Diversity." *CCC* 41 (1990): 409–29.

———. "Four Philosophies of Composition." *CCC* 30 (1979): 343–48.

———. "Technical Logic, Comp-Logic, and the Teaching of Writing." *CCC* 39 (1988): 436–52.

Fulwiler, Toby. "The Argument for Writing Across the Curriculum." *Writing Across the Curriculum: Research into Practice.* Ed. Art Young and Toby Fulwiler. Upper Montclair, NJ: Boynton/Cook, 1986. 21–32.

Fuss, Diana. *Essentially Speaking: Feminism, Nature, and Difference.* London: Routledge, 1989.

Gadamer, Hans-Georg. *Philosophical Hermeneutics.* Trans. and ed. David E. Linge. Berkeley: University of California Press, 1976.

Gaonkar, Dilip Parameshwar. "The Idea of Rhetoric in the Rhetoric of Science." *Rhetorical Hermeneutics, Invention and Interpretation in the Age of Science.* Ed. Alan Gross and William Keith. Albany: SUNY Press, 1997.

Garrison, Roger H. *How a Writer Works.* New York: Harper & Row, 1981.

———. "One-to-One: Tutorial Instruction in Freshman Composition." *NDCC* 2 (1974): 55–83.

Gendlin, Eugene. *Focusing.* New York: Everest House, 1978.

Geertz, Clifford. *The Interpretation of Cultures.* New York: Basic Books, 1973.

———. *Local Knowledge: Further Essays in Interpretive Anthropology.* New York: Basic Books, 1983.

Gere, Anne Ruggles. *Writing Groups: History, Theory, and Implications.* Carbondale: Southern Illinois University Press, 1987.

———. "Writing Well Is the Best Revenge." *CCC* 29 (1978): 256–60.

Gilligan, Carol. *In a Different Voice: Psychological Theory and Women's Development.* Cambridge: Harvard University Press, 1982.

Giroux, Henry A. "Paulo Freire and the Politics of Postcolonialism." *JAC* 12 (1992): 15–26.

———. *Theory and Resistance in Education: A Pedagogy for the Opposition.* Boston: Bergin and Garvey, 1983.

Gleason, Barbara. "Self-Reflection as a Way of Knowing: Phenomenological Investigations in Composition." *Into the Field: Sites of Composition Studies.* Ed. Anne Ruggles Gere. New York: MLA, 1993. 60–71.

Goleman, Judith. "The Dialogic Imagination. Something More than We've Been Taught." *Only Connect: Uniting Reading and Writing.* Ed. Thomas Newkirk. Upper Montclair, NJ: Boynton/Cook, 1986. 131–42.

Gorman, Michael E., Margaret E. Gorman, and Art Young. "Poetic Writing in Psychology." *Writing Across the Disciplines.* Ed. Art Young and Toby Fulwiler. Upper Montclair, NJ: Boynton/Cook, 1986. 139–59.

Gourdine, Angelletta. "Exploring the Rhetoric of Resistance." *WI* 10 (1991): 136–42.

Graff, Gerald. *Beyond the Culture Wars: How Teaching the Conflicts Can Revitalize American Education.* New York: W. W. Norton, 1992.

———. "The Politics of Composition: A Reply to John Rouse." *CE* 41 (1980): 851–56.

Graham, Margaret Baker, and Patricia Goubil-Gambrell. "Hearing Voices in English Studies." *JAC* 15 (1995): 103–19.

Graves, Richard L. "Levels of Skill in the Composing Process." *CCC* 29 (1978): 227–32.

Greenberg, Karen L. "Grading, Evaluating, Assessing: Power and Politics in College Composition." Rev. of *Alternatives to Grading Student Writing* by Stephen Tchudi, ed.; *Situating Portfolios: Four Perspectives* by Kathleen Blake Yancey and Irwin Weiser, eds.; and *Assessment of Writing: Politics, Policies, Practices* by Edward M. White, William D. Lutz, and Sandra Kamusikiri, eds. *CCC* 49 (1998): 275–84.

———. "Research on Basic Writers: Theoretical and Methodological Issues." *A Sourcebook for Basic Writing Teachers.* Ed. Theresa Enos. New York: Random House, 1987. 187–207.

Greene, Stuart. "Toward a Dialectical Theory of Composition." *RR* 9 (1990): 149–72.

Grego, Rhonda C. "Writing Academic Autobiographies. Finding a Common Language Across the Curriculum." *Pedagogy in the Age of Politics.* Ed. Patricia A Sullivan and Donna J. Qualley. Urbana, IL: NCTE, 1994. 214–29.

Gunner, Jeanne. "The Fate of the Wyoming Resolution: A History of Professional Seduction." *Writing Ourselves into the Story.* Ed. Sheryl I. Fontaine and Susan Hunter. Carbondale: Southern Illinois University Press, 1993. 107–22.

Gusfield, Joseph R. "The Bridge over Separated Lands: Kenneth Burke's Significance for the Study of Social Action." *The Legacy of Kenneth Burke.* Ed. Herbert W. Simons and Trevor Melia. Madison: University of Wisconsin Press, 1989. 28–54.

Hairston, Maxine. "Carl Rogers' Alternative to Traditional Rhetoric." CCCC Annual Convention. Philadelphia. 25–27 March 1976.

———. "Carl Rogers' Alternative to Traditional Rhetoric." *CCC* 27 (1976) 373–77.

———. *A Contemporary Rhetoric.* Boston: Houghton Mifflin, 1974.

———. "Diversity, Ideology, and Teaching Writing." *CCC* 43 (1992): 179–93.

———. "The Winds of Change: Thomas Kuhn and the Revolution in the Teaching of Writing." *CCC* 33 (1982): 76–88.

Halasek, Kay. "Feminism and Bakhtin: Dialogic Reading in the Academy." *RSQ* 22 (1992): 63–73.

Halloran, S. Michael. "From Rhetoric to Composition: The Teaching of Writing in America to 1990." *A Short History of Writing Instruction: From Ancient Greece to Twentieth Century America.* Ed. James J. Murphy. Davis, CA: Hermagoras Press, 1990. 151–82.

———. "On the End of Rhetoric, Classical and Modern." *CE* 36 (1975): 621–31.

Hamilton-Wieler, Sharon. "Empty Echoes of Dartmouth: Dissonance Between the Rhetoric and Reality." *WI* 8 (1988): 29–41.

Harkin, Patricia. "Bringing Lore to Light." *PRE/TEXT* 10 (1989): 55–67.

———. "The Postdisciplinary Politics of Lore." *Contending with Words: Composition and Rhetoric in a Post Modern Age.* Ed. Patricia Harkin and John Schilb. New York: MLA, 1991. 124–38.

———. "Research as Lore." CCCC Annual Conference. Nashville. 16–19 March 1994.

Harned, Jon. "Post-Structuralism and the Teaching of Composition." *FEN* 15 (1986): 10–16.

Harris, Joseph. "After Dartmouth: Growth and Conflict in English." *CE* 53 (1991): 631–46.

————. "Egocentrism and Difference." CCCC Annual Presentation. Atlanta. 19–21 March 1987.

————. "The Idea of Community in the Study of Writing." *CCC* 40 (1989): 11–22.

————. "Negotiating the Contact Zone." *JBW* 14 (1995): 27–42.

————. *A Teaching Subject: Composition Since 1966*. Upper Saddle River, NJ: Prentice Hall, 1997.

Harris, Muriel. "Composing Behaviors of One- and Multi-Draft Writers." *CE* 51 (1989): 174–91. Rpt. in *Background Readings for Instructors Using the Bedford Handbook*. 5th ed. Ed. Glenn Blalock. Boston: Bedford Books, 1998. 91–107.

————. "The Ins and Outs of Conferencing." *WI* 6 (1987): 87–96.

Hartwell, Patrick. "Creating a Literate Environment in Freshman English: Why and How." *RR* 6 (1987): 4–20.

Hassett, Michael. "Increasing Response-ability through Mortification: A Burkean Perspective on Teaching Writing." *JAC* 15 (1995): 471–88.

Haswell, Richard H. *Gaining Ground in College Writing: Tales of Development and Interpretation*. Dallas: Southern Methodist University Press, 1991.

Hatch, Gary Layne. "Reviving the Rodential Model for Composition: Robert Zoellner's Alternative to Flower and Hayes." CCCC Annual Meeting. Boston. 21–23 March 1991.

Hatch, Gary Layne, and Margaret Bennett Walters. "Robert Zoellner's Talk-Write Pedagogy." *Writing Ourselves into the Story*. Ed. Sheryl I. Fountaine and Susan Hunter. Carbondale: Southern Illinois University Press, 1993. 335–51.

Hayes, John R. "Taking Criticism Seriously." *RTE* 27 (1993): 305–15.

Hayes, John R., and Linda S. Flower. "Identifying the Organization of Writing Processes." *Cognitive Processes in Writing: An Interdisciplinary Approach*. Ed. Lee W. Gregg and Erwin Steinberg. Hillsdale, NJ: Lawrence Erlbaum, 1980. 3–30.

Heath, Shirley Brice. "A Lot of Talk about Nothing." *Reclaiming the Classroom: Teacher Research as an Agency for Change*. Ed. Dixie Goswami and Peter Stillman. Upper Montclair, NJ: Boynton/Cook, 1987. 39–48.

————. *Ways with Words: Language, Life, and Work in Communities and Classrooms*. New York: Cambridge University Press, 1983.

Heath, Robert L. *Realism and Relativism: A Perspective on Kenneth Burke*. Macon, GA: Mercer University Press, 1986.

Henry, George H. "The Council: How Shall It Survive?" *CE* 46 (1984): 668–78.

Herndl, Carl G. "Tactics and the Quotidian: Resistance and Professional Discourse." *JAC* 16 (1996): 455–70.

————. "Teaching Discourse and Reproducing Culture: A Critique of Research and Pedagogy in Professional and Non-Academic Writing." *CCC* 44 (1993): 349–63.

Herrington, Anne J. "Writing to Learn: Writing Across the Disciplines." *CE* 43 (1981): 379–87.

Herzberg, Bruce. "Composition and the Politics of the Curriculum." *Teaching with the Bedford Guide for College Writers*. 4th ed. Vol. 2: Background Readings. Ed. Shirley Morahan. Boston: Bedford Books, 1996. 97–117.

Higgins, Lorraine, Linda Flower, and Joseph Petraglia. "Planning Text Together: The Role of Critical Reflection in Student Collaboration." *WC* 9 (1992): 48–84.

Hill, Carolyn Ericksen. *Writing from the Margins*. New York: Oxford University Press, 1990.

Hillocks, George, Jr. *Research on Written Composition: New Directions for Teaching*. Urbana, IL: NCTE, 1986.

———. *Teaching Writing as Reflective Practice*. New York: Teachers College Press, 1995.

Hirsch, E. D., Jr. *Cultural Literacy: What Every American Needs to Know*. Boston: Houghton Mifflin, 1987.

———. "Culture and Literacy." *JBW* 3 (1980): 27–47.

———. "Cultural Literacy." *American Scholar* 52 (1983): 159–69.

———. *The Philosophy of Composition*. Chicago: University of Chicago Press, 1977.

———. "Reading, Writing and Cultural Literacy." MLA Annual Conference. New York. 27–30 December 1981.

———. "Reading, Writing, and Cultural Literacy." *Composition & Literature: Bridging the Gap*. Ed. Winifred Bryan Horner. Chicago: University of Chicago Press, 1983, 141–47.

———. *Validity in Interpretation*. New Haven, CT: Yale University Press, 1967.

Holzman, Michael. "Scientism and Sentence-Combining." *CCC* 34 (1983): 73–79.

Hook, J. N. *A Long Way Together: A Personal View of NCTE's First Sixty-seven Years*. Urbana, IL: NCTE, 1979.

Horner, Bruce. "Discoursing Basic Writing." *CCC* 47 (1996): 199–222.

———. "Students, Authorship, and the Work of Composition." *CE* 59 (1997): 505–29.

Horner, Winifred Bryan. *Nineteenth-Century Scottish Rhetoric: The American Connection*. Carbondale: Southern Illinois University Press, 1993.

———. "Speech-Act and Text-Act Theory." *CCC* 30 (1979): 165–69.

Horning, Alice. "Reflection and Revision: Intimacy in College Writing." *Composition Chronicle: Newsletter for Writing Teachers* 9 (1997): 4–7.

Hubbuch, Susan H. "Confronting the Power in Empowering Students." *WI* 9 (fall 1989/ winter 1990): 35–44.

Hunt, Kellogg. *Grammatical Structures Written at Three Grade Levels*. Urbana, IL: NCTE, 1965.

Huot, Brian. "Reliability, Validity, and Holistic Scoring: What We Know and What We Need to Know." *CCC* 41 (1990): 201–13.

Irmscher, William F. "Kenneth Burke." *Traditions of Inquiry*. Ed. John Brereton. New York: Oxford University Press, 1985. 105–35.

Jarratt, Susan C. "Feminism and Composition: The Case for Conflict" *Contending with Words*: Composition and Rhetoric in a Postmodern Age. Ed. Patricia Harkin and John Schilb. New York: MLA, 1991. 105–23.

———. *Rereading the Sophists: Classical Rhetoric Refigured*. Carbondale: Southern Illinois University Press, 1991.

Jensen, Julie, ed. *Stories to Grow On: Demonstrations of Language and Learning in K–8 Classrooms*. Portsmouth, NH: Heinemann, 1989.

Johnson, Jean Flanigan. "The New Ethnography in Literacy Studies: A Reconsideration." *WI* (1987): 102–13.

Jones, Robert, and Joseph J. Comprone. "Where Do We Go Next in Writing Across the Curriculum?" *CCC* 44 (1993): 59–68.

Kantor, Kenneth J. "Classroom Contexts and the Development of Writing Intuitions: An Ethnographic Case Study." *New Directions in Composition Research*. Ed. Richard Beach and Lillian S. Bridwell. New York: Guilford Press, 1984. 72–94.

————. "Creative Expression in the English Curriculum: An Historical Perspective." *RTE* 9 (1975): 5–29.

Kantor, Kenneth J., Dan R. Kirby, and Judith P. Goetz. "Research in Context: Ethnographic Studies in English Education." *RTE* 15 (1981): 293–309.

Kelly, Lou. "Toward Competence and Creativity in an Open Class." *CE* 34 (1973): 644–60. Rpt. in *Rhetoric and Composition: A Sourcebook for Writers and Teachers*. Ed. Richard Graves. Upper Montclair, NJ: Boynton/Cook, 1984. 49–64.

Kennedy, George. *Classical Rhetoric and Its Christian and Secular Tradition from Ancient to Modern Times*. Chapel Hill: North Carolina University Press, 1980.

Kent, Thomas. "Beyond System: The Rhetoric of Paralogy." *CE* 51 (1989): 492–507.

————. *Paralogic Rhetoric: A Theory of Communicative Interaction*. London: Associated University Press, 1993.

————. "Talking Differently: A Response to Gayatri Chakravorty Spivak." *(Inter)Views: Cross-Disciplinary Perspectives on Rhetoric and Literacy*. Ed. Gary A. Olson and Irene Gale. Carbondale: Southern Illinois University Press, 1991. 261–66.

Killingsworth, M. Jimmie. "Product and Process, Literacy and Orality: An Essay on Composition and Culture. *CCC* 44 (1993): 26–39.

King, Martha L. "Research in Composition: A Need for Theory." *RTE* 2 (1978): 193–202.

Kinneavy, James L. "The Process of Writing: A Philosophical Base in Hermeneutics."*JAC* 7 (1987): 1–9.

————. *A Theory of Discourse: The Aims of Discourse*. 2nd ed. New York: W. W. Norton, 1980.

————. "Writing Across the Curriculum." *Teaching Composition: Twelve Bibliographical Essays*. Ed. Gary Tate. Fort Worth: Texas Christian University Press, 1987. 353–77.

Kinney, James. "Classifying Heuristics." *CCC* 30 (1979): 351–56.

————. "Tagmemic Rhetoric: A Reconsideration." *CCC* 29 (1978): 141–45.

Kirsch, Gesa E. *Women Writing the Academy: Audience, Authority, and Transformation*. Carbondale: Southern Illinois University Press, 1993.

Kirsch, Gesa E., and Joy Ritchie. "Beyond the Personal: Theorizing a Politics of Location in Composition Research." *CCC* 46 (1995): 7–29.

Kneupper, Charles W. "Teaching Argument: An Introduction to the Toulmin Model." *CCC* 29 (1978): 237–41.

Knoblauch, C. H. "A Response to Gary Olson's Interview with Paulo Freire." *(Inter)Views: Cross-Disciplinary Perspectives on Rhetoric and Literacy*. Ed. Gary A Olson and Irene Gale. Carbondale: Southern Illinois University Press, 1991. 177–83.

————. "Rhetorical Contributions: Dialogue and Commitment." *CE* 50 (1988): 125–40.

————. "Some Observations on Freire's Pedagogy of the Oppressed." *JAC* 8 (1988): 50–54.

Knoblauch, C. H., and Lil Brannon. *Critical Teaching and the Idea of Literacy*. Portsmouth, NH: Boynton/Cook, 1993.

————. "Knowing Our Knowledge: A Phenomenological Basis for Teacher Research." *Audits of Meaning: A Festschrift in Honor of Ann E. Berthoff*. Ed. Louise Z. Smith. Portsmouth, NH: Boynton/Cook, 1988. 17–28.

————. *Rhetorical Traditions and the Teaching of Writing*. Upper Montclair, NJ: Boynton/Cook, 1984.

————. "Writing as Learning Through the Curriculum." *CE* 45. (1983): 465–74.

Knorr-Cetina, K. D. *The Manufacture of Knowledge: An Essay on the Constructivist and Contextual Nature of Science*. Oxford: Pergamon Press, 1981.

Kohlberg, Lawrence. "The Development of Modes of Thinking and Choices in Years 10 to 16." Ph.D. diss, University of Chicago, 1958.

————. *The Philosophy of Moral Development*. San Francisco: Harper & Row, 1981.

Kohler, Wolfgang. *The Mentality of Apes*. 2nd ed. Trans. Ella Winter. New York: Harcourt Brace, 1927.

Kozol, Jonathon. "Foreword." *Literacy and Revolution: The Pedagogy of Paulo Freire*. Ed. Robert Mackie. New York: Continuum, 1981. xi–xvii.

Kroll, Barry M. "Cognitive Egocentrism and the Problem of Audience Awareness in Written Discourse." *RTE* 12 (1978): 269–81.

————. "Developmental Perspectives and the Teaching of Composition." *CE* 41 (1980): 741–52.

————. "Rewriting a Complex Story for a Young Reader: Development of Audience-Adapted Writing Skills." *RTE* 19 (1985): 120–39.

————. "Writing for Readers: Three Perspectives on Audience." *CCC* 35 (1984): 172–85.

Kuhn, Thomas. *The Structure of Scientific Revolutions*. 2nd ed. Chicago: University of Chicago Press, 1970.

Lamb, Catherine E. "Beyond Argument in Feminist Composition." *CCC* 42 (1991): 11–24.

Langer, Judith. "Learning through Writing: Study Skills in the Content Areas." *JR* 29 (1986): 400–406.

Langer, Judith, and A. Applebee. *How Writing Shapes Thinking: A Study of Teaching and Learning*. Research Report No. 22. Urbana, IL: NCTE, 1987.

Langstraat, Lisa R. " 'Hypermasculinity' in Cultural Studies and Composition: Mapping a Feminist Response." *Composition Forum* 7 (1996): 1–16.

Larrabee, M. J., ed. *An Ethic of Care: Feminist and Interdisciplinary Perspectives*. New York: Routledge, 1993.

Larson, Richard L. "Classifying Discourse: Limitations and Alternatives." *Essays on Classical Rhetoric and Modern Discourse*. Ed. Robert Connors, Lisa Ede, and Andrea Lunsford. Carbondale: Southern Illinois University Press, 1984. 203–14.

————. "Competing Paradigms for Research and Evaluation in the Teaching of English." *RTE* 27 (1993): 283–92.

————. "Language Studies and Composing Processes." *The Territory of Language: Linguistics Stylistics, and the Teaching of Composition*. Ed. Donald McQuade. Carbondale: Southern Illinois University Press, 1986. 213–23.

Lassner, Phyllis. "Feminist Responses to Rogerian Argument." *RR* 8 (1990): 220–33

Latour, Bruno, and Steve Woolgar. *Laboratory Life: The Social Construction of Scientific Fact*. Beverly Hills, CA: Sage Publications, 1979.

Lauer, Janice. "Heuristics and Composition." *CCC* 21 (1970): 396–404.

————. "Response to Ann E. Berthoff, 'The Problem of Problem Solving.' " *CCC* 23 (1972): 208–10.

Lauer, Janice, and J. William Asher. *Composition Research/Empirical Designs*. New York: Oxford University Press, 1988.

Lawson, Bruce, Susan Sterr Ryan, and W. Ross Winterowd, eds. *Encountering Student Texts: Interpretive Issues in Reading Student Writing*. Urbana, IL: NCTE, 1989.

LeFevre, Karen Burke. *Invention as a Social Act*. Carbondale: Southern Illinois University Press, 1987.

Lensmire, Timothy J. "Writing Workshop as Carnival: Reflections on an Alternative Learning Environment." *HER* 64 (1994): 371–91.

Leverenz, Carrie Shively. "Collaboration, Race and the Rhetoric of Evasion." *JAC* 16 (1996): 297–312.

Liggett, Sarah. "Teaching Journals as Reflective Practice: From Graduate Teaching Assistant to Writing Instructor." CCCC Annual Convention. Phoenix. 12–15 March 1997.

Lindemann, Erika. "Ken Macrorie: A Review Essay." *CE* 44 (1982): 358–67.

———. *A Rhetoric for Writing Teachers*. 2nd ed. New York: Oxford University Press, 1987.

———. "Three Views of English 101." *CE* 57 (1995): 287–302. Rpt. in *Teaching with the Bedford Guide for College Writers*. 4th ed. Vol. 2 Background Readings. Ed. Shirley Morahan. Boston: Bedford Books, 1996. 2–14.

Lloyd-Jones, Richard. "A Balanced Survey Course in Writing." *Balancing Acts: Essays on the Teaching of Writing in Honor of William F. Irmscher*. Ed. Virginia Chappell, Mary Louise Buly-Meissner, and Chris Anderson. Carbondale: Southern Illinois University Press, 1991. 123–40.

———. "Primary Trait Scoring." *Evaluating Writing: Describing, Measuring, Judging*. Ed. Charles Cooper and Lee Odell. Urbana, IL: NCTE, 1977. 33–66.

———. "The Right to Write: Some History." NCTE Annual Conference. Louisville, KY. 18–23 November 1992.

———. "Who We Were, Who We Should Become." *CCC* 43 (1992): 486–96.

Lloyd-Jones, Richard, and Andrea Lunsford, eds. *The English Coalition Conference: Democracy Through Language*. New York: MLA, 1987.

Long, Russell. "Writer-Audience Relationships: Analysis or Invention." *CCC* 31 (1980): 221–26.

Lovejoy, Kim B. "The Gricean Model: A Revising Rubric." *JTW* 6 (1987): 9–18.

Lu, Min-Zhan. "Conflict and Struggle: The Enemies or Preconditions of Basic Writing?" *CE* 54 (1992): 887–913. Rpt. in *Background Readings for Instructors Using the Bedford Handbook*. 5th ed. Ed. Glenn Blalock. Boston: Bedford Books, 1998. 296–317.

———. "From Silence to Word: Writing as Struggle." *CE* 49 (1987): 437–48.

———. "Professing Multiculturalism: The Politics of Style in the Contact Zone." *CCC* 45 (1994): 442–58.

Lunsford, Andrea A. "Aristotelian vs. Rogerian Argument: A Reassessment." *CCC* 30 (1979): 146–51.

———. "Cognitive Development and the Basic Writer." *CE* 41 (1979): 38–46.

———. "Composing Ourselves: Politics, Commitment, and the Teaching of Writing." *CCC* 41 (1990): 71–82.

———. "The Content of Basic Writers' Essays." *CCC* 31 (1980): 278–90.

———. "Intellectual Property, Concepts of Selfhood, and the Teaching of Writing." *WI* 12 (1993): 67–77.

———. "The Nature of Composition Studies." *An Introduction to Composition Studies*. Ed. Erika Lindemann and Gary Tate. New York: Oxford University Press, 1991. 3–14.

———. "What We Know—and Don't Know—About Remedial Writing." *CCC* 29 (1978): 47–52.

Lunsford, Andrea A., and Lisa Ede. "Representing Audience: Successful Discourse and Disciplinary Critique." *CCC* 47 (1996): 167–79.

Lynch, Dennis, Dianna George, and Marilyn Cooper. "Moments of Argument: Agonistic Inquiry and Confrontational Cooperation." *CCC* 48 (1997): 61–84. Rpt. in *Background Readings for Instructors Using the Bedford Handbook*. 5th ed. Ed. Glenn Blalock. Boston: Bedford Books, 1998. 252–71.

Lynch, Dennis, and Stephen Jukuri. "Beyond Master and Slave: Reconciling Our Fears of Power in the Writing Classroom." *RR* 16 (1998): 270–88.

Mack, Nancy. "The Social Nature of Words: Voices, Dialogues, Quarrels." *WI* 8 (1989): 157–65.

Macrorie, Ken. *Searching Writing: A Contextbook*. Rochelle Park, NJ: Hayden, 1980.

———. *Telling Writing*. Rochelle Park, NJ: Hayden, 1970.

———. "To Be Read." *English Journal* 57 (1968): 686–92. Rpt. in *Rhetoric and Composition: A Sourcebook for Teachers and Writers*. Ed. Richard Graves. Upper Montclair, NJ: Boynton/Cook, 1984. 89–92.

———. *Uptaught*. 1970. 2nd ed. Rochelle Park, NJ: Hayden, 1976.

Mahala, Daniel. "Writing Across the Curriculum and the Promise of Reform." *CE* 53 (1991): 773–89.

Mahala, Daniel, and Jody Swilkey. "Remapping the Geography of Service in English." *CE* 59 (1997): 625–46.

Maimon, Elaine. "Knowledge, Acknowledgment, and Writing Across the Curriculum: Toward an Educated Community." *The Territory of Language: Linguistics, Stylistics, and the Teaching of Composition*. Ed. Donald A. McQuade. Carbondale: Southern Illinois University Press, 1986. 89–100.

Mallet, Susan. "It All Depends on What You're Trying to Do." *WI* 4 (1985): 126–34.

Marshall, James. "The Effects of Writing on Students' Understanding of Literary Texts." *RTE* 21 (1987): 30–63.

———. "Of What Does Skill in Writing Really Consist? The Political Life of the Writing Process Movement." *Taking Stock: The Writing Process Movement in the 90s*. Ed. Lad Tobin and Thomas Newkirk. Portsmouth, NH: Boynton/Cook, 1994. 45–56.

McGee, Patrick. "Truth and Resistance: Teaching as a Form of Analysis." *CE* 49 (1987): 67–78.

McLeod, Susan. "Pygmalion or Golem? Teacher Affect and Efficacy." *CCC* 46 (1995): 369–86.

———. "Writing Across the Curriculum: An Introduction." *Writing Across the Curriculum: A Guide to Developing Programs*. Ed. Susan McLeod and Margot Soven. Newbury Park, CA: Sage Publications, 1992. 1–11.

McPherson, Elisabeth. "Then, Now, and Maybe Then . . ." *CE* 46 (1984): 697–701.

Mellon, John. *Transformational Sentence-Combining*. Urbana, IL: NCTE, 1969.

Meyers, George Douglas. "The Scholar Who Helps Me Teach Better: Adapting Zoellner's Talk-Write Model to the Business Writing Classroom." *Bulletin of the Association of Business Communication* 48 (1985): 14–16.

Miller, Susan. "The Disciplinary Processing of Writing-as-Process." CCCC Annual Convention. Cincinnati. 19–21 March 1992.

———. "The Student's Reader Is Always a Fiction." *JAC* 5 (1984): 15–29.

——. *Textual Carnivals: The Politics of Composition*. Carbondale: Southern Illinois University Press, 1991.

Minock, Mary. "Toward a Postmodern Pedagogy of Imitation." *JAC* 15 (1995): 489–509.

Minot, Walter. "Response to Russell C. Long, Writer-Audience Relationships: Analysis or Invention?" *CCC* 32 (1981): 334–37.

Mishler, Elliot G. "Meaning in Context: Is There Any Other Kind?" *HER* 49 (1979): 1–19.

Moffett, James. *Teaching the Universe of Discourse*. Boston: Houghton Mifflin, 1968.

Moran, Charles. "Review: English and Emerging Technologies." *CE* 60 (1998): 2–209.

Mortensen, Peter, and Gesa E. Kirsch. "On Authority in the Study of Writing." *CCC* 44 (1993): 556–72.

——. eds. *Ethics and Representation in Qualitative Studies of Literacy*. Urbana, IL: NCTE, 1996.

Moss, Beverly J. "Ethnography and Composition: Studying Language at Home." *Methods and Methodology in Composition Research*. Carbondale: Southern Illinois University Press, 1992. 153–71.

Muller, Herbert J. *The Uses of English*. New York: Holt, Rinehart, and Winston, 1967.

Murphy, Ann. "Transference and Resistance in the Basic Writing Classroom: Problematics and Praxis." *CCC* 40 (1989): 175–87.

Murphy, James J. "Rhetorical History as a Guide to the Salvation of American Reading and Writing: A Plea for Curricular Courage." *The Rhetorical Tradition and Modern Writing*. Ed. James J. Murphy. New York: MLA, 1982. 3–12.

Murphy, Richard J., Jr. "Polanyi and Composition: A Personal Note on a Human Science." *Into the Field: Sites of Composition Studies*. Ed. Anne Ruggles Gere. New York: MLA, 1993. 72–83.

Murray, Donald M. "Teach Writing as a Process Not Product." *Leaflet* (November 1972): 11–14. Rpt. in *Rhetoric and Composition: A Sourcebook for Teachers and Writers*. Ed. Richard Graves. Upper Montclair, NJ: Boynton/Cook, 1984. 89–92.

Myers, Greg. "Reality, Consensus, and Reform in the Rhetoric of Composition Teaching." *CE* 48 (1986): 154–71.

——. "The Social Construction of Two Biologists' Proposals." *WC* 2 (1985): 219–45.

——. *Writing Biology: Texts in the Social Construction of Scientific Knowledge*. Madison: University of Wisconsin Press, 1990.

Nardini, Gloria. "Towards an Ethnographic Understanding of Adolescent Literacy." *WI* 9 (fall 1989/winter 1990): 45–56.

Nealon, Jeffrey T. "The Ethics of Dialogue: Bakhtin and Levinas." *CE* 59 (1997): 29–148.

Neel, Jasper. "Learning about Learning about Deconstruction: An Epi(trying-tobe)gone." *JAC* 15 (1995): 155–61.

Newkirk, Thomas. "Barrett Wendell's Theory of Discourse." *RR* 10 (1991): 20–30.

——. "The Politics of Composition Research: The Conspiracy Against Experience." *The Politics of Writing Instruction: Postsecondary*. Ed. Richard Bullock and John Trimbur. Gen. ed. Charles Schuster. Portsmouth, NH: Boynton/Cook, 1991. 119–35.

——. "Seduction and Betrayal in Qualitative Research." *Ethics and Representation in Qualitative Studies of Literacy*. Ed. Peter Mortensen and Gesa Kirsch. Urbana, IL: NCTE, 1996. 3–16.

Newman, Samuel. *A Practical System of Rhetoric.* Portland, ME: William Hyde, 1827.

Nichols, Marie Hochmuth. "Kenneth Burke and the New Rhetoric.' " *QJS* 38 (1952): 133–44. Rpt. in *Contemporary Theories of Rhetoric: Selected Readings.* Ed. Richard L. Johannesen. New York: Harper & Row, 1971. 96–113.

Noddings, Nell. *Caring: A Feminine Approach to Ethics and Moral Education.* Berkeley: University of California Press, 1984.

Nold, Ellen, and Sarah Washauer Freedman. "An Analysis of Readers' Responses to Essays." *RTE* 11 (1977): 164–74.

North, Stephen M. *The Making of Knowledge in Composition: Portrait of an Emerging Field.* Upper Montclair, NJ: Boynton/Cook 1987.

Nudelman, Jerrold, and Alvin H. Schlosser. "Experiential vs. Expository: Is Peaceful Coexistence Really Possible?" *A Sourcebook for Basic Writing Teachers.* Ed. Theresa Enos. New York: Random House, 1987. 497–506.

Odell, Lee. "The Classroom Teacher as Researcher." *EJ* 65 (1976): 106–11.

———. "The Process of Writing and the Process of Learning." *CCC* 31 (1980): 42–50.

———. "Writing Assessment and Learning to Write: A Classroom Perspective." *Theory and Practice in the Teaching of Writing: Rethinking the Discipline.* Carbondale: Southern Illinois University Press, 1993. 289–313.

O'Donnell, Thomas G. "Politics and Ordinary Language: A Defense of Expressivist Rhetorics." *CE* 58 (1996): 423–39.

O'Hare, Frank. *Sentence-Combining: Improving Student Writing Without Formal Grammar Instruction.* Urbana, IL: NCTE, 1973.

Ohmann, Richard. *English in America: A Radical View of the Profession.* New York: Oxford University Press, 1976.

———. "Generative Grammars and the Concept of Literary Style." *Word* 20 (1964): 423–39. Rpt. in *New Rhetorics.* Ed. Martin Steinmann, Jr. New York: Charles Scribner's Sons, 1967. 134–60.

———. "In Lieu of a New Rhetoric." *CE* 26 (1964): 17–22. Rpt. in *Professing the New Rhetorics.* Ed. Theresa Enos and Stuart C. Brown. Englewood Cliffs, NJ: Prentice Hall, 1994. 298–306.

———. "Instrumental Style: Notes on the Theory of Speech as Action." *Current Trends in Stylistics.* Ed. Braj B. Kachru and Herbert F. W. Stahlke. Edmonton, Canada: Linguistic Research, 1972. 115–41.

———. "Reflections on Class and Language." *CE* 44 (1982): 1–17.

———. "Speech, Action, and Style." *Literary Style: A Symposium.* London: Oxford University Press, 1971. 241–59.

Olson, Gary, and Joseph Moxley. "Directing Freshman Composition: The Limits of Authority." *CCC* 40 (1989): 51–60.

Ong, Walter J., S. J. "The Writer's Audience Is Always a Fiction." *PMLA* 90 (1975): 9–21.

Onore, Cynthia. "The Student, the Teacher, and the Text: Negotiating Meanings through Revision and Response." *Writing and Response: Theory, Practice, and Research.* Ed. Chris Anson. Urbana, IL: NCTE, 1989. 231–60.

Paine, Charles. "Relativism, Radical Pedagogy, and the Ideology of Paralysis." *CE* 51 (1989): 557–70.

Papillion, Terry. "Isocrates' Techne and Rhetorical Pedagogy." *RSQ* 25 (1995): 149–63.

Park, Douglas B. "The Meanings of 'Audience.' " *CE* 44 (1982): 247–57.

Pastore, Catherine Blair. "Opinion: Only One of the Voices: Dialogic Writing Across the Curriculum." *CE* 50 (1988): 383–89.

Payne, Michelle. "Rend(er)ing Women's Authority in the Writing Classroom." *Taking Stock: The Writing Process Movement in the 90's.* Ed. Lad Tobin and Thomas Newkirk. Portsmouth, NH: Boynton/Cook, 1994. 97–111.

Pemberton, Michael A. "Tales Too Terrible to Tell: Unstated Truths and Underprepa- ration in Graduate Composition Programs." *Writing Ourselves into the Story.* Ed. Sheryl I. Fontaine and Susan Hunter. Carbondale: Southern Illinois University Press, 1993. 154–73.

Penrose, Ann M. "To Write or Not to Write: Effects of Task and Task Interpretation on Learning Through Writing." *WC* 9.4 (1992): 465–500.

Perelman, Chaim. *The New Rhetoric and the Humanities.* Dordrecht, Holland: D. Reidel, 1949.

Perelman, Chaim, and Lucie Olbrechts-Tyteca. *The New Rhetoric: A Treatise on Argu- mentation.* Trans. John Wilkinson and Purcell Weaver. Notre Dame, IN: Univer- sity of Notre Dame Press, 1969.

Perelman, Les. "Approaches to Comprehensive Writing: Integrating Writing into the College Curriculum." *WI* (spring 1982): 71–80.

———. "The Context of Classroom Writing." *CE* 48 (1986): 471–79.

Perl, Sondra. "The Composing Processes of Unskilled College Writers." *RTE* 13 (1979): 317–36.

———. "Understanding Composing." *CCC* 31 (1980): 363–69.

Pfister, Fred R., and Joanne F. Petrick. "A Heuristic Model for Creating a Writer's Audience." *CCC* 31 (1980): 213–30.

Phillips, Donna Burns, Ruth Greenberg, and Sharon Gibson. "*College Composition and Communication*: Chronicling a Discipline's Genesis." *CCC* 44 (1993): 443–65.

Piaget, Jean. *The Language and Thought of the Child.* London: Routledge & Kegan Paul, 1978.

Piaget, Jean, and Barbel Inhelder. *The Child's Conception of Space.* Trans. F. J. Langdon and J. L. Lunger. New York: W. W. Norton, 1967.

Pike, Kenneth. "A Linguistic Contribution to Composition: A Hypothesis." *CCC* 15 (1964): 82–88.

Poincaré, Henri. *Science and Method.* Trans. Francis Maitland. London: T. Nelson and Sons, 1914.

Polanyi, Michael. *Personal Knowledge: Towards a Post-Critical Philosophy.* Chicago University of Chicago Press, 1958.

———. *The Tacit Dimension.* Garden City, NY: Doubleday, 1966.

Porter, James E "Divisio as Em-/De-Powering Topic: A Basis for Argument in Rhetoric and Composition." *RR* 8 (1990): 191–207.

Porter, Kevin J. "Methods, Truths, Reasons." *CE* 60 (1998): 426–40.

Poulakos, John. "Aristotle's Voice, Our Ears." *CCC* 47 (1996): 293–301.

Pratt, Mary Louise. "Arts of the Contact Zone." *Profession 91.* New York: MLA, 1991. 33–40.

Pritchard, Ruie Jane, and Jon C. Marshall. "Foreword." *RTE* 28 (1994): 259–85.

Probst, Robert E. "Transactional Theory and Response to Student Writing." *Writing and Response: Theory, Practice, and Research.* Ed. Chris Anson. Urbana, IL: NCTE, 1989. 68–79.

Pullman, George L. "Rhetoric and Hermeneutics: Composition, Invention, and Literature." *JAC* 14 (1994): 367–87.

Purves, Alan C. "NCTE: The House of Intellect or Spencer Gifts." *CE* 46 (1984): 693–96.

———. "Research on Written Composition: A Response to Hillocks' Report." *RTE* 22 (1988) 104–8.

Qualley, Donna J. "Being Two Places at Once: Feminism and the Development of 'Both/And' Perspectives." *Pedagogy in the Age of Politics.* Ed. Patricia Sullivan and Donna Qualley. Urbana, IL: NCTE, 1994. 25–42.

Qualley, Donna J., and Elizabeth Chiseri-Strater. "Collaboration as Reflexive Dialogue: A Knowing Deeper than Reason.' " *JAC* 14 (1994): 111–30.

Radcliffe, Terry. "Talk-Write Composition: A Theoretical Model Proposing the Use of Speech to Improve Writing." *RTE* 6 (1972): 187–99.

Rankin, Elizabeth. "Taking Practitioner Inquiry Seriously: An Argument with Stephen North." *RR* 8 (1990): 260–69.

Ray, Ruth E. "Afterword: Ethics and Representation in Teacher Research." *Ethics and Representation in Qualitative Studies of Literacy.* Ed. Peter Mortensen and Gesa Kirsch. Urbana, IL: NCTE, 1996. 287–300.

———. *The Practice of Theory: Teacher Research in Composition.* Urbana, IL: NCTE, 1993.

Recchio, Thomas E. "On Composing Ethnographically: Strategies for Enacting Authority in Writing." *RR* 10 (1991): 131–42.

Reid, Ronald. "The Boylston Professorship of Rhetoric and Oratory, 1806–1904: A Case Study in Changing Concepts of Rhetoric and Pedagogy." *QJS* 45 (1959): 239–57.

Resnick Stephen, and Richard Wolff. *Knowledge and Class: A Marxian Critique of Political Economy.* Chicago: University of Chicago Press, 1987.

Ried, Paul. "The Boylston Professor in the Twentieth Century." *QJS* 73 (1987): 474–81.

Ritchie, Joy S. "Beginning Writers: Diverse Voices and Individual Identity." *CCC* 40 (1989): 152–74.

———. "Resistance to Reading: Another View of the Minefield." *JAC* 12 (1992): 117–36.

Roberts, Patricia, and Virginia Pompei Jones. "Imagining Reasons: The Role of the Imagination in Argumentation." *JAC* 15 (1995): 527–41.

Rogers, Carl. "Communication: Its Blocking and Its Facilitation." Northwestern University's Centennial Conference on Communication. 11 October 1951. Rpt. in *Rhetoric: Discovery and Change.* Ed. Richard Young, Alton Becker, and Kenneth Pike. New York: Harcourt, Brace & World, 1970. 284–89.

Rohman, D. Gordon, and Alfred O. Wlecke. "Pre-Writing: The Construction and Application of Models for Concept Formation in Writing." U.S. Department of Health, Education, and Welfare Cooperative Research Project No. 2174. East Lansing: Michigan State University, 1964.

Rorty, Richard. "The Dangers of Over-Philosophication—Reply to Arcilla and Nicholson." *EdT* 40 (1990): 41–44.

———. *Philosophy and the Mirror of Nature.* Princeton, NJ: Princeton University Press, 1979.

———. Interview. "Social Construction and Composition Theory: A Conversation with Richard Rorty." By Gary A. Olson. *JAC* 9 (1989): 1–9.

Rose, Mike. *Lives on the Boundary: The Struggles and Achievements of America's Underprepared.* New York: Free Press, 1989.

———. "Remedial Writing Courses: A Critique and a Proposal." *CE* 45 (1983): 109–28.

Rose, Shirley K. "Down from the Haymow: One Hundred Years of Sentence-Combining." *CE* 45 (1983): 483–91.

Roth, Robert G. "The Evolving Audience: Alternatives to Audience Accommodation." *CCC* 38 (1987): 47–55.

Rouse, John. "The Politics of Composition." *CE* 41 (1979): 1–12.

Rueckert, William H. *Kenneth Burke and the Drama of Human Relations.* 2nd ed. Berkeley: University of California Press, 1982.

Russell, David R. *Writing in the Academic Disciplines, 1870–1990.* Carbondale: Southern Illinois University Press, 1991.

Salvatori, Mariolina. "Toward a Hermeneutics of Difficulty." *Audits of Meaning: A Festschrift in Honor of Ann E. Berthoff.* Ed. Louise Z. Smith. Portsmouth, NH: Boynton/Cook, 1988. 80–95.

Schell, Eileen E. *Gypsy Academics and Mother-Teachers.* Portsmouth, NH: Boynton/Cook, 1998.

Schilb, John. "Cultural Studies, Postmodernism, and Composition." *Contending with Words: Composition and Rhetoric in a Postmodern Age.* Ed. Patricia Harkin and John Schilb. New York: MLA, 1991. 173–88.

Schön, Donald. *Educating the Reflective Practitioner: Toward a New Design for Teaching and Learning in the Professions.* San Francisco: Jossey-Bass, 1987.

———. *The Reflective Practitioner: How Professionals Think in Action.* New York: Basic Books, 1983.

Schriver, Karen. "Theory Building in Rhetoric and Composition. The Role of Empirical Scholarship." *RR* 7 (1989): 272–88.

Schumacher, Gary M., and Jane Gradwohl Nash. "Conceptualizing and Measuring Knowledge Change Due to Writing." *RTE* 25 (1991): 67–95.

Schuster, Charles. "Mikhail Bahktin as Rhetorical Theorist." *Rhetoric: Concepts, Definitions, Boundaries.* Ed. William Covino and David Jolliffe. Boston: Allyn and Bacon, 1995. 530–44.

Schwartz, Joseph. "Kenneth Burke, Aristotle, and the Future of Rhetoric." *CCC* 17 (1966): 210–16.

Scott, Robert L. "On Viewing Rhetoric as Epistemic." *CSSJ* 18 (1967): 9–17.

Searle, John R. *Speech Acts: An Essay in the Philosophy of Language.* Cambridge, England: Cambridge University Press, 1969.

Searle, John R., Ferenc Kiefer, and Manfred Bierwisch, eds. "Introduction." *Speech Act Theory and Pragmatics.* Holland/Boston: D. Reidel, 1980. vii–xii.

Selzer, Jack. "Intertextuality and the Writing Process: An Overview." *Writing in the Workplace: New Research Perspectives.* Ed. Rachel Spilka. Carbondale: Southern Illinois University Press, 1993. 171–80.

Shaughnessy, Mina P. "Diving In: An Introduction to Basic Writing." *CCC* 27 (1976): 234–39. Rpt. in *The Writing Teacher's Sourcebook.* 2nd ed. Ed. Gary Tate and Edward P. J. Corbett. New York: Oxford University Press, 1988. 297–302.

———. *Errors and Expectations: A Guide for the Teacher of Basic Writing.* New York: Oxford University Press, 1977.

Sheard, Cynthia Miecznikowski. "Kairos and Kenneth Burke's Psychology of Political and Social Communication." *CE* 55 (1993): 291–310.

Shor, Ira. *Empowering Education: Critical Teaching for Social Change*. Chicago: University of Chicago Press, 1992.

Simmons, Jo An MacGuire. "The One-to-One Method of Teaching Composition." *CCC* 35 (1984): 222–29.

Sledd, James. "Why the Wyoming Resolution Had to Be Emasculated: A History of Quixotism." *JAC* 11 (1991): 269–81.

Slevin, James F. "Depoliticizing and Politicizing Composition Studies." *The Politics of Writing Instruction: Postsecondary*. Ed. Richard Bullock and John Trimbur. Gen. ed. Charles Schuster. Portsmouth, NH: Boynton/Cook, 1991. 1–21.

Sloan, Gary. "Transitions: Relationships Among T-Units." *CCC* 34 (1983): 447–53.

Smit, David W. "Hall of Mirrors: Antifoundationalist Theory and the Teaching of Writing." *JAC* 15 (1995): 35–52.

———. "Some Difficulties with Collaborative Learning." *JAC* 9 (1989): 45–58.

Smith, Louise. "Opinion: Why English Departments Should House Writing Across the Curriculum." *CE* 50 (1988): 390–95.

Smith, Nelson J., III. "Logic for the New Rhetoric." *CCC* 20 (1969): 305–13.

Soles, Derek. "Problems with Confrontational Teaching." *CCC* 49 (1998): 267–69.

Sommers, Nancy. "Revision Strategies of Student Writers and Experienced Adult Writers." *CCC* 31 (1980): 378–88. Rpt. in *The Writing Teacher's Sourcebook*. 2nd ed. Ed. Gary Tate and Edward P. J. Corbett. New York: Oxford University Press, 1988. 119–27.

Sosnoski, James J. "Postmodern Teachers in Their Postmodern Classrooms: Socrates Begone!" *Contending with Words.*: Composition and Rhetoric in a Postmodern Age. Ed. Patricia Harkin and John Schlib. New York: MLA, 1991. 198–220.

Sotirou, Peter. "Articulating a Hermeneutic Pedagogy: The Philosophy of Interpretation." *JAC* 13 (1993): 365–80.

———. "The Question of Authority in the Composition Classroom: A Godamerian Perspective." *WI* 1 (1993): 7–20.

Southwell, Michael G. "Free Writing in Composition Classes." *CE* 38 (1977): 676–81.

Spellmeyer, Kurt. "Being Philosophical About Composition: Hermeneutics and the Teaching of Writing." *Into the Field: Sites of Composition Studies*. Ed. Anne Ruggles Gere. New York: MLA, 1993. 9–29.

Spivak, Gayatri Chakravorty. *The Post-Colonial Critic*. Ed. Sarah Harasym. New York: Routledge, 1990.

Stanger, Carol A. "The Sexual Politics of the One-to-One Tutorial Approach and Collaborative Learning." *Teaching Writing: Pedagogy, Gender, and Equity*. Ed. Cynthia L. Caywood and Gillian R. Overing. Albany, SUNY Press, 1987, 31–44.

Stewart, Donald C. *The Authentic Voice: A Pre-writing Approach to Student Writing*. Dubuque; IA: W. C. Brown, 1972.

———. "Cognitive Psychologists, Social Constructionists, and Three Nineteenth-Century Advocates of Authentic Voice." *JAC* 12 (1992): 270–90.

———. "Collaborative Learning and Composition: Boon or Bane?" *RR* 7 (1988): 58–83.

———. "Composition Textbooks and the Assault on Tradition." *CCC* 29 (1978): 171–76.

———. "Fred Newton Scott." *Traditions of Inquiry*. Ed. John Brereton. New York: Oxford University Press, 1985. 26–49.

————. "Harvard's Influence on English Studies: Perceptions from Three Universities in the Early Twentieth Century." *CCC* 43 (1992): 455–71.

————. "A Real Audience for Composition Students." In "Staffroom Interchange." *CCC* 16 (1965): 35–37.

————. "Rediscovering Fred Newton Scott." *CE* 40 (1979): 539–47.

————. "Two Model Teachers and the Harvardization of English Departments." *The Rhetorical Tradition and Modern Writing*. Ed. James Murphy. New York: MLA, 1982. 118–29.

Stewart, Murray F., and Cary H. Grobe. "Syntactic Maturity and Mechanics of Writing." *RTE* 13 (1979): 207–15.

Stotsky, Sandra. "Research on Written Composition: A Response to Hillocks' Report." *RTE* 22 (1988): 89–99.

————. "Types of Lexical Cohesion in Expository Writing: Implications for Developing the Vocabulary of Academic Discourse." *CCC* 34 (1983): 430–46.

Strain, Margaret. "Hermeneutic Inquiry and the Possibilities for Composition History." CCCC Annual Convention. Nashville. 10–16 March 1994.

————. "Toward a Hermeneutic Model of Composition History: Robert Carlsen's 'The State of the Profession, 1961–1962.' " *JAC* 13 (1993): 217–40.

Sullivan, Francis J. "Critical Theory and Systemic Linguistics. Textualizing the Contact Zone." *JAC* 15 (1995): 411–34.

Sullivan, Patricia A. "Ethnography and the Problem of the Other.' " *Ethics and Representation in Qualitative Studies of Literacy*. Ed. Peter Mortensen and Gesa E. Kirsch. Urbana, IL: NCTE, 1996. 97–114.

————. "Feminism and Methodology in Composition Studies." *Methods and Methodology in Composition Research*. Carbondale: Southern Illinois University Press, 1992. 37–61.

Swearingen, Jan C. "Pistis, Expression, and Belief: Prolegomenon for a Feminist Rhetoric of Motives." *A Rhetoric of Doing: Essays on Written Discourse in Honor of James L. Kinneavy*. Ed. Stephen P. Witte, Neil Nakadate, and Roger D. Cherry. Carbondale: Southern Illinois University Press, 1992. 123–43.

Tate, Gary, ed. Teaching Composition: Twelve Bibliographical Essays. Fort Worth: Texas Christian University Press, 1987.

Tirrell, Mary Kay, Gordon M. Pradl, John Warnock, and James Britton. "Re-Presenting James Britton: A Symposium." *CCC* 41 (1990): 166–86.

Tobin, Lad. "Introduction: How the Writing Process Was Born—and Other Conversion Narratives." *Taking Stock: The Writing Process Movement in the '90s*. Ed. Lad Tobin and Thomas Newkirk. Portsmouth, NH: Boynton/Cook, 1994. 1–14.

————. *Writing Relationships: What Really Happens in the Composition Class*. Portsmouth, NH: Boynton/Cook, 1993.

Tobin, Lad, and Thomas Newkirk, eds. *Taking Stock: The Writing Process Movement in the Nineties*. Portsmouth, NH: Boynton/Cook, 1994.

Toulmin, Stephen. *The Uses of Argument*. Cambridge, England: Cambridge University Press, 1958.

Trimbur, John. "Collaborative Learning and Teaching Writing." *Perspectives on Research and Scholarship in Composition*. Ed. Ben W. McClelland and Timothy R. Donovan. New York: MLA, 1985. 87–109.

————. "Consensus and Difference in Collaborative Learning." *CE* 51 (1989): 602–16.

————. "Really Useful Knowledge in the Writing Classroom." *JEd* 172 (1990): 21–23.

Tronto, Joan. *Moral Boundaries: A Political Argument for an Ethic of Care*. New York: Routledge, 1993.

Troyka, Lynn Quitman. "Defining Basic Writing in Context." *A Sourcebook for Basic Writing Teachers*. Ed. Theresa Enos. New York: Random House. 1987. 2–15.

Tuman, Myron. "Class, Codes, and Composition: Basil Bernstein and the Critique of Pedagogy." *CCC* 39 (1988): 42–51.

———. "From Astor Place to Kenyon Road: The NCTE and the Origins of English Studies." *CE* 48 (1986): 339–49.

VanDeWeghe, Richard. "Writing Models, Versatile Writers." *JBC* 20 (1983): 13–23.

Varnum, Robin. "The History of Composition: Reclaiming Our Lost Generations." *JAC* 12 (1992): 39–55.

Veglahn, Nancy J. "Searching: A Better Way to Teach Technical Writing." In "Staffroom Interchange." *CCC* 39 (1988): 85–87.

Viertel, John. "Generative Grammars." *CCC* 5 (1964): 65–81.

Villanueva, Victor, Jr. "Considerations for American Freireistas." *The Politics of Writing Instruction: Postsecondary*. Ed. Richard Bullock, John Trimbur, and Charles Schuster. Portsmouth, NH: Boynton/Cook, 1991. 247–62.

Vitanza, Victor J. "Three Countertheses: Or, a Critical In(ter)vention into Composition Theories and Pedagogies." *Contending with Words: Composition and Rhetoric in a Postmodern Age*. Ed. Patricia Harkin and John Schilb. New York: MLA, 1991. 139–72.

Vopat, James B. "*Uptaught* Rethought—Coming Back from the 'Knockout.' " *CE* 40 (1978): 41–45.

Vygotsky, Lev. *Thought and Language*. Cambridge: MIT Press, 1962.

Wall, Susan V. "Rereading the Discourses of Gender in Composition: A Cautionary Tale." *Pedagogy in the Age of Politics: Writing and Reading in the Academy*. Ed. Patricia A. Sullivan and Donna J. Qualley. Urbana, IL: NCTE, 1994. 166–82.

Wall, Susan V., and Nicholas Coles. "Reading Basic Writing: Alternatives to a Pedagogy of Accommodation." *The Politics of Writing Instruction*. Ed. Richard Bullock, John Trimbur, and Charles Schuster. Portsmouth, NH: Boynton/Cook, 1991. 227–46.

Wallace, David. "Reconsidering Behaviorist Composition Pedagogies: Positivism, Empiricism, and the Paradox of Postmodernism." *JAC* 16 (1996): 103–17.

Wallas, Graham. *The Art of Thought*. New York: Harcourt, Brace and Co., 1926.

Walters, Frank D. "Writing Teachers Writing and Politics of Dissent." *CE* 57 (1995): 822–39.

Walvoord, Barbara E. "The Future of WAC." *CE* 58 (1996): 58–79.

Warnock, Tilly, and John Warnock. "Liberatory Writing Centers: Restoring Authority to Writers." *Writing Centers: Theory and Administration*. Ed. Gary Olson. Urbana, IL: NCTE, 1984. 16–23.

Weaver, Richard. *The Ethics of Rhetoric*. Chicago: Regnery, 1953.

———. "Language Is Sermonic." *Dimensions of Rhetorical Scholarship*. Ed. Robert E. Nebergall. Norman: University of Oklahoma Department of Speech, 1963. Rpt. in *Language Is Sermonic: Richard M. Weaver on the Nature of Rhetoric*. Ed. Richard L. Johannesen, Rennard Strickland, and Ralph Eubanks. Baton Rouge: Louisiana State University Press, 1970. 201–25.

Weber, Christian O. *Basic Philosophies of Education*. New York: Rinehart & Company, 1960.

Welch, Kathleen. "Ideology and Freshman Textbook Production: The Place of Theory in Writing Pedagogy." *CCC* 38 (1987): 269–82.

Welch, Nancy. *Getting Restless: Rethinking Revision in Writing Instruction*. Portsmouth, NH: Boynton/Cook, 1997.

White, Edward M. "Post-Structural Literary Criticism and the Response to Student Writing." *CCC* 35 (1984): 186–95.

———. *Teaching and Assessing Writing*: Recent Advances in Understanding, Evaluating, and Improving Student Performance. San Francisco: Jossey-Bass, 1985.

Wiener, Harvey S. "Collaborative Learning in the Classroom. A Guide to Evaluation." *CE* 48 (1986): 52–61. Rpt. in *The Writing Teacher's Sourcebook*. 2nd ed. Ed. Gary Tate and Edward P. J. Corbett. New York: Oxford University Press, 1988. 238–47.

Wiley, Mark. "Writing in the American Grain: Peter Elbow's and David Bartholomae's Emersonian Pedagogies of Empowerment." *WI* 9 (fall 1989/winter 1990): 57–66.

Williams, Joseph M. "Defining Complexity." *CE* 40 (1979): 595–609.

Wilson, Matthew. "Research, Expressivism, and Silence." *JAC* 15 (1995): 241–60.

Wink, Joan. *Critical Pedagogy, Notes from the Real World*. New York: Longman, 1997.

Winterowd, W. Ross. "Emerson and the Death of Pathos." *JAC* 16 (1996): 27–40.

———. *The English Department: A Personal and Institutional History*. Carbondale: Southern Illinois University Press, 1998.

———. "Linguistics and Composition." *Teaching Composition: Ten Bibliographical Essays*. Ed. Gary Tate. Fort Worth: Texas Christian University Press, 1976. 197–221.

Wixon, Vincent, and Patricia Wixon. "Using Talk-Write in the Classroom." *Theory and Practice in the Teaching of Composition*. Ed. Miles Myers and James Gray. Urbana, IL: NCTE, 1983. 129–35.

Wright, William. "Students as Ethnographers: Encouraging Authority." *TETYC* 18 (1991): 103–8.

Wolff, Janice. "Writing Passionately: Student Resistance to Feminist Readings." *CCC* 42 (1991): 484–92.

Yancey, Kathleen Blake, ed. *Voices on Voice, Perspectives, Definitions, Inquiry*. Urbana, IL: NCTE, 1994. 298–314.

Yin, Sue Hum. "Collaboration: Proceed with Caution." *WI* 12 (1992): 27–37.

Young, Art. "Considering Values: The Poetic Function of Language." *Language Connections: Writing and Reading Across the Curriculum*. Ed. Toby Fulwiler and Art Young. Urbana, IL: NCTE, 1982. 77–97.

Young, Art, and Toby Fulwiler. *Writing Across the Disciplines: Research into Practice*. Upper Montclair, NJ: Boynton/Cook, 1986.

Young, Richard E. "Concepts of Art and the Teaching of Writing." *The Rhetorical Tradition and Modern Writing*. Ed. James J. Murphy. New York: MLA, 1982. 130–41.

———. "Invention: A Topographical Survey." *Teaching Composition: Ten Bibliographical Essays*. Ed. Gary Tate. Fort Worth: Texas Christian University Press, 1976. 1–43.

———. "Paradigms and Problems. Needed Research in Rhetorical Invention." *Research on Composing: Points of Departure.* Ed. Charles Cooper and Lee Odell. Urbana, IL: NCTE, 1978. 29–47.

———. "Recent Developments in Rhetorical Invention." *Teaching Composition: Twelve Bibliographical Essays.* Ed. Gary Tate. Fort Worth: Texas Christian University Press, 1987. 1–38.

Young, Richard E., Alton Becker, and Kenneth Pike. *Rhetoric: Discovery and Change.* New York: Harcourt, Brace & World, 1970.

Zaharlick, Amy, and Judith L. Green. "Ethnographic Research." *Handbook of Research on Teaching the English Language Arts.* Ed. James Flood et al. New York: Macmillan, 1991. 205–25.

Zoellner, Robert. "Talk-Write: A Behavioral Pedagogy for Composition." *CE* 30 (1969): 267–320.

Name Index

Page numbers for main entries are set in **boldface** type.

Ackerman, John, 6, 266

Adams, John Quincy, 132

Addams, Jane, 224

Agar, Michael, 163

Allen, Michael, 124

Althusser, Louis, 274, 275

Anderson, Larry, 216, 243

Anderson, Virginia, 190, 191, 227, 228

Anderson, Worth, 191

Annas, Pamela, 169

Anson, Chris, 231, 232, 233

Applebee, Arthur N., **1–2**, 166, 223, 225, 266, 267, 280, 283

Aristotle, 9, 35, 48, 60, 62, 74, 76, 82, 90, 104, 150, 157, 187, 188, 197, 219

Aronowitz, Stanley, 144, 145, 208, 209, 228, 276

Asher, J. William, 65, 189, 249, 254, 261

Atwan, Robert, 71

Augustine, St., 74

Austin, J. L., 244, 246

Axelrod, Rise, 25, 200

Bacon, Francis, 196, 197

Bain, Alexander, **2–3**, 150, 200, 201

Baird, Theodore, 44

Baker, Nancy W., 216, 223

Bakhtin, Mikhail, 122, 123, 135, 136, 151, 152, 153, 155, 186, 192, 193, **271–272**

Barthes, Roland, 49

Bartholomae, David, **3–4**, 10, 33, 71, 92, 114, 115, 116, 124, 126, 129, 133, 134, 153, 154, 194, 195, 268

Barton, Kerri Morris, 57

Bauer, Dale, 125, 152, 190, 228

Bazerman, Charles, **4–5**, 140, 144, 198, 240, 242, 265

Beach, Richard, 15, 176

Beauvais, Paul, 245

Becker, Alton L., **5**, 86, 108, 110, 181, 187, 196, 197, 236, 237, 243, 248, 249, 257, 281

Bee, Barbara, 180, 181

Belanoff, Pat, 33, 139, 178, 216, 223

Belenky, Mary Field, 39, 125, 131, 138, 139, 156, 168, 169

Benjamin, Walter, 274

Bennett, William, 126, 127, 147, 148

Berkenkotter, Carol, **6–7**, 118, 121, 124, 137, 142, 154, 191, 223, 227, 230

Berlin, James, **7–8**, 61, 86, 90, 93, 118, 127, 128, 131, 145, 146, 148, 149, 150, 151, 172, 173, 174, 187, 192, 196, 197, 200, 202, 203, 204, 205, 206, 207, 210, 217, 225, 228, 230, 237, 238, 241, 242, 243, 250, 253, 257, 258, 272, 278, 280, 283

Bernstein, Basil, 160, 161, 162, 235, 279

Berthoff, Ann E., **8–9**, 64, 128, 144, 145, 146, 151, 164, 181, 187, 188, 197, 217, 229, 230, 243, 251, 252, 257, 266, 267, 276

Bialostosky, Don, 121, 122, 123, 152, 153

Bierwisch, Manfred, 245

Birnbaum, June, 143

Bishop, Wendy, 171

Bissex, Glenda, 252

Bitzer, Lloyd F., **9–10**, 121

Bizzell, Patricia, 3, **10–11**, 53, 54, 92, 113, 114, 115, 116, 125, 126, 129, 136, 140, 141, 142, 144, 145, 146, 147, 148, 153, 154, 176, 177, 190, 191, 192, 209, 210, 212, 228, 241, 242, 247, 259, 263, 265, 279, 283

Black, Edwin, 10, 204, 205

Blair, Hugh, **11–12**, 20, 25, 31, 104, 148, 150, 196, 237, 238

Blakeslee, Ann, 35

Bleich, David, 168

Blom, Thomas E., 210

Bloom, Allan, 126, 127, 148

Bloom, Lynn Z., 250, 263

Bloom, Martin, 250

Booth, Wayne C., **12–13**, 107, 118, 121, 151, 204, 205

Bourdieu, Pierre, 7

Boylston, Nicholas, 132

Braddock, Richard, **13–14**, 55, 66, 78, 166, 218

Brand, Alice, 137, 227

Brandt, Deborah, 137, 255

Brannon, Lil, **14–15**, 62, 146, 178, 188, 218, 228, 252, 259, 263, 267

Bratcher, Suzanne, 202

Brent, Doug, 236

Bridwell-Bowles (Bridwell), Lillian S., **15–16**, 163, 255

Britton, James, **16–17**, 34, 49, 75, 120, 151, 173, 174, 175, 191, 202, 214, 215, 222, 223, 252, 258, 259, 263, 265, 266, 267, 272

Brockriede, Wayne, 31, 100, 256, 257

Brodkey, Linda, **17–18**, 144, 171, 244, 261

Brooke, Robert E., 263

Brown, Rexford, 117, 221

Brown, Stuart, 206

Bruffee, Kenneth A., **18–19**, 115, 116, 119, 122, 125, 126, 137, 138, 139, 140, 144, 177, 192, 193, 194, 197, 198, 207, 208, 240, 242, 247, 248, 253, 279, 283

Bruner, Jerome, 34, 136, **272**

Bullock, Richard, 252

Burgess, Tony, 214, 258

Burke, Kenneth, **19–20**, 23, 28, 48, 58, 96, 101, 103, 104, 108, 118, 121, 157, 183, 184, 187, 189, 190, 191, 196, 197, 205, 206, 207, 252, 253

Burnham, Christopher C., 216

Burton, Frederick R., 252

Butler, Maureen, 45

Calfee, Robert, 40

Camargo, Martin, 74

Campbell, George, 2, 9, 12, 14, **20**, 25, 31, 104, 105, 121, 148, 150, 196, 200, 201, 237, 238

Canagarajah, Suresh A., 209

Castell, Suzanne de, 225

Castellano, Marisa, 88

Caywood, Cynthia, 125

Channing, William Ellery, 132

Charney, Davida, 188, 189, 213, 217

Chase, Geoffrey, 115, 116, 209, 234

Cherry, Roger, 37

Child, Francis James, 132

Chiseri-Strater, Elizabeth, 163, 171, 193

Chodorow, Nancy, 39

Chomsky, Noam, 79, 106, 238, 239, 259, 260, 261
Christensen, Francis, **21**, 29, 63, 181, 182, 205, 207
Church, Robert, 224
Cicero, 35, 48, 74, 197
Cixous, Helene, 101
Clark, Gregory, 48, 154
Clark, Irene, 138, 139
Clark, Suzanne, 258
Clinchy, Blythe McVicker, 131, 138, 156, 168
Coe, Richard M., 157, 158, 182
Coles, Nicholas, 195
Coles, William E., Jr., **21–22**, 44, 49, 121, 122, 163, 172, 173, 175, 223, 257
Coley, W. B., 81
Collins, James L., 160
Colomb, Gregory, 12, 107
Comprone, Joseph, **22–23**, 157, 223, 252, 265
Connors, Robert J., 20, **23–24**, 30, 61, 67, 68, 131, 133, 148, 149, 152, 153, 200, 201, 204, 205, 210, 211, 252, 253
Cooper, Charles R., **24–25**, 78, 117, 188, 189, 200, 223
Cooper, Marilyn, 131, 145, 152, 154, 156, 157, 158, 226, 227, 243, 244
Corbett, Edward P. J., **25–26**, 97, 132, 133, 190, 204, 205, 206, 257
Corder, James W., **26–27**, 127, 197, 236, 237
Courts, Cynthia, 24
Covino, William A., **27–28**, 144, 145, 146, 153, 197, 255
Cowan, Elizabeth, 127
Crane, Ronald S., 204, 205
Crosswhite, James, 154
Crowley, Sharon, **28–29**, 131, 149, 150, 164, 188, 189, 196, 197, 200, 201, 211, 212, 270, 273
Crusius, Timothy, 185, 210

Daiker, Donald, 239, 260
Daly, John, 37
D'Angelo, Frank, **29–30**, 71, 182, 200, 201
Daniell, Beth, 233, 234, 252

Dasenbrock, Reed Way, 194, 241, 245, 246
Davidson, Donald, 213, 241
Day, Henry, 200
De Beaugrande, Robert, 182, 238, 239
de Saussure, Ferdinand, 273
Deleuze, Gilles, 101
Denney, Joseph, 90
Derrida, Jacques, 76, 108, 176, 213, **272–273**
Descartes, René, 14, 62
Dewey, John, 85, 90, 93, 224, 225, 231, 232, 233, **273–274**, 281, 282
Dickson, Marcia, 216
Dilthey, Wilhelm, 184, 185
Dixon, John, 150, 151, 263
Dobrin, David N., 226, 227
Doheny-Farina, Stephen, 154, 170, 171, 213, 261
Donelson, Ken, 127
Dowst, Kenneth, 175
Duhamel, P. Albert, 204, 205

Eagleton, Terry, **274–275**
Ede, Lisa, 23, 25, **30–31**, 67, 119–121, 139, 152, 160, 166, 186, 204, 205, 236, 244
Edlund, John R., 123, 155, 193
Ehninger, Douglas, **31–32**, 100, 256, 257
Eichhorn, Jill, 174, 218
Elbow, Peter, 3, **32–33**, 44, 59, 73, 75, 114, 118, 121, 122, 124, 129, 130, 131, 139, 155, 156, 164, 165, 172, 173, 175, 178, 179, 185, 187, 188, 200, 216, 218, 223, 228, 229, 257, 262, 263, 267, 268
Eldred, Margaret, 265
Emig, Janet, **33–35**, 38, 45, 46, 65, 68, 85, 136, 137, 142, 143, 217, 222, 230, 247, 248, 251, 252, 257, 264, 266, 267, 272, 274, 283
Emig, Peter, 223
Enkvist, Nils Erik, 261
Enos, Richard Leo, **35**, 187, 188
Enos, Theresa, **36**, 129, 160, 206
Erickson, Frederick, 234
Ewald, Helen, 135, 186, 236

Faigley, Lester, **36–38**, 116, 117, 121,
    122, 126, 154, 171, 173, 175, 182,
    186, 188, 189, 212, 213, 220, 221,
    223, 226, 227, 238, 246, 268
Fairbanks, A. Harris, 257
Farmer, Frank, 135, 136, 153, 193
Farrell, Thomas, 115
Felman, Shoshana, 234
Fish, Stanley, 49, 140, 167, 176, 177,
    184, 193, 194, 198, 240, 242, 245,
    248, 253, 254
Fishman, Stephen M., 174, 225, 274
Flower, Linda S., 6, **38–39**, 50, 121, 129,
    136, 137, 159, 160, 192, 200, 223,
    226, 227, 228, 229, 230, 232, 267, 268
Flynn, Elizabeth A., **39–40**, 125, 169,
    175, 204, 205, 265, 268
Foertsch, Julie, 192
Fogarty, Daniel, 148, 150, 207
Fontaine, Sheryl, 178
Fort, Keith, 124
Foster, David, 187, 239
Foucault, Michel, 53, 125, 274, **275**
Fox, Thomas, 162, 221, 223
Franklin, Phyllis, 165
Fraser, Kay Losey, 88
Freedman, Sarah Washauer, **40–41**, 126,
    189, 246
Freire, Paulo, 8, 9, 10, 62, 85, 93, 108,
    127, 128, 144, 145, 146, 152, 153,
    180, 181, 208, 209, 219, 221, 222,
    227, 228, 232, 233, 234, **276**, 277
Freisinger, Randall R., 122, 173, 251
Freud, Sigmund, 234
Fulkerson, Richard, 158, 172, 174, 175,
    257, 265
Fulwiler, Toby, **41–42**, 109, 174, 175,
    214, 215, 218, 258, 263, 264, 265, 267
Fuss, Diana, 167

Gadamer, Hans-Georg, 85, 125, 184, 185,
    186
Gaonkar, Dilip Parameshwar, 185
Garrison, Roger H., 179, 180
Gates, Henry Louis, Jr., **276–277**
Geertz, Clifford, 170, 171, 176, 208, 242,
    254, 255, **277**
Gendlin, Eugene, 84, 175, 176

Genung, John Franklin, **42–43**, 54, 131,
    132, 148, 150, 197, 200
George, Dianna, 131
Gerber, John, 133
Gere, Anne Ruggles, **43–44**, 138, 139,
    220, 252, 265, 267
Gibson, Sharon, 3
Gibson, Walker, **44–45**, 122, 172, 173,
    175, 218
Gilligan, Carol, 39, 125, 138, 139, 168,
    169
Giroux, Henry, 144, 145, 146, 174, 208,
    209, 222, 228, 232, 233, 234, 242,
    276, **277–278**
Gleason, Barbara, 187
Glenn, Cheryl, 24
Goetz, Judith P., 143, 170, 171, 254
Goldberger, Nancy Rule, 131, 138, 156,
    168
Golden, James, 25
Goleman, Judith, 152
Gorman, Margaret E., 214, 258
Gorman, Michael E., 214, 258
Goswami, Dixie, **45**, 78, 171, 252
Goubil-Gambrell, Patricia, 212
Gourdine, Angelletta, 233
Gradwohl, Jane, 266
Graff, Gerald, 7, 124, 144, 161, 162, 194,
    228, 235, **278**
Graham, Margaret Baker, 212
Grasi, Ernesto, 186
Gratz, Ronald, 175, 268
Graves, Donald H., **46**, 171, 223, 239,
    263
Gray, James, 201
Green, Judith, 163
Greenberg, Karen, 160, 171, 216
Greenberg, Ruth, 3
Greene, Stuart, 140, 144, 198
Grego, Rhonda C., 251
Grice, Paul, 246
Grobe, Cary H., 246
Guatari, Felix, 101
Gunner, Jeanne, 269, 270
Gusfield, Joseph R., 252

Haas, Christina, 38
Hairston, Maxine, **47–48**, 149, 150, 151,

183, 184, 210, 211, 212, 222, 223, 236, 237, 279, 281
Hake, Rosemary, 107
Halasek, Kay, 123, 135, 152
Halloran, S. Michael, **48–49**, 133, 149, 150, 190, 200
Hamilton-Wieler, Sharon, 150, 151, 211
Harkin, Patricia, 161, 167, 168, 198, 199, 254
Harned, Jon, 137
Harris, Joseph, **49–50**, 114, 115, 116, 129, 141, 142, 147, 151, 154, 160, 195, 228
Harris, Muriel, 180, 229
Hartwell, Patrick, 147
Hassett, Michael, 253
Haswell, Richard H., 185
Hatch, Gary L., 249, 250, 251
Havelock, Eric, 81
Hawisher, Gail, 91
Hayes, John R., 6, 38, **50–51**, 129, 136, 137, 192, 217, 218, 223, 226, 227, 230
Heath, Robert L., 184
Heath, Shirley Brice, **51–52**, 170, 171, 251, 252
Heidegger, Martin, 184, 185, 186, 281
Henry, George, 203
Herbert Beall, 101
Herndl, Carl, 150, 234
Herrington, Anne J., **52–53**, 78, 265, 267
Herzberg, Bruce, 11, **53–54**, 145, 190, 225, 263, 265
Higgins, Lorraine, 232, 233
Hill, Adams Sherman, 42, **54–55**, 131, 132, 148, 150, 197, 200, 201
Hill, Carolyn, 164, 192, 255
Hillocks, George, Jr., **55–56**, 166, 171, 178, 231, 232, 233
Hirsch, E. D., Jr., **56–57**, 126, 127, 146, 147, 148, 184, 186, 241
Holzman, Michael, 226, 227, 239, 247
Hook, J. N., 203
hooks, bell, 125, 156, 228
Horner, Bruce, 129, 141, 142
Horner, Winifred Bryan, **57–58**, 157, 196, 237, 238, 245, 246
Horning, Alice, 232
Hubbuch, Susan H., 242

Huckin, Thomas N., 6
Hull, Glynda, 88
Hunt, Kellogg, 79, 238, 239, 246, 247, 261
Huot, Brian, 188
Hutcheson, Francis, 237, 238

Inhelder, Barbel, 158
Inkster, Robert, 149, 187, 210
Irmscher, William F., **58**, 157, 197

James, William, 281
Jarratt, Susan, **59**, 125, 126, 130, 131, 145, 156, 174, 194, 228
Jensen, Julie, 164, 165
Johnson, Jean F., 262
Joliffe, David A., 28, 37, 103
Jones, Robert, 23, 265
Jones, Virginia Pompei, 171, 177
Judith Langer, 2
Judy, Stephen. See Tchudi, Stephen
Jukuri, Stephen, 125

Kant, Immanuel, 62
Kantor, Kenneth J., 143, 170, 171, 214, 224, 254, 262
Kaufer, David, 110
Kelly, Lou, 118, 120
Kennedy, George, 196
Kent, Thomas, 168, 212, 213, 241, 242
Kerek, Andrew, 239, 260
Kiefer, Ferenc, 245
Killingsworth, M. Jimmie, 243
Kilpatrick, William, 224
King, Martha, 170
Kinneavy, James L., **59–61**, 71, 184, 185, 186, 265
Kinney, James, 249
Kirby, Dan R., 143, 170, 171, 254
Kirsch, Gesa E., 114, 125, 126, 169, 170, 219, 234, 254
Kitzhaber, Albert, 7, 49, **61–62**, 131, 132, 148, 151, 207
Klaus, Carl H., 66, 219
Kneupper, Charles W., 256, 257
Knoblauch, C. H., 14, **62–63**, 144, 146, 148, 178, 188, 218, 219, 221, 228, 252, 259, 263, 267

Knorr-Cetina, K. D., 240
Koen, Frank, 5
Kohlberg, Lawrence, 72, 168, 280
Kohler, Wolfgang, 191
Kozol, Jonathan, 181
Krashen, Stephen, 108
Kroll, Barry, 119, 120, 121, 159, 160, 224
Kuhn, Thomas, 18, 47, 100, 138, 140, 143, 176, 197, 198, 207, 209, 210, 211, 212, 239, 242, 247, 248, **278–279**, 281

Labov, William, **279–280**
Lacan, Jacques, 234
Lamb, Catherine E., 135, 169, 236
Langer, Judith, 2, 137, 266, 267
Langstraat, Lisa R., 243
Larson, Richard L., **63–64**, 71, 97, 197, 200, 210, 211, 230, 261
Lassner, Phyllis, 236
Latour, Bruno, 197, 198, 240
Lauer, Janice, 8, 34, **64–65**, 68, 187, 188, 189, 197, 249, 254, 257, 261
Lawson, Bruce, 185
LeFevre, Karen Burke, 122, 192, 196, 197
Lensmire, Timothy, 136
Lentricchia, Frank, 28, 270
Leverenz, Carrie, 144
Liggett, Sarah, 231, 232
Lindemann, Erika, **65–66**, 98, 157, 158, 163, 189, 249, 256, 260
Lindquist, E. F., 116, 117
Lloyd-Jones, Richard, 13, 55, **66–67**, 68, 78, 116, 117, 127, 133, 134, 164, 165, 166, 189, 219, 221, 258
Locke, John, 14, 62
Long, Russell, 119, 121
Lovejoy, Kim, 245
Lu, Min-Zhan, 116, 129, 141, 142
Luke, Allan, 225
Lunsford, Andrea, 23, 25, 30, 34, 65, 66, **67–69**, 97, 119, 120, 121, 128, 129, 134, 139, 142, 152, 159, 164, 165, 186, 204, 205, 235, 236, 263
Luria, A. R., 34

Lynch, Dennis, 125, 131
Lyotard, Jean-François, 101, 102, 212, 213

Macedo, Donaldo, 276
Machey, Pierre, 274
Mack, Nancy, 186, 268
Macrorie, Ken, 22, 32, 44, **69**, 75, 118, 121, 122, 163, 164, 172, 173, 175, 178, 179, 187, 218, 252, 255, 256, 257
Mahala, Daniel, 165, 176, 263, 264
Maimon, Elaine, **70**, 139, 193, 218, 264, 265
Mallet, Susan, 245, 246
Marshall, James, 225, 266
Marshall, Jon C., 202
Martin, Nancy, 214, 258, 265
Marx, Karl, 62
Maxwell, Jack, 165
McCarthy, Lucille, 154, 174, 225, 274
McCormick, Kathleen, 194
McCulley, George, 175, 268
McGee, Patrick, 234
McKean, Rev. Joseph, 132
McKeon, Richard, 204, 205
McLeod, Alex, 214, 258
Mcleod, Susan, 198, 199, 265, 266, 270
McLuhan, Marshall, 206
McPherson, Elisabeth, 203
McQuade, Donald, **71**, 95
Mead, Margaret, 170
Mellon, John C., 79, 238, 239, 260
Memering, Dean, 79
Meyers, George Douglas, 250
Milic, Louis, 48
Miller, James, 175
Miller, Richard, 142
Miller, Susan, **72–73**, 135, 185, 201, 202, 211, 212, 222
Minock, Mary, 123, 230
Minot, Walter, 119, 121
Mishler, Elliot G., 142, 143, 217
Moffett, James, **73–74**, 75, 151, 159, 175, 182, 260, 261, 280, 283
Moglen, Helene, 68
Montague, Gene, 34, 65, 68
Moran, Charles, 53
Morenberg, Max, 239, 260

Morris, Paul, 99
Mortensen, Peter, 125, 126, 169, 170, 254
Moss, Beverly J., 163, 171, 261
Moxley, Joseph, 270
Muller, Herbert J., 150, 151
Murphy, Ann, 234
Murphy, James J., **74–75**, 132, 133, 196
Murphy, Richard J., 218
Murray, Donald M., 6, 44, 73, **75–76**, 118, 122, 124, 172, 173, 175, 218, 222, 223, 263
Myers, Greg, 138, 139, 140, 198, 240, 242
Myers, Miles, 189, 251, 252

Nancarrow, Paula Reed, 15
Nardini, Gloria, 128
Nash, Jane G., 51
Nash, Jane Gradwohl, 266, 267
Nealon, Jeffrey T., 152, 242
Neel, Jasper, **76–77**, 273
Newkirk, Thomas, 103, 131, 143, 162, 166, 174
Newman, Samuel, 200
Nichols, Marie Hochmuth, 206
Nietzsche, Friedrich, 101, 275
Noddings, Nell, 168, 169
Nodine, Barbara, 70
Nold, Ellen, 40, 246
North, Stephen M., **77–78**, 85, 184, 185, 197, 198, 199, 202, 211, 218, 229
Nudelman, Jerrold, 256

O'Connor, Finnbar, 70
Odell, Lee, 24, 45, 52, **78–79**, 171, 189, 213, 220, 223, 251, 261, 263, 265
O'Donnell, Thomas, 130, 175
Ogden, C. K., 86
O'Hare, Frank, **79–80**, 238, 239, 260, 261
Ohmann, Richard, **80–81**, 133, 161, 205, 206, 207, 235, 243, 245, 246, 249, 257, 260, 261
Olbrechts-Tyteca, Lucie, 82, 83, 121, 206, 207
Olson, Gary, 270, 282

Ong, Walter J., S J., **81–82**, 118, 119, 121
Onore, Cynthia, 222
Overing, Gillian, 125

Paine, Charles, 228
Park, Douglas, 119, 120, 121
Pastore, Catherine Blair, 152, 264
Payne, Michelle, 150, 174
Pemberton, Michael, 199
Penrose, Ann, 266
Perelman, Chaim, **82–83**, 121, 205, 206, 207
Perelman, Les, 229, 244, 265
Perl, Sondra, **83–84**, 92, 129, 136, 137, 175, 176, 223, 227, 230, 283
Perry, William, 280
Peterson, Jane, 134
Petraglia, Joseph, 232
Petrick, Joanne F., 119
Petrosky, Anthony, 3
Pfister, Fred R., 119
Phelps, Louise Weatherbee, 34, **84–86**, 233
Phillips, Donna Burns, 3
Piaget, Jean, 72, 73, 78, 136, 150, 158, 159, 160, 267, 272, **280**, 283
Pike, Kenneth L., 5, **86**, 108, 110, 187, 196, 197, 206, 236, 237, 243, 248, 249, 257, 281
Plato, 35, 76, 90, 96, 103, 172
Poincaré, Henri, 191
Polanyi, Michael, 191, 247, 248, **280–281**
Ponsot, Marie, 71
Porter, James, 176, 177
Porter, Kevin J., 241
Poulakos, John, 205
Pratt, Mary Louise, 49, 141, 142, 246
Pritchard, Ruie Jane, 202
Probst, Robert E., 220
Pullman, George, 197
Purves, Alan, 166, 203

Qualley, Donna J., 167, 193
Quick, Doris, 78
Quintilian, 74, 197

Radcliffe, Terry, 250
Ramus, Peter, 81, 196, 197

Rankin, Elizabeth, 218
Ray, Ruth E., 134, 163, 252
Recchio, Thomas, 170
Redman, George, 164
Reid, Ronald, 132
Reid, Thomas, 237, 238
Resnick, Stephen, 167, 168
Rice, Warner G., 61
Richards, Ivor A., 8, **86–87**, 205, 206, 207
Ricoeur, Paul, 85, 185, 186
Ried, Paul, 132
Ritchie, Joy S., 114, 155, 209, 219, 234, 263
Roberts, Patricia, 171, 177
Robertson, Linda R., 28, 270
Rodgers, Paul, Jr., 181
Rogers, Carl, 47, 235, 237, **281**
Rohman, D. Gordon, 96, 173
Rorty, Richard, 18, 138, 140, 143, 144, 176, 177, 197, 198, 207, 208, 239, 240, 242, **281–282**
Rose, Mike, **87–89**, 92, 114, 128, 129
Rose, Shirley, 238
Rosenblatt, Louise, **282–283**
Ross, Donald, 15
Roth, Robert, 120
Rouse, John, 124, 161, 162, 227, 235
Rousseau, Jean-Jacques, 224, 225
Royster, Jacqueline Jones, **89–90**
Rueckert, William H., 183
Russell, David R., 202, 237, 238, 265
Ryan, Susan S., 185
Ryle, Gilbert, 254

Salvatori, Mariolina, 185
Sams, Henry, 204
Schell, Eileen E., 169, 269
Schilb, John, 208
Schleiermacher, Friedrich, 184
Schlosser, Alvin H., 256
Schoer, Lowell, 13, 55, 66, 78, 166
Scholes, Robert, 7
Schön, Donald A., 231, 232, 233
Schriver, Karen, 137
Schumacher, Gary M., 266, 267
Schuster, Charles, 155
Schwartz, Helen, 15

Schwartz, Joseph, 206, 207
Schweickart, Patrocinio, 39
Scott, Fred Newton, 54, **90–91**, 96, 131, 132, 148, 149, 150, 200, 203
Scott, Robert L., 7, 242
Searle, John, 244, 245, 246
Selfe, Cynthia L., **91–92**, 145
Selfe, Richard J., 91
Selzer, Jack, 186
Shaughnessy, Mina, 67, **92–93**, 97, 113, 115, 124, 128, 129, 159, 161, 218, 223, 238, 251
Sheard, Cynthia M., 184
Shor, Ira, **93–94**, 126, 144, 145, 146, 181, 209, 221, 222, 228, 234, 242, 276
Simmons, Jo An McGuire, 180
Simon, Linda, 95
Skinner, Anna, 37
Skinner, B. F., 249
Sledd, James, 269
Slevin, James F., 68, **94–95**, 109, 126, 134, 269, 270
Sloan, Gary, 246
Smit, David W., 138, 139, 166, 177, 194, 208, 253
Smith, Adam, 238
Smith, Louise, 264
Smith, Nelson J., III, 206
Soles, Derek, 227
Sommers, Nancy, 15, 71, **95–96**, 136, 137, 223, 230
Sotirou, Peter, 125, 185
Southwell, Michael, 178
Spellmeyer, Kurt, 185
Spivak, Gayatri Chakravorty, 167, 168
Squires, Geoffrey, 43
Stanger, Carol, 124, 140, 179
Stenhouse, Lawrence, 251
Stewart, Donald C., 90, **96–97**, 118, 121, 122, 131, 132, 133, 134, 149, 173, 175, 208, 241, 242, 249
Stewart, Murray F., 246
Stillman, Peter, 252
Stotsky, Sandra, 114, 179
Strain, Margaret, 185
Stroble, Elizabeth, 202
Sullivan, Francis, 141

Sullivan, Patricia, 110, 114, 115, 171, 214
Sunstein, Bonnie Stone, 163
Swearingen, Jan, 169
Swilky, Jody, 165

Talbert, Carol, 171
Tarule, Jill Mattuck, 131, 138, 156, 168
Tate, Gary, 25, 66, **97–98**
Tchudi (Judy), Stephen, **98–99**, 175, 265
Tirrell, Mary Kay, 218
Tobin, Lad, 130, 174, 175, 183, 184, 192, 216, 223
Toulmin, Stephen, 31, 32, **99–100**, 205, 256, 257
Trilling, Lionel, 115
Trimbur, John, **100–101**, 126, 138, 139, 140, 143, 144, 198, 208
Troyka, Lynn Quitmann, 129
Tuman, Myron, 161, 203

VanDeWeghe, Richard, 250
Varnum, Robin, 131, 252
Viertel, John, 259, 260
Villanueva, Victor, 233, 234
Vitanza, Victor J., **101–103**, 195, 212, 213, 253, 275
Vopat, James, 255, 256
Vygotsky, Lev, 18, 34, 137, 150, 159, 240, 242, 267, **283**

Wall, Susan V., 169, 195
Wallace, David, 217, 250
Wallas, Graham, 191
Walters, Frank, 140
Walters, Margaret, 249, 250, 251
Walvoord, Barbara, 264, 265, 266
Warnock, John, 144
Warnock, Tillie, 144
Weaver, Richard, **103–104**, 183, 184, 189, 190, 197, 204, 205
Weber, Christian O., 224

Welch, Kathleen, 200, 201
Welch, Nancy, 242, 268
Wells, Ida B., 89
Wendell, Barrett, 54, **104**, 131, 132, 148, 150, 200
West, Susan, 68
Whately, Richard, 12, 20, 25, 31, **104–105**, 148, 150, 196, 238
White, Edward M., **105–106**, 116, 117, 189, 194, 216, 220, 221
Wieler, Kathleen, 156
Wiener, Harvey, 124, 138, 139, 140
Wiley, Mark, 122, 172
Williams, Joseph M., 12, **106–107**, 246
Williams, Raymond, 7, 49, 274
Williamson, Michael M., 160
Wilson, Matthew, 171
Wilson, Nancy, 84
Wink, Joan, 153, 219
Winterowd, W. Ross, 71, **107–109**, 185, 199, 230, 243, 245, 246, 253, 258, 263
Witte, Stephen, 37, 226, 227
Wixon, Patricia, 251
Wixon, Vincent, 251
Wlecke, Albert O., 96, 173
Wolff, Janice, 233
Wolff, Richard, 167, 168
Woolgar, Steve, 197, 198, 240
Wright, William, 170
Wykoff, George S., 134

Yancey, Kathleen Blake, 173, 174, 216
Yin, Sue Hum, 138
Young, Art, 42, 94, **109**, 174, 175, 214, 215, 233, 234, 258, 265
Young, Richard E., 5, 71, 86, 108, **110–11**, 148, 149, 150, 182, 187, 196, 197, 209, 210, 211, 212, 223, 236, 237, 243, 248, 249, 257, 281

Zaharlick, Amy, 163
Zoellner, Robert, 249–251, 257

Subject Index

ᴄᴙ

Page numbers for main entries are set in **boldface** type. Terms in *italics* are category headings used in Section I, part "a."

Abnormal Discourse, **207–208**, 281

Academic Discourse, 3, 11, 33, 88, **113–115**, 152, 195, 234, 262

Academic Discourse Community, 3, 10, 18, 49, 88, 113, **115–116**, 124, 129, 154

Analytic Scoring, 24, 37, 105, **116–117**, 220

Anthropology, 169, 171, 277

Anti-Essentialism, **167–168**, 199, 273

Anti-Foundationalism, 117, **176–177**, 194, 239, 253

Argument, 19, 26, 31, 42, 47, 82, 99, 103, 104

Aristotelian Rhetoric, 19, 35, 76, 148, 204, 236

Arrangement, 2, 21, 29, 42, 54, 63, 82, 99, 104

Assessment, 36, 105

Audience, 4, 6, 9, 12, 16, 19, 20, 30, 31,32, 37, 38, 42, 44, 48, 60, 67, 73, 81, 82, 83, 90, 95, 98, 103, 105, **117–21**, 159, 172, 190, 200, 206, 215, 222, 228, 234, 243, 245, 262, 267, 268, 280, 282

Authentic Voice, 22, 44, 75, 96, **121–122**, 150, 172, 241

Authoritative Word (Discourse), **122–123**, 193

Authority, 26–27, 89, 100, **123–126**, 169, 224, 233, 262, 275; student, 95, 150, 170, 222; teacher, 41, 73, 93, 139, 149, 161, 174, 179, 215, 235, 255

Back to Basics Movement, **126–127**

Banking Concept of Education, 93, **127–128**, 221, 227, 276

Basic Writing, 3, 10, 36, 49, 67, 83, 87, 92; Basic writers (writing), 71, 77, 114, 124, **128–129**, 159, 161, 194, 276, 279, 280

Bay Area Writing Project, **201–202**

Believing Game, 32, 59, **130–131**, 155

Bibliography, 7, 10, 13, 15, 18, 22, 25,

26, 35, 53, 57, 59, 63, 65, 74, 91, 92, 96, 97, 107, 110

Big Four, 42, 54, 90, 104, **131–132**, 150, 200

Boylston Professorship, 54, **132–133**

Carnival, 72, **135–136**, 186

Censorship, 73–74

Cognitive Theories of Composition, 7, 10, 33–34, 37, 38, 40, 50, 83, 101, 110, 118, 128, **136–137**, 158, 159, 168, 172, 173, 175, 191, 192, 205, 222, 225, 226, 228, 230, 241, 242, 243, 244, 249, 257, 266, 268, 272, 280, 283

Collaboration, 30, 43, 67, 70, 100; Collaboration (collaborative learning/writing), 10, 18, 30–31, 39, 42, 45, 52, 68, 75, 96, 119, 124, 130, **138–140**, 150, 152, 156, 161, 170, 179, 183, 186, 193, 194, 207, 208, 222, 232, 234, 240, 244, 250, 262, 271, 279, 282, 283

Communication triangle, 60

Community, 115, 125, 190, 193, 197, 207, 209, 274, 279

Composing Processes, 1, 6, 16, 21, 22, 24, 32, 33, 38, 46, 47, 50, 75, 78, 83, 95, 110. *See also* Process

Computers and Composing, 15, 82, 91, 97, 152, 262

Conference on College Composition and Communication (CCCC), 3, 13, **133–135**, 164, 203, 269; chairs of, 134–135

Conferences (as pedagogical tools), 41, 46, 104, 179–180, 222

Conflict Model of Education, 278

Consensus, 18, 100, 125, 138, **140**, 197, 208, 239, 262, 278, 279

Consubstantial, 19, 141, 190

Contact Zones, 49, 91, 125, 129, **141–142**

Context Stripping, **142–143**, 254

Conversation, 4, 17, 18, 70, 140, **143–144**, 197, 207, 239, 281

Cooking, 32

Critical Consciousness, 9, 10–11, 54, 93, 127, **144–145**, 227, 232, 276, 277

Critical Literacy, 7, 28, **145–146**, 180, 227, 276, 278

Critical Pedagogy, 14, 54, 59, 62, 93, 146, 227. *See also* Radical Pedagogy

Cultural Literacy, 56, 145, **146–147**

Cultural Studies, 7, 36, 51, 56, 72, 80, 93, 94, 100; Cultural Studies, 7–8, 80, 100–101, 127, 146, 233, 234, 275, 276, 278

Current-Traditional Rhetoric, 2, 11, 16, 22, 24, 28, 42, 48, 54, 78, 90, 101, 104, 105, 110, 117, 123, 127, 131, **148–150**, 166, 172, 196, 198, 200, 204, 205, 210, 211, 217, 218, 222, 237, 252, 279

Curriculum Development, 272, 280

Dartmouth Seminar, 49, 61, 73, **150–151**, 165, 172, 262, 280, 283

Deconstruction, 28, 120, 253, 272–273

Deep Structure, 259

Dialogic, 31, 68, 93, 125, **151–153**, 155, 186, 193, 240, 264, 271, 276

Discourse Community, 6, 49, 60, 70, 83, 114, 119, 121, 124, 136, 141, 143, **153–154**, 160, 192, 194, 207, 240, 241, 243, 258, 262, 264

Dissensus, 100, 140. *See also* Consensus

Double-Voicedness, **155**, 186, 271

Doubting Game, 32, 130, **155–156**

Dramatistic Pentad, 19, 23, 58, 96, 108, **157**, 187, 196

Ecological Model of Writing, **157–158**

Educational Testing Service, 188–189

Egocentrism, 118, 128, **158–160**, 267, 280, 283

Elaborated Code, **160–162**, 235, 280

Eloquence, 74

Emic, **162–163**, 171

Empathetic rhetoric. *See* Rogerian Rhetoric

Engfish, 22, 69, **163–164**

English as a Second Language, 52, 279

English Coalition Conference, 33, 67, 68, 99, **164–165**

Environmental Mode of Instruction, 55, **166**

Epistemic, 7, 8, 35, 62, 80, 86, 87, 90, 93, 99, 107, 149, 197, **242–243**, 257, 258, 272

Essay and Personal Writing, 21, 23, 32, 41, 44, 69, 73, 75, 96

Essentialism, 156, **167–168**, 183, 241

Ethic of Care, 125, **168–169**

Ethnography, 14, 17, 34, 37, 41, 45, 46, 51, 55, 58, 78, 84, 142, 152, 162, **169–171**, 213, 217, 240, 251, 254, 255, 261, 272, 277

Ethos, 20, 26, 27, 48, 74, 113–114

Etic, **162–163**, 171

Expressionism, 7, 101, 118, 150, **172–173**, 174, 204, 224, 240, 242, 257, 262, 267

Expressivism, 21, 32–33, 37, 41, 44, 59, 69, 73, 75, 96, 98, 121–122, 123, 125, 151, 166, 172, **173–175**, 179, 202, 205 214, 222, 228, 243, 244, 255, 258, 266; expressive writing, 16, 88, 109, 173, 258

Faculty psychology, 20, 199

Felt Sense, 84, **175–176**

Feminist: theory, 39–40, 59, 68, 72, 81, 85, 114, 124–125, 130, 135, 138, 152, 156, 167–169, 174, 179, 193, 204, 205, 219, 234, 236, 241; pedagogy, 190, 271; research, 217

Foundationalism, 10, 11, 101, 167, **176–177**, 253

Freewriting, 32, 42, 44, 55, 69, 121, 163, **178–179**, 187, 196

Garrison Approach, **179–180**

Gender and Composition, 17, 23, 36, 39, 43, 59, 67, 72, 84, 89

Generative, **180–181**

Generative Rhetoric, 21, 29, **181–182**

Generative-Transformational Grammar, 181. *See also* Transformational Grammar

God-Terms, 19, 103, **183–184**

Grammar and Usage, 42, 54, 104, 106

Hermeneutics, 56, **184–186**, 241

Heteroglossia, **186**, 271

Heuristic, 5, 19, 32, 35, 64, 69, 86, 87, 96, 110, 118, 120, 157, 178, **187–188**, 195, 196, 236, 248, 266

History of Rhetoric and/or Composition, 1, 7, 9, 10, 14, 23, 25, 27–31, 35, 36, 48, 49, 53, 57, 59, 61, 64, 67, 72, 74, 76, 77, 80–82, 96, 98, 101, 107

Holistic Evaluation, 24, 37, 40–41, 66, 78, 105–106, 117, **188–189**, 220

Identification, 19, 20, 23, 103, 118, **189–191**, 206, 227

Incubation, **191**, 281

Inner Speech, 73, 159, 267

Inner-Directed Theories, 10, 136, **191–192**

Intellectual Property, 67–69

Internally Persuasive Word, 122, **192–193**

Interpretive Communities, 176, **193–194**

Inventing the University, 3, 114, 124, 153, **194–195**

Invention, 5, 8, 19, 27, 28, 42, 58, 64, 69, 86, 110; Invention, 5, 8, 9, 12, 16, 19, 20, 26, 27, 28, 29, 35, 42, 43, 54, 58, 63, 64, 65, 69, 81, 103–104, 105, 108, 110–111, 120, 148–149, 157, 187, **195–197**, 206, 210, 248

I-Search Paper, 69

Journals, 41–42, 44, 266, 272; Teaching Journal, 231

Kairos, 60–61

Knowledge (as Socially Constructed), 59, 143, 192, **197–198**, 208, 209, 239, 243, 247, 251, 252, 262, 275, 278, 281

Liberatory Pedagogy, 144, 152, 233, 276, 277

Linguistics, 21, 51, 71, 86, 106, 107, 110; Linguistics, 5, 21, 51, 71, 80, 86, 90, 108, 110, 150, 181, 205, 248–249, 259–260, 280

Literacy, 3, 10, 14, 17, 51, 56, 73, 80, 81, 87, 89, 93, 94, 107; Literacy, 1, 10, 14, 15, 17, 22, 27, 35, 37, 43, 51, 62, 68, 81–82, 88, 89, 91, 94, 99, 108, 126, 128, 141, 145, 146, 180, 181, 195, 203, 219, 233, 241, 265, 276,

277, 283. *See also* Critical Literacy; Cultural Literacy

Literature and Composition, 11, 12, 22, 41, 57, 86, 109; Literature and Composition, 25, 26, 29, 42, 56, 81, 94, 98, 108, 109, 132, 141, 144, 203, 269, 276, 278, 282

Lore, 85, 167, **198–199**, 218

Marxist Theory, 37, 80, 101, 114, 121, 135, 144, 219, 227, 241, 274, 276, 277, 281, 283

Meta-Analysis, 55, 166

Modes of Discourse, 2, 16, 20, 23–24, 29–30, 54, 148, **199–201**

Monitor, 38

Narrative Theory, 272

National Council of Teachers of English (NCTE), 13, 90, 133–134, 164, **202–204**, 219, 225; Founding Members, 204

National Writing Project, **201–202**

Neo-Aristotelians, 172, **204–205**

Neo-Platonism, 172, 204

New Pragmatism, 240, 281

New Rhetoric, 7, 19, 21, 26, 30, 32, 36, 67, 80, 82–83, 86, 110, 118, 172, 190, **205–207**, 243, 245

Nonfoundational, 273, 282

Normal Discourse, **207–208**, 281

Objective Rhetoric, 7, 257–258

Opposition, **208–209**, 233, 278

Orality, 81–82

Outer-Directed Theory, 10, **191–192**

Paradigm, 2, 23, 34, 47, 53, 110, 207, **209–210**, 278, 279

Paradigm Shift, 28, 47, 148, 150, 210, **211–212**, 222, 279

Paralogy, 102, **212–213**

Participant Observer, 170, **213–214**, 254

Pedagogy, 2, 8, 21, 25, 46, 49, 58, 63, 65, 69, 71, 73, 75, 77, 79, 87, 90, 93, 94, 97, 98, 107

Peer Tutoring, 18, 78, 100, 119, 139, 240. *See also* Tutor Training

Personal Knowledge. *See* Tacit Knowledge

Poetic Writing, 16, 109, 173, **214–215**, 258, 264, 266

Portfolio Evaluation, 33, 105, **215–216**, 232

Positivism, 34, 103, 149, 172, 196, 204, **216–218**, 227, 257

Postmodernism, 17, 39–40, 85, 101, 217

Poststructuralism, 105–106, 120, 122, 156, 167, 174, 176, 198, 233, 252, 271, 277, 281

Practitioner, 77, 98, 167, 198, 202, **218**

Pragmatism, 172, 240, 273

Praxis, 62, **219**

Primary Trait Scoring, 37, 66, 78, 105, **219–221**

Problematize, 93

Problem-Posing Education, 127, 144, **221–222**, 276

Process (Writing-as-a-Process Movement), 2, 5, 6, 14, 16, 25, 27, 28, 32, 34, 35, 37, 45, 47, 50, 58, 61, 62, 63, 67, 69, 72, 75, 77, 78, 83–84, 85, 90, 95, 96, 104, 105, 117, 120, 123, 126, 127, 136, 148, 150, 158, 161, 166, 172, 174, 175, 185, 186, 191, 193, 196, 202, 210, 211, 215, **222–223**, 225, 226, 230, 239, 245, 247, 249, 262, 272, 279, 281, 283; post, 223. *See also Composing Processes*

Progressive Education, 90, **223–225**, 273

Progymnasmata, 29

Protocol Analysis, 38, 50, 171, 222, **225–227**; Protocol, 6, 83, 87, 136–137, **225–227**

Psychoanalysis, 233–234

Radical Pedagogy, 125, 174, 180, 208–209, **227–228**, 233, 242–243, 276, 277, 278

Reader-Based Prose, 38, 118, 128, 159, **228–229**, 267

Reader-Response Theory, 39, 245, 282–283

Real Voice, 32, 69, 121, 229. *See also* Authentic Voice

Recipe Swapping, **229–230**

Recursive, 33, 84, 95, 136, 175, 222, **230**
Reflective/Reflection, 55, 85, 170, 209, 215, **231–233**, 266, 274
Relative Readability, 56
Research Methodology, 1, 6, 13, 15, 24, 33, 38, 40, 45, 46, 50–52, 55, 64, 66, 71, 77–79, 83, 87, 92, 95
Research Paper, 63–64, 69, 149, 170
Resistance, 18, 28, 40, 72, 93, 101, 190, 209, 227, **233–234**, 278
Response and Evaluation, 14, 24, 32, 36, 40, 62, 66, 78, 95, 105
Restricted Code, 161, **235**, 280
Revision, 15, 38, 40, 75, 95; Revision, 6, 10, 15, 16, 32, 36–37, 38–39, 41, 46, 50–51, 75–76, 84, 95–96, 118, 215, 220, 222–223, 230, 245, 262–263, 267–268, 280
Rhetoric and/or Composition Theory, 3, 4, 5, 6, 7, 8, 9, 10, 11, 12, 14, 16, 17, 18, 19, 20, 21, 23, 25, 26, 27, 28, 29, 30, 31, 32, 33, 36, 38, 39, 44, 47, 48, 50, 53, 54, 55, 56, 58, 59, 61, 62, 63–65, 67, 72, 73, 76, 77, 81, 82, 83, 84, 86, 90, 97, 99, 100, 101, 103, 104, 107, 110
Rhetorical Situation, 9–10, 118, 120–121, 123, 157, 182, 221, 238, 247, 257
Rogerian Rhetoric, 5, 27, 47, **235–237**, 281

Scottish Common Sense Realism, 20, 148, **237–238**
Semantic Triangle, 87
Sentence Combining, 21, 25, 43, 55, 79, 108, 182, **238–239**, 246, 260
Service Learning, 38, 39, 53, 225, 232, 274
Social Construction, 3, 7, 10, 18, 90, 93, 96, 119–121, 124, 136, 138–140, 143, 151, 156, 163, 167, 168, 174–176, 179, 186, 193, 194, 197, 198, 205, 208, **239–242**, 243, 247, 252, 277, 278, 279, 282
Social Epistemic Rhetoric, 7, 101, 127, 146, 172, 241, **242–243**, 278
Sociocognitive Theory, 6–7, 38, 137
Solitary Author, 17, **243–244**

Sophist, 28, 35, 59, 76, 102
Speech Act Theory, 80, **244–246**
Spontaneous Inventiveness, 75
Structuralism, 106, 271, 272–273
Style, 2, 11, 21, 25, 42, 44, 54, 71, 79, 80, 104, 106; Style, 12, 25–26, 29, 44, 48, 54, 60, 71, 80, 83, 97, 102, 104, 105, 106–107, 148, 149, 169, 179, 195, 196, 204, 206, 245, 258, 260–261, 279
Subjective Rhetoric, 7, 257–258
Surface Structure, 259
Surprise, 75, 79

Tacit Knowledge, 34, **247–248**, 280
Tagmemic Invention, 5, 86, 96, 108, 110, 187, 196, 236, **248–249**
Talk-Write Pedagogy, **249–251**, 257
Teacher-Researcher/Teacher-Research, 14, 45, 62, 162, 213, 217, **251–252**
Technology and Composition, 15, 36, 81, 91. *See also* Computers and Composing
Terministic Screens, 19, 23, **252–253**
Themewriting, 22, 163
Theory Hope, 176, **253–254**
Thick Description, 142, 170, 171, **254–255**, 261, 277
Third Way, 69, **255–256**
Topoi, 29, 82, 104, 110, 187
Toulmin Model of Argument, 31, 99, **256–257**
Transactional Rhetoric/Theory, 7, 242, **257–258**
Transactional Writing, 16, 109, 173, 214, **258–259**, 264, 266
Transformational Grammar (Generative-Transformational Grammar), 79, 80, 238, **259–261**
Triangulation, 254, **261–262**
True voice, 163. *See also* Authentic Voice; Real Voice
T-Unit, 16, 21, 79, 106, 238, **246–247**
Tutor Training, 77. *See also* Peer Tutoring

Voice, 3, 12, 16, 18, 22, 32, 42, 49–50, 59, 70, 84, 89, 95, 100, 102, 114, 116,

125–126, 130, 134, 138–139, 140, 149, 151–153, 154, 155, 156, 163–164, 168, 173, 174, 181, 186, 194, 195, 197, 237, 241, 245, 262–263, 271–272, 278. *See also* Authentic Voice; Real Voice; True Voice

WAC. *See* Writing Across the Curriculum

Workshop, 14, 33, 42, 43, 75, 104, 108, 119, 136, 150, 161, 222, 240, **262–263**, 264–265, 266, 272

Writer-Based Prose, 38, 118, 159, 228, 229, **263–265**

Writing Across the Curriculum, 4, 16, 22, 41, 43, 52, 59, 70, 98, 109; Writing Across the Curriculum, 4, 16, 23, 40, 41–42, 43, 45, 53, 60–61, 70, 91, 97, 99, 101, 109, 115, 152, 154, 174, 193, 214, **265–267**, 266–267, 271

Writing Apprehension, 37, 91; Writer's Block, 88

Writing Centers, 77; Writing Centers, 14, 77–78, 272

Writing in the Workplace, 4, 45, 52, 78

Writing Process. *See* Process

Writing Program Administration, 18, 47, 105

Writing To Learn, 2, 41, 264, **267–268**, 272, 283

Wyoming Conference Resolution, 28, 134, 165, 268–270

About the Authors

EDITH BABIN is Assistant Professor of English and ESL Coordinator at Louisiana State University, where she has taught composition for more than 30 years.

KIMBERLY HARRISON is Assistant Professor of English at Mississippi College, where she teaches courses in composition theory, women's writing, professional writing, and beginning and advanced composition.

ISBN 0-313-30087-9

EAN

9 780313 300875

90000>

HARDCOVER BAR CODE